Anna Cora Ogden Mowatt Ritchie

Fairy Fingers

A Novel

Anna Cora Ogden Mowatt Ritchie

Fairy Fingers
A Novel

ISBN/EAN: 9783744661331

Printed in Europe, USA, Canada, Australia, Japan

Cover: Foto ©Thomas Meinert / pixelio.de

More available books at **www.hansebooks.com**

IN PRESS:

BY THE AUTHOR OF THIS VOLUME,

THE MUTE SINGER;

𝔄 𝔑𝔬𝔳𝔢𝔩.

FAIRY FINGERS.

A Novel.

..

BY

ANNA CORA RITCHIE,

AUTHOR OF "THE AUTOBIOGRAPHY OF AN ACTRESS," "MIMIC LIFE," "TWIN ROSES,"
"ARMAND," "FASHION," ETC.

"Labor is Worship."

NEW YORK:

CARLETON, PUBLISHER, 413 BROADWAY.

CONTENTS.

(v)

FAIRY FINGERS.

CHAPTER I.

NOBLESSE.

They were seated in the drawing-room of an ancient château in Brittany, — the Countess Dowager de Gramont and Count Tristan, her only son, — a mansion lacking none of the ponderous quaintness that usually characterizes ancestral dwellings in that locality. The edifice could still boast of imposing grandeur, especially if classed among "fine ruins." Within and without were harmoniously dilapidated, and a large portion of the interior was uninhabitable. The limited resources of the count precluded even an apologetic semblance of repairs.

The house was surrounded by spacious parks and pleasure-grounds, in a similarly neglected condition. Their natural beauty was striking, and the rich soil yielded fruits and flowers in abundance, though its only culture was received from the hands of old Baptiste, who made his appearance as gardener in the morning, but, with a total change of costume, was metamorphosed into butler after the sun passed the meridian. In his button-hole a flower, which he could never be induced to forego, betrayed his preference for the former vocation.

The discussion between mother and son was unmistakably tempestuous. A thunder-cloud lowered on the noble lady's brow;

her eyes shot forth electric flashes, and her voice, usually subdued to aristocratic softness, was raised to storm-pitch.

"Count Tristan de Gramont, you have taken leave of your
senses!"

A favorite declaration of persons thoroughly convinced of their
own unassailable mental equilibrium, when their convictions encounter the sudden check of opposition.

As the assertion, unfortunately, is one that cannot be disproved
by denial, the count sank resignedly behind the shield of silence.
His mother returned to the attack.

"Do you mean me to understand that, in your right mind, you
would condescend to mingle with men of business? — that you
would actually degrade yourself into becoming a shareholder, or
manager, or director, or whatever you please to term it, in a railway company? — *you*, Count Tristan de Gramont! The very
proposal is a humiliation; to entertain it would be an absurdity
— to consent, an impossibility. I repeat it, you have taken leave
of your senses!"

"But, my dear mother," answered the count, with marked deference, "you are forgetting that this railway company chances
to be an American association; my connection with it, or, rather,
its very existence, is not likely to be known here in Brittany, —
therefore, my dignity will not be compromised. The only valuable property left us is the transatlantic estate which my roving
brother purchased during his wanderings in the New World, and
bequeathed to my son, Maurice, for whom it is held in trust by
an American gentleman. The members of the association, who
desire to interest me in their speculation, assert that the proposed
railroad may pass directly through this very tract of land. Should
that be the case, its value will be greatly increased. At the present moment the estate yields us nothing; but the advent of this
railroad must insure an immense profit. We estimate that, by
judicious management, the land may be made to bring in" —

His mother interrupted him with a haughty gesture. "'*Speculation!*' '*yield!*' '*profit!*' '*bring in!*' What language to
grow familiar to the lips of a son of mine! You talk like a
tradesman already! My son, give up all idea of this plebeian
enterprise!"

The count did not answer immediately. He seemed puzzled
to determine what degree of confidence it was necessary to repose
in his stately mother. After a brief pause, he renewed the conversation with evident embarrassment.

"It is very difficult to make a lady, especially a lady of your rank, education, and mode of life, understand these matters, and the necessity " —

"It ought to be equally difficult to make the nobleman, my son, comprehend them," answered the countess, freezingly.

The count rejoined, as though driven to extremity, "It is the very fact of my being a nobleman, that has made these people, Americans as they are, and despisers of titles as they profess to be, seek me with eagerness. The *prestige* of my *title*, and the promise of obtaining some privileges respecting Maurice's Maryland estate, are all that I can contribute toward the success of their undertaking. It is true I am a nobleman; but even rank, my dear mother, must have the means of sustaining its existence, to say nothing of preserving its dignity. Even rank is subject to the common, vulgar need of food and raiment and shelter, not to mention the necessity of keeping horses, carriages, domestics, and securing other indispensable but money-consuming luxuries. Our narrow income is no longer sufficient to meet even our limited expenditures. The education of Maurice at the University of Paris, and your own charities, have not merely drained our purse, but involved us in debt. I hail the offer made me by this American company, because it may extricate us from some very serious difficulties. I am much mortified at your resolute disapproval of the step I contemplate."

Count Tristan de Gramont was a widower, the father of but one child. It must not be supposed that, although he seriously purposed embarking in a business enterprise, he had failed to appropriate a goodly share of that pride which had both descended by inheritance, and been liberally instilled into his mind by education. His character was strongly stamped with the Breton traits of obstinacy and perseverance, and he was gifted with an unaristocratic amount of energy. When an idea once took possession of his brain, he patiently and diligently brought the embryo thought to fruition, in spite of all disheartening obstacles. He was narrow-minded and selfish when any interests save his own and those of his mother and son were at stake. These were the only two beings whom he loved, and he only loved them because they were *his* — a portion of *himself;* and it was merely himself that he loved through them. In a certain sense, he was a devoted son. His education had rendered him punctilious, to the highest degree, in the observance of all those forms that betoken filial veneration. He always treated his august mother with the most profound reverence. He paid her the most courteous attentions, — opened the doors when she desired to pass, placed

footstools for her feet, knelt promptly to pick up the handkerchief or glove she dropped, was ever ready to offer her his arm
for her support, and seldom combated her opinions.

The first time he had openly ventured to oppose her views
was in the conversation we have just related.

She looked so regal, as she sat before him in a richly carved
antique chair, which she occupied as though it had been a throne,
that, in spite of the blind obstinacy with which she refused to see
her own interests and his, Count Tristan could not help regarding her with admiration.

She was still strikingly handsome, notwithstanding the sixty
winters which had bleached her raven locks to the most uncompromising white. Those snowy tresses fell in soft and glossy
curls about her scarcely furrowed countenance. Her forehead
was somewhat low and narrow; the face, a decided oval; the
nose, almost straight; the eyes almond-shaped, and of a jetty
blackness, flashing out from beneath brows that were remarkable
for the fine, dark line that designated their arch. The mouth
was the least pleasing feature,—it was too small, and unsug-
gestive of varied expression; the lips not only lacked fulness,
but wore a supercilious curl that had become habitual.

Her form was considerably above the medium height, and
added to the sense of grandeur conveyed by her presence. Her
carriage was erect to the verge of stiffness, and her step too firm
to be quite soundless. Advancing years had not produced any
unseemly *embonpoint*, nor had her figure fallen into the opposite extreme, and sharpened into meagre angularity; its outline
retained sufficient roundness not to lose the curves or grace.

She had made no reply to her son's last remark, which forced
him to begin anew. He thought it politic, however, to change the
subject.

"You remember, my mother, that some seven of our friends
are engaged to dine with us to-morrow. I trust you will not
disapprove of my having invited two American gentlemen to
join the party. After the letters of introduction they brought
me, I was forced to show them some attention and"—

He paused abruptly, without venturing to add that those
gentlemen were directors of the railway company of which he
had before spoken.

"My son, you are aware that I never interfere with your
hospitalities, but you seem to have forgotten that my Sèvres
china is only a set for twelve, and I can use no other on ceremonious occasions. With Bertha and Madeleine we have one guest
too many."

"That is a matter readily arranged," replied the count. "Madeleine need not appear at table. She is always so obliging and manageable that she can easily be requested to dine in her own room. In fact, to speak frankly, I would *rather not* have her present."

"But, should she be absent, Bertha will be annoyed," rejoined Madame de Gramont.

"Bertha is a simpleton! How strange that she does not see, or suspect, that Madeleine always throws her into the background! I said a while ago, my mother, that *your charities* had helped to drain our purse, and this is one which I might cite, and the one that galls me most. Here, for three years, you have sheltered and supported this young girl, without once reflecting upon the additional expense we are incurring by your playing the benefactress thus grandly. It is very noble, very munificent on your part; still, for a number of reasons, I regret that Madeleine has become a permanent inmate of this château."

"Madeleine was an orphan," replied the countess, "the sole remaining child of the Duke de Gramont, your father's nephew. When she was left homeless and destitute, did not the *honor of the family* force me to offer her an asylum, and to treat her with the courtesy due to a relative? Have we not always found her very grateful and very agreeable?"

"I grant you — very agreeable — *too* agreeable by half," returned the count; "so agreeable that, as I said, she invariably throws your favorite Bertha into the shade. I confess that the necessity of always reserving for this young person, thrust upon us by the force of circumstances, a place at table, a seat in the carriage, room upon every party of pleasure, makes her presence an inconvenience, if not a positive burden. And will you allow me to speak with great candor? May I venture to say that I have seen you, my dear mother, chafed by the infliction, and irritated by beholding Bertha lose through contrast with Madeleine?"

His mother replied with animation: "Bertha is my grandniece, — the granddaughter of my only sister; the ties of blood, if nothing more, would bind me more closely to her than to Madeleine. Possibly there may have been times when I have not been well pleased to see one so dear, invariably, though most inexplicably, eclipsed. Bertha may shine forth in her most resplendent jewels, — her most costly and exquisite Parisian toilet; Madeleine has only to enter, in a simple muslin dress, a flower, or a knot of ribbons in her hair, and she draws all eyes magnetically upon her."

"That is precisely the observation I have made," answered Count Tristan; "and, my mother, have you never reflected how seriously your *protégée* may interfere with our prospects respecting Maurice?"

The countess started. "Impossible! He could not think of Madeleine when a union with Bertha would be so much more advantageous."

"Youth does not think — it chooses by the attraction it experiences towards this or that object," answered the count. "Before Maurice last returned to the university, nine months ago, his admiration for Madeleine was unmistakable. Now that he is shortly to come home, and for an indefinite period, — now that our plans must ripen, I have come to the conclusion that Madeleine must be removed, or they will never attain fruition; she must not be allowed to cast the spell of her dangerous fascination over him; something must be done, and that before Maurice returns; in a fortnight he will be here."

Before the countess could reply, a young girl bounded into the room, with a letter in one hand, and a roll of music in the other.

It would be difficult to find a more perfect type of the pure blonde than was manifested in the person of this fair young maiden. The word "dazzling" might be applied without exaggeration to the lustrous whiteness of a complexion tinged in the cheeks as though by the reflection of a sea-shell. Her full, dewy lips disclosed milky rows of childlike teeth within. Her eyes were of the clearest azure; but, in spite of their expression of mingled tenderness and gayety, one who could pause to lay the finger upon an imperfection, would note that something was wanting to complete their beauty; — the eyebrows were too faintly traced, and the lashes too light, though long. The low brow, straight, slender nose, the soft curve of the chin, the fine oval of the face, were obviously an inheritance. At a single glance it was impossible not to be struck with the resemblance which these classic features bore to those of the countess. But the sportive dimples, pressed as though by a caressing touch, upon the cheeks and chin of the young girl, destroyed, even more than the totally opposite coloring, the likeness in the two countenances. The hair of the countess had been remarkable for its shining blackness, while the yellow acacia was not more brightly golden than the silken tresses of Bertha, — tresses that ran in ripples, and lost themselves in a sunny stream of natural curls, which seemed audaciously bent on breaking their bounds, and looked as though they were always in a frolic. In vain they were smoothed back by the skilful fingers of an expert *femme de chambre*, and confined in an elaborate knot at the back of Bertha's small head; the rebellious locks *would* wave and break into fine rings upon the white brow, and lovingly steal in stray ringlets adown the alabaster throat, ignoring conventional restraint as sportively as their owner.

Bertha de Merrivale, like Madeleine, was an orphan, but, unlike Madeleine, an heiress. The Marquis de Merrivale, Bertha's uncle, was also her guardian. He allowed her every year to spend a few months with her mother's relatives, who warmly pleaded for these annual visits. Her sojourn at the château de Gramont was always a season of delight to Bertha herself, for she dearly loved her great-aunt, liked Count Tristan, enjoyed the society of Maurice, and was enthusiastically attached to Madeleine.

"A letter! a letter from Maurice!" exclaimed Bertha, dancing around her aunt as she held out the epistle.

The countess broke the seal eagerly, and after glancing over the first lines, exclaimed, "Here is news indeed! We did not expect Maurice for a fortnight; but he writes that he will be here to-morrow. How little time we shall have for preparation! And I intended to order so many improvements made in his chamber, and to quite remodel" —

"Oh, of course, everything will have to be remodelled for the Viscount Maurice de Gramont! Nothing will be good enough for *him!* Every one will sink into insignificance at *his* coming! We, poor, forlorn damsels, will henceforth be of no account, — no one will waste a thought on *us!*" said Bertha.

"On the contrary," replied her aunt, "I never had your happiness more in my thoughts than at this moment. Be sure you wear your blue brocade to-morrow, and the blue net interwoven with pearls in your hair, and that turquoise set which Maurice always admired."

"Be sure that I play the coquette, you mean, as my dear aunt did before me," answered Bertha, merrily. "No, indeed, aunt, that may have done in *your* day, but it does not suit *ours*. We, of the present time, do not wear nets for the express purpose of ensnaring the admiration of young men; or don our most becoming dresses to lay up their hearts in their folds. I am going to seek Madeleine to tell her this news, and I have another surprise for her."

"What is it?" inquired the countess, in an altered tone.

2

" This great parcel of music, which I sent to Paris to obtain expressly for her. But I have something else which she must not see to day, — this bracelet, the exact pattern of the one my uncle presented to me upon my last birthday, and Madeleine shall receive this upon her birthday ; that will be *to-morrow.*"

As she spoke, she clasped upon her small wrist a band of gold, fastened by a knot formed of pearls, and gayly held up her round, white arm before the eyes of the count and countess.

The latter caught her uplifted hand and said gravely, " Bertha, music and bracelets are very appropriate for *you*, but they do not suit Madeleine. Madeleine is poor, worse than poor, wholly dependent upon " —

" There you are mistaken, aunt," returned Bertha, warmly. " As *I* am rich, she is not poor ; — that is, she will not always be poor, and she shall *not* be dependent upon any one — not even upon *you*. I mean to settle upon her a marriage portion if she choose to marry, and a handsome income if she remain single."

" Very generous and *romantic* on your part," replied the countess, ironically ; " but, unfortunately for her, you have no power at present over your own property ; you cannot play the benefactress without the consent of your guardian, and that you will never obtain."

" But if I marry, I will have the right," answered Bertha, naïvely.

" You will have the consent of your husband to obtain, and that will be equally difficult."

" That is true, but I am not discouraged. I suppose when I am of age I shall have the power, and I need not marry before then. I am sixteen, nearly seventeen ; it will not be so *very* long to wait, and I am determined to serve Madeleine."

" Many events may occur to make you change you mind before you attain your majority. Meanwhile you are fostering tastes in Madeleine which are unsuited to her condition. I know you think me very severe, but " —

" No, no, aunt, you are never severe toward me ; you are only too kind, too indulgent ; you spoil me with too much love and consideration ; and it is because you *have* spoiled me so completely that I mean to be saucy enough to speak out just what I think."

Bertha seated herself on the footstool at her aunt's feet, took her hand caressingly, and with an earnest air prattled on.

" It is with Madeleine that you are severe, and you grow more and more severe every day. You speak to her so harshly, so disdainfully at times, that I hardly recognize you. One would not imagine that she is your grandniece as much as I am, — that is, *almost* as much, for she was the grandniece of the Count de Gramont, my uncle. You find incessant fault with her, and she seems to irritate you by her very presence. Oh! I have seen it for a long time, and during this last visit I see it more than ever."

" Bertha!" commenced her aunt, in a tone which might have awed any less volatile and determined speaker.

" Do not interrupt me, aunt; I have not done yet, and I *must* speak. Why do you put on this manner towards Madeleine? You *do put it on*, — it is not natural to you, — for you are kind to every one else. And have you not been most kind to her also? Were you not the only one of her proud relatives who held out a hand to her when she stood unsheltered and alone in the world? Have you not since then done everything for her? Done everything — but — but — *but love her?* "

" Bertha, you are the only one who would venture to " —

" I know it, aunt, — I am the only one who would venture, so grant me one moment more; I have not done yet. Madeleine cannot be an incumbrance, for who is so useful in your household as she? Who could replace her? When you are suffering, she is the tenderest of nurses. She daily relieves you of a thousand cares. When you have company, is it not Madeleine who sees that everything is in order? If you give a dinner, is it not Madeleine who not only superintends all the preparations, but invents the most beautiful decorations for the table, — and out of nothing — out of leaves and flowers so common that no one would have thought of culling them, yet so wonderfully arranged that every one exclaims at their picturesque effect? When you have dull guests, — guests that put me to sleep, or out of patience, — is it not Madeleine who amuses them? How many evenings, that would have been insufferably stupid, have flown delightfully, chased by her delicious voice! "

" You make a great virtue of what was simply an enjoyment to herself. She delights as much, or more, in singing than any one can delight in hearing her."

" That is because she delights in everything she does; she always accomplishes her work with delight. She delighted in making you that becoming cap, with its coquettishly-disposed knots of violet ribbons; she delighted in turning and freshening and remaking the silk dress you wear at this moment, which fits you to perfection, and looks quite new. She delighted in embroidering my cousin Tristan that pretty velvet smoking-cap he has on his head. She delighted in making me the wreath which I wore at the Count de Caradaré's concert the other evening, and which every one complimented me upon. It was her own invention; — and did not you yourself remark that there was not a head-dress in the room half as beautiful? Everything she touches she beautifies. The commonest objects assume a graceful form beneath her fingers. The "*fingers of a fairy*" my cousin Maurice used to call them, and, there certainly is magic in those dainty, rapidly-moving hands of hers. They have an art, a skill, a facility that partakes of the supernatural. Madeleine is a dependent upon your bounty, but her magic fingers make her a very valuable one; and, if you would not think it very impertinent, I would say that we are all *her debtors*, rather than *she ours*. There, I have done! Now, forgive me for my temerity, — confess that you have been too severe to Madeleine, and promise not to find fault with her any more."

"I will confess that she has the most charming advocate in the world," answered the countess with affection.

"Madeleine must not see this bracelet until to-morrow; so I must hasten to lock it up," resumed the young girl; "after that I will let her know that our cousin will be here to honor her birthday. How enchanted she will be! But she makes entirely too much of him, — just as you all do. The instant she hears the news, away she will fly to make preparations for his comfort. I shall only have to say, 'Maurice is coming,' and what a commotion there will be!"

Bertha tripped away, leaving the countess alone with her son.

"Is she not enchanting?" exclaimed the former, as Bertha disappeared. "Maurice will have a charming bride."

"Yes, *if* the marriage we so earnestly desire ever take place."

"If? If? I intend that it *shall* take place. It is my one dream, my dearest hope!" said the countess.

"It is mine also," replied the count; "and yet I have my doubts — my fears; in a word, I do not believe this union ever *will* take place if Madeleine remain here."

The countess drew herself up with indignant amazement. "What do you mean? Do you think Madeleine capable of"—

"I do not think Madeleine capable of anything wrong; but she has such versatility of talent, she is so fascinating, her character is so lovable, that I think those talents and attractions capable of upsetting all our plans and of making Maurice fall deeply in love with her."

"But is not Bertha fascinating, and lovely as a painter's ideal?" asked the countess.

"Yes, but it is not such a striking, such. an impressive, such a bewitching, bewildering style of beauty," replied her son. "Mark my words: I understand young men. I know what dazzles their eyes and turns their heads. If Maurice is thrown into daily communication with Bertha and Madeleine, it is Madeleine to whom he will become attached."

"It must not be!" said the countess, emphatically, and rising as she spoke. "It shall not!"

"I echo, it shall not, my mother. But we must take means of prevention. It is most unfortunate that Maurice returns a fortnight before we expected him. I had my plans laid and ready to carry into execution before he could arrive. Now we must hasten them."

"What is your scheme?" asked his mother.

"Madeleine has other relations, all richer than ourselves. I purpose writing to each of them, and proposing that they shall receive her, not for three years, as we have done, but that they shall each, in turn, invite her to spend three months with them. They surely cannot refuse, and her life will be very varied and pleasant, visiting from house to house every three months, enjoying new pleasures, seeing new faces, making new friendships. And her relatives will, in reality, be our debtors, for Madeleine is the most charming of inmates. She is always so lively, and creates so much gayety around her; she has so many resources in herself, and she is so *useful!* In fact, we are bestowing a valuable gift upon these good relatives of hers, and they ought to thank us, as I have no doubt they will."

The countess approved of her son's plan to rid them of their dangerously agreeable inmate, and the count, without further delay, sat down to pen the projected epistles.

CHAPTER II.

THE COUSINS.

BERTHA's prediction was verified, and the whole château was thrown into confusion by preparations for the coming of the young viscount. Old Baptiste forsook his garden-tools for the

whole day, to play in-door domestic. Gustave, who daily doubled
his *rôle* of coachman with that of *valet*, slighted his beloved horses
(horses whose mothers and grandmothers had supplied the de
Gramont stables from time immemorial) to cleanse windows,
brighten mirrors, and polish dingy furniture. Bettina, the antiquated *femme de chambre* of the countess, who also discharged
the combined duties of housekeeper and housemaid, flew about
with a bustling activity that could hardly have been expected
from her years and infirmities. Elize, the cook, made far more
elaborate preparations for the coming of the young viscount than
she would have deemed necessary for the dinner to be given to
her master's guests. This band of venerable domestics had all
been servants of the family before the viscount's birth, and he
was not only an idol among them, but seemed, in a manner, to
appertain to them all.

The countess, alone, did not find the movement of gladness
around her contagious. The coming of Maurice before the departure of Madeleine, distressed her deeply; but small troubles
and great were incongruously mingled in her mind, for, while she
was tormented by the frustration of her plans, she fretted almost
as heartily over that set of Sèvres porcelain which, with the addition of her grandson, would not be sufficient for the expected
guests, even if Madeleine dined in her own chamber. Besides,
the arrival of Maurice made *that* arrangement out of the question. He would certainly oppose her banishment, just as Bertha
had done; and the day, unfortunately, was Madeleine's birthday.
This circumstance would give her cousins additional ground for
insisting upon her presence at the festive board. The countess
saw no escape from her domestic difficulties, and was thoroughly
out of humor.

Before Madeleine had awoke that morning, Bertha had stolen
to her bedside and clasped the bracelet upon her arm. Light as
was Bertha's touch, it aroused the sleeper, and she greeted her
birthday token with unfeigned gratitude and delight. But Mad-
cleine had few moments to spend in contemplation of the precious
gift. She dressed rapidly, then hastened away to make the château bright with flowers, to complete various preparations for the
toilet of her aunt, to perform numerous offices which might be
termed menial; but she entered upon her work with so much
zest, she executed each task with such consummate skill, she took
so much interest in the employment of the moment, that no labor
seemed either tedious or debasing.

Maurice de Gramont had just completed his twenty-first year

when he graduated with high honor at the University of France. After passing a fatiguing examination, he had gladly consented to act upon his father's suggestion, and devote a few weeks to enjoyment in the gay metropolis. The count had no clew to the cause of his sudden return to Brittany.

"Aunt, aunt! There is the carriage,—he is coming!— Baptiste, run and open the gate!" cried Bertha, whose quick eyes had caught sight of a coach which stopped at the farther end of a long avenue of noble trees, leading to the château.

Baptiste made all the speed which his aged limbs allowed; Gustave hastened to throw open the front door; Bertha was on the porch before the carriage drew up; the count and countess appeared at the entrance just as Maurice sprang down the steps of the lumbering vehicle.

His blue eyes sparkled with genuine joy, and his countenance glowed with animation, as he embraced his grandmother warmly, kissed his father, according to French custom, then turning to Bertha, clasped her extended hands and touched either cheek lightly with his lips. She received the cousinly salutation without any evidence of displeasure or any token of confusion.

As the maiden and youth stood side by side, they might easily have been mistaken for brother and sister. The same florid coloring was remarkable in the countenances of both, save that the tints were a few shades deeper on the visage of Maurice. His eyes were of a darker blue; his glossy hair was tinged with chestnut, while Bertha's shone with unmingled gold; but, like Bertha's, his recreant locks had a strong tendency to curl, and lay in rich clusters upon his brow, distressing him by a propensity which he deemed effeminate. His mouth was as ripely red as hers, but somewhat larger, firmer, and less bland in its character. His eyebrows, too, were more darkly traced, supplying a want only too obvious in her countenance. The resemblance, however, disappeared in the forehead and classic nose, for the brow of Maurice was broad and high, and the nose prominent, though finely shaped.

His form was manly without being strikingly tall. It was what might be designated as a noble figure; but the term owed its appropriateness partly to his refined and graceful bearing.

"My dear father, I am so glad to see you!—grandmother, it is refreshing to find you looking as though you bade defiance to time;—and you, my little cousin, how much you have improved! How lovely you have grown! A year does a great deal for one's appearance."

"Yours, for instance," replied Bertha, saucily. "Well, there was abundant room for improvement."

Maurice replied to her vivacious remark with a laugh of assent, and, looking eagerly around, asked, "Where is Madeleine?"

"Madeleine is busy as usual," answered Bertha. "I warrant she is in some remote corner of the château, mysteriously employed. She does not know that you have arrived."

"And is she well? My father never once mentioned her in his letters. And has she kept you company in growing so much handsomer during the last year?"

"*Her* beauty needed no heightening!" exclaimed Bertha, affectionately. "But she develops new talents every day; she sings more delightfully than ever; and lately she has commenced drawing from nature with the most wonderful ease. You should see the flowers she first creates with her pencil and then copies with her needle! I really think her needle can paint almost as dexterously as the brush of any other artist."

The count exchanged a look with his mother, and whispered, "Do stop her!"

The latter turned quickly to her grandson, and said, "Are you and Bertha determined to spend the morning out of doors? Come, let us go in."

As they entered the drawing-room, the countess pointed to a seat beside her.

"Maurice, leave your chattering little cousin, and sit down and give us some account of yourself. What have you been doing? How have you been passing your time?"

Maurice obeyed; Bertha placed herself on the other side of her aunt; the count took a chair opposite.

"Behold a most attentive and appreciating audience!" cried Bertha. "Now, Mr. Collegian and Traveller, — hero of the hour! — most noble representative of the house of de Gramont! hold forth! Let us hear how you have been occupying your valuable time."

"In the first place, I have been studying tolerably hard, little cousin. It seems very improbable, does it not? The midnight oil has not yet paled my cheeks to the sickly and interesting hue that belongs to a student. Still the proof is that I have passed my examination triumphantly. I will show you my prizes by and by, and they will speak for themselves. Next, I have joined a debating society of young students who are preparing to become lawyers. Our meetings have afforded me infinite pleasure. At our last reunion, I undertook to plead a cause, and achieved a wonderful success. I had no idea that language would flow so readily from my lips. I was astonished at my own thoughts, and the facility with which I formed them into words, and they say I made a capital argument. I received the most enthusiastic congratulations, and my associates, in pressing my hand, addressed me, not as the Viscount de Gramont, but as the *able orator.* I really think that I could make an orator, and that I have sufficient talent to become a lawyer."

"A lawyer!" exclaimed the countess with supreme disdain. "What could introduce such a vulgar idea into your head? A lawyer! There is really something startling, something positively appalling in the vagaries of the rising generation! A lawyer! what an idea!"

"It is something more than an *idea*, my dear grandmother : it is a project which I have formed, and which I cherish very seriously," replied Maurice.

"A project,—a project! I like projects. Let us hear your sublime project, Mr. Advocate," cried Bertha.

"The project is simply to test the abilities which I am presumptuous enough to believe I have discovered in myself, and to study for the bar. My father wrote me that he intended to become a director in a railway company, and descanted upon the advantage of embarking in the enterprise. He also confided to me, for the first time, the real state of our affairs, — in a word, the empty condition of our treasury. Why should my father occupy himself with business matters and I live in idleness? Once more, I repeat, I am convinced I have sufficient ability to make a position at the bar, and with my father's consent, and yours, grandmother, I propose to commence my law studies at once."

"A pettifogger! impossible! I, for one, will never countenance a step so humiliating! It is not to be thought of!" replied his grandmother, in a tone of decision.

"No, Maurice, your project is futile," responded his father. "My joining this railroad association is quite a different matter. I shall in reality have nothing to do. It is only my name that is required; besides, America is so far off that nobody in Brittany will be aware of my connection with the company. Your becoming a lawyer would be a public matter. I cannot recall the name of a single nobleman in the whole list of barristers" —

"So much the better for me! My title may, *in this solitary*

instance, prove of service to me. It may help to bring me
clients. People will be enchanted to be defended by a viscount."

"You conjure up a picture that is absolutely revolting!"
cried the countess, warmly. "*My grandson* pleading to defend
the rabble ! "

"Why not, if the rabble should happen to stand in need of
defence ? "

"Why not ? — because you should ignore their very existence!
What have you and they in common ? "

Maurice was about to reply somewhat emphatically, but noticing his grandmother's knitted brow, and his father's troubled
expression, he checked himself.

The countess added, with an air of determination that forbade discussion, "Maurice, you will never obtain my consent,
never ! "

"But if I may not study for the bar, what am I to do ? "
asked the young man with spirit.

"Do ? " questioned the countess, proudly. "What have the
de Gramonts done for centuries past ? Do nothing ! "

"*Nothing?* Thank you, grandmother, for your estimate of my
capacities and of the sluggish manner in which my blood
courses through my veins. Doing *nothing* was all very well in
dead-alive, by-gone days, but it does not suit the present age of
activity and progress. In our time everything that has heart
and spirit feels that labor is a law of life. Some men till the
earth, some cultivate the minds of their fellow-men, some
guard their country's soil by fighting our battles ; that is,
some vocations enable us to live, some teach us how to live, and
some render it glorious to die. Now, instead of adopting any of
these pursuits, I only wish to " —

"To become a manufacturer of fine phrases, a vender of
words ! " replied the countess, disdainfully.

"An advantageous merchandise," answered Maurice, — "one
which it costs nothing, to manufacture but which may be sold
dear."

"Sold ? You shock me more and more ! Never has one who
bore the name of de Gramont earned money ! " replied the
countess, with increased *hauteur.*

"Very true, and very unfortunate ! We are now feeling the
ill effects of the idleness of our ancestors. It is time that the
new generation should reform their bad system," replied
Maurice.

" Maurice " — began his father.

" My dear father, let me speak upon this subject, for I have it greatly at heart. I have an iron constitution, buoyant spirits, a tolerably good head, a tolerably large heart, an ample stock of imagination, an unstinted amount of energy, and an admiration for genius; now, all these gifts — mind, heart, imagination, spirit, energy — cry out for action, — ask to vindicate their right to existence, — need to find vent! *That* is one ground upon which I plant my intention to become a lawyer. Another is that a man of my temperament, liberal views, and tendencies to extravagance, also needs to have the command of means " —

" Have we ever restricted you, Maurice?" asked his father, reproachfully.

" No, it is only yourselves you have restricted. But do you suppose I am willing to expend what has been saved through your economy? Until lately I never knew the actual state of our finances. Now I see the necessity for exertion, that I may be enabled to live as my tastes and habits prompt."

" That you may obtain by making an advantageous marriage," remarked the countess, forgetting at the moment that Bertha was present.

" What! owe my privileges, my luxuries, my very position, to my wife? Never! Every manly and independent impulse within me rises in arms against such a suggestion; while the emotion I experienced when I felt I could become something *of myself*, — that I had talents which I could employ, — that I had a future before me, — renown to win, — great deeds to achieve, — filled me with a strange joy hitherto unknown. I tell you, my father, there is a force and fire in my spirit that must have some outlet, — must leap into action, — *must* and *will!*"

" It shall find an outlet," replied the countess, " without making you a hired declaimer of fine words, — a paid champion of the low mob. Let us hear no more of this absurd lawyer project. The matter is settled: you will never have your father's consent, nor mine."

" Then I warn you," exclaimed Maurice, starting up, and speaking almost fiercely. " You will drive me into evil courses. I shall fall into all manner of vices for the sake of excitement. If I cannot have occupation, I must have amusement. I shall run in debt, I may gamble, I may become dissipated, I may commit offences against good taste and good morals, which will degrade me in reality; and all because you have nipped a pure intention in the bud. The root that bore it is too vigorous not to blossom out anew, and the chances are that it will bring forth some less creditable fruit. You will see! I do not jest; I know what is in me!"

"Content! we will run the risk!" replied the countess, trying to speak cheerfully.

The grave manner of Maurice and his impressive tone, as he stood before her with an air half-threatening, half-prophetic, made her experience a sensation of vague discomfort.

"We will trust you, for you are a de Gramont, and cannot commit a dishonorable action. Now, pray, go to your room and make your toilet. We are expecting guests to dinner."

Maurice turned away without uttering another word, without even heeding the hand which Bertha stretched in sympathy towards him; and, with a clouded brow and slow steps, ascended to his own apartment.

CHAPTER III.

MADELEINE.

"FOURTEEN at table, and the Sèvres set only sufficient for twelve! Truly it *is* untoward, but I wish, my dear aunt, you would not let it trouble you so much. If you will allow the two extra plates to be placed before Bertha and myself, we will endeavor to render them invisible by our witchcraft. Do compliment us by permitting the experiment to be tried."

"Bertha is entitled to the best of everything in my mansion," answered the countess, unsoothed by this proposition.

"*That* I admit," was Madeleine's cordial reply; "but to meet this unlooked-for emergency, I thought you might possibly consent to let her exert her witchery in making an intrusive plate disappear from general view."

"And you, it seems, are quite confident of possessing witchcraft potent enough to accomplish the same feat!"

Madeleine, without appearing to be hurt by the taunting intonation which pointed this remark, replied frankly, "I suppose I must have been guilty of imagining that I had; but, indeed, it was unpremeditated vanity. I really did not reflect upon the subject. I was only anxious to get over the dilemma in which we are placed by these troublesome plates."

"Not *premeditated* vanity, I dare say," remarked the countess, dryly; "only vanity so spontaneous, natural, and characteristic that *premeditation* is out of the question."

Madeleine remained silent, and went on with her task, dexterously rolling around her slender fingers her aunt's soft, white curls, and letting them lightly drop in the most becoming positions.

The toilet of the countess for her son's dinner-party was in process of completion.

She wore a black velvet dress, which, after being on duty for a fabulous number of years, and finally pronounced past all further active service, had been resuscitated and remodelled, to suit the style of the day, by Madeleine. We will not enter into a description of the adroit method by which a portion of its primitive lustre had been restored to the worn and pressed velvet, nor particularize the skilful manner in which the corsage of the robe had been refashioned, and every trace of age concealed by an embroidery of jet beads, which was so strikingly tasteful that its double office was unsuspected. Enough that the countess appeared to be superbly attired when she once more donned the venerable but rejuvenated dress.

The snow-white curls being arranged to the best advantage, Madeleine placed upon the head of her aunt a dainty cap, of the Charlotte Corday form, composed of bits of very old and costly lace, — an heir-loom in the de Gramont family, — such lace as could no longer be purchased for gold, even if its members had been in a condition to exchange bullion for thread. This cap was another of the young girl's achievements, and she could not help smiling with pleasure when she saw its picturesque effect. The countess, in spite of the anxious contraction of her dark brows, looked imposingly handsome. Hers was an old age of positive beauty, — a decadence which had all the lustre of

"The setting moon upon the western wave."

It was only when her features were accidentally contrasted with those of such a mild, eloquent, and soul-revealing face as the one bending over her that defects struck the eye, — defects which the ravages of time had done less to produce than the workings of a stern and haughty character.

But Madeleine's countenance how shall we portray? The
3

lineaments were of that order which no painter could faithfully
present by tracing their outline correctly, and no writer conjure
up before the mind by descriptive language, however minutely
the color of eyes, complexion, and hair might be chronicled.
Therefore our task must necessarily be an imperfect one, and
convey but a vague idea of the living presence.

It was a somewhat pale face, but pure and unsallow in its pallor. The vivid blood rushed, with any sudden emotion, to cheek
and brow, but died away as quickly; for late hours, too little
sunlight, fresh air, and exercise, forbade the flitting roses to be
captured and a permanent bloom insured. The hue of the large,
dreamy eyes might be called a light hazel; but that description
fails to convey an impression of their rare, clear, topaz tint, — a
topaz with the changing lustre of an opal: a combination difficult to imagine until it has once been seen. The darkly-fringed
lids were peculiarly drooping, and gave the eyes a look of exceeding softness, now and then displaced by startling flashes of
brilliancy. The finely-chiselled mouth was full of grave sweetness, decision, and energy, and yet suggestive of a mirthful temperament. The forehead was not too high, but ample and
thoughtful. The finely-shaped head showed the intellectual and
emotional nature nicely balanced. Through the long, abundant
chestnut hair bright threads gleamed in and out until all the
locks looked burnished. They were gathered into one rich braid
and simply wound around the head. At the side, where the
massive tress was fastened, a single cape jasmine seemed to
form a clasp of union. A more striking or becoming arrangement could hardly have been devised.

Madeleine was somewhat above the ordinary stature, and her
height, combined with the native dignity of her bearing, would
have given her an air of stateliness, but for the exceeding grace
which dispelled the faintest shadow of stiffness,— a stiffness very
noticeable in the formal carriage of the countess.

The wardrobe of the young girl was necessarily of the most
limited and uncostly character; and, though she was dressed for
a ceremonious dinner, her attire consisted merely of a sombre-
hued barege, made with the severest simplicity, and gaining its
only pretension to full dress by disclosing her white, finely-
moulded neck and arms. Her sole ornament was the bracelet
which had been Bertha's birthday gift.

While giving the last, finishing touches to her aunt's toilet,
Madeleine talked gayly. Hers was not one of those bright, sil-
very voices which make you feel that, could the sounds become

visible, they must *shine;* but there was a rich depth in her tones, which imparted to her lightest words an intonation of feeling, and told the hearer that her vocal chords were in close communication with her heart. Though her countenance did not lack the radiance of youthful gladness, there was so much thought mingled with its brightness that even her mirth conveyed the impression that she had suffered and sorrowed.

The only daughter of the Duke de Gramont, at eighteen she suddenly found herself an orphan and wholly destitute. Her father was one of that large class of impoverished noblemen who keep up appearances by means of constant shifts and desperate struggles, of which the world knows nothing. But he was a man of unquestionable intellect, and had given Madeleine a much more liberal education than custom accords to young French maidens of her rank.

The accident of his birth the Duke de Gramont regarded as a positive misfortune, and daily lamented the burden of his own nobility, for it was a shackle that enfeebled and enslaved his large capacities.

He once said to his young daughter, " You would have been far happier as a peasant's child; I should have had a wider field of action and enjoyment as an humble laborer; we should both have been more truly *noble.* I envy the peasants who have the glorious privilege of doing just that which they are best fitted to do; who are not forced to *vegetate* and call vegetation existence, — not compelled to waste and deaden their energies because it is an aristocratic penalty, — not doomed to glide into and out of their lives without ever living enough to know life's worth."

Such words sank into Madeleine's spirit, took deep root there, and, growing in the bleak atmosphere of adversity, bore vigorous fruit in good season.

She had known only the intangible shadow of pomp and luxury, while the substance was actual penury. But her inborn fertility of invention, her abundant resources, her tact in accommodating herself to circumstances, and her inexhaustible energy, had endowed her with the faculty of making the best of her contradictory position, and the most of the humblest materials at her command.

Though she had several wealthy relatives, the Countess de Gramont was the only one who offered her unsheltered youth an asylum. Perhaps we ought not to analyze too minutely the motives of the noble lady, for fear that we might find her actuated less by a charitable impulse than by pride which would not allow it to be said that her grandniece ever lacked, or had to solicit, a home. Be that as it may, the orphan Madeleine became a permanent inmate of the Château de Gramont.

Her gratitude was deep, and found expression in actions more eloquent than words. - She was thankful for the slightest evidence of kindness from her self-constituted protectors. She even exaggerated the amount of consideration which she received. She was not free from the hereditary taint of *pride;* but in her it took a new form and unprecedented expression. The sense of indebtedness spurred her on to discover ways by which she could avoid being a burden upon the generosity of her benefactors, — ways by which her obligations might be lightened, though she felt they could never be cancelled. She became the active, presiding spirit over the whole household; her skilful fingers were ever at work here, there, and everywhere; and her quick-witted brain was always planning measures to promote the interest, comfort, or pleasure of all within her sphere. The thought that an employment was menial, and therefore she must not stoop to perform it, never intruded, for she had an internal consciousness that she dignified her occupation. What she accomplished seemed wonderful; but, independent of the rapidity with which she habitually executed, she comprehended in an eminent degree the exact value of time, — the worth of every minute; and the use made of her *spare moments* was one great secret of the large amount she achieved.

The toilet of the countess for the dinner was completed, but she kept Madeleine by her side until they descended to the drawing-room.

Madeleine had not yet welcomed Maurice, who had retired to his chamber to dress before she was aware of his arrival. When she entered the *salon* with the countess, he was sitting beside Bertha, but sprang up, and, advancing joyfully, exclaimed, "Ah! at last! I thought I was never to be permitted to see the busy fairy of the family, who renders herself invisible while she is working her wonders!"

He would have approached his lips to Madeleine's cheek, but the countess interfered.

"And why," asked Maurice, in surprise which was not free from a touch of vexation, — "why may I not kiss my cousin Madeleine? You found no fault when I kissed my cousin Bertha just now!"

"That is very different!" replied the countess, hastily.

"Different! What is the difference?" persisted Maurice.

"There is none that I can discover. . Both are equally near of kin, — both my cousins, — both second cousins, or third cousins, some people would call them; the one is kin through my grandmother, the other through my grandfather. What *can* be the difference?"

"*My will* makes the difference!" answered the countess, in a severe tone. "Is not *that* sufficient?"

"It ought to be so, Maurice," Madeleine interposed, without appearing to be either wounded or surprised at her aunt's manner. "If not, I must add *my will* to my aunt's." Then, as though in haste to change the subject, she said, extending her hand, "I am very, *very* glad to see you, Maurice."

"You have not changed as much as my pretty Bertha here," remarked Maurice. "She has gained a great deal in the last year. But you, Madeleine, look a little paler than ever, and a little thinner than you were. I fear it is because you still keep that candle burning which last year I used to notice at your window when I returned from balls long after midnight. You will destroy your health."

"There is no danger of *that*," answered Madeleine, gayly. "I am in most unpoetically robust health. I am never ailing for an hour."

"Never ailing and never weary," joined in Bertha. "That is, she never complains, and never admits she is tired. She would make us believe that her constitution is a compound of iron and India-rubber."

Maurice took a small jewel-case from his pocket, and, preparing to open it, said, "Nobody has yet asked why I am here one fortnight before I was expected. Has curiosity suddenly died out of the venerable Château de Gramont, that none of the ladies who honor its ancient walls by their presence care to know?"

"We all care!" exclaimed Bertha.

"That we do!" responded Madeleine. "Why was it, Maurice?"

"The reason chiefly concerns you, Madeleine."

"Me! You are jesting."

"Not at all; I came home because I remembered that to-day was your twenty-first birthday. I would not be absent upon your birthday, though I did not know that your reaching your majority was to be celebrated by a grand dinner."

"Madeleine's birthday was not thought of when your father invited his friends to dinner," remarked the countess, curtly.

Maurice went on without heeding this explanation.

3 *

"I have brought you a little birthday token. Will you wear it for my sake?"

As he spoke, he opened the case and took out a Roman brooch. Madeleine's eyes sparkled with a dewy lustre that threatened to shape itself into a tear. Before she could speak, Bertha cried out, —

"A dove with a green olive-branch in its mouth, — what a beautiful device! And the word '*Pax*' written beneath! That must be in remembrance that Madeleine not only bears peace in her own bosom, but carries it wherever she goes. Was not that what you intended to suggest, Cousin Maurice?"

"You are a delightful interpreter," replied the young man.

"Yet she left me to read the sweet meaning of her own gift," said Madeleine, recovering her composure. "See, a band of gold with a knot of pearls, — a '*manacle of love*,' as the great English poet calls it, secured by purity of purpose."

As she fastened the brooch in her bosom, she added, "I am so rich in birthday gifts that I am bankrupt in thanks; pray believe *that* is the reason I thank you so poorly."

The countess impatiently interrupted this conversation by summoning Maurice to her side.

As he took the seat she pointed out, he said, in an animated tone, "I have not told you all my good news yet. Listen, young ladies, for some of it especially concerns you. On my way here, I encountered the equipage of the Marchioness de Fleury. She recognized me, ordered her carriage to stop, and sent her footman to apprise me that she was on her way to the Château de Tremazan, and to beg that I would pause there before going home, as she had a few words to say to me. I gladly complied. At the château I found quite a large and agreeable company. I need not tell you that the amiable host and hostess received me with open arms."

The countess remarked, approvingly, "Our neighbors the Baron and Baroness de Tremazan are among the most valued of my friends. I have no objection to their making much of you."

"Nor have I," answered Maurice, vivaciously. "But, to continue" —

Bertha interrupted him: "I have so often heard the Marchioness de Fleury quoted as a precedent, and her taste cited as the most perfect in Paris, that I suppose she is a very charming person; — is she not?"

A comical expression, approaching to a grimace, passed over the bright countenance of Maurice, as he answered, "*Charming?*

I suppose the term is applicable to her. At all events, her toilets are the most charming in the world: she dresses to perfection! In her presence one never thinks of anything but the wonderful combination of colors, and the graceful flowing of drapery, that have produced certain artistic effects in her outward adorning. She is style, fashion, elegance, taste personified; consequently she is very *charming as an exhibition of the newest and most captivating costumes,* — as an inventor and leader of modes that become the rage when they have received her stamp."

"But her face and figure, — are they not remarkably handsome?" asked Bertha.

"Her figure is the *fac-simile* of one of those waxen statues which are to be seen in the windows of some of the shops in Paris, and would be styled faultless by a mantua-maker, though it might drive a sculptor distracted if set before him as a model. As for her face, the novel arrangement of her hair and the coquettish disposition of her head-ornaments have always so completely drawn my attention away from her countenance, that I could not tell you the color of her eyes, or the character of any single lineament."

"Perhaps, too," suggested Madeleine, "she is so agreeable in conversation, that you never thought of scanning her features."

"Of course she is agreeable, — that is, in her own peculiar way; for she has an archly graceful manner of discussing the only subjects that interest *her,* and always as though they must be of the deepest interest to *you.* If you speak to her of her projects for the winter or the summer, she will dwell upon the style of dress appropriate in the execution of such and such schemes. If you express your regret at her recent indisposition, she will describe the exquisite *robes de chambre* which rendered her sufferings endurable. If you mention her brother, who has lately received an appointment near the person of the emperor, she will give you a minute account of the most approved court-dresses. If you allude to the possibility that her husband (for such is the rumor) may be sent as ambassador to the United States, she will burst forth in bitter lamentations over the likelihood that American taste may not be sufficiently cultivated to appreciate a Parisian toilet, or to comprehend the great importance of the difficult art of dressing well. If you give the tribute of a sigh to the memory of the lovely sister she lost a year ago, she will run through a list of the garments of woe that gave expression to her sorrow, — passing on to the shades of second, third, and fourth mourning through which she gradually laid aside her grief. You laugh, young ladies. Oh, very well; but I declare to you she went through the catalogue of those mourning dresses, rehearsing the periods at which she adopted such and such a one, while we were dancing a quadrille. In short, the Marchioness de Fleury is an animated fashion-plate! — a lay-figure dressed in gauze, silk, lace, ribbon, feathers, flowers, that breathes, talks, dances, waltzes! — a mantua-maker's, milliner's, hair-dresser's puppet, set in motion, — not a woman."

"Has she really no heart, then?" questioned Bertha.

"I suppose that, anatomically-speaking, a bundle of fibres, which she courteously designates by that name, may rise and fall somewhere beneath her jewel-studded bodice; but I doubt whether the pulsations are not entirely regulated by her attire."

"You are too severe, Maurice," remarked his grandmother, rebukingly. "The Marchioness de Fleury is a lady of the highest standing and of great importance."

"Especially to the Parisian modistes who worship her!" replied Maurice. "But, while we are discussing the lady herself, I am forgetting to tell you her reasons for delaying me half an hour. It was to inquire whether you would be disengaged to-morrow morning, as she purposes paying you a visit to make a proposition which she thinks may prove agreeable to the Countess de Gramont and Count Tristan."

"We are ever proud to receive the Marchioness de Fleury," responded the countess, graciously.

"I dare say you think I have emptied my budget of news," Maurice went on; "but you are mistaken: several bits of agreeable intelligence remain behind. At the Château de Tre-mazan, I saw three of our relatives on the de Gramont side, Madame de Nervac, the Count Damorean, and M. de Bonneville. They inquired kindly after you, Madeleine, and I told them you were the most " —

The countess interrupted him with the inquiry, "Are they upon a visit of several days?"

"I believe so. Now for the last, most pleasant item. As there are so many lively young persons gathered together at the château, some one proposed an impromptu ball. Madame de Tremazan seized upon the idea, and commissioned me to carry invitations to the Countess dowager de Gramont, Mademoiselles Madeleine and Bertha, and Count Tristan, for the evening after to-morrow. I assured her in advance that the invitations would be accepted; — was I not right?"

"Oh, yes," replied Bertha; "I am so glad!"

"We will enjoy a ball greatly!" exclaimed Madeleine.

"And so will I!" said Maurice. "I engage Madeleine for the first quadrille, and Bertha for the first waltz."

"And we both accept!" answered his cousins, with girlish delight.

"Not so fast, young ladies," interrupted the countess. "It is quite out of the question for you to attend a ball of such magnificence as may be expected at the Château de Tremazan."

"And why not, aunt?" asked Bertha, in a disappointed tone. "You surely will not refuse your consent?"

"I deny you a pleasure very unwillingly, dear child, but I am forced to do so. You did not expect to appear at any large assemblies while you were in Brittany, and you have brought no ball-dress with you. You have nothing ready which it would be proper for you to wear at such a brilliant reunion; for the de Tremazans are so rich that everything will be upon the most splendid and costly scale. Mademoiselle Bertha de Merrivale cannot be present upon such an occasion, unless she is attired in a manner that befits her rank and fortune. I, also, have no dress prepared."

"What a pity, what a pity!" half sighed, half pouted Bertha.

"It is too bad, too provoking!" ejaculated Maurice.

"If there be no obstacle but the lack of a ball-dress for yourself and for Bertha, aunt," remarked Madeleine, "we may console ourselves; for we will go to the ball."

"Oh, you dear, good, ingenious Madeleine!" exclaimed Bertha, throwing her arms around her cousin. "I wonder if the time ever *will* arrive when you have not some resource to extricate us from a difficulty?"

"Madeleine forever! Long live Madeleine!" shouted Maurice, with enthusiasm.

"And now, good, fairy godmother, where is the robe of gold and silver to deck your Cinderella?" asked Bertha.

"I did not promise gold and silver apparel; you must be content with a toilet simple, airy, fresh, and spring-like as yourself. And for you, aunt, I will arrange an autumn arraying,— a costume soft, yet bright, like the autumn days which the Americans call 'Indian summer,'—something which will almost make one wish to fall into the sere and yellow leaf of life in the hope of resembling you."

"But how is it possible to make two ball-dresses between this time and night after next?" inquired the countess, evidently not at all averse to the project, if it could be carried into execution.

"I answer for the possibility!" replied Madeleine.

"Yes, Madeleine answers for it!" repeated Maurice.

"Madeleine answers for it!" echoed Bertha; "and you know Madeleine has *the fingers of a fairy;* she can achieve whatever she undertakes. But your own dress, Madeleine?"

"Do not be uneasy about that; we will think of that when the others are ready."

"But if you do not wear a dress that becomes you?" persisted Bertha.

"Why, then I shall have to look at yours, and, remembering that it is my handiwork, be satisfied."

"There is no one like you, Madeleine!" burst forth Maurice, uncontrollably,—"no one! You never think of yourself; you"—

"But, as some one is always good enough to think of me, I deserve little credit on that account," rejoined Madeleine.

"Who could help thinking of you?" murmured Maurice, tenderly.

The countess had not heard the enthusiastic encomium of Maurice, nor his last, involuntary remark. The young man had risen and joined his cousins. His father had taken the vacant seat beside the countess, and was talking to her in a low tone. From the moment he learned that Madeleine's relatives were accidentally assembled at the Château de Tremazan, he had determined to seize that favorable opportunity, and send them the letters requesting that they would by turns offer a home to their poor and orphan relative. These letters, though written upon the day previous, fortunately had not yet been posted. Count Tristan whisperingly communicated his intention to his mother, and received her approval.

Their conversation was interrupted by the entrance of M. Gaston de Bois, who invariably arrived before other guests made their appearance. M. de Bois was such a martyr to nervous timidity, that he could not summon courage to enter a room full of company, even with some great stimulating compensation in view. On the present occasion, though only the family had assembled, his olive complexion crimsoned as he advanced towards the countess, and his expressive, though irregular and not strictly handsome features became almost distorted; he unconsciously thrust his fingers through his hair, throwing it into startling disorder, and twisted his dark moustache until it stood out with sufficient ferocity to suit the face of a brigand in a melodrama.

But the most painful effect of this bewildering embarrassment evinced itself when he attempted to speak. His utterance became suddenly impeded, and, the more violent his efforts to articulate, the more difficult it seemed for him to utter a distinct sentence. He was painfully near-sighted; yet he always detected the faintest smile upon the countenance of any one present, and interpreted it into an expression of derision.

These personal defects, however, were liberally counterbalanced by mental attributes of a high order. His constitutional diffidence caused him to shun society; but he devoted his leisure to books, and was an erudite scholar, without ever mounting the pompous stilts of the pedant. All his impulses were noble and generous, though his best intentions were often frustrated by that fearful self-consciousness which made him dread the possibility of attracting attention. There was a slight shade of melancholy in his character. Life had been a disappointment to him, and he was haunted by a sense of the incompleteness of his own existence.

His estate joined that of the Count de Gramont, and was even more impoverished. Gaston de Bois led a sort of hermit-like life in the gloomy and empty château of his ancestors. He chafed in his confinement, like a caged lion ready to break loose from bondage. But the lion freed might take refuge in his native woods, while Gaston, if he rushed forth into the world, knew that his bashfulness, his stammering, his near-sightedness, would render society a more intolerable prison than his solitary home.

At the Château de Gramont he was a frequent guest, for the countess and her son held him in the highest esteem.

After saluting his host and hostess, he warmly grasped the hand of Maurice, and then addressed Madeleine, with but little hesitation apparent in his speech; but when he turned to Bertha, and essayed to make some pleasant remark, he was suddenly seized with a fit of hopeless stammering.

The beaming smile with which Bertha greeted him was displaced by an expression almost amounting to compassion. Madeleine, with her wonted presence of mind, came to his aid; finished his sentence, as though he had spoken it himself; and went on talking *to him* and *for him*, while he regarded her with an air of undisguised thankfulness and relief.

Between Madeleine and Gaston de Bois there existed that sort of friendship which many persons are sceptical that a

young and attractive woman and an agreeable man can enter
tain for each other without the sentiment heightening into a
warmer emotion. But love and friendship are totally distinct
affections. A woman may cherish the truest, kindliest friendship for a man whom it would be impossible for her to love;
nay, in whom she would totally lose her interest if he once presented himself in the aspect of a lover; and we believe a certain class of men are capable of experiencing the same pure
and kin-like devotion for certain women.

M. de Bois felt that he was comprehended by Madeleine, — that
she sympathized with his misfortunes, appreciated the difficulties of his position, and, without pretending to be blind to his
defects, always viewed them leniently: thus, in her presence he
was sufficiently at ease to be entirely himself; his *amour propre*
received fewer wounds, and he was conscious that he appeared
to better advantage than in the society of other ladies.

Madeleine, on her side, had more than once reflected that
there was no one to whom she could more easily turn to impart
a sorrow, intrust a secret, solicit a favor, or receive consolation and advice, — no one in whom she could so thoroughly confide, as M. de Bois.

Gaston had only commenced to regain his self-possession
when the two American gentlemen, Mr. Hilson and Mr. Meredith, were announced.

The countess received them with a freezing formality which
would have awed any visitors less unsuspicious of the cause of
this augmented stateliness.

They were both gentlemen who held high positions in their
own country; they had brought letters to Count Tristan de
Gramont, with a view of enlisting his interest in the railway
company of which we have before spoken; they had been
cordially received by him, and invited to partake of his hospitality; it therefore never occurred to either of them that the
haughty demeanor of the countess was designed to impress
them with a sense of their inferiority.

Mr. Hilson was what is termed a "self-made" man, — that
is, he owed nothing to the chances of birth; he had received
little early cultivation, but he had educated himself, and therefore all the knowledge he had acquired was positive mental gain,
and brought into active use. He had · inherited no patrimony,
and started life with no advantages of position; but he had made
his own fortune, and earned his own place in the social sphere.
He had been one of the most successful and scientific engineers

which the United States ever produced, and was now the president of an important railroad, and a highly influential member of society.

Mr. Meredith was born in the State of Maryland, — a " man of family," as it is styled. He had not encountered the difficulties and experienced the struggles of his associates; his was therefore a less strong, less highly developed, character. He had travelled over the larger portion of Europe, yet preferred to make his home in America; he had once retired from business, but, finding that he was bored to death without the necessity for occupation, connected himself with the railroad company of which Mr. Hilson was president.

The other guests were gentlemen residing or visiting in the neighborhood. They were the Marquis de Lasalles, the Count Caradore, Messieurs Villiers, Laroche, and Litelle. The two former, being the most important personages, occupied seats at table on the right and left of the countess. Gaston de Bois was well pleased to find himself beside Madeleine; for he was opposite to Bertha, and could feast his eyes upon her fair, unclouded face, and now and then he spoke to her in glances which were far more eloquent than his tongue.

Mr. Hilson sat on the other side of Madeleine. A few naturally suggested questions about his native land unloosed his tongue, and she soon became deeply interested in the information he gave her concerning America, — the habits, views, and aspirations of its people.

After listening for some time, she almost involuntarily murmured, with a half-sigh, " I should like to visit America."

There was something in her own nature which responded to the spirit of self-reliance, energy, and industry, which are so essentially American characteristics.

Bertha sat between the Marquis de Lasalles and Maurice. She was in the highest spirits, and looked superlatively lovely. The brow of the countess gradually smoothed as she noticed how gayly the heiress chatted with her cousin.

The two plates which intruded into the Sèvres set had been a terrible eyesore to Madame de Gramont at first; but Madeleine's suggestion had been acted upon, — they were placed before the young ladies, and, as the countess rose from the table, she comforted herself with the reflection that they had escaped observation.

The gentlemen accompanied the ladies to the drawing-room, and then Maurice lured Madeleine to the piano, and was soon in

raptures over the wild, sweet melodies which she sung with untutored pathos. His grandmother could scarcely conceal her
vexation. Approaching the singer, she took an opportunity,
while Bertha and Maurice were searching for a piece of music,
whisperingly to suggest that Baptiste was old and clumsy, and
the Sèvres set in danger until it was safely locked up again.

Madeleine murmured, in return, " I will steal away unnoticed
and attend to it."

She stole away, but not unperceived, for one pair of eyes
was ever upon her. She found so much besides the valuable
china that demanded attention, and her aid was so heartily welcomed by the old domestics, who had become confused by the
multiplicity of their duties, that it was late in the evening before
she reappeared in the drawing-room. The guests were taking
their leave.

" I am highly flattered by the interest you have expressed in
my country," said Mr. Hilson, in bidding her adieu. " If you
should ever visit America, as you have expressed the desire to
do, and if you should pass through Washington, as you certainly will if you visit America, will you not promise to apprise
me? Here is my address?" and he placed his card in her
hands.

Madeleine looked not a little surprised and embarrassed at
this unexpected and informal proceeding, which she knew
would greatly shock the countess; but, taking the card, answered,
courteously, " I fear nothing is more unlikely than that I should
cross the ocean; but, if such an unlooked-for event should ever
occur, I promise certainly to apprise you."

CHAPTER IV.

PROPOSALS.

On the morrow, at the usual hour for visitors, the count and
his mother sat in the drawing-room awaiting the promised guest.
Maurice, at Count Tristan's solicitation, had very unwillingly
consented to postpone his customary equestrian exercise, and
was sauntering in the garden, wondering over the caprice that
prompted his father to desire his presence at the expected inter-

view. The tramp of hoofs broke his revery; and a superb equipage, drawn by four noble horses, postilion-mounted, dashed up the long avenue that led to the château. He hastened to the carriage-door, and aided the Marchioness de Fleury to alight.

The living embodiment of graceful affability, she greeted him with a volley of slaying smiles; then, with an air which betrayed her triumphant certainty of the execution done, glided past him into the drawing-room, almost disappearing in a cloud of lace, as she made a profound obeisance to the countess, and partially rising out of her misty *entourage* in saluting Count Tristan.

Her voice had a low, studied sweetness as she softly syllabled some pleasant commonplaces, making affectionate inquiries concerning the health of the countess, and simulating the deepest interest as she apparently listened to answers which were in reality unheard. Ere long, she winningly unfolded the object of her visit. Her brother, the young Duke de Montauban, had prayed her to become his ambassador. He recently had the felicity of meeting the niece of the Countess de Gramont, Mademoiselle Bertha de Merrivale. He had been struck and captivated by her grace and surpassing beauty; he now charged his sister to apprise the family of Mademoiselle Bertha that he sought the honor of her hand in marriage, and hoped to obtain a favorable response to his suit.

The consternation created by those words did not escape the quick eyes of the marchioness. The count half rose from his seat, white with vexation, then sat down again, and, making an attempt to hide his displeasure, answered, in a tone of forced courtesy, —

"Though Mademoiselle Bertha de Merrivale is my mother's grandniece, we have no control over her actions or inclinations. Her uncle, the Marquis de Merrivale, who is her guardian, is morbidly jealous of any influence exerted over his niece, even by relatives equally near."

The Countess de Gramont, though she also had been greatly disconcerted, recovered herself more quickly than her son, and answered, with such an excess of suavity that it had the air of exaggeration, —

"We feel deeply indebted for the proposed honor. An alliance with a nobleman of the high position and unblemished name of the Duke de Montauban is all that could be desired for my niece; but, as my son has remarked, her guardian is very punctilious respecting his rights, and would not tolerate an interference with her future prospects. I beg you will believe that we are highly flattered by the proposal of the Duke de Montauban, though we have no power to promote his suit."

Maurice could not help wondering why his father looked so thoroughly vexed, and why his grandmother made such an effort to conceal her displeasure by an assumption of overacted gratification.

The Marchioness de Fleury betrayed neither surprise, disappointment, nor emotion of any kind, except by gently tapping the ground with the exquisitely gaitered little foot that peeped from the mazes of her ample drapery.

She answered, in the most honeyed voice, "Oh! I was misinformed, and I knew that your charming niece was at this moment visiting you."

Then, spreading her bespangled fan, and moving it gently backward and forward, though the day was far from sultry, she dismissed the subject by asking Maurice if he had delivered Madame de Tremazan's invitations to the ball.

Almost before he had concluded his reply, she rose, and, with the most enchanting of smiles, courtesied, as though she were making a reverence in a quadrille of the Lancers, and the lace cloud softly floated out of the room, the human being it encircled being nearly lost to sight when it was in motion.

Maurice could not resist the impulse to turn to his father, and express his amazement that the complimentary proposals made for Bertha by the Marchioness de Fleury had been so definitely declined, adding, "If my little cousin had been already engaged, you could not more decidedly have shut the door upon the duke."

The count bit his lips, and strode up and down the room.

The countess replied, "We have other views for Bertha, — views which we trust would be more acceptable to herself; but here she comes, and I have a few words to say to her in private. Take a turn with your father in the park, Maurice, while I talk to your cousin."

She gave the count a significant glance as she spoke.

Father and son left the room as Bertha entered.

For some minutes the two gentlemen walked side by side in silence. Finding that his father did not seem inclined to converse, Maurice remarked, abruptly, —

"Now that the visit of the marchioness is over, I shall take my postponed ride, if you have no further need of me."

"I *have* need; let your horse wait a few moments longer," replied the count. Can you conceive no reason why we did not for one instant entertain the proposition of the Marchioness de Fleury?"

"None: it was made entirely according to rule; and, if you will allow me to say so, common courtesy seemed to demand that it should have been treated with more consideration."

"Suppose Bertha's affections are already engaged?" suggested the father.

"Ah, that alters the aspect of affairs; but it is hardly possible, — she is so young, and appears to be so heart-free."

"Still, I think she has a preference; and, if I am not mistaken, her choice is one that would give us the highest satisfaction."

"Really!" ejaculated Maurice, unsuspiciously. "Whom, then, does she honor by her election?"

"A very unworthy person!" rejoined the count, in a tone of irritation, "since he is too dull to suspect the compliment."

"You cannot mean"—began Maurice, in confused amazement, but paused, unwilling to finish his sentence with the words that rose to his lips.

"I mean a most obtuse and insensible young man, walking by my side, who has learned to interpret Greek and Latin at college, but not a woman's heart."

"Impossible! You are surely mistaken. Bertha has only bestowed upon me a cousinly regard," answered Maurice, evidently more surprised and embarrassed than pleased by the unexpected communication.

"I presume you do not expect the young lady herself to make known the esteem in which she holds you, undeserving as you are? You must take our word for her sentiments. What this alliance would be to our falling house, I need not represent; it is not even necessary that you should enter into the merits of this side of the question. You must see that Bertha is beautiful and lovable, and would make the most delightful companion for life. Is this not so?"

"Yes, she is beautiful, lovable, and would make a delightful companion," answered Maurice, as though he echoed his father's words without knowing what he said.

"Is she not all you could desire?"

"All, — all I could desire as — as — as a *sister!*" replied Maurice.

"But the question is now of a wife!" rejoined the count, angrily. "Are you dreaming, that you pore upon the ground and answer in that strange, abstracted manner?"

4 *

Maurice looked up, as if about to speak, but hesitated, dubious what reply would be advisable.

The count went on.

"Maurice, your grandmother and I have this matter deeply at heart. Besides, Bertha loves you; you cannot treat her affection with disdain. Promise me that you will at once have an understanding with her, and let this matter be settled. It must not be delayed any longer. Why do you not reply?"

"Yes,—you are right. I ought to have an understanding with her,—*I will have!*" replied Maurice, still in a brown study.

"That is well; and let it be as soon as possible,—to-day, or to-morrow at the latest,—before this ball takes place,—before you meet the Marchioness de Fleury again."

Maurice answered, hastily, "You need not fear that I desire any delay. You have put an idea into my head which would make suspense intolerable. I will speak to her without loss of time. And now will you allow me to wish you good-morning? My horse has been saddled for an hour."

Saying this, he walked toward the stable and called to Gustave, who at once appeared, leading the horse. The viscount vaulted upon its back, and, starting off at full gallop, in a few moments was out of sight.

His father was mystified, doubtful of the real feelings of Maurice, and uncertain what course he meant to pursue, but well assured that he would keep his word; and, if he did, it would be impossible for him to introduce this delicate subject without compromising himself,—nay, without positively offering himself to Bertha. The very mention of such a theme would be a proposal; and, with this consolatory reflection, he returned to the château.

As he passed the drawing-room, he caught a glimpse of Bertha, sitting at his mother's feet. The latter was holding both of the young girl's hands, and talking to her earnestly. Bertha's countenance wore an expression of maidenly confusion and perplexity which, even if the count had not been aware of his mother's intentions, would have betrayed the nature of her discourse.

CHAPTER V.

HEART—BEATS.

MAURICE must have found his equestrian exercise particularly agreeable upon that day, for he returned to the château so late that no one saw him again until the family assembled at dinner.

Bertha was unusually silent and *distraite*, not a single smile rippled her slumbering dimples, and she answered at random. She did not once address Maurice, to whom she usually prattled in a strain of merry *badinage*, and he evinced the same constraint toward her.

As soon as the ladies rose from table, Madeleine retired to her own chamber. Her preparations for the morrow demanded all her time. The count retreated to the library. Maurice and Bertha were on the point of finding themselves *tête-à-tête*, for the countess just remembered that she had a note to write, when her little plot to leave the cousins together was frustrated by the entrance of the Marquis de Lasalles.

The clouds suddenly melted from Bertha's countenance when the dull old nobleman was announced. She greeted him with an air of undisguised relief, as though she had been happily reprieved from an impending calamity. The lively warmth of her salutation attracted the marquis to her side, and he remained fascinated to the spot for the rest of the evening. The countess was too thoroughly well-bred to allow herself to look annoyed, or, even in secret, to acknowledge that she wished the marquis elsewhere; but she was disconcerted, and puzzled by the unaccountable change in Bertha's deportment.

So passed the evening.

The next morning, when Bertha appeared at breakfast, every one, Maurice perhaps excepted, remarked that she seemed weary and dispirited. Her brilliant complexion had lost something of its wonted lustre; her usually clear blue eyes looked heavy and shadowed; her rosy mouth had a half-sorrowful, half-fretful expression. It was evident that some nightmare preyed upon her mind, and had broken the childlike sound sleeping that generally visited her pillow. When the ball that was to take place that evening was mentioned, she brightened a little, but quickly sank back into her musing mood.

"You must give me some assistance this morning, Bertha,"

said Madeleine, as she poured a few drops of almond oil into a tiny cup. "Your task shall be to gather, during your morning walk, this little basket full of the greenest and most perfect ivy leaves you can find, and bring them to the *châlet*. Then, if you feel inclined to aid me further, I will show you how to impart an emerald brilliancy to every leaf by a touch of this oil and a few delicate manipulations."

"I suspect you are inventing something very novel and tasteful," remarked Bertha, with more indifference than was natural to her.

"You shall judge by and by," replied Madeleine, as she left the room, with the cup in her hand.

She carried it, with her work, to a dilapidated summer-house, embowered by venerable trees. Madeleine's taste had given a picturesque aspect to this old *châlet*, and concealed or beautified the ravages of time. With the assistance of Baptiste, she had planted vines which flung over the outer walls a green drapery, intermingled with roses, honeysuckle, and jasmine; and, within doors, a few chairs, a well-worn sofa, a table, and footstool gave to the rustic apartment an appearance of habitableness and comfort. This was Madeleine's favorite resort when the weather was fine, and not a few of the magic achievements of her "fairy fingers" had been created in that romantic and secluded locality. There was glamour, perhaps, in the sylvan retreat, that acted like inspiration upon hands and brain.

Bertha usually flitted about her as she worked, wandering in and out, now and then sitting down for a few moments, and reading aloud, by fits and starts, or occasionally taking up a needle and making futile efforts to busy herself with the womanly implement, but always restless, and generally abandoning her attempt after a brief trial; for Bertha frankly confessed that she admired industry in her cousin without being able to practise it in her own person.

This morning, however, Madeleine sat alone; the fleecy tarlatan, that rolled in misty whiteness around her, gradually assuming the shape of female attire. Bettina had been despatched to Rennes on the day previous to procure this material for Bertha's ball-costume, and had not returned until late in the evening; yet the dress was cut out and fitted before Madeleine closed her eyes that night. The first auroral ray of light that stole into her chamber the next day fell upon the lithe figure of the young girl folding tucks that were to be made in the skirt, measuring distances, placing pins here and there for guides; and, as the dawn broke, she sat down unwearily, and sent her needle in and out of the transparent fabric with a rapidity of motion marvellous to behold.

After a time, the rickety door of the *châlet* was unceremoniously pushed open, and old Baptiste entered. He deposited a basket filled with ivy leaves upon the table, and said that Mademoiselle Bertha desired him to gather and deliver them to Mademoiselle Madeleine.

"Has she not taken her usual walk this morning, then?" asked Madeleine, in surprise.

"No, mademoiselle; Mademoiselle Bertha only came to me as I was weeding the flower-beds, and immediately went back to the château. Have I brought mademoiselle enough ivy?"

"Quite sufficient, thank you; but I did not mean to consume your time, my good Baptiste. I thought Mademoiselle Bertha would take pleasure in selecting the ivy herself."

"Mademoiselle Madeleine knows how glad I always am to serve her," answered Baptiste.

For another hour Madeleine sat alone, singing, in a soft murmur, as she sewed, while

> "Her soul was singing at a work apart
> Behind the walls of sense."

The sound of a manly step upon the pathway silenced her plaintive melody. The next moment the vines, that formed a verdant curtain about the otherwise unprotected casement, were gently drawn back, and a face appeared at the window.

"I thought I should find you here on this bright morning, Mademoiselle Madeleine. May I en — en — enter?" asked Gaston de Bois, speaking with so much ease that his only stammer came upon the last word.

"If you please."

"A noble slave of the needle," he continued, still looking in at the window. "The daughter of a duke, with the talents of a dressmaker! *Where* will ge — ge — genius next take up her abode?"

"Genius — since you are pleased to apply that sublime appellation to my poor capacities for wielding the most familiar and harmless weapon of my sex — is no respecter of persons, as you see. You are an early visitor to-day, M. de Bois. Of course, you are on your way to the château?"

"I have let — let — letters for the count. He intrusted me yes — es — esterday with a package to take with me to the Château de Tremazan, where I was engaged to pass the evening, and I have brought him the replies. But before I play the post-man, let me come in and talk to you, since you are the only person I can ever manage to talk to at all."

" Come in then, and welcome."

Gaston accepted the invitation with alacrity. He took a seat, and, regarding her work, remarked, " This must be for to-night's ball ; is it your own dress ? "

" Mine ? All these tucks for a dress of *mine* ? No, indeed, it is Bertha's, and I hope she will like the toilet I have planned ; each tuck will be surmounted by a garland of ivy, left open at the front, and fastened where it breaks off, on either side, with blush roses. Then among her luxuriant curls a few sprigs of ivy must float, and perhaps a rose peep out. You may expect to see her looking very beautiful to-night."

M. de Bois sighed, and remained silent for a moment. Then he resumed the conversation by asking, " And the dress will be ready in time ? "

" Before it is needed, I trust, for it is now well advanced. Fortunately my aunt's dress was completed last night. But it was not new, — only a fresh combination of materials that had already been employed. Yet she was kind enough to be highly pleased."

" Well she might be ! You are always wor — wor — working for the good of the whole family."

" What other return can I make for the good I have received ? " replied Madeleine, with emotion. " Can I ever forget that, when I was left alone in the world, without refuge, without friends, almost without bread, my great-aunt extended to me her protec-tion, supplied all my wants, virtually adopted me as her own child ? Can I offer her too much gratitude in return ? Can I lavish upon her too much love ? No one knows how well I love her and all that is hers ! How well I love that dwelling which received the homeless orphan ! People call the old château dreary and gloomy ; to me it is a palace ; its very walls are dear. I love the trees that yield me their shade, — the parks that you no doubt think a wilderness, — the rough, un-weeded walks which I tread daily in search of flowers, — this ruined summer-house, where I have passed hours of delicious calm, — all the now familiar objects that I first saw through my tears, before they were dried by the hand of affection ; and I reflect with joy that probably I shall never quit the Heaven-pro-vided home which has been granted me. I have been so very happy here."

"Real — eal — eally?" asked Gaston, doubtingly. "I fancied sometimes, when I saw the Countess and Count Tristan so — so — so severe to you, that" —

"Have they not the right to find fault with me when I fail to please them? That is only what I expect, and ought to bear patiently. I will not pretend to say that sometimes, when I have been misunderstood, and my best efforts have failed to bring about results that gratify them, — I will not say that my heart does not swell as though it would burst; but I console myself by reflecting that some far off, future day will come to make amends for all, and bring me full revenge."

"Re — re — revenge! You re — re — revenge?" cried Gaston, in astonishment.

"Yes, *revenge!*" laughed Madeleine. "You see what a vindictive creature I am! And I am positively preparing myself to enjoy this delightful revenge. I will make you the confidant of my secret machinations. This old château is lively enough now, and the presence of Bertha and Maurice preserve to my aunt the pleasant memory of her own youth. But by and by Maurice will go forth into the world, and perhaps we shall only see him from time to time, at long intervals. Bertha will marry" —

At these words M. de Bois gave a violent start, and, stammering unintelligibly, rose from his seat, upsetting his chair, walked to the window, brought destruction upon some of Madeleine's vines by pulling them violently aside, to thrust out his head; then strode back, lifted the fallen chair, knocking down another, and with a flushed countenance seated himself again.

Madeleine went on, as if she had not noticed his abrupt movement.

"Solitude and *ennui* might then oppress the Countess and even Count Tristan, and render their days burdensome. I am laying up a store of materials to enliven these scenes of weariness and loneliness. I have made myself quite a proficient in *piquet,* that I may pass long evenings playing with the count; I have noted and learned all the old airs that his mother delights to hear, because they remind her of her girlhood, and I will sing them to her when she is solitary and depressed. I will make her forget the absence of the dear ones who must leave such a void in her life; in a thousand ways I will soften the footsteps of age and infirmity as they steal upon her; — that will be the amends time will bring me, — that is the *revenge* I seek."

"Ah! Mademoiselle Mad — ad — adeleine, you are an angel!"

"So far from an angel," answered Madeleine, gayly, "that you make me feel as though I had laid a snare, by my egotism, to entrap that ill-deserved compliment. Now let us talk about yourself and your own projects. Do you still hold to the resolution you communicated to me in our last conversation?"

"Yes, your advice has decided me."

"I should have been very impertinent if I had ventured to give you advice. I can hardly be taxed with that presumption. We were merely discussing an abstract question, — the use of faculties accorded us, and the best mode of obtaining happiness through their employment; and you chose to apply my general remarks to your particular case."

"You drew a picture which made me feel what a worth — orth — orthless mortal I am, and this incited me to throw off the garment of slothfulness, and put on armor for the battle of life."

"So be it! Now tell us what you have determined upon."

"My unfortunate imped — ed — ediment is my great drawback. Maurice hopes to become a lawyer; but that profession would be out of the ques — es — estion for me who have no power to utter my ideas. I could not enter the army, for what kind of an officer could I make? How should I ever manage to say to a soldier, 'Go and brave death for your coun — oun — ountry'? I should find it easier to do myself than to say it. Some diplomatic position I *might* possibly fill. As speech, according to Talleyrand, was given to men to disguise their thoughts, a man who st — st — stammers is not in much danger of making known his private medita — a — ations."

"That is ingenious reasoning," replied Madeleine. "I hope something will grow out of it."

"It is grow — ow — ing already. Yesterday, at the Château de Tremazan, I had a long interview with the Marquis de Fleury. He expects to be sent as ambassador to the United States. We are old friends. We talked, and I tol — ol — old" —

"You told him your views," said Madeleine, aiding him so quietly and naturally that her assistance was scarcely noticeable. "And what was concluded upon? for your countenance declares that you have concluded upon something. If the marquis goes to America, you will perhaps accompany him?"

"Yes, as sec — sec — sec —"

"As secretary?" cried Madeleine. "That will be an admirable position. But America — ah! it is a long, long distance from Brittany! This is good news for you; but there are two persons to whom it will cause not a little pain."

" To who — o — om ? " inquired Gaston, with suppressed agitation.

" To my cousin Bertha, and to me."

" Mademoiselle Ber — er — ertha! Will *she* heed my absence? She — she — she, — will she ? " asked Gaston, confusedly.

" Yes — but take care ; if you let me see how deeply that idea affects you, you will fail to play the diplomat in disguising your thoughts, for I shall divine your secret."

" My secret, — what — what secret? What is it you divine? What do you imagine? I mean."

" That you love Bertha, — love her as she deserves to be loved ? "

" I? I? " replied M. de Bois, trying to speak calmly; but, finding the attempt in vain, he burst forth : " Yes, it is but too true ; I love her with my whole soul ; I love her passionately ; love her despairingly, — ay, *despairingly !* "

" And why *despairingly ?* "

" Alas ! she is so rich ! " he answered, in a tone of chagrin.

" True, she is encumbered with a large and *un*-encumbered estate."

" A great misfortune for me ! " sighed Gaston.

" A misfortune which you cannot help, and which Bertha will never remember when she bestows her heart upon one who is worthy of the gift."

" How can she ever deem *me* worthy? Even if I succeed in making myself a name, — a position ; even if I become all that you have caused me to dream of being, — this dreadful imped — ed — ediment, this stammering which renders me ridiculous in the eyes of every one, in her eyes even, will " —

" Your stammering is only the effect of timidity," answered Madeleine, soothingly. " Believe me, it is nothing more ; as you overcome your diffidence and gain self-possession, you will find that it disappears. For instance, you have been talking to me for some time with ease and fluency."

" To *you*, ah, yes ; with *you* I am always at my ease, — I have always confidence. It is not difficult to talk to one for whom I have so much affection, — so *much*, and yet not *too much*."

" That proves fluent speech possible."

" But to any one else, if I venture to open my heart, I hesitate, — I get troubled, — I — I stammer, — I make myself ridic — ic — iculous ! "

" Not at all."

" But I do," reiterated Gaston, warmly. " Fancy a man

5

saying to a woman he adores, yet in whose presence he trembles
like a school-boy, or a culprit, " I — I — I — lo — ov — ov — ove
you ! "

"The fact is," began Madeleine, laughing good-naturedly.

" *There! there!* " cried M. de Bois, with a gesture of impatience and discouragement; "the fact is, that you laugh yourself, — *you*, who are so forbearing ! "

" Pardon me ; you mistook " —

" You could not help it, I know. It is precisely that which
discourages me. And yet it is very odd ! I have one method
by which I can speak for five minutes at a time without stopping or hesitating."

" Indeed ! Why, then, do you not always employ that magical
method in society ? "

" It would hardly be admissible in polite circles. Would you
believe it ? — it is very absurd, but so is everything that apper-
tains to us unfortunate tongue-tied wretches."

" Tell me what your method is."

" I — I — I do not dare ; you will only laugh at me again."

" No ; I promise I will not."

" Well, then, my method is to become very much animated, —
to lash myself into a state of high excitement, and to hold forth as
though I were making an exordium, — to talk with furious rapidity, using the most forcible expressions, the most emphatic ejaculations ! Those unloose my tongue ! My words hurl themselves
impetuously forward, as zouaves in battle ! Only, as you may
conceive, this discourse is not of a very classic nature, and
hardly suited to the drawing-room, — especially, as I receive
great help, and rush on all the faster, for a few interjections that
come under the head of — of — of swear — ear — earing ! "

"*Swearing?*" was all Madeleine could say, controlling a strong
inclination to merriment.

" Yes, downright swearing; employing strong expletives, —
actual oaths ! Oh, it helps me more than you can believe. But
just imagine the result if I were to harangue Mademoiselle
Bertha in this style ! She would — would — "

" Would think it very original, and, as she has a joyous temperament, she might laugh immoderately. But she likes originality, and the very oddity of the discourse might impress her
deeply. Then, too, she is very sympathetic, and she would
probably be touched by the necessity which compelled you to
employ such an extraordinary mode of expression."

" Ah, if that were only true ! "

" I think it *is* true.

"Thank you! thank you!"

Madeleine was opening a skein of silk, and, extending it to M. de Bois, she said : " Will you assist me ? It is for Bertha I am working. Will you hold this skein ? It will save time."

Gaston, well pleased, stretched out his hands. Madeleine adjusted the skein, and commenced winding.

"Besides, who knows?" she went on to say. "It seems to me very possible that the very singularity of such an address might captivate her, and give you a decided advantage over lovers who pressed their suit in hackneyed, stereotyped phrases."

"You think so?"

"I should not be surprised if such were the case, because Bertha has a decided touch of eccentricity in her character."

"If I only dared to think that she had ever given me the faintest evidence of favorable regard!"

"When she sees you embarrassed and hesitating, does she not always finish your sentences?"

"Is it pos — pos — pos —" stammered Gaston.

"Possible?" said Madeleine. "Yes, I have observed that she invariably does so if she imagines herself unnoticed. I have besides remarked a certain expression on her transparent countenance when we talked of you, and she has dropped a word, now and then," —

"What — what — what words? But no, you are mocking me cruelly! It cannot be that she ever thinks of me! I have too powerful a rival."

"A rival! what rival?" asked Madeleine, in genuine astonishment.

"The Viscount Maurice."

The silken thread snapped in Madeleine's hand.

"You have broken the thread," remarked M. de Bois; "I hope it was not owing to my awkward hold — old — olding."

"No, no," answered Madeleine, hurriedly, and taking the skein out of his hand, but tangling it inextricably as she tried to draw out the threads.

"You — you — you — think my cousin Maurice loves Bertha?" she asked, hardly aware of the pointedness of her own question.

"I do not exactly say *that;* but how will it be possible for him to help loving her? Good gracious, Mademoiselle Madeleine! what have I said to affect you? How pale you have become!"

Madeleine struggled to appear composed, but the hands that held the snarled skein trembled, and no effort of will could force the retreating blood back to her face.

" Nothing — you have said nothing, — you are quite right, I — I — I dare say."

" Why, you are just as troubled and embarrassed as I was just now."

" I? nonsense! I'm — I'm — I'm only — only — "

" And you stammer, — you actually stammer almost as badly as I do! " exclaimed Gaston, in exultation. " Ah, Mademoiselle Madeleine! I have betrayed to you *my* secret, — you have discovered *yours* to me! "

" Monsieur de Bois, I implore you, do not speak another word on this subject! Enough that, if *I had a secret*, there is no one in the world to whom I would sooner confide it."

" Why, then, do you now wish to hide from me the preference with which you honor your cousin? "

Madeleine replied, in a tremulous tone, " You do not know how deep a wound you are probing, how heavy a grief you " —

" Why should it be a grief? What obstacle impedes your union? "

" An insurmountable obstacle, — one that exists in my own heart."

" How can that be, since that heart is his? "

" Those to whom I owe everything," replied Madeleine, " cherish the anticipation that Maurice will make a brilliant marriage. Even if my cousin looked upon me with partial eyes, could I rob my benefactors of that dearest hope? Could I repay all their benefits to me by causing them such a cruel disappointment? I could never be so ungrateful, — so guilty, — so inhuman. Therefore, I say, the obstacle lies in my own heart: that heart revolts at the very contemplation of such an act. I pray you never to speak to me again on this subject; and give me your word that no one shall ever know what I have just confided to you, — I mean what you suspect — what you suspect, it may be, *erroneously!* "

" I promise you on the honor of a gentleman."

" Thank you."

A step was heard on the path leading to the summer-house.

Gaston looked towards the open door and said, "It is the count."

At the same moment he withdrew to the window.

Madeleine, who had risen, resumed her seat, and, as she plied her needle, half buried her agitated face in the white drapery which lay in her lap.

The count entered with downcast eyes, and flung himself into a chair. He had not perceived that any one was present. Madeleine found it difficult to command her voice, yet could not allow him to remain unaware that he was not alone.

After a brief interval, she said, in a tolerably quiet tone, " I am afraid you have not chosen a very comfortable seat. I told Baptiste to remove that chair, for its legs are giving signs of the infirmities of age."

At the sound of her voice the count glanced at her over his shoulder, and said, brusquely, " What are you doing there ? "

" Playing Penelope, as usual."

The count returned harshly, " Always absorbed in some feminine frippery, just as if " —

" Just as if I were a woman ! " answered Madeleine, forcing a laugh.

" A woman in your position should find some less frivolous employment."

Madeleine replied, in a tone of badinage that would have disarmed most men, " How cruelly my cousin pretends to treat me ! He actually makes believe to scold me when I am occupied with the interests of his family,—when I am literally *shedding my blood* in their behalf ! " she added playfully, holding towards him the white dress upon which a slight red stain was visible ; for the needle grasped by her trembling hands had pricked her.

" Good heavens, Madeleine ! when will you lay aside those intolerable airs and graces which you invariably assume, and which would be very charming in a young girl of sixteen, — a girl like Bertha ; but, in a woman who has arrived at your years, — a woman of twenty-one, — become ridiculous affectation ? "

M. de Bois, enraged at the injustice of this rebuke, could control himself no longer, and came forward with a lowering visage. The count turned towards him in surprise.

" Ah, M. de Bois, I was not aware of your presence. I must have interrupted a *tête-à-tête*. You perceive, I am, now and then, obliged to chide."

Gaston answered only by a bow, though his features wore an expression which the count would not have been well pleased to see if he had interpreted aright.

" But," continued the latter, " we are most apt to chide those whom we love best, as you are aware."

" I am a — a — ware," began M. de Bois, trying to calm his indignation, yet experiencing a strong desire to adopt his new method of speaking fluently by using strong interjections.

The count changed the subject by asking, " Did you deliver

the letters, of which you had the goodness to take charge, to the Count Damoreau, Madame de Nervac, and Monsieur de Bonneville?"

"Our relatives!" exclaimed Madeleine, unreflectingly. "Have you forgotten that you will see them to-night at the ball? But I beg pardon; perhaps you had something very important to write about."

"It *was* very important," answered the count, dryly.

"I im — im — imagined so," remarked M. de Bois, "by the sensation the letters created. Madame de Nervac turned pale, and the Count Damoreau turned red, and M. de Bonneville gnawed his nails as he was reading."

"Had they the kindness to send answers by you, as I requested?"

"Yes, the object of my early vi — vi — visit was to deliver them. I heard Mademoiselle Madeleine singing as I passed the *châlet*, and paused to pay my respects."

He drew forth three letters, and placed them in the count's hand.

The latter seized them eagerly, and seemed inclined to break the seals at once, but changed his mind, and putting them in his pocket, said, "Shall I have the pleasure of your company to the château?"

M. de Bois could not well refuse.

He left the *châlet* with the count, but, after taking a few steps, apologized for being obliged to return in search of a glove he had dropped. He went back alone. Madeleine was occupied with her needle as when he left her. There were no traces of tears upon her cheeks; there was no flush, no expression of anger or mortification upon her serene countenance.

M. de Bois regarded her a moment in surprise, for he had expected to find her weeping, or looking vexed, or, at all events, in a state of excitement.

"Is the count often in such an amiable temper?" he asked.

"No; pray, do not imagine *that;* he is evidently troubled to-day. You saw how preoccupied he was. Something has gone wrong, something annoys him. He did not mean to be harsh."

"And *you* can excuse him? Well, then *I* cannot! I felt as though I must speak when he rated you so unreasonably. And, if I had spoken, I should certainly have had my tongue loosened by swearing; perhaps I shall yet"—

"Pray, M. de Bois," urged Madeleine, "do not try to defend

me, or allude to what you unfortunately heard. It will only make my position more trying."

" So I fear ; but I have something to say to you. *You* have given *me* good counsels; you must listen to some I have to give you in return, — but not now. You are going to the ball to-night? "

" Yes, certainly."

" Perhaps I may find an opportunity of talking to you there."

Saying these words, he picked up the glove, and hastened to rejoin the count, who was too much absorbed in his own thoughts to remark the length of his friend's absence.

———————

CHAPTER VI.

UNMASKING.

MADELEINE, left alone in the old *châlet*, remained for some time absorbed in her work, which progressed rapidly. The ivy leaves were dexterously polished, and a graceful garland laid above every tuck of the transparent white dress. The last leafy band was nearly completed, when the door again creaked upon its rusty hinges, and the young girl, looking up, beheld Maurice.

" Is not Bertha here? " he asked, in a tone that sounded very unlike his usual cheerful voice. " I came to seek her, and felt sure she must be with you."

" I have not seen her since early morning," answered Madeleine. " She promised to bring me this basket full of ivy leaves, but sent Baptiste instead."

" I looked for her in the library, the *boudoir*, the drawing-room, and the garden, before I came here," Maurice continued, in the same grave tone. " She has disappeared just at the moment when I have made up my mind to have an understanding without further delay."

Madeleine's speaking countenance betrayed her surprise, for it seemed strange that Maurice should desire an especial interview with his cousin, whom he saw at all hours; and stranger still that he appeared to be so much disturbed.

" How serious you look, Maurice ! Are you troubled ? Has anything occurred to cause you unhappiness ? "

"I can have no disguises from you, Madeleine. I am thoroughly sick at heart. In the first place, my father and my grandmother have violently opposed my determination to embark in an honorable and useful career of life; — *that* threw a cloud over me almost from the hour I entered the château. I tried to forget my disappointment for the moment, that no shadow might fall upon your birthday happiness; besides, I clung to the hope that I might yet convince them of the propriety, the policy, the actual necessity of the step I propose to take. My father, yesterday, stunned me with a piece of intelligence which renders me wretched, yet forces me to act. I have given him my promise; there is no retreat. I must bring this matter to a climax, be the sequence what it may; and yet I dread to make the very first movement."

"I am too dull to read the riddle of the sphinx, and your words are as enigmatical. I have not begun to find their clew," replied Madeleine, pausing in the garland she was forming, and letting the ivy drop unnoticed around her.

The first impulse of Maurice was to gather the fallen leaves; the second prompted him gently to force the dress, she was so tastefully adorning, out of her hands, and toss it upon the table.

" I see your task is nearly completed, and Bertha's toilet for the ball will be sufficiently picturesque to cause the Marchioness de Fleury to die of envy ; can you not, therefore, rest from your labors, good fairy dressmaker, and talk awhile with me? I need consolation, — I need advice, — and you alone can give me both."

" I ? " Madeleine spoke that single word tremulously, and a faint flush passed over her soft, pale face.

" *You*, Madeleine, you, and *you* only ! "

"There is Bertha, at last," she exclaimed, rising hastily, and approaching the door. " Do you not see her blue dress yonder through the trees ? Bertha ! Bertha !" and, leaving Maurice, she went forth to meet Bertha.

" Where have you hidden yourself all the morning, little truant ? Why ! what has happened to distress you ? Your eyes look as though you had been weeping. Dear Bertha ! what ails you ? "

" I could not bear it any longer," almost sobbed Bertha, laying her head upon her cousin's shoulder. " I could not help coming to you, though I wanted to act entirely upon my own responsibility, and I had determined not even to consult you, for I am always fearful of getting you into trouble with my aunt."

Madeleine was so completely mystified that she could only

murmur half to herself, "More enigmas! What can they mean?"

Then, passing her arm around Bertha's slender waist, they walked to the summer-house. The position of Bertha's head caused her bright ringlets completely to veil her face, and it was not until after she entered the *châlet,* and shook the blinding locks from before her eyes, that she saw Maurice. She drew back with a movement of vexation and confusion never before evinced at his presence, — clung to Madeleine as though for protection, and seemed on the point of bursting into tears.

"Maurice came here expecting to find you with me," observed Madeleine. "He wanted to speak to you."

"Did he? — yes, I know he did. I know what he is going to say; I kept out of his way on purpose, until I could make up my mind about it all; I mean, I thought it best to postpone; but it does not matter, — I would rather have it over; no, — I don't mean *that,* — I mean " —

Bertha's perturbation rendered any clearer expression of her meaning out of the question.

Madeleine took up the dress, which Maurice had flung upon the table, and said, "When you return to the house, Bertha, will you not come to my room and try on your dress? It is just completed."

"Stay, stay, Madeleine!" exclaimed Bertha and Maurice together.

"You see, we *both* desire you to stay," added Maurice; "therefore you cannot refuse. We have no secrets from you, — have we, Bertha?"

"*I* had none until yesterday; but my aunt is inclined to be so severe with Madeleine, that I feared I might make mischief by taking her into my confidence. Do not go, Madeleine. Sit down, for you *must* stay. If you go, I will go with you; and Maurice wants to speak to me, — I mean, I want to speak to him, — that is to say, he intends to " —

Madeleine resumed her seat.

"Since you so tyrannically insist upon my remaining, I will finish this garland while you are having your mysterious explanation."

Maurice approached Bertha with a hesitation which had some slight touch of awkwardness. Feeling that it was easier to induce *her* to break the ice than to take the first step upon this delicate ground himself, he remarked, "You wanted to speak to me; what did you desire to say, my dear little cousin?"

Bertha looked up innocently into his face, as though she was scanning his features for the first time.

"What my aunt says is all very true. You *are* exceedingly handsome; I never denied it, except in jest; and you *are* decidedly agreeable, except now and then; and you *have* a noble heart,—I never doubted it; and a fine intellect,—though I do not know much about *that;* and any woman might be proud of you, —that is, I dare say most women would."

"And I have a little cousin who is an adroit flatterer, and who is herself beautiful enough for a Hebe, and whose fascinations are sufficiently potent to captivate any reasonable or unreasonable man."

"Oh! but that is not to the point. I did not mean that we should exchange compliments. What I want to say is that such an attractive and agreeable young man as you are will naturally find hosts of young girls, who would any of them be proud to be chosen as his wife."

"And you, with your grace and beauty, your lovable character, and your large fortune, will have suitors innumerable, from among whom you may readily select one who will be worthy of you."

"But that is not to the point either! I told my aunt that I was not insensible to all your claims to admiration. I assure you I did you ample justice!"

"You were very kind and complimentary, little cousin; but I said as much of you to my father. I gave him to understand that I acknowledged you to be one of the most charming beings in the world, and that I thought the man to whom you gave your hand would be the happiest of mortals, and that I did not believe *that man* could value you more as a wife than I should as a sister."

"*A sister! A sister!* Oh! I am so glad!—a *sister?* You do not really love me, then?"

"Have I said that?"

"You have said the same thing, and I am overjoyed! I can never thank you half enough!"

"*You* do not love *me* then?" asked Maurice.

"I love you with all my heart! I never loved you half as well as at this moment!—that is as—as—a *brother;* for you love me as a *sister,* while my aunt declared you hoped to make me your wife,—that you were crazily in love with me, and that if I refused you, I should ruin all your future prospects, for the blow would almost kill you. I cannot tell you how chagrined I was at the deplorable prospect. And it's all a mistake, — is it not?"

"My father assured me that you had formed the most flattering attachment for me. Is that a mistake also?" inquired Maurice, skilfully avoiding the rudeness of a direct reply to her question.

"Oh! I never cared a straw for you except as the dearest cousin in the world!"

"But why," asked Maurice, resuming his usual gay tone of raillery, "why, if I am the incomparable being you pretend to think me, why are you so particularly averse to becoming my wife? What do you say to that? I should like to have an explanatory answer, little cousin; or else you must take back all your compliments."

"Not one of them!" replied Bertha, merrily. "I am so charmed with you at this moment that I feel inclined to double their number. Yet there is a reason why I should have refused you, even if you had offered yourself to me."

"Is it because you like somebody else better?"

"No, no," answered Bertha, hastily; "how can you suggest such an idea? But I suppose *you do so because that is your reason* for desiring to refuse my hand?"

"I shall be obliged to think my suggestion correct, unless you tell me why you are so glad to escape becoming my wife."

"It was because," said Bertha, approaching her rosy mouth to his ear, and speaking in a low tone, "because there is another woman, who is far more worthy of you, who would make you a better wife than I could, and who — who does not exactly *hate* you."

"Another woman?"

"Hush! do not speak so loudly. There is nothing in the world I desire so much as to see that other woman happy; for there is no one I love half so well."

"The garland is finished!" Madeleine broke in, starting up abruptly, for she had caught the whispered words. "Come, Bertha, we must hasten back to the château. I must try on your dress immediately."

"Oh, since it is finished, we have plenty of time," said Bertha. "It is quite early in the day yet, and Maurice and I are deeply interested in our conversation. We were never before such fast friends and devoted cousins."

"Never," replied Maurice.

"But the dress may need some alteration," persisted Madeleine. "Pray, pray come!"

She spoke almost imploringly, and in an excited tone, which the mere trying on of a dress did not warrant.

"Oh, you dear despot! I suppose you must be obeyed."

Bertha snatched the ivy-garlanded dress, and bounded away. Madeleine would have followed, but Maurice seized her hand detainingly.

"One moment, Madeleine, — grant me one moment!"

"Not now. Bertha will be waiting for me!" And she made an effort to free her imprisoned hand.

"You shall tell her that you were taken captive, and she will forgive you, if it be only for the sake of your *jailer*. There's vanity for you!"

"But my arrangements for this evening are not all completed. It is growing late, Maurice; I entreat you to release me; I *cannot* remain — I *must* go!"

"Not until I have spoken to you. The time has come when you must hear me."

Madeleine felt that there was no escape, and, forcing herself to assume an air of composure, answered, "Speak, then; what can you have to say, Maurice, to which I ought to listen?"

"Must I tell you? Have you not divined? Must I show you my heart? If no responsive pulse in your own has revealed to you what is passing in mine, I am truly unfortunate, — I have been deceived indeed!"

"Maurice, Maurice! for the love of Heaven" —

"You do well to say for the love of Heaven; for I love Heaven all the better for loving a being who bears the impress of Heaven's own glorious hand! Yes, Madeleine, ever loved, — loved from the first hour we met."

The rustling of silk interrupted his sentence. Madeleine tremblingly withdrew her hand. The Countess de Gramont stood before them! Her tall figure dilated until it seemed to shut out all the sunlight beyond; her countenance grew ashy with suppressed rage; her black eyes shot out glances that pierced like arrows; not a sound issued from her tightly-compressed lips.

Maurice, recovering himself, tried to assume an unconcerned air, and stooped to gather some of the ivy leaves scattered around him. Madeleine bowed her head as a culprit who has no defence to make, and no hope of concealment to cling to as a last refuge.

The countess broke the painful silence, speaking in a hollow, scornful tone: "I am here at an unfortunate moment, it seems!"

There was no reply.

" Perhaps I ought to apologize for disturbing you," she continued, sarcastically.

" Not at all — not at all," said Maurice, who felt that it was his duty to answer and shield Madeleine, as far as possible, from his grandmother's displeasure.

" Why, then, is Madeleine covered with confusion ? Why did she so quickly withdraw her hand ? How — how came it clasped in yours ? "

" Is she not my cousin ? " answered Maurice, evasively. " Have I no right to show her affection ? Must I renounce the ties of blood ? "

" It is not you, Maurice, whom I blame," said the countess, trying to speak less sternly. " It is Madeleine, who should not have permitted this unmeet familiarity. I well know by what arts she has lured you to forget yourself. The fault lies with her."

For the first time the countess beheld a flash of indignation in the eyes Madeleine lifted from the ground.

" Madame — aunt ! " she began.

The countess would not permit her to proceed.

" I know what I say ! You have too much tact and quickness not to have comprehended our hopes in regard to Maurice and Bertha ; and it has not escaped my notice that you have sought, by every artful manœuvre in your power, to frustrate those hopes."

" I ? " ejaculated Madeleine, aghast at the charge, and too much bewildered to be able to utter a denial.

" Yes, *you !* Have you not sought to fascinate Maurice by every species of wily coquetry ? Have you not " —

" Grandmother ! " cried Maurice, furiously.

" Be silent, Maurice, — it is Madeleine to whom I am addressing my remarks, and her own conscience tells her their justice."

" Aunt, if ever by word, or look, or thought " —

" Oh ! it was all done in the most apparently artless, natural, *purposeless* manner ! But the same end was always kept steadily in view. What I have witnessed this morning convinces me of your aims. Your movements were so skilfully managed that they scarcely seemed open to suspicion. The most specious coquetry has governed all your actions. You were always attired more simply than any one else ; but by this very simplicity you thought to render yourself remarkable, and attract a larger share of attention. You always pretended to shun observation,

6

that you might be brought into more positive notice. You affected to avoid Maurice, that he might feel tempted to follow you, — that he might be lured to seek you when you were alone, as you were a moment ago, — that he might" —

Maurice could restrain his ire no longer. He broke forth with vehemence, —" Grandmother, I cannot listen to this injustice. I cannot see Madeleine so cruelly insulted. Were it my mother herself who spoke, I would not stand by and see her trample thus upon an innocent and defenceless heart."

Madeleine turned to Maurice beseechingly. "Do not utter such words to one whom you are bound to address with reverence ; — do not, or you will render my sufferings unendurable ! "

"Your *sufferings ?*" exclaimed the countess, catching at a word that seemed to imply a reproof, which galled the more because she knew it was deserved. "Your *sufferings ?* That is a fitting expression to drop from your lips ! I had the right to believe that, far from causing you *suffering*, I had put an end to your suffering when I threw open my doors to admit you."

"You misunderstood me, aunt. I did not intend to say " —

"You have said enough to prove that you add ingratitude to your other sins. And, since you talk of *sufferings*, I will beg you to remember the sufferings you have brought upon us, — you, who, in return for all you have received at my hands, have caused my very grandson to treat me with disrespect, for the first time in his life. *Your* sufferings ? I can well conceive that she who creates so much affliction in the house that has sheltered her, — she who so treacherously pierces the hearts that have opened to yield her a place, — she who has played the viper warmed upon almost a mother's bosom, — she may well have sufferings to wail over ! "

Madeleine stood speechless, thunderstruck, by the rude shock of these words. The countess turned from her, and, preparing to leave the *châlet*, bade Maurice give her his arm. He silently obeyed, casting a look of compassionate tenderness upon Madeleine. But she saw it not ; all her vast store of mental strength suddenly melted away ! For the first time in her life she was completely crushed, overwhelmed, — hopeless and powerless. For a few moments she remained standing as motionless as one petrified ; then, with a heart-broken cry, dropped into a seat, and covering her face with her hands, sobbed convulsively, — sobbed as though all the sorrows of her life were concentrated in the anguish of that moment, and found vent in that deluge of tears, — that stormy whirlwind of passion ! All

the clouds in the firmament of her existence, which she had,
day after day, dispelled by the internal sunshine of her patient,
trustful spirit, culminated and broke in that wild flood. Hope
was drowned in that heavy rain; all the flowers that brightened, and the sweet, springing herbs that lent their balm to her
weary pilgrimage, were beaten down into the mire of despair.
There was no ark, no Ararat; she was alone, without refuge,
on the waste of waters.

Her heavy sobs prevented her hearing the entrance of Bertha, and it was only when the arms of the young girl were
fondly twined about her, that she became aware of her
presence.

"Madeleine, dear, dear Madeleine! What has happened?
Why do you weep thus?"

"Do not speak to me, Bertha!" replied Madeleine in a stifled voice. "You cannot, cannot help me; there is no
hope left, — none, none! My father has died to me again to
day, and I am alone once more! — alone in a desert that has no
place of shelter for me, but a grave beneath its swathing
sands!"

Her tears gushed forth with redoubled violence.

"Do not treat me so cruelly! Do not cast me off!" pleaded
Bertha, as her cousin tried to disengage herself from her encir-
cling arms. "If you are wretched, so am I — *because* you are!
Only tell me the reason for this terrible sorrow. I was awaiting
you in your room; but, as you did not come, I felt sure my cousin
Maurice had detained you."

At those last words an involuntary cry of intense suffering
burst from Madeleine's lips.

"Then I saw my aunt and Maurice returning together, and
Maurice appeared to be talking in an excited manner, and my
aunt looked blacker than any thunder-cloud. Still you did not
come, and I went in search of you. Tell me why I find you
thus? — you, who have always borne your griefs with such silent
fortitude. What *has* my aunt said or done to you?"

"She has ceased to love me, — she has ceased to esteem me,
— she even repents of the benefits she has conferred upon me."

"No, no, Madeleine; you are mistaken."

"Oh, I am not mistaken, — my eyes are opened at last. The
thin, waxen mask of assumed kindness has melted from her face!
I am a burden to her, — an encumbrance, — an offence. She
only desires to be rid of me!"

"You, — the fairy of good works in her household? What

could she do without you? It is only excitement which makes
you imagine this."

"I never guessed, never dreamed it before; but I have wilfully deceived myself. *Now* all is too clear! A thousand recollections rise up to testify to the truth; a thousand suspicions,
which I repulsed as unworthy of me and of her, return to convince me; words and looks, coldness and injustice, slights and
reproaches start up with frightful vividness, and throw a hideous
light upon conduct I never dared to interpret aright."

"What looks? what words? what actions?" asked Bertha,
though her heart told her with what a catalogue she could
answer her own question.

"They could not be rehearsed in an hour or in a day. But it
is not to my aunt alone that my presence is offensive. Cousin
Tristan also chafes at the sight of his dependent relative. I have
seen it when I took my seat at table; I have seen it when room
was made for me in the carriage; I have seen it on numberless
occasions. His glances, his accents, his whole demeanor, have
seemed to reproach me for the place I occupied, for the garments
I wore, for the very bread I ate, — the bread of bitter, bitter
charity! And oh!" she groaned, "*must this be so still? Must
I still accept these bounties, which are begrudged me? Must I
still be bowed to the dust by the weight of these charities?* Alas!
I *must*, because I have nothing of my own, — because I am nothing of myself!"

"Madeleine! one of these days"—

Madeleine did not heed her. "Oh, my father! my father!
To what torturing humiliations you subjected me in bequeathing
me nobility with poverty! Well may you have wished that you
had been born a peasant! Had I been a peasant's child, I might
have lived by, and rejoiced in, honest labor! Had I been the
daughter of a mechanic, I might have gained my bread by some
useful trade. Had I even been the child of some poor gentleman, I might have earned a livelihood by giving lessons in music, in drawing, by becoming a governess, or teaching in a school.
But, the daughter of the Duke de Gramont, it is one of the curses
of my noble birth that I must live upon charity, — charity unwillingly doled out and thrown in my face, even when I am receiving it with meekness!"

"But, Madeleine, if you will but listen to me"—

Madeleine went on bitterly. "And I am young yet, — young
and strong, and capable of exertion; and I have dared to believe
that, while one is young, some of the benefits received could be

repaid by the cheerful spirit of youth, — by the performance of needful offices, — by hands ever ready to serve, and a heart ever open to sympathize; but, if I am an encumbrance, an annoyance while I am *young*, what an intolerable burden I must become when youth passes away! Then I shall either be repulsed with aversion, or sheltered with undisguised reluctance, — forced to remember every moment that the hospitality I receive is an *alms!* Oh! it is too horrible! Death would be a thousand times preferable."

"And you can forget how dreadful it would be for us, who love you, to lose you?"

"I forget *everything*, except the misery of my own degraded position! I ask for nothing save that God, in his mercy, will free me from it, I care not how! I look despairingly on all sides, and see no escape! I am bound, hand and foot, by the chains of my own noble birth, and shut within the iron walls of circumstance. I struggle vainly in my captivity; no way of freedom is open to me! And yet I can never again resign myself to passive endurance."

"If you only knew how wretched you make me by talking in this strain!"

"I make you wretched, as I have made all others, by my presence here, — yes, I know it! You see how ungrateful, how selfish misery has rendered me, since I am cruel even to you whose pure love I never doubted."

Before Bertha could make a fresh attempt to console her cousin, Baptiste entered, bearing a letter. He looked dismayed when he beheld Madeleine's face of woe, and Bertha's tearful countenance; but the latter checked his glance of inquiry by asking abruptly what he wanted.

Still regarding Madeleine with an expression of deep concern, he replied, "The *valet* of Count Damoreau has just left this letter for Mademoiselle Madeleine, and desired that it should be delivered to her at once."

"Very well; that will do."

Bertha took the letter, and motioned to Baptiste to withdraw.

"What *can* Count Damoreau have to write to you about? Do open the letter and tell me."

"Not now, Bertha. Leave me to myself for a little while. I scarcely know what I am doing or saying. I entreat you to leave me!"

"Madeleine, if I were in trouble, I would not send you from me."

6 *

" Go, if you love me ! And you — *you*, at least, *do* love me !"

" *If* I love you ? I will even leave you to prove that I do ; but it is very hard."

Bertha walked slowly away, taking the path that led from the château. In a few moments she paused, turned suddenly, and quickened her steps in the opposite direction, prompted by an impulse to seek Maurice and tell him of Madeleine's grief. Perhaps he might have the power to console her.

Count Tristan had been prevented opening the letters which M. de Bois had delivered. When the two gentlemen reached the château, several visitors were awaiting the count, and their stay was protracted. The instant his guests took their leave, he hastened to the library, which his mother entered at the same moment. He listened impatiently as she briefly recounted the scene which had taken place in the summer-house.

" The time has come when we must put an end to this madness," answered the count ; " and I trust that I hold the means in my hands. These are the replies of Madeleine's relations."

He broke one of the seals, and glanced over the contents of the letter, gnawing his under lip as he read.

" Well, my son, what reply ? "

" This letter is from M. de Bonneville. He writes that his château is only large enough for his own family, — that it would be a great inconvenience to have any addition to his home circle ; and *we* — I suppose *we* have not been inconvenienced for the last three years " —

" I am not astonished at such a reply from M. de Bonneville. I expected nothing else. Give me Madame de Nervac's letter. She is a charming woman, whom every one admires and respects, and I know her kindness of heart."

The count handed the letter. His mother opened it, and read, —

" MY DEAR COUSIN :

" Are you not aware that a woman of any tact, who has still some claims to admiration, could hardly commit the absurd *faux pas* of establishing in her own house, and having always by her side, a person younger and handsomer than herself ? To consent to your proposition concerning Madeleine would therefore be a suicidal act " —

" This is insupportable ! " ejaculated the count. " It seems that we are to be forced into continuing to bear this burden, though it may bring us to ruin. What insupportable vanity Madame de Nervac betrays! You see what her kindness of heart is worth!"

"There is still one letter to open," remarked his mother, clinging to a faint hope.

"Oh, it will be a repetition of the others, — you may be sure of that!" He tore it open angrily; but, glancing at the first lines, exclaimed, "What do I see? Have we found one reasonable and charitable person at last? The Count Damoreau writes, —

"'A thousand thanks, my dear cousin for the opportunity you afford me of being useful to that lovely and unfortunate relative of ours. I have always regarded her with admiration and affection, and always appreciated the noble generosity which prompted your kindness to the orphan.'"

"The count is a man endowed with most excellent judgment," remarked the countess with complacency.

Her son continued reading the letter, —

"'I am at this moment about to make a number of necessary repairs in my château, which will cause me to absent myself for some time. I shall probably spend a year or two on the continent.'"

"So much the better! He will doubtless take Madeleine with him," suggested the countess.

Count Tristan in an altered tone read on, —

"'As I shall travel entirely *en garçon*, of course it will be impossible for Madeleine to accompany me, but an admirable opportunity presents itself for placing her in a situation that is very suitable. My friend, Lady Vivian, of Edinburgh, who forms one of the party here, is in search of an humble companion. I have spoken to her ladyship concerning Madeleine. She made some slight demur on account of the young lady's attractive person, but finally consented to offer her this situation.'"

"A de Gramont hired out as an humble companion! What an indignity!" ejaculated the countess.

The count continued reading, —

"'I will myself write to Madeleine and apprise her of what I have done, and present the many advantages of such a position.'"

"She must not receive the letter!" said the countess, earnestly. "She is capable of accepting this offer for the sake of wounding us. But Count Damoreau has insulted us grossly How has he dared to entertain such an offer for a member of our family,—one in whose veins flows the same untainted blood? Why do you not speak, my son? But indignation may well deprive you of speech!"

"I can only say that in *some manner we must at once rid our-selves of Madeleine.*"

"I would rather see her dead than in a situation which disgraced her noble name," answered the countess, violently.

"I quite agree with you," returned the count, with a sardonic look; "but, unfortunately, life and death are not in our hands!"

As he spoke, there was a gleam in his malignant eye, almost murderous. His foot was lifted to crush the worm in his path, and, could he have trodden it out of existence in secret, the deed would have been accomplished with exultation. His hatred for Madeleine had strengthened into a fierce passion as his fears that Maurice loved her threatened to be confirmed. Far from sharing his mother's indignation at the proposal of Count Damoreau, he had made up his mind to force Madeleine into acceptance, if no other presented itself for freeing the château from her presence.

CHAPTER VII.

A CRISIS.

COUNT TRISTAN was in the heat of argument with his haughty mother, when the door of the library opened, and Madeleine entered. One who had beheld the tempestuous burst of grief, the torrent of tears, the heart-rending despair that convulsed her frame but half an hour before, in the little *châlet*, would scarcely have recognized the countenance upon which the eyes of the Countess de Gramont and her son were now turned. Not the faintest shadow of that whirlwind of passionate anguish was left upon Madeleine's face, unless it might be traced in the great calm which succeeds a heavy storm; in the death-like pallor which overspread her almost rigid features; in the steady light that shone from her soul-revealing eyes; in the firm outline of her colorless lips; in the look of heroic resolve which imparted to her noble lineaments a higher beauty than they ever before had worn.

She approached Count Tristan with an unfaltering step, holding a letter in her hand. That letter had given a sudden check to her vehement sorrow, and restored her equilibrium.

"I have received this communication from Count Damoreau."

As she spoke, she extended the epistle to the count, who for one instant quailed before her clairvoyant eyes. It seemed as though a prophetic judgment spoke out of their shining depths.

He took the letter mechanically, without opening it. His gaze was riveted, as though by a magnetism too powerful for him to resist, upon her purposeful countenance.

Madeleine went on, —

"Count Damoreau tells me that you and my aunt desire to withdraw your protection from me; that you feel I have sufficiently long enjoyed the shelter of your roof; that you wish to provide me with some other asylum."

There was no hesitation in her voice as she uttered these words. She spoke in a tone rendered clear and quiet by the dignity of self-respect.

"Count Damoreau had no authority to write in such a strain to you," observed the countess, with asperity.

"There is his letter. He informed me that he has the Count Tristan's authority. To prove it, he encloses the letter yesterday delivered to him by M. Gaston de Bois."

Count Tristan was too thoroughly confounded to attempt any reply. He was painfully aware of the unmistakable character of that epistle.

"Count Damoreau announces to me," continued Madeleine, undisturbed, "that he is unable to comply with your request, and extend an invitation for me to join his family circle; and that my other relatives have also declined to accede to a solicitation of yours that they should by turns receive me as an inmate. He adds that his friend, Lady Vivian, is seeking an humble companion to accompany her to Scotland; and he trusts that I will thankfully accept this situation."

"It is an insult, — a deliberate insult to us and you!" broke forth the countess.

Madeleine's lips trembled with a half smile.

"I do not deem it an insult to myself: I am as thankful as Count Damoreau can desire me to be; but I decline his well-intentioned offer."

Count Tristan ground his teeth, and cast u
glance of fury and menacing detestation. Th
she returned the look with an expression which
she recognized what was passing in his mind.

"You did right to decline : I should never ha
to accept," remarked the countess, in a somewl

She deemed it politic to conciliate Madeleine
fearing that she might be driven to take some
which would cast a reflection upon her kindred.

"I regret that my son has acted hastily. If
self with the propriety which I have the right to
still find a home in the Château de Gramont,
mother I have ever been to you."

"Mother !" at that word Madeleine's glacial c
"A *mother !* — oh, my aunt, thank you for that w
know how much good it does me to hear it from
the Château de Gramont can never more be m
settled : I came to tell you so."

"What do you mean?" asked the count, wi
disguised satisfaction.

"I mean that I purpose shortly to quit this
return !"

"Then you *do* intend to accompany Lady Viv
he inquired.

"You — my niece — *a de Gramont* — become
panion of Lady Vivian !" exclaimed the cour
astonishment. "Can you even contemplate sucl

"No, madame," returned Madeleine, with an
might have been interpreted into a tone of pri
become the humble companion of any lady."

"With whom do you expect to live?" demai

"I shall live alone."

"*Live alone,* at your age, — without fortune,
It is impracticable, — impossible !" replied her :

"I have reached my majority. I shall try t(
I have some small possession : the family diamo
still remain to me."

"But your noble name."

"Rest assured that it will never be disgraced

"I tell you that your project is impossible,'
countess, resolutely. "I forbid you to even a
into execution. I forbid you by the gratitude
forbid you in the name of all the kindnesses

" And do you not see, my aunt, it is because I would still be grateful for these kindnesses that I would go hence? From the moment I learned I was a burden to you, that my presence here was unwelcome, this was no longer my home. If I leave you now, the memory of your goodness only, will dwell in my heart. If I were to remain longer, each day my presence would become more intolerable to you; each day your words and looks would grow colder and harsher; each day I should feel more degraded in my own eyes. *You* would spoil your own benefactions: *I* perhaps, might forget them, and be stained with the crime of ingratitude. No, let us now part, — now, while I may still dare to hope that you will think of me with tenderness and regret, — now, while I can yet cherish the recollection of the happy days I have passed beneath your roof. My resolution is taken: it is unalterable. I could not rest here. You will, perhaps, accord me a few days to make needful preparations; then I must bid you farewell."

She turned to quit the room, but encountered Maurice and Bertha, who had entered in time to hear the last sentence.

Bertha, on leaving her cousin, had sought Maurice and told him of Madeleine's prostrating sorrow. They hastened back to the *châlet* together, but she had disappeared. They were in search of her when they entered the library.

" Bid us farewell, Madeleine?" cried Bertha. " What do you mean? Where are you going? Surely you will never leave us?"

" I must."

" But my aunt will not let you; Cousin Tristan will not let you; Maurice will not let you. Speak to her, some of you, and say that she shall not go."

" Bertha," answered the count, "you do not know all the circumstances which have caused Madeleine to form this resolution; and, if my mother will pardon me for differing with her, I must say, frankly, that I approve of the course Madeleine has chosen. I honor her for it. I think she acts wisely in remaining here no longer!"

Then Maurice came forward boldly, and placing himself beside Madeleine, with an air of manly protection, spoke out, —

" And *I* agree with you, my father. I honor Madeleine for her resolution. I think she acts wisely in remaining here no longer."

" O Maurice, Maurice! how can you speak so? Don't let her go, unless you want to make me miserable!" pleaded Bertha.

Madeleine's hueless face was overspread with a brilliant glow as she cast upon Maurice one hasty look of gratitude.

"I speak what I mean. Madeleine cannot, without sacrificing her self-respect, accept hospitality which is not freely given, — protection which is unwillingly accorded. She cannot remain here as an inferior, — a dependent; one who is under daily obligation, — who is merely tolerated because she has no other place of refuge. My father, there is only *one* position in which she *can* remain in the Château de Gramont, and that is as an equal; as its future mistress; as your daughter; *as my wife!* "

The countess was stricken dumb with rage; and a sudden revulsion of feeling toward the shrinking girl, whose deep blushes she interpreted into a token of exultation, made her almost as willing to drive her forth, no matter whither, as her son himself.

Bertha, with an exclamation of delight, flung her arms joyfully about Madeleine's neck.

"Maurice, are you mad? Do you forget that you are my son?" was all that the count could gasp out, in his indignant amazement.

"It is as your son that I speak; it is as the inheritor of your name, — that name which Madeleine also bears."

"You seem to have forgotten" — began his father.

Maurice interrupted him, —

"I have not forgotten that I have not reached my majority, and that your consent is necessary to render Madeleine my wife."

(Our readers are doubtless aware that the law in France fixes the majority of a young man at twenty-five, and that he has no power to contract marriage or to control property until that period.)

"But, believe me, my father, even if this were not the case, I should not desire to act without your approval, and I know I could never induce Madeleine to forego your consent to our union. But what valid objections can you have? You desired that Bertha should become my wife. Is not Madeleine precisely the same kin to me as Bertha? Is she not as good, as beautiful?"

"Oh, a thousand times better and lovelier!" exclaimed Bertha, with affectionate enthusiasm.

"There is but one difference: she is poor and Bertha is rich. Think you Bertha's fortune could have one feather's weight in deciding my choice? I thank Heaven for teaching me to account it more noble, more honorable, to ask what the woman I would marry *is*, than to inquire what she *has*."

His father made a vain attempt to speak. Maurice went on without noticing the futile effort.

"But this is not all: I dare to hope that Madeleine's heart is mine, while Bertha's is not. My father, you requested that Bertha and I should have an understanding with each other; and we have had one. Bertha has told me that she does not love me. Is it not so, Bertha?"

"I told you that I loved you with all my heart, as the dearest, most delightful cousin in the world!" answered Bertha, naïvely.

"Just as I love you!" replied Maurice, smiling upon her tenderly. "But, as a lover, you definitely rejected me, — did you not?"

"Oh, yes; just as you refused me. We are perfectly agreed upon that point," she rejoined, with childlike frankness and simplicity.

"For shame, Maurice!" said the countess, in a tone of angry rebuke.

"Grandmother, hear me out. For once my heart must speak, even though it may be silent forever after. I feel that my whole future destiny hangs upon the events of this moment. You love me as a de Gramont should love; you love me with an ambition to see me worthy of my name, — to see that name rendered more lustrous in my person. How far that is possible, my father's decision and yours this hour will determine. I am ardent, impetuous, fond of excitement, reckless at times, — as prone, I fear, to be tempted to vice as to be inspired by virtue. If you withhold your consent to my union with the only woman I can love, — if you drive me to despair, — I am lost! Every pure and lofty aspiration within my nature will be crushed out, and in its place the opposite inclination will spring. I warned you before, when you thwarted the noblest resolution I ever formed. There is yet time to save me from the evil effects of that disappointment, and to spare me the worst results of *this*. If you grant me Madeleine" —

"Maurice, for pity's sake!" supplicated Madeleine, extending her clasped hands toward him.

Maurice caught the outstretched hands in his, and bent over her with an expression of ineffable love irradiating his countenance.

"Do not speak yet, Madeleine; do not answer until you have heard me, — until you have well comprehended my meaning. You do not know the thousand perils by which a young man is beset in Paris, — the siren lures that are thrown in his

way to ensnare his feet, be they disposed to walk ever so
warily. You do not know that your holy image, rising up before me, shining upon the path I trod, and beckoning me into
the right road when I swerved aside, has alone saved me from
falling into that vortex of follies and vices by which men are
daily swallowed up, and from which they emerge sullied and
debased. You do not know that, while I am here beside you,
listening to the sound of your voice, holding your hand, gazing
upon your face, I feel like one inspired, who has power to make
his life glorious and keep it pure! Madeleine, would you have
me great, distinguished?. I shall become so if it be your will.
Would you have me lift up our noble name? It shall be exalted at your bidding. Would you reign over my soul and keep
it stainless? It is under your angel guardianship. Madeleine,
best beloved, will you not save me?"

Madeleine only answered with a look which besought Maurice
to forbear.

"Is your rhapsody finished at last?" asked Count Tristan,
scornfully. "Is any one else to be permitted to speak?"

"It seems there is but one person whose voice is of any importance to your son, ʳ_____ sneered the countess, "and that is Madeleine. It is for *her* to speak; it is for her to accomplish her
work of base ingratitude; it is for her to give the last finishing
stroke to the fabric she has secretly been laboring to build up
for the last three years."

Madeleine — who, when the voice of Maurice was sounding in
her ears, had been unable to control the agitation which caused
her breast to heave, and her frame to quiver from head to foot,
while confusion flung its crimson mantle over her face — grew
suddenly calm when she heard these taunts. The same icy,
pallid quietude with which, but a few moments before, she
entered the library, returned. She withdrew the hands Maurice
had clasped in his, lifted her bowed head, and stood erect, preparing to reply.

"Speak!" commanded the count, furiously. "Speak! since
we are nothing and nobody here, and *you are everything*. Since
you are sole arbiter in this family, speak!"

Madeleine could not at once command her voice.

The countess, arguing the worst from her silence, cried, with
culminating wrath, "Speak, viper! Dart your fangs into the
bosom that has sheltered you: it is bared to receive the deadly
stroke; it is ready to die of your venom! Nothing remains
but for you to strike!"

"Take courage, dearest Madeleine," whispered Bertha. "They will not be angry long. Speak and tell them that you love Maurice as he loves you, and that you will be the happiest of women if you become his wife."

"Well, your answer, Mademoiselle de Gramont?" urged the countess.

"It will be an answer for which I have only the pardon of Maurice to ask," said Madeleine, speaking slowly, but firmly. "Maurice, my cousin, I shall never be able to tell you, — you can never know, — what emotions of thankfulness you have awakened in my soul, nor how unutterably precious your words are to me. Thus much I may say; for the rest, *I can never become your wife!* "

"You refuse me because my father and my grandmother have *compelled* you to do so by their reproaches, — their *menaces*, I might say!" cried Maurice, wholly forgetting his wonted respect in the rush of tumultuous feelings. "This and this only is your reason for consigning me to misery."

The fear that she had awakened unfilial emotions in the bosom of Maurice infused fresh fortitude into Madeleine's spirit.

"No, Maurice, you are wrong. If my aunt and Count Tristan had not uttered one word on the subject, my answer to you would have been the same."

"How can that be possible? How can I have been so deceived? There is only *one* obstacle which *can* discourage me, only one which can force me to yield you up, and that is an admission, from your own lips, that your affections are already bestowed, — that your heart is no longer free."

Madeleine, without hesitation, replied in a clear, steady, deliberate tone, looking her cousin full in the face, and not by the faintest sign betraying the poniard which she heroically plunged into her own devoted breast, —

"My affections are bestowed; my heart is *no longer free!* "

"Madeleine, Madeleine! you do not love Maurice, — you love some one else?" questioned Bertha, in sorrowful astonishment.

Maurice spoke no word. He stood one moment looking at Madeleine as a drowning man might have looked at the ship that could have saved him disappearing in the distance. Then he murmured, hardly conscious of his own words, —

"And I felt sure her heart was mine! O Madeleine! may you never know what you have done!"

"Forgive me if you can, Maurice. Be generous enough to

pardon one who has made you suffer. A bright future is before you. The darkness of this hour will gradually fade out of your memory."

" Say, rather, that you have taken from me my future, — withdrawn its guiding star, and left me a rayless and eternal night. But why should I reproach you? What right had I to deem myself worthy of you? You love *another.* All is spoken in those words : there is nothing more for me to say, except to thank you for not discarding me without making a confession which annihilates all hope."

There was a dignity in his grief more touching than the most passionate outburst would have been. Even his grandmother, in spite of her joy at Madeleine's declaration, was not wholly unmoved as she contemplated him. Count Tristan's exultation broke through all polite disguise, —

" Madeleine has atoned for much of the past by her present conduct ; it has restored her in a measure to " —

Madeleine, as far as her gentle nature permitted, experienced an antipathy toward Count Tristan only surpassed by that which he entertained for her. The sound of his voice grated on her ears ; his commendation made her doubt the wisdom and purity of her own act; his approval irritated her as no rebuke could have done. Without waiting for him to conclude his sentence, she grasped Bertha's hand, whispering, " I cannot stay here ; I am stifling ; come with me."

They left the room together, and took their way in silence to Madeleine's chamber. Bertha carefully closed the door, and, drawing her cousin down into a seat, placed herself beside her, and strove to read her countenance.

" Madeleine, is it possible? How mistaken I have been ! You do not love our cousin Maurice. Poor Maurice ! It is a dreadful blow to him. And you love some one else. But whom ? I know of no gentleman who comes here often, — who is on an intimate footing at the château, — except " —

A painful suspicion for the first time shot through her mind, and made her pause. Could it be Gaston de Bois whom Madeleine preferred? She always treated him with such marked courtesy. There was no one else, — it must be he ! Bertha could not frame the question that hovered about her lips, though to have heard it answered in the negative would have made her heart leap for joy.

Madeleine was too much absorbed by her own reflections to divine those of her cousin.

"At all events," said Bertha, trying to rally and talk cheerfully, though she could not chase that haunting fear from her thoughts, "my aunt is no longer angry with you, and cousin Tristan was well pleased. They will treat you better after this, and your home will be happier."

"*My home?*" ejaculated Madeleine, in a tone that made Bertha start.

"Yes, yours, until you exchange it for that of the favored lover, of whose name you make such a mystery."

"*That will never be!*"

"Never? Does he not love you, then? But I know `he does, — he must. Every one loves you; no one can help it, — you win all hearts!"

"*Count Tristan's, for instance*," remarked Madeleine, bitterly.

"Ah, not *his*, that is true. How wickedly he looked at you when Maurice pictured how dear you were to him! I noticed Cousin Tristan's eyes, and they frightened me. He looked positively fiendish; and when Maurice said" —

To hear those precious words Maurice had spoken, — those words which she could never more forget, — repeated, was beyond Madeleine's powers of endurance: she sprang up, exclaiming, "Do not let us talk of these matters any more to-day, Bertha. It is growing late, — almost six o'clock. It is time for you to dress for dinner. And you have not forgotten the ball to-night?"

"I could not bear to go now. I am sure Maurice will not go; and you, — would you go, even if we did?"

"You will not refuse me a favor, Bertha, though it may cost you some pain to grant it? Go to this ball, and persuade, entreat Maurice to go. If you do not, you will draw down my aunt's displeasure upon me anew, for she will know why you remain at home, — especially as it will be impossible for me to appear in public to-night."

"I would do anything rather than have my aunt displeased with you again; and then there is the beautiful dress you have taken such pains to make."

"I should be very much disappointed if you did not wear it this evening. Now let us prepare for dinner."

As she spoke, Madeleine commenced her own toilet. Bertha stood looking at her as she unbound her long silken hair, and, after smoothing it as carefully as was her wont, rapidly formed the coronal braid, and wound the rich tress about the regal head.

"I cannot comprehend you, Madeleine: you are a marvel to

7*

me. A couple of hours ago you were almost frantic with grief, — I never saw any one weep so immoderately; and now you are as serene as though nothing had happened. If your lips were not so very, very white, and your eyes had not such a fixed, unnatural look, I could almost think you had forgotten that anything unusual had occurred."

" Forget it yourself, dear, and make ready for dinner."

Bertha obeyed at least part of the injunction, still wondering over Madeleine's incomprehensible placidity.

The young maidens entered the dining-room together. Maurice came in late. The meal passed almost in silence, though the Countess and Count Tristan made unusual efforts to keep up a conversation.

Bertha was right in imagining Maurice had lost all inclination to appear at the ball. When she brought up the subject, he answered impatiently that he did not intend to go. His grandmother heard the remark, and made an especial request that he would change that decision and accompany them. Bertha added her entreaties; but Maurice seemed inclined to rebel, until she whispered, —

" If you stay at home, my aunt will say it is Madeleine's fault, and she will be vexed with her again. Madeleine begged you would spare her this new trial, and bade me entreat you to go."

Maurice looked across the table, for the first time during dinner, and found Madeleine's eyes turned anxiously upon him.

" I will go," he murmured.

His words were addressed rather to her than to Bertha. A scarcely perceptible smile on the lips of the former was his reward.

No comment was made upon Madeleine's determination to remain at home. But the tone of the countess to her niece, when she was officiating as usual at her aunt's toilet, was gentler than she had ever before used. Not the faintest allusion to the events of the morning dropped from the lips of either.

At last the carriage drove from the door, and Madeleine was left alone with her own thoughts. The mask of composure was no longer needed, yet there was no return of the morning's turbulent emotion.

Are not great trials sent to incite us to great exertions, which we might not have the energy, the wit, perhaps the *humility*, to undertake, but for the spurring sting of that especial grief? Madeleine had resolutely looked her affliction full in the face; had grown familiar with its sternest, saddest features; had bowed before them, and dashed the tears from her eyes, to see more clearly as that sorrow pointed out a path which all her firmness would be taxed in treading,—a path which she had never dreamed existed for her, until it had been opened, hewn through the rocks of circumstance by that day's heavy blows, that hour's piercing anguish.

Her greatest difficulty lay in the necessity of concealing the step she was about to take from her aunt, whose violent opposition would throw a fearful obstacle in the way. It was easier to avoid than to surmount such a barrier; but if it could not be avoided, it *must* be surmounted. In that decision she could not waver.

CHAPTER VIII.

FLIGHT.

CAN there be a more dreary solitude, to a mind writhing under the throes of some new and hidden sorrow, than a brilliant ball-room? The stirring music jars like harshest discord upon the unattuned ear; the glaring lights dazzle the pained vision until utter darkness would seem grateful; the merry voices and careless laughter catch a tone of bitter mockery; the gayly apparelled forms, the faces decked with soulless smiles, are more oppressive than all the apparitions with which a fevered imagination can people the gloomiest seclusion. Maurice soon found the festive scene at the Château de Tremazan intolerable, and took refuge in the illuminated conservatory, the doors of which were thrown invitingly open. It was mid-summer, but the flowers had been restored to brighten their winter shelter during the fête. He had thought to find himself alone; but yonder, bending over richly-tinted clusters of azaleas and odorous heliotropes, a group of youthful heads unconcernedly thrust their lifeless chaplets in challenging contrast with nature's living loveliness, while flowing robes recklessly swept their floral imitations against her shrinking originals. In a different state of mind Maurice might not have been struck by the incongruous contact of the painted semblance with the blushing reality; but now it reminded him too keenly that the sphere within which he was bound, a social Ixion upon the petty wheel of conventionalism, was one grand combination of artificial trivialities and senseless shams. Goaded beyond endurance by the reflection, he impatiently made his escape into the open air.

Bertha had never mingled with a gay crowd in so joyless a mood. The presence of the heiress created no little sensation; but good-breeding kept its manifestation within such delicate limits that she was unconscious of its existence. She was not even aware that it was a sign of her own importance when the Marchioness de Fleury glided up to Count Tristan, on whose arm Bertha was leaning, and, in a softly cadenced voice, asked if she had not the pleasure of seeing Mademoiselle de Merrivale. In reply, the count presented Bertha. As she returned the courtesy of the marchioness, she could not help remembering the declaration of Maurice, that he had never perused the countenance of the distinguished belle, because his attention was irresistibly riveted upon the wondrous details of her toilet: for Bertha found her own eyes involuntarily wandering over the graceful folds of the amethyst velvet, and the exquisite disposition of the *point de Venise* by which it was elaborately ornamented; the artistic head-dress in perfect accordance with the costly robe, and the Cleopatra-like drops of pearls which seemed to have been showered over the wearer from brow to foot.

Bertha's eyes were too ingenuous not to betray their occupation; but those of the marchioness seemed only to be looking, with the most complimentary expression of interest, into the face of her new acquaintance, while, in reality, she was scanning Bertha's picturesque attire, and longing to discover by what tasteful fingers it had been contrived; examining the polished ivy intertwined among her bright ringlets, and the half-blown roses just bursting their sheaths in a glossy covert of amber tresses; and wondering that a coiffure with such poetic taste could have existed unknown in Brittany. As the marchioness stood, dropping sweet, meaningless words from her dewy lips, Bertha's hand was claimed by the Duke de Montauban, and she was led to the dance.

She was moving through the quadrille with a languid, unelastic motion, very unlike her usual springing step, when she caught sight of M. de Bois, standing at a short distance, with his face turned toward her. The smile that accompanied her bow of greeting drew him nearer. As the dance ended, and her partner was reconducting her to the countess, M. de Bois overcame his timidity sufficiently to join her.

" Where is Mademoiselle Mad-ad-adeleine ? " he inquired. " I
have not seen her."

" She is not here. She would not come," sighed Bertha,
stopping abruptly, though they had not quite reached her chape-
rone's side.

" Is she ill? She told me this morning that she would certainly be here. Has anything happened ? " asked M. de Bois,
speaking as distinctly as though he had never stammered in his
life, and throwing off, in his growing excitement, all the awkwardness of his constitutional diffidence.

Bertha could not but remark his anxious expression, and a
suspicion, which she had essayed to banish, once more took possession of her mind. But she loved Madeleine with such absolute devotion, that this vague, uncomfortable sensation was
quickly displaced by a purer emotion. Glancing at the countess
to see that she was not within hearing distance, she disengaged
her arm from that of the duke, with a bow which he interpreted
into a dismissal, and then, turning eagerly to M. de Bois, recounted
to him, in a low, hurried tone, the occurrences of the morning.
She fancied she heard words which sounded very like muttered
imprecations. He was perhaps putting into practice his new
method of loosening his tongue, and doubtless imagined that the
emphatic utterances were inaudible.

Bertha went on. " It was a terrible blow to Maurice! He
felt so sure until then that Madeleine loved him ; so did I. But
we were both mistaken. It is plain enough now that she does
not."

" What makes it plain? How can you be sure ? " asked M.
de Bois, becoming more and more disturbed.

" Her own declaration has placed the fact beyond doubt. She
even confessed that she loved another."

Her listener did not attempt to conceal his consternation at
these words.

" Mademoiselle Madeleine said she loved another! She, who
would not stoop to breathe a word which was not the strictest
truth, — *she told you so?* You heard it yourself? You are
certain, very certain, Mademoiselle Bertha ? "

" I dare say that I ought not to have repeated this to you,"
replied Bertha, who now experienced some self-reproach at betraying her friend's secret to one whom it, perhaps, so deeply
concerned ; " but I am very certain that Madeleine distinctly rejected Maurice, and, when he attributed her refusal to his grandmother's and his father's disapproval of his suit, she denied that

she was influenced by them, and confessed that her heart was not free, — that she had bestowed it upon another."

"By all that is heroic, she is a noble woman!" exclaimed M. de Bois, fervently. "She has the grandest nature! She is incom-com-com " —

"Incomparable," said Bertha, finishing his sentence, and checking a sigh. "Yes, I never knew any one like her. She has no equal."

"I don't exactly say *that*. I don't mean *that*. She is not su-su-superior — to " —

Bertha did not assist him by completing *this* disjointed phrase, even if she suspected what he desired to say.

At that moment Count Damoreau approached, accompanied by a gaunt, overdressed lady, with harsh and forbidding features.

"Lady Vivian is looking for Mademoiselle de Gramont. Did she not accompany you?" inquired the count.

"She intended to do so, but changed her mind."

"She received a letter from me to-day, — did she not?" continued Count Damoreau.

"Yes, I remember delivering one to her myself, which Baptiste said was brought by your valet."

"Did she not apprise you of its contents?"

"No. I was not present when she opened the letter."

"Then you do not know how she received my proposition?" remarked Lady Vivian, in a grating voice. "I begin to be a little doubtful myself how it will do. Is your cousin as handsome as they say she is?"

"In my eyes she is the most beautiful person in the world," answered Bertha, in a tone of admiration the sincerity of which could not be mistaken.

Lady Vivian looked vexed, and replied, "That's a pity. Beauty is a decided objection in such a position."

"I beg your ladyship's pardon," returned Bertha, with spirit; "but I cannot perceive that my cousin's position renders her beauty objectionable."

"Beauty is very suitable to you, my dear; but for an humble companion " —

"An *humble companion?* Madeleine is not my aunt's humble companion, nor mine. She is " —

"To become *mine*, I believe!" rejoined Lady Vivian, brusquely. "And I already begin to regret that I acceded to Count Damoreau's wishes."

"Madeleine your ladyship's humble companion? *That* she

shall never be. O Count Damoreau! how *could* you have suggested such an idea? I would go on my knees to implore her not to consent! I am sure your ladyship will find yourself mistaken."

Bertha, as she said these words, bowed with a degree of hauteur which no one had ever seen her assume, and, taking M. de Bois's arm, approached her aunt with a troubled countenance. Before the Countess de Gramont could ask the cause of her evident disquietude, she said, —

"I wish we could go home, aunt: I am wearied to death. I cannot enjoy anything to-night. And that horrid Lady Vivian has made me so angry, talking of Madeleine as her humble companion! Such impertinence! Surely you would never permit anything of the kind?"

"Never! I do not wonder you were indignant. But do you really wish to go?"

"Oh, yes. I am stifling here. I never was at such a dull ball. Pray, pray take me home!"

Her aunt could not refuse a request so vehemently urged, and begged M. de Bois to seek Maurice. Fearing that Madame de Tremazan would be mortified by their early departure, the countess took an opportunity to leave the ballroom, accompanied by her niece and son, without attracting the observation of the hostess. M. de Bois joined them in the antechamber, with the intelligence that Maurice was nowhere to be found. After a second search, and half an hour's delay, the carriage started without him.

As soon as they reached the château, Bertha bade her aunt good-night, and hastened to Madeleine's chamber. Madeleine, who did not anticipate her speedy return, and had not heard her light foot upon the floor, was sitting beside a small table, her head supported by her hands, and bent over some object which she contemplated with intense interest. At the sound of Bertha's voice she hastily closed the lids of a couple of ancient-looking caskets, which stood before her, and rose from her seat.

"Is it you, Bertha? How soon you have returned!"

"Yes; I was glad to get away. The ball was wretchedly stupid; and, after that disagreeable Lady Vivian irritated me by talking of you, I could not stay. She seemed to have the audacity to expect that you would become her humble companion. *You!* our noble, *doubly noble* Madeleine, the humble companion of any one, but especially of such a coarse person as Lady Vivian! It was unendurable."

"It is very possible that Count Damoreau assured her I would accept the proposition she made me through him," was Madeleine's calm reply.

"But you never could have entertained it for a moment?"

"No. There is the answer I have just written to Count Damoreau. You may read it."

Bertha glanced over the letter approvingly. As she laid it upon the table, she noticed the caskets.

"What are these, Madeleine?—jewel-cases?"

"They were my mother's diamonds. They have been in the family, I can hardly tell you for how many generations."

"Do let me see them."

Bertha opened one of the cases. A necklace, brooch, and ear-rings of brilliants sparkled within. The precious stones emitted a clear lustre which would have caused a connoisseur at once to pronounce them of the first water; but their setting was quaint and old-fashioned. The necklace was composed of diamonds *fleur-de-lis*, divided by emerald shamrock-leaves. A single *fleur-de-lis*, surrounded by the emerald shamrock, formed the brooch and ear-rings.

"Some of your ancestors must have come from the emerald isle : so, at least, we may infer from this shamrock."

"Yes, my great-great-great-grandfather married the beautiful Lady Katrine Nugent, and these were her bridal jewels. You see that the shamrock of Erin is mingled with the *fleur-de-lis* of France."

Bertha unclosed the other case. It held a bracelet and a tiara-shaped comb. The shamrock and lily were blended as in the necklace.

"These diamonds are very lustrous," said Bertha, clasping the bracelet admiringly upon her delicate wrist. "But what are you doing with them, and at this time of night?"

"Looking at them," answered Madeleine, with some hesitation. "I have not seen them before for years."

"You shall wear them for your bridal *parure*, Madeleine."

Madeleine tried to laugh.

"Then I should carry my whole fortune on my back; all that remains of my ancient house I should bear, snail-fashion, upon my head and shoulders. No, little dreamer, of two facts you may rest assured : one is that I shall never wear these jewels; the other that I never shall be a bride. Come, let me undress you; your blue eyes are so sleepy they are growing gray as the heavens at twilight."

The Château de Tremazan was seven miles from his father's mansion, but Maurice, after his abrupt exit from the conservatory, walked leisurely home. The next morning, before the count had risen, his son entered the room, in travelling attire, to make the communication that he had ordered the carriage to drive him to Rennes, in time to meet the early train that started for Paris. He trusted his father would offer no objection, and would make the traveller's apologies to the ladies of the household, for avoiding the pain of leave-taking. Count Tristan approved of the journey; and, a few moments later, Maurice leaped into the coach, glancing eagerly up at a window, surrounded by a framework of jasmine vines; but no face looked forth; no hand waved a farewell and filled the vernal frame with a living picture.

The intelligence of his sudden departure was received differently by the three ladies. The countess was inclined to be displeased that he had foregone the ceremony of an adieu. Any shortcoming in the payment of the full amount of deference, which she considered her due, was a great offence. Of late, Maurice had several times wounded her upon this tender point, and her sensitiveness was thereby increased.

Bertha was loud in her lamentations over the disappearance of her cousin. Her deep chagrin revived the hopes of Count Tristan and his mother, and awakened the welcome suggestion, that he, in reality, held a tenderer place in her heart than she had ever admitted to herself.

Madeleine's face instinctively brightened when she heard that Maurice was gone; his departure smoothed away a difficulty from the path she was about to tread. Count Tristan watched her closely, and was perplexed by the gleam of genuine satisfaction that illumined her countenance. For the first time he was half deceived into the belief that the passion of Maurice was unrequited. He had been puzzled in what manner to interpret Madeleine's determined rejection of her cousin. He was unable to comprehend a purity of motive which his narrow mind was equally incapable of experiencing. He finally attributed her conduct partly to a dread of her aunt's and his own displeasure, partly to a desire to render herself more highly valued by Maurice, and to gain a firmer hold upon his affections.

M. de Bois was an early visitor on the day after the ball, but never had he seemed more ill at ease, or found more difficulty in controlling his restless nervousness, or in expressing himself intelligibly. When he heard that Maurice was on his way to Paris, he dashed down an antique vase by his sudden movement of vexation, and, in stooping to gather the fractured china, upset the stand upon which it had stood. This manifestation of awkwardness, of course, increased his *mal-aise;* and, although the countess remained as unmoved as though she wholly ignored the accident, he could not recover his equanimity. Madeleine left the drawing-room with the fragments of the vase in her hand, and did not return. After a prolonged and unsatisfactory visit, M. de Bois took his leave.

As he issued from the château, Baptiste dropped his spade and followed him, keeping at a short distance behind, until he neared the gate; then the old gardener approached, looking cautiously around to see that he was not observed, stealthily held out a note, whispering, "Mademoiselle Madeleine bade me give this to monsieur," turned on his heel, and walked away as rapidly as though he feared to be pursued.

The note contained these words: —

"A friend in my great emergency is indispensable to me. I have no friend in whom I can confide but you. I shall be at the little *châlet* to-morrow morning, at five o'clock.

"MADELEINE M. DE GRAMONT."

A radiant change passed over the shadowed features of Gaston de Bois, as he read these lines. That one so self-reliant as Madeleine proffered him her confidence, trusted him, appealed to him for aid, was surely enough to raise him in his own esteem; and he almost forgot the recent mortification caused by an unfortunate awkwardness and miserable diffidence, which seemed the haunting demons of his existence.

Impatience chased all slumber from his eyes that night, and the dawn had scarcely broken when he hastened to the *châlet* to await the coming of Madeleine. The appointed time had just arrived, as the watch he constantly consulted informed him, when she entered the summer-house. Their interview, occupied but half an hour; but, when M. de Bois left the *châlet,* his countenance wore an expression of earnestness, responsibility, and composure, totally opposite to its usual characteristics.

Madeleine, as she tripped back through the dew, smiled with moist eyes, — a smile of gratitude rather than of pleasure. More than once she drew a long breath, as though some heavy pressure had been lifted from her breast; and, as she dashed away the tears that gathered in her eyes, she seemed eagerly looking into the distance, as though a mist had rolled from before her steps, and she now saw her way clearly. All was silent in the château, and she reached her chamber unperceived.

That day passed as usual, and another, and another. Madeleine never once alluded to the determination which she had announced to her aunt as unalterable, and the countess was satisfied that her niece had spoken under the influence of excitement, without any fixed purpose; and gradually dismissed from her mind the fear that her dependent relative would take some rash and dignity-compromising step.

Bertha had not forgotten that Madeleine had declared the Château de Gramont was no longer her home; but as the latter went through the daily routine of her wonted avocations as though they were always to continue, and as no change was apparent in her manner, save that she was more silent and meditative, and her once ready smiles grew rarer, Bertha, also, was lulled into the belief that her cousin had abandoned her intention.

Count Tristan fell into no such error. Madeleine's preoccupied mien, her unwonted reserve, the tender sadness with which she sometimes gazed around her, as though bidding farewell to dear, familiar objects, assured him that she had not spoken lightly, and that her threat would be carried into execution at no distant period. Well was it for her that he had come to this satisfactory conclusion, for it spared her further persecution at his hands.

On the fourth morning after the departure of Maurice, Bertha entered Madeleine's chamber, according to her custom, — for the young maidens always descended to breakfast together. Her room was empty.

"She has not waited for me to-day," thought Bertha, hurrying down, and expecting to find Madeleine in the breakfast-room.

The countess and her son were at table, but Madeleine was not there.

"Has Madeleine breakfasted?" inquired Bertha, cutting short her morning salutations.

The answer was in the negative.

"Have you not seen her?" she asked.

"No, not this morning," replied the countess.

"I suppose she is taking an early walk," continued Bertha. "It seems odd that she does not come back, for she is never late."

Bertha seated herself, but the coffee remained untasted before her; and her head was constantly turned towards the window which commanded a view of the garden and park. Gustave passed, and she cried out to him, —

"Gustave, have you seen Mademoiselle Madeleine, this morn‧ing?"

"No, mademoiselle."

"Why, where *can* she be?" exclaimed Bertha, impatiently. "If you will excuse me, aunt, I will go in search of her. Since she has not broken her fast yet, we will breakfast together, as usual." And away darted Bertha into the garden.

The countess had not attached any importance to Madeleine's absence, and resumed the conversation with her son.

Through Count Tristan's mind the suspicion at once had flashed that Madeleine was gone, and he chuckled inwardly at the verification of his own unspoken predictions. A quarter of an hour passed, and then he beheld Bertha coming rapidly from the direction of the *châlet.* He felt no surprise in observing that she was alone. The windows of the breakfast-room opened to the ground, and she entered by one of them, — her face crimsoned, her fair hair unbound and floating over her shoulders, for she had been running.

"I cannot find Madeleine!" she faltered out. "It is *very* strange! She is not in the *châlet,* nor in the garden. I have called until I am hoarse. I picked up this handkerchief in the *châlet,* — it is marked 'G. de Bois,' yet it is three days since M. de Bois was here; and Madeleine and I have spent every morning since then at the *châlet.* When could M. de Bois have dropped this handkerchief there?"

The count took the handkerchief from her hand, and examined the mark without comment: he could not trust his voice at that moment.

"I presume Madeleine will be here presently, to account for herself," remarked the countess, not apparently discomposed. "Take your breakfast, Bertha; there is no need of your fasting until she chooses to make her appearance."

Bertha obediently sat down, sipped her coffee for a few moments, and then, declaring that she wanted nothing more, left the room and returned to Madeleine's apartment. It was in perfect order, but so it was always; the bed was made, but Madeleine was in the habit of making her own bed; there was no sign of change. Bertha opened the wardrobe, — the dresses Madeleine usually wore were hanging within; she wandered about the ‧room, examining every nook and corner, hardly conscious of what she was doing, — what she expected to find or to miss. All at once she remarked that a few books, which were favorites of Madeleine and once belonged to her father, had been removed from the table; but what of that?—they had probably been placed somewhere else. Continuing her almost purposeless search, Bertha now drew out the drawers of the bureau: they usually held Madeleine's linen; they were empty! In violent agitation the kneeling girl sprang to her feet; her undefined fear was taking shape. She ran to the antechamber and looked for a little trunk which had come to the château with Madeleine: it was no longer there!

Bertha darted down the stair and rushed into her aunt's presence, sobbing out in agony of grief,—"She has gone! Madeleine has gone! I know she has gone, and she will never, never return to us! Her dresses are there; everything you have given her is there; she has only taken with her what she had when she came to the château, and she has surely gone!"

Count Tristan pretended to laugh at Bertha's fears, and maintained that Madeleine would presently walk in, and feel very much flattered by the sensation she had created, and by her cousin's lamentations over her supposed flight; adding, jocosely, that it was not easy for a young lady to disappear in that dramatic manner, except from the pages of a novel.

The countess, who began to be alarmed, desired her son to ring the bell. Gustave appeared in answer, and, after being closely questioned, was desired to summon the other domestics. Bettina and Elise promptly obeyed the command. Their answers were precisely the same as those of Gustave: they had not seen Madeleine; they could not imagine where she was.

"Baptiste,—where is he?" asked the countess.

Baptiste was in the garden.

"I am going out,—I will speak to him myself, and also institute further inquiries to satisfy our dear little Bertha; but I warn her that her dreams of a romantic adventure, and the flight of a young lady from an ancient château and her natural protectors, will probably meet with a sudden check by Madeleine's walking in from a long ramble."

Thus speaking, the count left Bertha to be consoled by his mother, and went forth in search of Baptiste. Count Tristan well knew that, although the domestics were all warmly attached to Madeleine, the devotion of Baptiste was unsurpassed. The count did not, for one instant, doubt that she had really gone. Some assistance she must have had, and Baptiste's was the aid she would naturally have selected. He chose to interrogate the old man himself, to *prevent his giving* rather than to extract information from him.

8 *

The simple-hearted gardener was not an adept in deception. He was digging among his flower-beds when his master approached him, and it did not escape the nobleman's observation that the spade went into the ground and was drawn out again with increased rapidity as he drew near, and that the head of Baptiste, instead of being lifted to see who was coming, was bent down as though he wished to appear wholly engrossed in his occupation.

"Baptiste?"

"Monsieur?"

The tremulous voice in which that one word was uttered, and his guilty countenance, scarcely raised as he spoke, were enough to convict him.

"Has Mademoiselle Madeleine passed you in walking out, this morning?"

"No, monsieur. I have been very busy, monsieur; these flower-beds are in a terrible state; it is not easy for one pair of hands to keep them even in tolerable order. I have not noticed who passed. I don't generally look about me, — I" —

"Oh, very well; we thought perhaps you might have seen Mademoiselle Madeleine to-day, as she must have walked out; but, as you know nothing at all about her, I will inform the countess and Mademoiselle Bertha."

"I am much obliged to monsieur," replied Baptiste, gratefully.

He could not conceal his thankfulness at escaping the cross-examination which he had anticipated with the dread natural to one wholly unpractised in dissimulation.

"This handkerchief of M. de Bois was found in the *châlet*," continued the count. "I suppose he sometimes strolls over here in the morning, at an hour too early for visiting; it is very natural, as we are such near neighbors."

"As monsieur says, it would be very natural."

The count had gained all the information that he desired, and without letting Baptiste suspect he had betrayed his secret. That Madeleine had actually fled, that M. de Bois had lent his aid, and that Baptiste had been taken into their confidence, was indubitable.

The count returned to the château, and joined his mother, who was making vain attempts to soothe Bertha. The only comfort to which she would listen was the assurance that, if Madeleine had really gone, she would be traced and entreated to return to her former home.

The count now thought it politic to assume an air of the

"I am grieved to bring you such unsatisfactory news; but Baptiste knows nothing,— he has not seen Madeleine. I am very much shocked, but the fear that she has really left us forces itself upon me. I will order my horse and ride over to Rennes. She probably obtained a conveyance last night or this morning to take her there, as it is the nearest town; and then, by railroad or stage-coach, she must have proceeded upon her journey."

"But how could she have obtained a conveyance if none of the servants were in her confidence? She must have walked, though it is five miles; but that cannot be, for she could not have carried her trunk. Some one *must* have aided her. Oh, who *can* it be?"

Bertha wiped her streaming eyes with the handkerchief in her hand; it was the handkerchief found in the *châlet*,— that of Gaston de Bois. It seemed to answer her question. She hesitated for some moments before she could persuade herself to communicate her suspicion; but her strong love for Madeleine, and her desire that she should be restored to them, prevailed. She handed the handkerchief to Count Tristan.

"Before you go to Rennes, will you not return this handkerchief to M. de Bois? As it was picked up in the *châlet*, he must have been there lately,— possibly this morning. Perhaps he knows something of Madeleine's flight. Oh, he *must* know! —he must! Make him tell you,— implore him to tell you!"

The count took the handkerchief, saying, "It is an admirable suggestion of yours, my dear Bertha. I will go to M. de Bois at once. Meantime, do not spoil your beautiful eyes with weeping. Never fear,— we will have Madeleine back shortly; and if you will only be consoled, I promise to forgive her all the anxiety she has occasioned us."

Count Tristan found M. de Bois at home, burrowing among musty volumes, which were the daily companions of his solitude. When he received his handkerchief, a violent fit of stammering rendered the words he attempted to utter wholly incomprehensible, and the count made no effort to understand them. He proceeded to inform M. de Bois of Madeleine's sudden disappearance, and of the great unhappiness it had caused, adding that he came to him as a neighbor, to ask his advice concerning the best method of tracking the fugitive.

If M. de Bois offered any counsel (which his guest pretended to imagine he did), the impediment in his speech increased to such an extent that his suggestions were unintelligible. His perturbation might have passed for surprise at the startling intelligence so abruptly communicated; but it could hardly be translated into sorrow or sympathy, and was a very imperfect simulation of astonishment.

"I am going to Rennes, for the purpose of making inquiries at the railroad depôt. Will not that plan be a good one?" asked the count.

"Ver — ver — ery good," stammered M. de Bois.

"Can you think of any mode that will facilitate my search?"

"I fear not, — none at all; I am very dull in such m — m — matters."

The count took his leave, congratulating himself that his neighbor had not been subjected to the scrutiny of the Countess de Gramont or Bertha, and especially of Maurice, whose absence at this crisis he looked upon as doubly fortunate.

Count Tristan returned to the château with as dejected a mien as he could assume.

Bertha was watching at the window, and ran out to meet him. "What news? When did M. de Bois lose his handkerchief? When did he last see Madeleine?"

"Dear child, I am deeply pained not to bring more cheering information. M. de Bois must have dropped his handkerchief some days ago, — the morning after the ball; he has not been here since; he has no recollection of the circumstance; he has not seen Madeleine at all."

"Was he not amazed to hear that she had gone?"

"Very much confounded; the shock quite bewildered him. We consulted about the best means of tracing her at Rennes. You may rest assured that M. de Bois was totally ignorant of her intention to leave us. And, if you will allow me to make a suggestion, I would charge you not to let him suspect, when you meet, that you for a moment imagine he was in Madeleine's confidence. It would be highly indelicate, — the very supposition would be derogatory to her dignity. I have said all that was necessary to him, and, as he had nothing to do with the affair, it is a topic which cannot with propriety be touched upon again."

"Assuredly not," coincided the countess. "Madeleine, with all her faults, would not so entirely forget her own self-respect as to have a clandestine understanding with a young man. I cannot believe she would disgrace herself and us by such unmaidenly conduct."

"Unmaidenly! Would it be unmaidenly?" questioned Bertha, innocently. "If it would be an impropriety to confide in

M. de Bois, then Madeleine certainly has not made him her confidant. Oh, my poor Madeleine ! It is dreadful to think that she must have gone away alone, — quite alone !"

" You may well call it *dreadful,* Bertha. An occurrence of this kind has never blotted the annals of our family! What will be said of her and of us? Such a step, taken by a woman of her birth, will set hundreds of tongues discussing our domestic concerns; our names will be bandied about from lip to lip; our affairs will be in all sorts of common people's mouths. Hasten, for heaven's sake, my son, and find Madeleine before this story gets wind."

Count Tristan dutifully obeyed, — that is to say, he assumed an appearance of compliance, for in a few moments he was galloping toward Rennes.

Evening set in before he returned. His long absence had kindled in the minds of the countess and Bertha a hope that he had discovered some clew, and the latter had worked herself up to such a pitch of excitement that she almost anticipated the return of Madeleine in Count Tristan's company. Her disappointment when, at last, he entered, looking weary and dejected, was proportionate to her expectations. He had made all possible search, — *so he said,* — and no information concerning the fugitive could be gathered; she was gone! He feared they must now wait patiently until they heard from her. She would doubtless write soon, — a letter might come at any moment. Very possibly she had changed her mind in regard to Lady Vivian's offer, and had accepted it without communicating her intention, because she feared her aunt's displeasure. This was the most likely explanation of her sudden departure. He had called at the Château de Tremazan, and Lady Vivian had left for Scotland two days after the ball. Madeleine was doubtless at this moment on her way to Edinburgh.

The count, though he made this assertion with an air of perfect credence, did not, for a moment, believe that such was Madeleine's destination ; but he thought to check persistent inquiries which might accidentally bring to light some fine thread that

Bertha would very gladly have followed the count's advice; but, even if she had made the effort, it would have been impossible to drive anxiety for Madeleine out of her thoughts. Several times during the evening she started up, thinking that she heard her voice; if a step echoed in the antechamber, she turned eagerly to the door, her blue eyes greatening with expectation. Once, when the roll of wheels sounded in the distance, she uttered a cry of joy and rushed out upon the porch. Every moment she grew more and more restless and feverish; and when the usual hour for retiring came, she wandered into Madeleine's room, instead of her own, and once more minutely examined the whole chamber. There might, perhaps, be a note somewhere which she had overlooked: after the most diligent search, none was to be found. There were pens, ink, and paper upon the little table which Madeleine generally used, but not a word of writing was visible.

The sight of pen and ink suggested an idea which had not before occurred to Bertha. She sat down and wrote to Maurice. She poured out all her grief upon paper, and it was soothed as if dropped into words upon the blank sheet before her. How often a full heart has had its burden lifted and lightened at the pen's point, as if the sorrow it recorded grew less heavy beneath the calming touch of that potent instrument!

CHAPTER IX.

THE EMPTY PLACE.

It chanced that Bertha's letter to Maurice was posted the next morning without the knowledge of Count Tristan and his mother; not, however, through any preconcerted arrangement on the part of Bertha. Her character was so frank, so transparent, — her actions were always so unveiled, — her thoughts flowed in such an instinctive current toward her lips, — that the idea of concealment could have no spontaneous existence in her mind. She made no allusion to the letter until it was gone; but that was purely accidental, though not the less fortunate. Had Count Tristan been aware that such a letter had been written, it would never have reached its destination.

It was somewhat singular that the count, whose code of honor would have forced him to resent, at the sword's point, the faintest hint that he could be guilty of an unworthy action, would not have scrupled to intercept a letter, to distort a fact (we use the mildest phrase), to stoop to any deception, to be guilty of any treachery, if he were powerfully prompted by what he termed family considerations, — which simply meant his own personal interest.

He had determined to keep Maurice in ignorance of Madeleine's flight as long as possible, that the chances of discovering her retreat might be diminished; and great was the wily schemer's consternation when he learned that Bertha had unadvisedly frustrated his plans by writing to her cousin.

Madeleine's value had never been estimated to its just height until her place was empty. It is not in human nature to prize that which we possess to its full worth, until it is "lacked and lost!" Alas! in how many households there moves, with noiseless feet, some placid, patient, yet potent spirit, with hands ever ready to toil, or soothe; a smile ever kindled to comfort or encourage; a voice that "turns common words to grace," imparting hope and dispensing joy; a presence full of helpfulness and peace; a being, grown familiar to our eyes by every day's association, whom we carelessly greet, or jostle against unheeding, or thrust aside impatiently, never dreaming that our working-day mortal, could she cast off this garment of clay, would stand revealed one of God's holy messengers commissioned to minister! — that is, *never until* we suddenly find her place empty, yet trace the touch of her delicate fingers, the print of her light footsteps everywhere around us, and feel the dreary void made in our hearts by her absence, and recognize, too late, that we have entertained an angel unawares.

Throughout the Château de Gramont there was no one, save Count Tristan, who did not make some such reflection (though vague and undefined, perhaps) while thinking of Madeleine. The ancient domestics seemed completely lost without her guiding hand, — her spirit of order systematizing and lightening all their duties. Everything was in confusion, everything went wrong. Dearly as they loved her, they had never before realized that Mademoiselle Madeleine had been of so much importance and assistance to them all.

The countess missed her every moment; and, interested as were her regrets, they were not unmingled with some faint self-reproach when she remembered how lightly she had prized her services. The antiquated *femme de chambre* had never appeared so clumsy, purblind, and stupid; and the more her stately mistress chided her, the more bewildered Bettina became, the more blunders she committed.

Even a bearing as majestic as that of the noble lady could not neutralize the caricaturing effect of a robe pinned awry; curls with long straight ends standing out porcupine fashion; a cap obstinately bent upon inclining to one side; and a collar with a strong tendency to avoid a central position.

As for Bertha, naturally restless, excitable, and untutored in the art of calming the agitation of her mind by active employment, she could do nothing but wander in and out of her aunt's apartment; stand at the window watching for the postman, beating the devil's tattoo upon the panes; counting the hours, fretting over their insupportable length, and breaking out, at intervals, into piteous lamentations.

It was with difficulty that she could be persuaded to appear at table, and she scarcely tasted food. Glancing up at the faded flowers in the hanging baskets suspended before the windows, and to the withered bouquets in the tall vases that stood on either side, — baskets and vases which Madeleine had ever kept freshly supplied, — Bertha could scarcely restrain her tears, as she murmured mournfully. —

"Ah, I know now what the English poet's Ophelia meant, when she said all the violets withered when her father died! All our flowers faded when Madeleine went!"

Baptiste, who was standing beside her chair, rubbed his eyes, and the sigh, that would not be checked, was audible to her quick ears. She turned to give him a glance which recognized his sympathy, and noticed that there was no gay-looking blossom in his button-hole that day. This was an unmistakable expression of sorrow on the part of Baptiste; for he never assumed the compulsory office of butler without asserting his preference for his legitimate vocation of gardener by a flower in his coat. Bertha had never seen him dispense with the floral decoration before, and she comprehended its absence but too well.

Her nervous disquietude increased every hour, and caused her aunt a species of petty martyrdom resembling the torture of perpetual pin-pricking, the incessant buzzing and stinging of a gnat, the endless creaking of rusty door-hinges, — minor miseries often more unendurable than some great mental or physical suffering. But although the patience of the countess was wearied out, Bertha was too great a favorite to be rebuked. Count

Tristan discreetly fled the field, and thus avoided his share of the infliction.

Bertha's letter reached Maurice the day after it was written, and found him in a state of such torpid despondency that any summons to action, even the most painful, was a blessing. He had felt that the only chance of combating his sorrow, and preventing its obtaining full mastery over all his faculties, was to work off the sense of depression by hard study, — to battle against it with the arms of some engrossing occupation; but how could he spur himself up to study without an object? — and he was as far as ever from obtaining his father's consent to fitting himself for the bar, or for any other professional pursuit. No, — there was only one pursuit left open to him, the pursuit of pleasure, and he had not sufficiently recovered from his late shock to start off in chase of that illusive phantom. Bertha's letter roused him out of this miserable, mind-paralyzing apathy. In the very next train which left for Rennes he was on his way back to Brittany.

It was the fourth day after Madeleine's departure. Those days had seemed months to Bertha, the weariest months of her brief, glad life. She was standing at a window that commanded the road, — her favorite post, and the only locality where she ever remained quiet for any length of time, — when the carriage in which Maurice was seated drove up the avenue. With a joyful exclamation she rushed out of the room, darted down the stair, through the hall, into the porch, and had greeted Maurice before any one but the old gardener knew that he had arrived.

"You have heard from her?" were her cousin's first words, gaspingly uttered.

"No, not a line. She will never write; she will never come back! O Maurice! I have lost all hope," sighed Bertha.

"Dear Bertha, we will find her! Let her go where she may, I will find her! — be sure of that. I will not rest until I do."

His grandmother, attracted by Bertha's exultant ejaculation, had followed her, though with more deliberate steps, and now appeared. The cruel words the countess had spoken to Madeleine were ringing in the ears of Maurice, and he saluted his noble relative respectfully, but not with his usual warmth.

"I am glad you have come back to us, Maurice. Bertha is so lonely."

The lips of Maurice parted, but some internal warning checked the bitter words before they formed themselves into sound. He bowed gravely, and, entering the house, remarked to Bertha, —

"You wrote that all the servants had been examined?"

9

"Yes, all; and they know nothing of Madeleine's flight."

"That is *impossible*. One of them at least must have some knowledge."

Maurice rang the bell. It was Bettina, who replied. Gustave, she said, was in the stable, and Baptiste in the garden. The answers of the *femme de chambre* to the young viscount were clear and unhesitating: no one could doubt, for a moment, that she was wholly ignorant of Madeleine's movement; and her tone and manner evinced, as forcibly as any language could have done, how deeply she mourned over her absence. Elise was next summoned, and her replies were but a repetition of Bettina's.

"I will not send for Gustave and Baptiste," he observed, dismissing the two female domestics, — "I will walk out and see them."

"And I will go with you," said Bertha.

The countess was too well pleased to see the cousins together to object.

Gustave was grooming a horse as they passed by the stable. He paused in his work to welcome the viscount, and added, in the same breath, —

"Monsieur will find it very dull at the château, now. It does not seem like the same place since Mademoiselle Madeleine left!"

"Have you no idea how she went, Gustave? Some of you surely must know!"

"I know nothing, monsieur. When they told me that Mademoiselle Madeleine was gone, it was as though a thunder-bolt had struck me. I have never felt good for anything since!"

There was too much sincerity, too much feeling in his tone for Maurice to doubt him, or deem further questioning necessary. He walked sadly away, accompanied by Bertha.

Baptiste was busied near the little *châlet;* he seemed to hover about it constantly of late. He was aware of the return of his young master, — he had bowed to him as he was descending from the carriage. When Bertha and her cousin approached the venerable domestic, his trepidation was too obvious to escape their notice. He was pruning the luxuriant growth of some of the vines Madeleine had planted, and the hand which held his knife shook and committed unintentional havoc among the blossoming branches.

"Baptiste, come in; I have something to talk to you about," said Maurice, entering the *châlet* with Bertha.

How painfully that pleasant little retreat reminded him of Madeleine! For a moment he was overpowered, and dropped into a chair, covering his eyes with his hands; perhaps because he could not bear the sight of objects which called up such agonizing recollections; perhaps because his eyes were dim with too womanish a moisture.

"Dear Maurice," said Bertha, bending over him compassionately, "if Madeleine only knew how wretched she has made us both, surely she would not forsake us so cruelly."

Maurice, by a gesture, prayed her to sit down. Baptiste stood in the doorway; his attitude betokened a reluctance to enter, and a desire to be quickly dismissed. After a long interval, the viscount, slowly raising his head, was again struck by the perturbed mien of the guileless old man, whose native simplicity, warmth, and ingenuousness would have melted any mask he attempted to assume. Maurice had almost abandoned all expectation that he would receive any information from the domestics; but he now experienced a sudden renewal of hope.

"Baptiste," he said, scrutinizing the ancient gardener closely, "do you not know where Mademoiselle Madeleine is?"

"No, monsieur."

The reply was uttered in a tone of genuine sadness.

"You cannot even guess?"

"No, monsieur."

"Do you know how she left here?"

"No, monsieur."

"Baptiste, you are not speaking falsely?—you are not trifling with me? If you *are*, you can hardly know how cruelly you are adding to my sorrow."

"I have spoken the exact truth, monsieur."

"I am sure he has, Maurice," interrupted Bertha. "I never knew Baptiste to utter even a *white lie:* he has as great a horror of falsehood as Madeleine herself."

Baptiste looked at her gratefully.

"Then you know *nothing at all*," ejaculated Maurice, in a tone of discouragement. "You did not help Mademoiselle Madeleine in any way? She must have had some assistance; but from *you* she had none? You did not even know that she intended to leave us?"

Baptiste hesitated; his mouth twitched,—his eyes were fixed upon the ground

"Why do you not answer, Baptiste?" asked Bertha. "You *did not* know that Mademoiselle Madeleine was going,—did you?"

"Yes, mademoiselle."

The answer was spoken almost in a whisper.

" *You knew it?* And why, *why* have you not told us this before?" she almost shrieked out.

"No one asked me that question, mademoiselle; and Mademoiselle Madeleine requested me not to give any information concerning her which I could possibly, and without uttering a falsehood, avoid."

Maurice sprang up and laid his hand upon the old man's shoulder.

"Speak *now* then! You cannot avoid telling us all you know! You were aware that she was going; you assisted her flight. *How* did you aid her? *What* did you do? *What* do you know?"

"Very little, monsieur. I did very little and know very little. The evening before Mademoiselle Madeleine left, she came to me in the garden; she asked me if I would do her a favor. I would have done her a thousand. Did I not owe her enough? Was it not she who watched beside my bed when I had that terrible rheumatic fever two years ago? Did she not pour out my medicine with her own white hands? Did she not talk to me when I was racked with pain, until I thought the room was full of heavenly music, and I forgot I was suffering? Did she not keep me from cursing God when the pangs were so sharp that I felt I was tortured beyond my strength? Did she not tell me why all anguish of soul or body should be borne patiently? Was there, oh, was there *anything* I would not have done for Mademoiselle Madeleine? When she left the château, was her loss greater to any one than it was to me? And she would not have gone if she could have staid any longer. I was sure of *that*. When she said she must go, I knew she *must*, and I never even dared to pray her to remain."

It was seldom that Baptiste spoke so much, for he was taciturn by nature; but the emotion, forcibly suppressed for so many days, once breaking bondage, burst forth into a torrent of words.

"You did well, Baptiste, — good, faithful old man! Mademoiselle Madeleine needed a friend; and I thank Heaven she had one like you. Do not think we blame you; only tell us all you know. She came to you the evening before she left: what favor did she ask?"

"Mademoiselle Madeleine only asked, monsieur, that I would come to her room when the house was all quiet, that night, and carry down her trunk and place it in the *châlet*. I could not help saying, 'Oh, Mademoiselle Madeleine, are you going to leave us?' She answered, 'I *cannot* stay, Baptiste. I am *compelled* to go. You are the only person here who is aware of my intention. When I am gone do not give any information concerning me that you can possibly, and without uttering a falsehood, avoid. It will be better that no one should know I had your aid.' Those were her exact words, monsieur."

" Go on, — go on!" urged Maurice, as the narrator paused.

" When the house was all quiet, I put off my shoes and stole softly to Mademoiselle Madeleine's room. She opened the door, and, without speaking, pointed to the little trunk. Old and weak as I am, I had no trouble in carrying it. It was light enough. It could not have held much."

" Did she not bid you adieu, then?" asked Bertha.

" Just as I was stooping to lift the trunk, Mademoiselle Madeleine stretched out her hand and took mine. I felt her warm, soft touch the whole day after. She did not say adieu, but she looked it. She looked as though she were blessing me and thanking me. I never saw a face that said so much, — so much that went to my very soul and comforted me! When she let go my hand, I took up the trunk and carried it out. She closed the door behind me without a sound, and I brought the trunk here that night and left it. That is all I know, monsieur."

" But how was the trunk conveyed hence?"

" I do not know, monsieur."

" Did you see Mademoiselle Madeleine the next morning?" inquired Bertha.

" No, mademoiselle. I could not help going to the *châlet* the first thing when I came out to work. I pushed the door open and looked in; the trunk was not there, and I knew that Mademoiselle Madeleine was gone too!"

" But did not Mademoiselle Madeleine drop some hint, even the faintest, of her plans?" asked Maurice, earnestly.

" I have told monsieur every word Mademoiselle Madeleine spoke to me on the subject."

" *Some one* must have aided her further! Who could it be? *Who could it possibly be?*" mused Maurice.

Baptiste was certain he knew who alone it could be; and he was pondering within himself whether he had the right to mention the note Madeleine had ordered him to deliver to M. de Bois. Her request had been that he would give no information he could honestly avoid; if it *could* be avoided, it was plain, then, that the intelligence ought not to be communicated.

"Has monsieur done with me?" he asked, as Maurice stood reflecting in silence.

"Yes, if you have nothing further to tell me."

"Nothing further, monsieur." Saying these words, Baptiste withdrew.

"After Madeleine was missed," said Bertha, when the old gardener was gone, "I was the first person who came to the *chàlet*. I found a handkerchief lying just by this table. It was marked G. de Bois."

"Gaston de Bois! Then it is clear *he* was Madeleine's confidant. He promoted her flight!"

"So I thought, at first," rejoined Bertha; "but it seems this is not so. Your father took him the handkerchief, and he could not tell when or where he had lost it. He was amazed to hear that Madeleine had left us, and disclaimed all knowledge concerning her."

"Who, then, could it have been? But I will see M. de Bois myself."

"First let me tell you"—began Bertha, and faltered.

"Why do you hesitate? For Heaven's sake, dear Bertha, tell me everything which can throw the faintest glimmer of light upon the path Madeleine has taken."

"I do not know how to say what I was thinking; perhaps I ought not to allude to it at all; yet it seems as if it must be true. Do you not remember that Madeleine confessed she had bestowed her affections upon *some one*? Since they were not given to you, as I once believed, I cannot help imagining that perhaps she might — might have meant"—

"Gaston de Bois?"

"Yes."

Maurice did not answer, and Bertha could say no more. There was a painful struggle going on in her mind, though less torturing than that which convulsed the spirit of her cousin.

When he had somewhat recovered himself, he said, —

"At all events I will see M. de Bois. If there is nothing to be learned from him, if he really knows nothing concerning Madeleine's departure, I must seek information at Rennes. There is no time to lose. I will call upon M. de Bois at once."

The cousins parted at the door of the *chàlet*. Bertha turned toward the château, pausing on her way to talk with Baptiste; Maurice went in the direction of his neighbor's residence.

Count Tristan's visit had taken M. de Bois aback, chiefly because he was confounded by a new proof of his own awkwardness (stupidity, he plainly termed it) in leaving his handkerchief behind him, as a witness of his presence at the *châlet*. But there was no such confusing testimony to destroy his composure when he received Maurice. Besides, he had ample time to collect himself; for he was walking in the park when his valet announced that the young viscount was awaiting him in the library. He had looked forward to the return of Maurice to Brittany as soon as the latter heard of Madeleine's mysterious disappearance. M. de Bois knew that it would be more difficult to prevent her being traced by her cousin than by any other person, and that it was by him Madeleine herself most feared to be discovered. Gaston was therefore fully on his guard against betraying her confidence.

Maurice, on his part, was keenly sensible of the difficulty of his undertaking. He could not openly inquire of M. de Bois whether Madeleine had apprised him of her intentions. The very question would have a tendency to compromise his cousin, by suggesting that she was capable of holding clandestine communication with a young gentleman. Then, too, if M. de Bois was really the object of her attachment, he might not be aware of the preference with which she honored him; and it would be the height of indelicacy for Maurice to allow him to suspect a circumstance which her modesty would scrupulously conceal. He was sitting in the library pondering over the embarrassments of his position, when his host entered. The gentlemen greeted each other with wonted cordiality.

"Did you return from Paris to-day?" asked M. de Bois. "Have you just come?"

"About an hour ago. I came to you at once to"—

M. de Bois interrupted him. It was the policy of the former to lead the conversation, that he might avoid direct questions.

"Had you heard that Mademoiselle de Gramont had left the château?"

"Yes; my cousin Bertha wrote to me, and"—

Again M. de Bois seized upon the thread of conversation.

"Have you no news from Mademoiselle Madeleine?—no letter?"

"None," sighed Maurice, convinced that, as M. de Bois plunged into the subject in this straightforward, calm manner, he could not possibly be in her confidence.

The host went on.

"Has not Count Tristan been able to obtain any trace of her?"

"Thus far, none at all! What *could* have become of her! Where *could* she have gone!" exclaimed Maurice; but not in a tone of interrogation, for he now felt assured that M. de Bois could not answer.

"One thing is certain; what Mademoiselle Mad — ad — adeleine has done must have been prompted by a noble motive. She could not cause you all this sorrow unless she imagined herself compelled to take the step which we must all lament."

"You are right, you only do her justice!" rejoined Maurice.

"What course do you propose to ado — op —opt?" inquired M. de Bois, with a perfectly natural air of friendly interest.

"I hardly know what to do. I should be thankful for any advice. I shall first visit the Prefecture at Rennes, to see if she obtained a passport. She could not surely run the risk of attempting to travel without one. If the passport be for Great Britain, I may go to Scotland. Possibly she may have changed her mind, and accepted Lady Vivian's offer, — do you not think so?"

"It does not appear to me likely. She definitely decli — i — ined."

"Did she tell you so? Did she speak to you on the subject?" asked Maurice, hastily.

For the first time during the interview, M de Bois betrayed a slight disquietude, but he quickly collected himself and answered, —

"I heard Lady Vivian speak to Mademoiselle Bertha of the offer she had made her cousin, and after that, Mademoiselle Mad — ad — adeleine told me she had declined the prop — op — oposition. But, if you imagine she has changed her mind, would not a letter to Lady Vivian answer every pur — ur — urpose?"

"No; if she should be there, I must see her, and use arguments which would have no force upon paper. *She must be there!* Where else could she be? I will start for Scotland to-night. Now I must bid you adieu."

"If you are going back to the château, I will accompany you. I must make my *adieux* to the ladies. I leave for Paris to-morrow."

"Indeed! Do you make a long stay?"

"Prob — ob — obably. The Marquis de Fleury had promised me a secretaryship, if he were sent as ambassador to America. It is uncertain when he may get the appointment, but he has offered me the post of confidential sec — ec — ecretary at once."

"And you have accepted?"

" Gladly."

" Ah, M. de Bois, how I envy you ! *You* will have an object in life, while *I*, who feel as though a pent-up volcano were roaring within me, am condemned to let my struggling energies smoulder beneath the ashes of my father's autocratic will ! You have heard of his opposition to my studying for the bar ? What is to become of me if I am deprived of every stimulating incentive to action ? — especially now — now that " — he checked himself suddenly. He was not aware that M. de Bois had been informed by Bertha of Madeleine's rejection, and Maurice could not dwell upon his own disappointment to one who might be a rival.

" Count Tristan may gradually be . brought to contemplate your wishes with more favor."

" Hardly ; but come — if you will accompany me, let us go."

Bertha, who had been waiting impatiently for the return of Maurice, did not fly to meet him when she saw M. de Bois walking . by his side, as they approached the château. The countess was in the drawing-room when the gentlemen entered, and her majestic presence stemmed the stream of inquiries that was ready to gush from Bertha's lips.

M. de Bois, who during his interview with Maurice had been so self-possessed that the impediment in his speech was scarcely observable, was seized anew and cast into chains by his invisible enemy. The captive struggled in vain ; the avenues of speech were barricaded ; all his limbs were shackled ; his movements became uncertain and spasmodic, menacing tables, chairs, vases, which, had they been gifted with consciousness, must have trembled at his approach ; his nervous fingers thrust themselves into his hair, and threw it into ludicrous disorder ; his countenance was suffused with scarlet ; he stammered out something about bidding adieu, which the ladies were evidently at a loss to comprehend, until Maurice explained that M. de Bois expected to start on the morrow for Paris, where he purposed to take up his residence.

" We shall regret losing so valued a neighbor ! " observed the countess, condescendingly.

Bertha made no remark, though she looked as though she wished to speak, and could not summon resolution. She took an opportunity, while the countess was conversing with their guest, to whisper to her cousin, —

" You asked M. de Bois, and he could give you no information concerning Madeleine ? "

"None at all," replied Maurice in a low tone.   Then, turning
to the countess, he said aloud, " I also must bid you adieu, my
grandmother ; I am going immediately to Rennes ; if I obtain
the information there, which I think probable, I shall start
at once for Scotland and seek Lady Vivian."

" You have not consulted your father, Maurice," the countess
answered, with an emphasis which was intended to remind him
that he was not a free agent.

" I must beg you to make my apologies to him."

Maurice, though he treated his grandmother with deference
which left her no room for complaint, could not force himself to
assume his wonted air of affection ; his love for her had waned
from the hour he listened to the unjust accusation, the reproaches, the contumely she had heaped upon the innocent and
unfortunate orphan placed at her mercy.   The softening veil
had fallen from her character, and disclosed its harsh, proud
selfishness and policy.   He now knew that she had offered her
destitute relative shelter, not from any genuine, womanly feeling
of tenderness and compassion, but simply because she deemed it
humiliating to allow one who bore her name to be placed in a
doubtful and friendless position.   All Madeleine's gentleness,
cheerfulness, diligence to please, had failed to melt her aunt's
impenetrable heart and make it expand to yield her a sacred
place ; the countess had misinterpreted her highest virtues, —
grossly insulted her by attributing shameful motives to her most
disinterested conduct, and destroyed all the merit of her own
benefactions by reminding the recipient of her indebtedness.
Maurice felt that, truly to venerate a person, he must be moved
by esteem for noble qualities possessed.   The recent revelation
of his grandmother's actual attributes estranged and revolted
him, until it became difficult to treat her with even the outward
semblance of reverence.

When the viscount bade farewell, M. de Bois also took his
leave.

" You will write to me as soon as you reach Edinburgh ? "
pleaded Bertha to her cousin.

" I will certainly write," answered Maurice ; " meantime
comfort yourself with the assurance that I will not relinquish my
search until Madeleine is restored to us."

And Bertha did solace herself with that pledge, for hope was
a dominant characteristic of her buoyant temperament.

The monotonous round of blank, weary days that ensued was
happily broken, before the week closed, by the promised letter

from Maurice. Bertha, whose only exciting occupation consisted in watching for the arrival and distribution of letters, was in possession of the precious missive before her aunt and Count Tristan were aware of its arrival. She tore it open, and, glancing through the contents, uttered a cry of joy that rang through the château, and reached the ears even of the countess and her son in the library. The next moment Bertha burst into the apartment, laughing and crying, waving the letter triumphantly over her head, and exclaiming, in a voice now stifled with sobs, now broken by hysterical mirth, —

"She is found! she is found! Maurice has traced her! Oh, my dear, dear Madeleine, I shall see her again!"

Her blinding tears, or her overwhelming transport, prevented her noticing the totally different effect produced upon her two relatives by this rapturously uttered communication. The face of the countess expressed a haughty satisfaction that her noble family had been spared some impending disgrace; but Count Tristan's black brows contracted; his malignant eyes flashed fiercely; he ground his teeth with suppressed rage as he snatched the letter out of Bertha's hand. She flung her arms about her aunt, and laid her head lovingly upon her unsympathetic bosom, as though she must caress some one in the exuberant outburst of her joy! Meanwhile the count perused the letter.

"My son, let me hear what Maurice says."

Count Tristan read, —

"I hasten to send you good news, my dearest Bertha. At Rennes I visited the Prefecture to examine the list of passports, knowing that Madeleine must have obtained one to travel unmolested. I found that her passport had been taken out for England. This confirmed my impression that she had joined Lady Vivian in Scotland. The passport which, as you are aware, requires two responsible witnesses, was signed by Messrs. Picard and Bossuet. I sought those gentlemen to extract further information from them, but, singularly enough, both had left Brittany the day after Madeleine. I cannot conceive how she obtained their signatures, for surely she had no acquaintance with them. Following this clew I started immediately for Edinburgh, and arrived here on Wednesday evening. I had no difficulty in finding the residence of Lady Vivian. She is in London, but is expected home shortly. I had an interview with her venerable housekeeper, who answered all my inquiries with great patience. From her I learned that Lady Vivian was accompanied by a young French lady whom she had recently engaged as a *dame de compagnie.* The housekeeper could not remember her foreign name, but when I mentioned Mademoiselle de Gramont, she said it sounded like that. She had been informed that the young lady was very accomplished and belonged to an excellent family; also that Lady Vivian had first heard of her during her late visit in Brittany. In answer to the question whether this young lady arrived with Lady Vivian in London, the housekeeper replied that she did not, — she had joined her ladyship only a few days ago. Thus I feel certain that Madeleine is found. I leave for London at once, and, not many days after you receive this letter, you may expect to see us both; for I will never cease my supplications until Madeleine yields and returns with me to the Château de Gramont. I know what joy this intelligence will give you, my dear little cousin, and my joy is increased by the reflection of yours."

The count broke off without reading the concluding lines of the letter, and remarked, —

"Maurice came to a hasty conclusion. If Lady Vivian's *dame de compagnie should* prove to be Madeleine, as it *may* be, there is no certainty that she will yield to his persuasions and return to us. Madeleine is very obstinate and self-willed. You must pardon me, Bertha, for throwing a damper upon your hopes, but I would spare you too severe disappointment."

"I shall *not* be disappointed. I feel sure Maurice has discovered Madeleine : *that* is all I ask for the present. You may be right about her refusing to return here, — I dare say you are ; but *that* will not make me miserable, which I should be if we could not find her at all. I mean to ask my uncle's permission to allow Madeleine to reside with us. I do not see how he can refuse, and he is very indulgent ; so that, whether Madeleine consents to return here, or not, we shall not be wholly parted."

Bertha did not suspect into what a fury her words were lashing the count, nor did she divine the machinations already at work within his perfidious spirit to defeat her kindly purpose.

CHAPTER X.

THE HUMBLE COMPANION.

RAPIDLY as Maurice travelled from Edinburgh to London, the distance seemed interminable to his impetuous spirit. Multitudes of arguments were driven through his mind in long array, and he was impatient to prove their power in persuading Madeleine to return. Was it possible that she could refuse to see their force? If calm reasoning, if entreaties and prayers failed to move her, he would test the potency of a threat, — she should learn that he had vowed never to return to his paternal home, never to forgive those who had driven her forth by their cruelty, until *she* had proclaimed their pardon by again taking up her abode at the Château de Gramont. Madeleine, who shrank from all strife, who moved in an atmosphere of harmony, which seemed to envelop her wherever she went, would not lift her hand to sever the sacred bond of union between father and son, grandmother and grandchild. Whatever anguish it might cost her to yield, however great her sacrifice, she would endure the one and accept the other rather than become the instrument that, with fatal blow, struck such an unholy severance.

Maurice vividly pictured to himself his approaching interview under a tantalizing variety of circumstances. Now he imagined that he saw Madeleine only in the presence of her new friends, — that she was cold and reserved, and allowed him no opportunity of uttering a word that could reach *her* ear alone. Now he fancied she had granted him a private interview, — that she was sitting by his side, but resolute, unconvinced, unmoved, while he besieged her with arguments, appealed to her with all the passionate fervor that convulsed his soul, portrayed in darkest colors the fearful results of her inflexibility. Now he painted her overwhelmed by his reasoning, melted by his application, terrified by that terrible menace, and finally consenting to his petition.

It was past ten o'clock when the train reached the London terminus. The loquacious Edinburgh housekeeper had informed him that Lady Vivian was the guest of Lady Augusta Langdon. The lateness of the hour forbade a visit that night; yet, after having engaged a room at Morley's hotel, he could not

10

help strolling in the direction of Grosvenor Square, and was
soon searching for the number he had written upon his tablets.
It was easily found, and Maurice stood before one of the most
sumptuous of the magnificent edifices which adorn that aristocratic locality. The windows were thrown open, and the richly
embroidered lace curtains drawn back, for the evening was
more than usually sultry. He crossed to the opposite side of
the street, and took up a position which enabled him to distinguish forms moving about the spacious drawing-room. With
what straining eyes and breathless anxiety he scrutinized them!
Now he saw a lady of noble carriage walking to and fro, —
that might be Lady Langdon; by and by he caught sight of a
gaunt, ungainly figure, and recognized Lady Vivian. Who
would have believed that a glimpse of that angular, unsymmetrical form could ever have called such radiance to the eyes of a
young and handsome man? — could have kindled such a glow
upon his cheeks? — could have quickened his pulses with so
joyful a motion?

Not long after, a group of young ladies clustered together,
just beneath the chandelier, to examine some object which one
of them held in her hand; and now the heart of Maurice
throbbed so tumultuously that its beats became audible. He
had singled out one maiden whose height and graceful proportions distinguished her from her companions, — Madeleine!
Her face was turned from him; but surely that statuesque outline,
that slender, flexible throat, that exquisitely-shaped head,
about which he thought he traced the coronal braid that usually
crowned her noble brows, — these could belong to Madeleine
only! Could he fail to recognize them anywhere or at any distance? The longer he gazed the more certain he became that
it was she herself, — that she was found at last! How eagerly
he watched to see her turn, and render "assurance doubly
sure" by revealing her lovely countenance! She remained
some time in the same position; then the little group dispersed,
and she glided away, but not in the direction of the window.
The eyes of Maurice never moved from the place where she
had disappeared, though he was conscious of attracting the attention of passers-by, and now and then a whispered comment
of derision fell upon his ear.

Several equipages drove up to Lady Langdon's door, and her
guests gradually departed. Soon after the drawing-room was
deserted, the lights were extinguished, the windows closed.
Other lights brightened the casements above. Still Maurice re-

mained riveted to the spot, unreasonably hoping to behold Madeleine for one fleeting moment again. By and by, one window after another grew dark; but not until the last light went out could he force himself to turn away and retrace his steps to the hotel.

"Will the dawn never come?" How often that question rises involuntarily to the lips, through the long night of expectation that precedes a wished-for day! *Time* — that is, the sense of its duration — is but another word for *state*, — state of mind. The length or briefness of the hour is so completely governed by the mood of one's spirits that it becomes easy for those who have learned this truth from experience to conceive a thousand years but as a day to the blessed, — a day of torture, an age to the miserable; and to comprehend that *time itself* can have no existence, and its computation must be replaced by *state* in the eternal hereafter where we shall live in the spirit only.

"Will the dawn never come?" Maurice repeated hundreds of times as that night dragged its leaden, lagging feet with the slow movement of centuries.

The dim, late London morning came at last to bring with it a new perplexity. It would be a breach of etiquette to call upon Lady Vivian at too early an hour; yet, how was Maurice to curb the headlong rush of his impatience until the prescribed period for ceremonious visits arrived? A stranger in London, it might be supposed that the numberless noteworthy objects by which he was environed might have diverted his attention; but one engrossing thought so completely filled his whole being that it rendered him blind to all the marvels of art or beauties of nature. Yet to remain imprisoned at the hotel was out of the question. He concluded to spend his morning in Hyde Park, chiefly because it was not far distant from Grosvenor Square. But the attractions of the noble park, through which he listlessly sauntered, and of the adjacent Kensington Gardens, to which he unconsciously extended his rambles, were entirely lost upon the abstracted wanderer. Grand old trees, romantic walks, delicious flowers, had no existence for him; the whole world was one great, hueless, formless void, in which he beheld nothing but the spectral image mirrored in his own soul.

He had decided not to pay his visit until after one o'clock; but, before the sun reached its meridian, he absolved himself from the propriety of waiting, and, with rapid steps, once more took his way to Lady Langdon's residence.

The door was opened by a solemn footman.

"Is Lady Vivian at home?"

"Not at home, sir."

"Is Mademoiselle de Gramont—I mean the young lady who accompanied Lady Vivian—at home?"

"Not at home, sir."

"Can you tell me when I shall be likely to find them?"

"Her ladyship gave no orders on the subject, sir."

Maurice stood perplexed, and hesitating.

"Your card, if you please, sir," suggested the demure domestic.

"No, I will call again by and by."

Maurice walked directly back to the park. His suspense was intolerable; he could only endure it for another hour, and then returned to Lady Langdon's.

The same staid attendant reappeared at his knock.

"Has Lady Vivian returned?"

"Not returned, sir."

"Can you tell me when I may depend upon seeing her? I call upon a matter of great importance."

The stately footman looked as though he were pondering upon the propriety of making any satisfactory answer to this question.

Maurice repeated the inquiry with such an anxious intonation, such a perturbed air, that the stolid domestic, accustomed to behold only the conventional composure which allows no pulse to betray its beating, was moved out of the even tenor of his way by astonishment.

"Lady Vivian went with my lady and a large party to Hampton Court. Their ladyships will probably spend the day."

"The day!" exclaimed Maurice, in an accent of consternation.

The footman evidently thought that he had proffered more than sufficient information, and made a dignified attempt to put a close to the interview, by extending his hand, and saying, "I will see that your card reaches her ladyship."

"No, there is no need of my leaving a card: I shall return. At what hour does Lady Langdon dine?"

"At seven, sir."

"I will take the liberty of calling after dinner."

The footman looked as though he decidedly thought it was a liberty, and Maurice turned slowly away from the closing door.

What could be done to shorten the endless hours that stretched their weary length between that period and evening? Hampton Court! What was to prevent his going to Hampton Court? He might meet Lady Vivian and Madeleine, there; nothing was more likely, since they were to spend the day. His spirits revived as he signalled an empty cab, and requested to be driven as rapidly as possible to Hampton Court. He took no note of the length of time occupied in reaching his destination: it was a relief to be in motion, and to know that every moment brought him nearer a locality where the lost one might be found.

Was he more likely to encounter her in the palace or in the grounds? he asked, internally, as he sprang out of the cab. He would try the palace first. He strode through its magnificent apartments, one after another, without noticing their gorgeous grandeur, without glancing at their superb decorations, without wasting a look upon the wondrous products of brush, or chisel, or loom. His disconcerted guide paused before each world-renowned master-piece in vain; Maurice hurried on, and silenced him by saying that he was in search of a friend.

Neither Lady Vivian nor Madeleine was to be seen. They were doubtless rambling in the beautiful pleasure-grounds.

Maurice took his way through noble avenues of trees, — through groves, gardens, conservatories, — without letting his eyes dwell upon any object but the human beings he passed. Still no Madeleine. He made the tour of the palace the second time, and then traversed the grounds once more. The result was the same. Lady Vivian must have returned home.

It was growing late. He reëntered his cab, and ordered the driver to take him to Morley's Hotel; paid the exorbitant price which the man, knowing he had to deal with a stranger, demanded, and took refuge in his chamber, without remembering that he had not broken his fast since morning, until a waiter knocked at the door to know if he would dine.

Yes; dinner might assist in whiling away the time. But it helped less effectually than he had anticipated; for to dine without appetite is a tedious undertaking. His own busy thoughts supplied him with more than sufficient food, and precluded all sense of hunger.

Maurice had but a slight acquaintance with Lady Vivian. An evening visit certainly was not *selon les regles;* but all ceremony must give way before the urgency of his mission. He compelled himself to wait until nine o'clock before he again appeared in Grosvenor Square.

That imperturbable footman again! The very presence of the automaton chilled and dispirited the impatient visitor.

"Is Lady Vivian at home?"

"Her ladyship is indisposed and has retired, sir."

"Can I see Mademoiselle de Gramont?"

"Whom, sir?"

"The young lady who accompanies Lady Vivian."

"She is with Lady Vivian ; but I will take your card, sir."

Maurice had no alternative and handed his card.

"Say that I earnestly beg to see her for a few moments."

Did he imagine that human machine could deliver a message which conveyed the suggestion that any one very earnestly desired anything in creation?

The viscount was ushered into the drawing-room. A long interval, or one Maurice thought long, elapsed before the messenger returned.

"The ladies will be happy to see you, sir, to-morrow, at two o'clock."

Another night and another morning to struggle through, haunted by the murderous desire of killing that which could never be restored, — *time!* But here, at least, was a definite appointment, — a fixed period when he should certainly see Madeleine ; this was a great step gained.

He had heard some gentlemen, at the hotel, loud in praise of Charles Kean's impersonation of "King John," which was to be represented that evening, and the recollection of their encomiums decided him to visit the Princess' Theatre.

Our powers of appreciation are limited, governed, crippled or expanded, by the mood of the moment, and a performance, which might have roused him to a high pitch of enthusiasm at another time, now seemed dull and tedious. But duller and more tedious still was the night that followed. And when morning came, how was he to consume the hours between breakfast and two o'clock? He must go somewhere ; must keep on his feet ; must give his restless limbs free action. He bethought him of St. Paul's and Westminster Abbey. These majestic edifices were associated with the memory of those who had done with time, and might assist him in the time-annihilating process which was then his chief object. He was mistaken ; he could not interest himself in monuments to the dead ; he was too closely pursued by a living phantom. He walked through the aisles, the chapels, the crypt, with as much indifference as he had wandered through Hyde Park, and Kensington Gardens, and Hampton Court.

The appointed hour drew near, at last, and with rising excitement he ordered the coachmen to drive to Grosvenor Square, number ——. It was just two, — hardly two, perhaps. The inevitable footman received his card, with the faintest *soupçon* of a grin, and conducted him to the drawing-room.

Lady Vivian entered a few moments afterwards. She was delighted to see him, — very flattered at his visit. When did he come to London? Would he make a long stay? How did he leave their friends in Brittany?

Maurice replied as composedly as possible to her inquiries, and then asked, "May I be allowed to see Mademoiselle de Gramont?"

"Mademoiselle de Gramont!" exclaimed Lady Vivian, raising her bushy eyebrows.

"Yes, she is with you. She is engaged as your humble companion, — is she not?"

"No, I have not the pleasure of her acquaintance."

If a bullet had passed through Maurice, he could not have sprung from his seat with a wilder bound, and hardly have dropped back more motionless.

Lady Vivian looked at him in amazement, — asked what had happened. Was he ill? Would he take anything? He had been very much fatigued, perhaps. He was so very pale! She felt quite alarmed; really it was distressing.

Making a desperate effort to recover from the stunning blow, he faltered out, "I heard that you made Mademoiselle de Gramont a proposition to" —

"To become my humble companion? Yes, I did so at the request of Count Damoreau. But she definitely declined, and I felt much relieved, for she was entirely too handsome for that position. Shortly afterward I heard of a young person who suited me much better. I thought it was a mistake of the footman's, last night, when he said you desired to see the young lady who accompanied me. It was somewhat singular to have one's humble companion included in a visit to one's self! Now I comprehend that you thought she was your cousin. I hope you are feeling better; your color is coming again."

Maurice was not listening. He had lost Madeleine anew. The agony of a second bereavement, the mystery that enveloped her fate, the dreadful uncertainty of tracing her, pressed upon him and rent his soul with fiercer throes than before. Muttering some hurried apology, he rose, staggered toward the door, and, to the amazement of the stoical footman, who was greatly scandalized thereby, the pertinacious stranger fairly reeled past him into the street.

CHAPTER XI.

PURSUIT.

MAURICE, when he took his abrupt leave of Lady Vivian, did not return to the hotel. He felt as though he could not breathe, could not exist, shut within four walls, with the oppressive weight of his new disappointment crushing and stifling his spirit. He traversed the streets with a rapid pace, not knowing nor caring whither he went, if he only kept in motion. His own torturing thoughts pursued him like haunting fiends, driving him mercilessly hither and thither, and he sped onward and onward, as though by increased celerity he could fly from his intangible persecutors.

Now sprang up the tantalizing suggestion, that, as Lady Vivian had never seen Madeleine, the latter had presented herself under a feigned name, for the sake of concealing her rank, and baffling the friends who sought to discover her abode. Was not *that* very possible, very natural? He recalled the tall, finely-moulded form, of which he had caught a glimpse in Lady Langdon's *salon*, and for awhile he cherished this chimera; then its place was usurped by one more painful: Madeleine was perhaps travelling alone, subjected by her very beauty to the curious scrutiny, the heartless insults of brutal men; and, perchance, through her ignorance of the world, trapped into some snare from which she could never be extricated unharmed. Then his mind was filled with the horrible idea that, in her friendliness and despair, finding no place of refuge on earth, she had flung away her burdensome life with violent hands. Nothing was more improbable than that a being endowed with her self-controlled, serene, sorrow-accepting temperament, should be driven to such an act of unholy madness. Yet Maurice allowed the frightful fantasy to work within his brain until it clothed itself with a shape like reality, and drove him to the verge of distraction.

Where could she have gone? *Where? oh, where?*

Hundreds of times he asked himself that perplexing question! All the pursuing demons seemed to shout it in his ears, and defy him to answer. If she had escaped the perils he most dreaded, where had she hidden herself? Perhaps she had only taken out a passport for England, with a view of throwing those who sought to track her steps, off the right scent. If she had gone to England, her passport must have been *viséd* as she passed through Paris. If it had not been presented at the *bureau des passeports*, she must have remained in Paris. If she had conceived any plans by which she thought to earn a livelihood, where could they so well be carried into execution? In that great city she might reasonably hope to be lost in the crowd, and draw breath untraced and unknown. If she had left the metropolis, the fact could easily be ascertained by examining the list of passports. Maurice walked on and on, until gradually the clamorous city grew silent, and the streets were deserted. Besides the vigilant police, only a few, late revellers, with uncertain steps, and faces hardly more haggard than his own, passed him, from time to time. Still he walked, carrying his hat in his hand, that the night-breeze might cool his fevered brow.

There was a stir of wheels again, a waking-up movement around him; shop-windows lifting their shutter-lids, and opening their closed eyes; men and women bustling forward, with busy, refreshed morning faces. Another day had dawned and brought its weight of anguish for endurance. Maurice had paced the streets all night. The light that struck sharply upon his bloodshot eyes first made him aware of the new morning. The season for action then had arrived; the night had flown as a hideous dream. He did not know into what part of London he had wandered, but hailed a cab, sprang in, and gave the order to be driven to Morley's. The distance seemed insupportably long. He was now tormented by the fear that he should not reach his destination in time to take the first train for Dover. When he alighted at the hotel, he learned that in less than an hour the train would start. He dashed off a few, incoherent, sorrowful lines to Bertha, hastily crammed his clothes into his trunk, paid his bill, drove to the station, and secured a seat one moment before the railway carriages were in motion.

After he had crossed the channel, and entered a railway coach at Calais, utter exhaustion succeeded to his state of turbulent wretchedness. Nature asserted her soothing rights, and poured over his bruised spirit the balm of sleep. With reviving strength came renewed hope, and when he awoke at the terminus, in Paris, he was inspired with the conviction that he should find Madeleine in that vast metropolis, — a conviction as firm as the belief he had entertained that he would behold her in Scotland, and afterwards that he would discover her in London. He hastened to the *bureau des passeports*, and examined the list. No passport had been *viséd* to which her name was attached. It was then certain that she was still in Paris. But what method could he devise for a systematic search? He thought of the argus-eyed, keen-scented police, who, with the faintest clew, can trace out any footprint once made within the precincts of the far-spreading barriers; but could he drag his cousin's name before those public authorities? Could he describe her person to them, and enter into details which would enable them to hunt her down like a criminal? Delicacy, manly feeling, forbade. He must seek her himself, unaided, unguided; and a superstitious faith grew strong within him that, through his unremitting search, never foregone, never relaxed, he would discover her at last.

His plan was sufficiently vague and wild. He resolved to scour Paris from end to end, scanning every face that passed him, until the light shone upon hers, and kindled up once more his darkened existence.

When he last returned from Brittany, he had engaged one small, plain apartment in the Rue Bonaparte, the *Latin* quarter of the city, — a favorite locality of students. Here he again took up his abode, or, rather, here he passed his nights; he could scarcely be said to have a dwelling-place by day. From dawn until late in the evening he wandered through the streets, peering into every youthful countenance that flitted by him, quickening his pace if he caught sight of some graceful female form above the ordinary stature, and plunging onward in pursuit, with his heart throbbing madly, and his fevered brain cheating him with phantoms. His search became almost a monomania. His mind, fixed strainingly upon this one, all-engrossing object, lost its balance, and he could no longer reason upon his own course, or see its futility, or devise a better. The invariable disappointment which closed every day's search, by some strange contradiction, only confirmed him in the belief that Madeleine was in Paris, and that he would shortly find her there ; that he would meet her by some fortunate chance ; would be drawn to her by some mysterious magnetic instinct. Every few days he visited the *bureau des passeports*, to ascertain whether her passport had been presented to be *viséd.*

To the friends he daily encountered he scarcely spoke, but hurried past them with hasty greeting, and a painfully engrossed look, which caused the sympathetic to turn their heads and gaze after him, wondering at the disordered attire and unsettled demeanor of the once elegant and vivacious young nobleman, who had graced the most courtly circles, and was looked upon as the

Maurice had been nearly a month in Paris, passing his days in the manner we have described, when, for the first time, he encountered Gaston de Bois. The former would have hastened on, with only the rapid salutation which had grown habitual to him, but M. de Bois stopped with outstretched hand, and said, —

" Where have you hidden yourself? I have been expecting to see you ever since I came to Paris; but I could not discover where you lod — od — odged."

" My lodgings are in the Rue Bonaparte, numero—," returned Maurice, abruptly; " but I am seldom at home."

" You will allow me to take my chance of finding you?" asked M. de Bois, forcibly struck by his friend's altered appearance. " Or," he added, " you will come to see me instead? I am at the Hotel Meurice at present."

" Thank you," said Maurice, absently, and glancing around him at the passers-by as he spoke. " Good-morning."

M. de Bois would not be shaken off thus unceremoniously. He was too much distressed by the evident mental condition of the viscount. He turned and walked beside him, though conscious that Maurice looked annoyed.

" When we parted, did you go to Scotland, as you pro — o — po — sed? " inquired Gaston.

" Yes; but Lady Vivian was in London. I sought her there. She knew nothing of my cousin. I returned to Paris; for I am sure Madeleine is here."

" Here? " almost gasped M. de Bois, stopping suddenly.

Maurice walked on without even noticing the strange confusion that arrested his companion's steps.

The latter recovered himself and rejoined him, asking, in as unconcerned a tone as he could command, " What has caused you to think so? "

" I am certain of it ; — her passport was taken out for England, but it has not been *viséd* in Paris. She must be here still, and I know that I shall find her. I have walked the streets day after day, hoping to meet her, and I tell you I shall — I must! "

M. de Bois, whose equanimity had only been disturbed for a moment, shook his head sorrowfully, saying, " I fear *not ;* it does not seem likely."

" To me it *does.* Fifty times I have thought I caught sight of her, but she disappeared before I could make my way through some crowd to the spot where she was standing. This will not last forever, — ere long we shall meet face to face."

" I hope so! I heartily hope so! I would give all I possess, though that is little enough, to have it so ! "

These words were spoken with such generous warmth, that Maurice was moved. He had not before noticed the change in his Breton neighbor, — a change the precise opposite to the one which had taken place in himself, yet quite as remarkable.

Gaston's address was no longer nervous and flurried ; he had gained considerable self-command and repose of manner. The air of uncomfortable diffidence, which formerly characterized his deportment, had disappeared, and given place to a manly and cheerful bearing.

" If he loves Madeleine," thought Maurice, " how can he look so calm while she is — God only knows where, and exposed to what dangers ? "

" Have you heard from Mademoiselle Ber — er — ertha ? " asked M. de Bois, with some hesitation.

" Yes, several times. My cousin Bertha was broken-hearted at the news I sent her from London ; but I trust that soon " —

He did not conclude his sentence : his wan face lighted up, his restless, straining eyes were fastened upon some form that passed in a carriage. Without even bidding M. de Bois good morning, he broke away and pursued the carriage ; for some time he kept up with it, then Gaston saw him motion vehemently to a sleepy coachman, who was lazily driving an empty fiacre. The next moment Maurice had opened the door himself and leaped into the vehicle ; it followed the carriage the young viscount had kept in view, and soon both were out of sight.

The imagination of Maurice had become so highly inflamed that forms and faces constantly took the outline and lineaments of those ever-present to his mind. And when, after some exhausting pursuits, he approached near enough for the illusive likeness to fade away, or when the shape he was impetuously making towards was lost to sight before it could be neared, he always felt as though he had been upon the eve of that discovery upon which all his energies were concentrated.

After their accidental encounter Gaston de Bois called upon Maurice repeatedly, but never found him at home.

Bertha continued to write sorrowful letters teeming with inquiries. Maurice answered briefly, as though he could not spare time to devote to his pen, but always giving her hope that the very next letter would convey the glad intelligence which she pined to receive. Four months was the limit of her yearly visit to the Château de Gramont, and the period of her stay was rapidly drawing to a close. She wrote that in a few days her uncle would arrive and take her back to his residence in Bordeaux.

The language in which this communication was made plainly indicated that she would rejoice at the change. She touched upon the probability of seeing Maurice before she left; but he was unmoved by the half-invitation; nothing could induce him to leave Paris while he cherished the belief that Madeleine was within its walls.

Count Tristan wrote and urged him to return home; but the summons was unheeded. He could not have endured, while his mind was in this terrible state of incertitude, to behold again the old château, which must conjure up so many harrowing recollections. Then, too, his natural affection for his father and his grandmother was embittered by the remembrance of their persecution of Madeleine. Until she had been found, — until he could hear from her own lips (as he knew he should) that she harbored no animosity towards them, — he could not force himself to forgive their injustice and cruelty. She alone had power to soften his heart and cement anew the broken link.

CHAPTER XII.

THE SISTER OF CHARITY.

The marvellous change in the bearing of Gaston de Bois, by which Maurice was struck, had been wrought by a triad of agents. A man who had passed his life in indolent seclusion, who had plunged into a tangled labyrinth of abstruse books, not in search of valuable knowledge, but to lose in its mazes the recollection of valueless hours; who had allowed his days to drag on in aimless monotony; who had fallen into melancholy because he lacked a healthy stimulus to rouse his faculties out of their life-deadening torpidity; who had allowed his nervous diffidence to gain such complete mastery over him that it tied his tongue, and clouded his vision, and confused his brain; who had despised himself because he was keenly conscious that his existence was purposeless and profitless; — this man, subjected to the sudden impetus of an occupation for which his mental acquirements and sedentary habits alike fitted him, found his new life a revelation. He had emerged from the dusty, beaten, grass-withered path his feet had spiritlessly trodden from earliest

11

youth, and entered a field of bloom and verdure where the very
stir of the atmosphere exhilarated, where the labor to be performed called dormant capacities into play and tested their
strength, where each day's achievement gave the delightful assurance of latent powers within himself hitherto unrecognized, —
in a word, where his manhood was developed through the re-
generating virtue, the glorious might, the blessed privilege of
work!

The second cause which had contributed to bring about the
happy metamorphosis in Gaston de Bois sprang out of the hope-
inspiring words Madeleine had dropped on that day which closed
so darkly on the duke's orphan daughter.   Those few, passing,
precious words had fallen like fructuous seed and struck deep
root in Gaston's spirit; and, as the germs shot upward, every
branch was covered with blossoms of hope which perfumed his
nights and days.   He dared to believe that Bertha did not look
upon him with disdain, — that she sympathized with the misfortune which debarred him from free intercourse with society, —
that a deeper interest might emanate from this compassionate regard.   The possibility of becoming worthy of her no longer appeared a dream so wild and baseless; but he was too modest,
too distrustful of himself, to have given that golden dream entertainment had it not been inspired by Madeleine's kindly breath.

The third cause which combined with the two just mentioned
to revolutionize his character will unfold itself hereafter.

The more cognizant M. de Bois became that powerful influences were vivifying, strengthening, and bringing order out of
confusion in his own mind, the more troubled he felt in pondering
over the disorded mental condition of Maurice.   During a whole
month after their accidental encounter in the street he called
repeatedly at the lodgings of the viscount, but never once found
him at home.   Half discouraged, yet unwilling to abandon the
hope of an interview, he persisted in his fruitless visits.   One
morning, to his unbounded satisfaction, when he inquired of the
concierge if M. de Gramont was within, an affirmative answer
was returned.   Gaston could hardly credit the welcome intelligence, and involuntarily repeated the question.

"Ah, yes, poor young gentleman! he's not likely to be out
again soon!" replied his informant, in a pitying tone.

Without waiting for an explanation of the mysterious words,
M. de Bois quickly ascended to the fifth story, and, being admitted
into the antechamber by a neat-looking domestic, knocked at the
door of the apartment which was indicated to him.

The voice of a stranger bade him enter. He turned the door-knob with shaking hand. The room was so small that it could be taken in at a single glance. It was a plain, almost furniture-less apartment. In the narrow bed lay Maurice. His eyes —those great, blue eyes which so strongly resembled Bertha's— were glittering with the wild lights of delirum ; fever burned on his cheeks and seemed to scorch his parched lips. The fair, clus-tering curls were matted and tangled about his brow ; his arms were tossing restlessly about. He sprang up into a sitting pos-ture as Gaston appeared at the door, and gazed at him eagerly ; then stared around, peering into every corner of the chamber, as though in quest of some one. Those searching glances were followed by a look of blank despair that settled heavily upon his pain-contracted features as he sank back and closed his eyes.

Beside the bed sat a woman, clad in the shapeless dress of black serge, and wearing the widely projecting white bonnet and cape, black veil, white band across the brow, and beneath the chin, which compose the attire of a sister *de bon secours.* She was one of that community of self-abnegating women, who, bound by holy vows, devote their lives to the care of the suffering, and are the most skilful, tender, and zealous nurses that France affords.

Just beyond the good "sister" stood a young man, poring over a piece of paper, which had the appearance of a medical prescription : a spirited-looking youth, whose harmonious and in-tellectual cast of features was heightened to rare beauty by richly mellow coloring, and the silken curves of a beard and moustache unprofaned by a razor, — curves softly traced above the fresh, rubious lips, and gracefully deepening about the cheeks and chin, — curves that disappear forever when the civilized barbarism of shaving has been accepted.

He came forward when M. de Bois entered, and accosted him in an earnest, rapid tone.

"I hope, sir, you are a friend of this gentleman. Am I right in my supposition ? "

" Yes — yes — what — what has happened? " asked M. de Bois, his countenance plainly betokening his alarm.

" I occupy the adjoining apartment," continued the stranger. " My name is Walton. Three nights ago I was startled by the sound of some object falling heavily near my door, followed by a deep groan. I found this gentleman lying on the ground, appa-rently insensible. I carried him into his chamber, laid him upon the bed, and summoned the *concierge.* The name inscribed upon her book is the Viscount Maurice de Gramont, and his last resi-

dence the château of his father, Count Tristan de Gramont, in
Brittany, near Rennes. I took upon myself the responsibility of
calling a physician, — Dr. Dupont, — and, through his advice, of
engaging this good 'sister,' one of the *'soeurs de bon secours,'* as
a nurse. Dr. Dupont wrote to his patient's father; but no answer has been received. I have been with your friend very constantly. You perceive he has a raging fever; he talks a great
deal, but too incoherently to be able to answer any questions or
to give any directions."

This information was communicated with a quick, energetic
intonation, while the speaker stood fanning Maurice, and preventing the hand which he flung about from striking against the wall.
There was a confident rapidity in the stranger's movements, a
vigorous manliness and self-dependence in his bearing, strikingly
dissimilar to the deportment which usually characterizes young
Parisians at the same age. Though he spoke the French language with fluent correctness, a slightly foreign accent betrayed
to M. de Bois that he was not a native of France.

Gaston thanked him as warmly as his troublesome impediment
permitted, and said that he would himself write to the Count de
Gramont. Then, bending over his friend, took his hot, unquiet
hand, and spoke to him again and again. His voice failed to
touch any chord of memory and cause it to vibrate in recognition. Maurice was muttering the same word over and over;
Gaston hardly needed to bow his head to catch the imperfect
sound; he knew, before he heard distinctly, that it was the
name of "Madeleine."

"Had you not better write your letter *immediately?*" asked
young Walton. "Will you walk into my room? I do not see
any writing materials here. Mine are at your service."

Gaston, as he followed the stranger into the adjoining chamber, could not but be struck by the easy, off-hand, decided manner in which he spoke, and the promptitude with which he
desired to accomplish the work to be done.

Mr. Walton's sitting-room, which was separated from his bed-
chamber, was much larger than the apartment of Maurice. It
had an air of great comfort, if not of decided elegance, and testified to the literary and artistic taste of its occupant. The walls
were decorated with fine photographic views, and some early
efforts in painting. Here stood an easel, holding an unfinished
picture; there an open piano; further on a convenient writing-
table; in the centre another table covered with books and portfolios; materials for writing and sketching were scattered about

"I will clear you a space here," said he, sweeping the contents of one table upon another, already overburdened. "Everything is in confusion; for I have been working at odd moments. I could not make up my mind to go to the studio. I would not leave that poor fellow until somebody claimed him. What an interesting face he has! If he were only better, I would make a sketch. His countenance is just my beau ideal of the young Saxon knight in a historical picture I am painting. A man always finds materials for art just beneath his hand, if he only has wit and thrift to stoop and gather them as he goes. But I fear I am interrupting you. Make yourself at home. I will leave you while you are writing. Really, I cannot express how glad I am that you have come at last. I have been looking for you — that is, for somebody who knew M. de Gramont — every moment for two days." ·

After drawing back the curtains to give M. de Bois more light, and glancing around to see that he was supplied with all he could require, the young artist returned to the apartment of Maurice.

Ronald Walton was born of South Carolinian parents, — their only child. His boyhood was not passed in a locality calculated to develop artistic instincts, nor had his education afforded him artistic advantages, nor had he been thrown into a sphere of artistic associates; yet from the time his tiny fingers could hold brush or pencil he had seized upon engravings of romantic scenery, copied them upon an enlarged scale, and painted them in oil, to the astonishment of his parents and friends. When his young companions extracted enjoyment from fish-hook and gun, and hilariously filled game-bags and fishing-baskets, he sat quietly drinking in a higher, more humane delight before his easel. These tastes, as they strengthened, caused his father, though a liberal and cultivated man, severe disappointment. At times he was even disposed to place a compulsory check upon his son's artist proclivities; but the soft, persuasive voice of the gentle, refined, clear-sighted mother interposed. She had made the most loving study of her child's character, and had faith in his fitness for the vocation he desired to adopt. She pleaded that his obvious gift might be tested, and proved spurious or genuine, before it was trampled under foot as unworthy of recognition; and her heart-wisdom finally prevailed.

Ronald was sent to Paris to study under a distinguished master. During three years he had made golden use of his opportunities. He was remarkable among his fellow-students for his

11 *

indomitable perseverance, and his power of concentrating all his thoughts upon his work. He experienced a desire to attain excellence *for its own sake,* not for the petty ambition of *excelling others.* Thus he became very popular among his associates, and excited their admiration without ever awakening the jealousies of wounded self-love. Though he had determined to devote his life to art, from the conviction that it was the vocation for which he came commissioned from the Creator's hand, there was nothing morbid in his passion for his profession. It was a healthy love of the beautiful in outward form, springing from the love of all which the beautiful typifies, combined with a strong impulse to represent and perpetuate the haunting images of varied loveliness which constantly floated through his brain.

The young Carolinian was called an enthusiast even by his French fellow-students, with whom enthusiasm is an inheritance; but his enthusiasm was allied to a severely critical taste,—a rare combination; and being grafted upon the tree of *practicability,* indigenous to the soil of his young country, it brought down his ideal conceptions into actual execution.

The philosopher of the present day scouts at *enthusiasm;* but what agent is half so mighty in giving the needful spur to genius? Enthusiasm kindles a new flame in the chilled soul when the ashes of disappointment have extinguished its fires; enthusiasm reinvigorates and braces the spirit that has become weary and enervated in the oppressive atmosphere of uncongenial *entourage;* enthusiasm is the cool, refreshing breeze of a warm climate and the blazing log of a cold. Ronald's unexhausted enthusiasm was the secret fountain whose waters nourished laurels for him in the gardens of success.

M. de Bois, when he had concluded his letter, found the art-student at the bedside of Maurice.

"I will post your letter, if you please," said Ronald; "then I will make a moment's descent into the studio, or some of those noisy madcaps will be rushing here after me. I will return, however, before long, if you have no objection."

Hardly waiting for M. de Bois's courteous, but rather slowly-expressed acknowledgment, he hurried away.

For a couple of hours Gaston sat beside Maurice, listening to his indistinct ravings, and tracing out that striking likeness to a countenance he had studied too closely for his own peace. Now and then he exchanged a word or two with the good "sister," as she moistened the lips, or bathed the brow of the sufferer.

The doctor came, but pronounced his patient no better, and

threw out a hint that he had some fears the fever was taking the form of typhus; adding a warning in regard to the danger of infection. That intelligence had no influence upon Gaston, who resolved to pass as many hours as possible with his friend. Nor did it affect Ronald Walton, when he returned and heard the physician's verdict.

The two young men for the next four days alternately shared the duties of the holy " sister."

The postal arrangements between Paris and Rennes chanced, at that moment, to be very imperfect; the letter of Dr. Dupont never reached its destination, and that of M. de Bois was delayed on its route. It was not until the fifth day after it was posted that Count Tristan, who obeyed the summons with all haste, arrived in Paris. His son had never once evinced sufficient consciousness to recognize Gaston de Bois, but, the instant the count was ushered into the room, was seized with a fit of frenzy, and broke forth in a torrent of reproaches, upbraided his father with the ruin and death of Madeleine, charged him with having wrought the destruction of his own son, and warned him that he had brought utter desolation upon his ancestral home.

Dr. Dupont, who entered the room during this paroxysm, suggested to the count the propriety of withdrawing. The latter, although every word Maurice uttered inflicted a deadly pang, could not, at first, be induced to tear himself away. The doctor was resolute in pronouncing his sentence of banishment, and declared that the viscount's life might be the sacrifice if he were subjected to further excitement.

We will not attempt to portray the poignant sufferings of the count, who, in spite of his wiliness and worldliness, was passionately attached to his only child, — the central axis upon which all his hopes, his schemes, his whole world moved.

Several times, while the invalid was sleeping, his father ventured to steal into the chamber; but, by some strange species of magnetism, his very sphere seemed to affect the slumberer, who invariably awoke, and recognized, or partially recognized him, and burst out anew in violent denunciations, to which respect would never have allowed him to give utterance, except under the stimulus of delirium. The count writhed and shrank beneath the fierce stabbing of those incisive words, and, in his ungovernable grief, flung himself beside the son, whom he feared death would shortly snatch from his arms, pouring forth assurances Maurice would once have hailed as words of life, but which now fell powerless upon his unheeding ears. While Count Tristan's overwhelming anguish lasted, there was no promise he would not have made to purchase his son's restoration, and no promise he would not have broken, if interest prompted, when the peril was past.

After one of these agitating interviews, the doctor's edict entirely closed the door of the patient's chamber against the count, who was forced to admit the wisdom of the order.

Gaston de Bois and Ronald Walton, between whom a pleasant intimacy was springing up, continued to watch by the bed of Maurice. Another fortnight passed, and though he lay, as it were, in a grave of fire, the doctor's prediction of typhus fever was not verified. At the expiration of this period, Ronald was the first to notice a favorable change, and to discover that the invalid had lucid intervals which showed his reason was reascending her abdicated throne. But he abstained from pointing out the improvement to Gaston, fearing that, in his joy, he might communicate the consolatory intelligence to the count, who would then insist upon seeing his son, and possibly reproduce the evil results by which his former visits had been attended.

Maurice had ceased to moan and mutter, and lay motionless as one thoroughly exhausted. He slept much, waking for but a few moments, and sinking again into a species of half-lethargy. There was something inexpressibly sweet and pleasant in his present calmness; his mind seemed to have been mysteriously soothed and satisfied; the turbulent waves, that dashed him hither and thither against the sharp rocks of doubt and fear, had subsided. His features, especially when he slept, wore an expression of the most serene contentment.

The *soeur de bon secours*, who had watched him through the night, had yielded her place to the "sister," who assumed the office of nurse during the day. Gaston entered soon after, and, finding the patient gently slumbering, sat down beside his bed. After a time, Maurice stirred, drew a long breath, and slowly opened his eyes. They met those of his watcher. For some time the invalid gazed at him without speaking, and then said, in a tone that was hardly audible, —

"M. de Bois."

"My dear Maurice — dear friend — you are better, — you know me at last," exclaimed Gaston, joyfully.

"I knew you before; you have been the most faithful of friends and nurses. I knew you quite well, and I knew *her* too!"

Gaston bounded from his chair, breathing so hard that he

could scarcely stammer out, "Her! who—o—o—om do you me—e—ean?"

"Madeleine," replied Maurice, confidently.

"Mademoiselle Mad—ad—adeleine; you are dream—eaming!"

"No! I thought so at first, and the dream was so sweet that I would not break it by word or motion, fearing that I should discover it was not reality. But it was no *dream*. Night after night,—how many I do not know—I could not count,—I have seen Madeleine beside me! When the good 'sister' moved about the room, in the dim light of the *veillense*, in spite of her coarse, unshapely garb, I recognized the outlines of Madeleine's form; notwithstanding the uncouth bonnet, and the white bandage that concealed her hair and brow, and, passing beneath her chin, almost hid her face, I recognized the features of Madeleine. I watched her as she glided about the room, and with her delicate, noiseless, rapidly moving touch created the most perfect order around her. I heard her as she softly sang sweet anthems, and I could not mistake the voice of Madeleine. I felt her hand, her cool, fresh, velvety hand, upon my burning forehead, and it soothed me deliciously. I lay with closed eyes as she bathed my temples, and passed her fingers through my hair to loosen its tangles. I was afraid of frightening her away, or finding I saw but a vision. The water she held to my lips was nectar; when she smoothed my pillow, all pain passed from the temples that rested upon it, throbbing with agony before, and I sank into a sweet slumber,—not unconscious slumber: I knew that I was sleeping; I knew that Madeleine sat there, filling the place of the sister of charity; I knew that when I opened my eyes I should see her,—*and I did*, again and again. I never once spoke to her; I feared some spell would be broken if I breathed her name. In the morning she disappeared; but I knew she would come again at midnight, when all was quiet, and the light was carefully shaded. M. de Bois, my dear Gaston, I tell you *I have seen Madeleine!*"

M. de Bois sat still, looking too much astounded to utter a word.

"I see you cannot believe me," Maurice continued. "She never came while you were here, and so you think it is a dream. A happy dream! a dream full of the balm of Gilead! for she has cured me! My brain was a burning volcano until her hand was laid upon my brow, and I gazed in her face, and knew it was no phantom. Do not look so much distressed, my dear Gaston. I am perfectly in my senses."

M. de Bois did not contradict him. Perhaps he remembered the good rule of never opposing a sick man's vagaries. After a pause he said, —

"Maurice, since you are quite yourself, would you not like to see your father ? "

The wan face of Maurice flushed slightly.

" Is he here ? "

" Yes, he has been here for more than a fortnight. The doctor forbade his entering. Will you not see him now ? "

The invalid assented languidly. He had perhaps spoken too much and overtaxed his strength.

The joy of Count Tristan was deep and voiceless when he was once more permitted to embrace his son. He was so fearful of touching upon some painful chord, and of again hearing those frantic ravings, that he had no language at his command. Maurice, in a faint tone, inquired after his grandmother and Bertha, and then seemed too weary to prolong the conversation. Glad at heart, as the count could not but feel, at the wonderful improvement in his son, he was ill at ease in his presence, and seemed always to have some haunting dread upon his mind. It was a relief when the doctor forbade his patient to converse, and hinted that the count should make his visits very brief.

The next day, when M. de Bois entered, Maurice greeted him in a mournful tone.

" She did not come last night. I watched for her in vain. The 'sister,' yonder, went as usual at midnight, and came back in the morning ; but, during the night, a stranger took her place."

What could M. de Bois answer? He gave a sigh of sympathy, but did not attempt to make any comment.

" She knows perhaps that my father is here, and she will come no more for fear of being discovered. But I have *seen her*, Gaston ! I know I have seen her ! I could not have lived if I had not. And her countenance was not sad, — it wore a look of patient hope that lent a glory to her face. The very remembrance of that saint-like expression put to shame the despair to which I have yielded."

" I — I — I — am " —

M. de Bois could get no further. If he meant to use any argument to persuade Maurice that it was only a vision, conjured up by his fevered imagination, which he had seen, the attempt would have been vain. Maurice clung to the belief that he had really beheld Madeleine, and that conviction soothed, strengthened, and reanimated him.

CHAPTER XIII.

WEARY DAYS.

Up to this period of his life the vigorous constitution of Maurice had suffered no exhausting drain. His habits had been so regular, his mode of life so simple, that his fine *physique* had been untrifled with, uninjured. As a natural sequence, the first inroads made upon its strength were rapidly repaired. The fever once conquered, in a week he was sufficiently convalescent to walk out, leaning on the arm of Gaston de Bois, or Ronald Walton. His gait was feeble, his form attenuated, his countenance had lost its ruddy glow, — the lines had sharpened until their youthful, healthful roundness was wholly obliterated; but the nervous, untranquil expression had passed away from his face, and the restless glancing from side to side had left his eyes. Through the stimulating medium of fresh air and gentle exercise he gathered new vitality, and the promise of speedy restoration was daily confirmed.

His favorite resort was the *atelier* of the celebrated master under whose direction Ronald was studying his art. Seated in the comfortable arm-chair devoted to the use of models, Maurice often remained for hours, watching the busy brushes and earnest faces, among which the genius-lighted countenance of the young Carolinian shone conspicuously. On one of these occasions, after sitting for some time lost in thought, when he chanced to turn his head Ronald surprised him by crying out, —

"My dear fellow, don't move! Keep that position another moment, — will you? I am making a sketch of your head. It has just the outline I want for my Saxon Knight after the battle.

Maurice could not but smile at this evidence of the national trait of the young American, who seized upon every material within his reach for the advancement of his art. Ronald's words, too, struck him, — "After the battle!" Well might he resemble one who had passed through a severe conflict; but it was also one who was prepared to fight valiantly anew, and not disposed to succumb to the army of adverse circumstances arrayed against his peace.

It was not possible for a young man, endowed with the impressible temperament of Maurice, to be thrown into constant communication with an associate as full of vigorous activity as Ronald Walton, without being stirred and inspired by the contact. The force, decision, aptitude, promptness, which distinguished Roland, had constituted him a sort of prince among his fellow-students, who gave him the lead in all their united movements, without defining to themselves his claim to supremacy. Ronald's character was not free from imperfections; but its very faults were essentially national, — were characteristics of that "fast-running nation" which is "indivertible in aim," and incredulous of the existence of the unattainable. His dominant failing was a self-dependence, which, in a weaker nature, would have degenerated into self-sufficiency, but just stopped short of that complacent, puerile egotism, which narrows the mind, and rears its own opinions upon a judgment-seat to pronounce verdicts upon the rest of the world. He never doubted his ability to scale any height upon which he fixed his eyes; he laughed at obstacles; he did not believe in impossibilities; what any other man could accomplish, that he had an internal conviction he might also achieve; and he held the faith of the poet-queen that all men were possible heroes.

These attributes were precisely those most calculated to impress and charm Maurice, and he regarded Ronald with unbounded admiration, mingled with a sickening sense of regret when he reflected upon the trammels which reined in the ready impulses and crushed the instinctive aspirations which were wrestling within himself.

Count Tristan, as soon as his son was sufficiently restored to travel, suggested that he should return with him to Brittany; but Maurice betrayed such uncompromising reluctance to this proposal that his father thought it wise not to press the point.

Though the count had escaped a calamity, which even to contemplate had almost driven him out of his mind, — though his son's life was spared, and his restoration to vigorous health assured, — at times the father felt as if that son were lost to him forever. An inexplicable reserve had risen up and thrust them asunder. In the count's presence Maurice was always abstracted and pensive; he uttered no complaints, made no petitions. He had come to the conclusion that both were useless; but his opinions and wishes were no longer frankly, boldly, iterated. He and his father stood upon different platforms, with an invisible, but an' insurmountable barrier looming up between them. Count Tristan, albeit irritated, galled, grieved, could discover no mode of reëstablishing the olden footing. After spending a month in Paris, he returned to Brittany, his mind filled with discomforting forebodings, to which he could give no definite shape.

Maurice was once more left in the great, gay capital, his own master, — at liberty to plunge into whatever sea of dissipation, to float idly down whatever tide of pleasure lured him. But he wronged himself when he warned his father, some months previous, that if he were debarred from studying a profession, he might seek excitement, or oblivion, in impure channels, and waste his exuberant energies in degrading pastimes. He spoke on the spur of some vague, restless impulse within him, that clamored for an outlet; but he misjudged himself in imagining that he could be compelled to drown the memory of his disappointment in the wine-cup, the vortex of the gaming-table, or the more fearful maelstrom of siren allurements. To a young heart which has not been sullied by familiar contact with evil, there is no ægis so invulnerable to the assaults of those deadly enemies, who make their attacks in the fascinating garb of licentious liberty, as a strong, pure, life-absorbing attachment. He who wears the shield of a first, stainless affection, carries Ithuriel's spear in his hand, and, at a single touch, the sensual enchanter in his path, however resplendent its disguise, drops the fair-featured mask and shining mantle, and stands revealed in native hideousness. The image of Madeleine, ever present to Maurice, drew around him a protecting circle which nothing vile could enter, and, wherever his own eyes turned, it seemed to him that her heavenly eyes followed. Could he profane their holy gaze by fixing his upon scenes of captivating degradation and rose-crowned vice?

Day after day, as his strength returned, it was but natural that he should grow more and more weary of monotonous indolence, and more and more impatient to escape from its depressing, deadening thraldom. The happy change, which a settled occupation had effected in Gaston de Bois, seemed to add to the discontent of his friend. Sometimes he was on the point of starting for Brittany, and making a fresh appeal to his father; then he was withheld by the dread that an angry discussion would be the only sequence. He knew that his father's pride, sustained by that of his grandmother, was unconquerable, and that the sentence, which condemned him to a dreary, inert, and profitless existence, would only be pronounced upon him anew.

Since his illness he had entirely abandoned his vain search for Madeleine. He always felt as though he had seen her, albeit, when he attempted to reflect upon the likelihood that she had actually sat beside his couch, and watched over him during his illness, reason essayed to efface the impression which could hardly have been made by the fingers of reality. Even granting that Madeleine, on leaving Brittany, had joined the sisterhood, and proposed to devote her life to holy offices, for which she was richly dowered by nature, was there not a novitiate to be passed? How could she so soon have entered upon her sacred duties? And if by some mysterious dispensation she had been absolved from the probation of a novice, how could she have learned that he was ill? How could she have come to him so promptly? Was it probable that Mr. Walton, an entire stranger, had, by mere accident, selected a nurse from the very society which she had joined? These questions, and other equally difficult to answer, sprang up constantly in his mind, and found no satisfactory solution. Yet the conviction that he had actually beheld her remained unshaken.

Bertha had been apprised by her aunt of the dangerous illness of Maurice, and had written to him when he was unable to read her letters. As soon as he was convalescent, they were placed in his hands.

"My dear Gaston, write a line to my cousin for me," begged Maurice, feeling that he had not strength to reply, and little dreaming what a thrill of joy ran through Gaston's frame at that request.

M. de Bois wrote, — wrote with an eloquence that could never have found utterance through his tongue.

If we may judge from the number of times Bertha perused that letter, or if we may draw an inference from her wearing it about her person (probably that she might be able to refresh her memory with its information concerning her cousin), the epistle was either very difficult of comprehension, or it had some witching spell which drew her eyes irresistibly to its cabalistic characters.

She had not recovered her wonted buoyancy. Beneath her uncle's roof she pined for Madeleine hardly less than at the Château de Gramont.

The Marquis de Merrivale, her guardian, was a bachelor. The chief object of his existence was an endeavor to "take life easy," and guard himself from all vexations and discomforts. His next aim was to pamper the cravings of an epicurean appetite, but always with such judicious ministry that his digestive organs might not be impaired thereby. He was good-natured on principle, because it was too much trouble to get excited and vexed. His equanimity was seldom disturbed, save by his cook's failure in the concoction of a favorite dish.

Count Tristan had drawn largely on his invention when he informed the Marchioness de Fleury that Bertha's uncle was exceedingly tenacious of his rights, and jealous of the inteference of his niece's relatives in regard to any future alliance she might form. The marquis never dreamed of troubling his brain with such a minor matter as matrimony. He was inclined to be governed entirely by Bertha's predilection, — to leave the affair wholly to her, throwing off the trouble with the responsibility. He could have no objection to see her affianced to the Duke de Montauban, — he would have had none to her union with Maurice de Gramont. He found it sufficient pleasure to have his bright-faced niece sitting opposite to him at table, so long as she was gay and had a good appetite. If he had thwarted her wishes he would have accused himself of making a base, unkinly attempt to injure her digestion by causing her annoyance. He considered himself quite incapable of so unworthy, so harmful so cruel an action.

When she returned from the Château de Gramont, he was discomposed at finding that she brought back a clouded visage, and seemed perfectly indifferent to the choicest dainties which he caused to be set before her as the most striking mark of his affection. Indeed, he became so uncomfortable when she rejected these delicate attentions day after day, that his mind was gradually prepared to look favorably upon a proposition which Bertha had resolved to make.

She had been at home about a month; they were dining, — that is, her uncle was enjoyingly partaking of the meal that rounded his day, while Bertha's fork played with the oyster *paté* on her plate, dividing it into tiny bits, but never lifting one to her mouth. The marquis, after descanting warmly upon the excellence of the *pate*, which he highly relished, interrupted his eulogium by saying, —

"My dear child, you have not tasted a morsel of this incomparable *paté!* It is a triumph of culinary art! If you will just oblige me by touching a small piece to your lips; the paste is so light it will magically melt! Really, you *must eat!*"

"I cannot, uncle."

"Try, try; it disturbs me greatly to see you sitting there looking so gloomy. It will really hurt my digestion, and that would be a frightful calamity. Don't you like Lucien's cooking? I think him a treasure; but if you cannot relish what he prepares he shall receive his dismissal."

"I dare say I should like the cooking in Paris better than any other," remarked Bertha, treacherously assailing her uncle in his vulnerable point.

"Paris! what are you talking about? We cannot have our dinners sent from Paris and kept warm on the road, — can we?"

"But we might go to Paris and take our dinners," she rejoined, coaxingly.

"Bless my heart! What an idea! It is a day's journey! Think of the trouble and discomfort of getting there!"

"Think of the new inventions of the Parisian *cuisine;* for they invent new dishes, my Cousin Maurice has told me, as often as they originate new fashions for dress. There are abundance of novel dishes every day issuing from the brains of accomplished cooks, — dishes of which you have never even heard. You really ought to taste some of them."

"That's a consideration, — positively it is. I must reflect upon it!" replied her uncle.

"And Maurice seems to cling to the idea that my Cousin Madeleine" — continued Bertha.

"There, there, my dear; that will do! don't touch on that unpleasant subject, especially at dinner; it will certainly injure your digestive organs, and give you the blues for the rest of the day. I assure you, my child, all low spirits come from indigestion. I am convinced indigestion is one great cause of all the sadness and sorrow, and, I dare say, of all the sin in the world."

"It seems to me change of air must be very beneficial," replied Bertha, recovering from the false step she had been on the point of making.

"Very wisely remarked! Change of air is beneficial, and gentle exercise is beneficial: both stimulate the digestive faculties and keep up their healthy action. And you really think, my dear, you would like to taste some of those new Parisian dishes?"

"I should indeed!"

"Then you shall. I look upon it as criminal, in the present low state of your appetite, to thwart its faintest craving. Of course we cannot procure anything fit to sustain nature on the road to Paris, but I can make Pierre pack up a basket of refreshments, and a bottle of old wine, so that we shall not be poisoned on the way. If we can only make the journey comfortably, I have no objection to investigate the gastronomic novelties of which you have heard. I could take Lucien with us, that he might learn some new mysteries in his art."

"To be sure you could. When shall we start, dear uncle? I am so anxious to go! When shall we start?"

"There! there! Don't get excited about it; that will interfere with the gastric juices. Let us conclude our dinner quietly. Try a wing of that pheasant, while we discuss the matter with wholesome calmness."

Bertha allowed herself to be helped to the wing, and tried to force down a few morsels for the sake of humoring the generously inclined *bon vivant*, who grew more and more genial and amiably disposed as he sipped his Château Margaux. Fine wine invariably had a softening, expansive effect upon his character, and, after a few glasses, he honestly looked upon himself as one of the most tender-hearted, soberly inoffensive, and morally disposed of mortals.

If Bertha had openly proposed to him that they should spend a few weeks in Paris for the gratification of any praiseworthy intention of her own, or of any harmless whim, he would have unhesitatingly refused, and opposed any number of objections to the proposition; but she had introduced the subject in its most favorable light, and was sure of a victory.

A few days later, the Marquis de Merrivale and his niece, attended by her maid, his valet and cook, were on their way to the metropolis. The marquis, having instituted many inquiries with the view of discovering what hotel rejoiced in the possession of the most scientific cook, concluded to engage a suite of apartments at the hotel *des Trois Empereurs.*

The meeting between Bertha and Maurice was as full of tenderness as though they had been in reality what their strong family resemblance caused them to appear, brother and sister.

"No word from Madeleine yet?" was Bertha's first inquiry, —hardly an inquiry, for she knew what the answer must be.

Then Maurice told her of the *soeur de bon secours* who had sat by his bed night after night.

"Could it really have been Madeleine?" she asked, breathlessly.

"M. de Bois seems to think not; yet I am unshaken in my conviction that it was she herself."

"But why did you not speak to her?"

"A feeling which I can scarcely define withheld me. At first I thought I was dreaming, and that the dream would be broken if I spoke or moved. Then I felt sure Madeleine was there, but that she believed herself unrecognized, and if I showed that I knew her she would leave me, — leave me when I could not

12 *

follow, and must again have lost all trace of her. It was such a luxury, such a joy to feel her by my side! It was her presence and not the skill of the physician which restored me."

"And you never once betrayed yourself?"

"No. What seems most singular is that from the very day I mentioned to M. de Bois that I had seen her, she came no more. Yet how could she have learned, or divined, that I knew her?"

"That circumstance, dear Maurice, makes it all look like a dream. As soon as the fever left you the phantom it conjured up disappeared."

Maurice shook his head, unconvinced, and Bertha was too willing to be deceived herself to attempt to persuade him that he was in error.

The Marquis de Merrivale now entered. Maurice, whom he had only known slightly, rose in favor when the epicure found that the young Parisian could give all requisite information concerning the best restaurants in Paris; and the viscount reached a higher summit of esteem, when he promptly promised to put Lucien *en train* to familiarize himself with certain valuable culinary discoveries. Maurice knew enough of the character of the marquis to be confident that his stay in the metropolis would be determined by the amount of comfort he enjoyed, and the quality of the dinners set before him.

Bertha's next visit was from M. de Bois, and could she have banished from her mind a vague impression that he loved Madeleine, or was beloved by her, the interview would have afforded her unmitigated happiness.

M. de Bois had not yet gained sufficient mastery over himself to command his utterance in the presence of the woman who had most power to confuse him. He still stammered painfully; but he could not help remarking that, even as Madeleine had said, Bertha finished his broken sentences, apparently unaware that she was doing so. And her greeting, surely it had been far from cold. And did she not say, with a soft emphasis which it almost took away his breath to hear, that it seemed an age since they met? Had she then felt the time long? And did she not drop some involuntary remark concerning the dulness of Brittany after he and Maurice left? Had she not coupled him with her cousin? Might he not dare to believe that Madeleine was right, and Bertha certainly did not scorn him?

CHAPTER XIV.

DIAMONDS AND EMERALDS.

"I wish you would go, Maurice. Do, for my sake!" pleaded Bertha, twisting in her slender fingers a note of invitation. "The Marquis de Fleury was one of the first persons who called upon my uncle, and he made a very favorable impression. Then Madame de Fleury has nearly crushed me beneath an avalanche of sweet civilities. I fancy that a humming-bird drowned in honey must experience sensations very similar to mine in her presence. Is it not the Chinese who serve as the greatest of delicacies a lump of ice rolled in hot pastry? The condiment with which she feeds my vanity reminds me of this singular and paradoxical dainty. If you penetrate the warm, sugared, outer crust, you find ice within. But, as my uncle does not anticipate Chinese diet at the table of the marchioness, he desires me to accept her invitation; and, as you are invited, I wish *you* to do the same, that I may have some familiar face near me."

"Gaston de Bois will be there," returned Maurice, "and so will the young American student, Ronald Walton, whom I presented to you; they are my dearest friends; pray let them represent me, little cousin."

But Bertha was obstinate; her character had a strong tincture of wilfulness, the result of invariably having her pleasure consulted, and always obtaining her own way. She did not relinquish her entreaties until Maurice, who had not lived long enough to be skilled in the art of successfully denying the petition of a person who will take no refusal, or of plucking the waspish sting out of a "no," consented to be present at the dinner.

The Marquis de Fleury had learned, through his secretary, that Mademoiselle Merrivale and her guardian were in Paris. Though the matrimonial proposition of the marchioness on behalf of her brother, the Duke de Montauban, had been so unfavorably received by Bertha's relatives in Brittany, and though Bertha herself, when she met the duke at the Château de Tremazan, had treated him somewhat coldly, the young duke was too much enamored of the fair girl herself, — to say nothing of a tender leaning towards her attractive fortune, — to be discouraged by a passing rebuff. His relatives hailed the anticipated opportunity of making the acquaintance of Bertha's guardian, and were prompt in paying their devoirs. An invitation to dine followed quickly on the footsteps of the visit.

We pass over the days that preceded the one appointed for the dinner party; they were unmarked by incidents which demand to be recorded.

The bond of intimacy between Ronald and Maurice was drawn closer and closer each day. Little by little the latter had communicated the history of his own trials; his father's determined opposition to his embracing a professional career; his attachment to Madeleine; her unaccountable rejection of his hand; her sudden disappearance, and the mad pursuit, which terminated by casting him insensible at Ronald's door, and brought to his succor one who not only watched beside him with all the devotion of a brother, mingled with the tenderness of womanhood itself, but whose buoyant, healthy tone of mind had infused new hope and vigor into a broken, despondent, prostrate spirit.

Ronald Walton was placed in an advantageous position in Paris by the very fact of being an American. His intellect, talents, manners, person, fitted him to grace the most refined society; and, coming from a land where distinctions of rank are not arbitrarily governed by the accident of birth, but where men are assigned their positions in the social scale through a juster, higher, more liberal verdict, the young Carolinian gained facile admission into the most exclusive circles abroad, and even took precedence of individuals who made as loud a boast of noble blood and hereditary titles as though the concentrated virtues of all their ancestors had been transmitted to them through these dubious mediums.

Ronald, as the intimate friend of Maurice de Gramont, had received an invitation to the dinner given by the Marchioness de Fleury to the relatives of the viscount.

The young men entered Madame de Fleury's drawing-room together, and, after having basked for a few seconds in smiles of meridian radiance, and been inundated by a flood of softly syllabled words, moved away to let the beams of their sunny hostess fall upon new-comers.

Maurice glanced around the room in search of his cousin.

"She has just entered the antechamber," said Ronald, comprehending his look. "Her Hebe-like face this minute flashed upon me."

While he was speaking, Bertha and her uncle were announced, and advanced toward their hostess.

The low genuflection of the marchioness had been responded

to by Bertha's unstudied courtesy, and the lips of the young girl had just parted to speak, when she suddenly gave a violent start, and uttered a cry as sharp and involuntary as though she had trodden upon some piercing instrument. As she tottered back, her dilated eyes were fixed upon Madame de Fleury in blank amazement.

"What is it, my dear? Are you ill?" asked her uncle with deep concern.

Bertha did not reply, but still gazed at the marchioness, or rather her eyes ran over the lady's toilet, and she clung to her uncle's arm as though unable to support herself.

"I am afraid you really are ill," continued the Marquis de Merrivale. "Something has disagreed with you; it must have been the truffles with which that pheasant we had for *déjeuner* was stuffed. I toyed with them very timidly myself."

"Pray sit down, my dear Mademoiselle de Merrivale," said Madame de Fleury, leading her to a chair which stood near. "Sit down while I order you a glass of water."

She turned to address a servant, but Bertha stretched out her hand, almost as though she feared to lose sight of her. "Don't go! Don't go! Let me look! Can they be hers? Let me look again!"

Madame de Fleury, as unruffled as though these broken exclamations were perfectly natural and comprehensible, bent over Bertha caressingly, laying the tips of her delicately gloved fingers on her shoulder. Bertha wistfully examined the bracelet on the lady's arm, then fixed her eyes upon the necklace, brooch, and ear-rings, and lastly upon the tiara-like comb, about which the hair of the marchioness was arranged in a dexterous and novel manner.

Madame de Fleury was gratified, without being moved by the faintest surprise that her toilet had produced such an overpowering sensation. Bertha's emotion did not appear to her in the least misplaced or exaggerated.

"You admire this set of diamonds and emeralds very much, then?" she asked, complacently.

"The *fleur-de-lis* and shamrock," faltered Bertha, "where — where did they come from?"

Interpreting the unceremonious abruptness and singularity of the question into a spontaneous tribute paid to her costly ornaments, the marchioness graciously answered, —

"This *parure* was a delicate attention from M. de Fleury. Not long after he presented these diamonds to me, by a very strange coincidence Vignon sent this dress for my approval.

You observe how dexterously the device of the necklace is imitated. Can anything be more perfect than these lilies and shamrock leaves?"

Bertha hastily glanced at the rich white silk robe, trimmed with *revers* of pale violet, upon which the lilies and shamrock were embroidered with some species of lustrous thread, which counterfeited not only the design but the sparkle of the gems. The marchioness went on, —

"Was it not odd that Vignon, famed as she is for novelties, should have chanced upon a dress which so exactly matched my new set? It quite makes me a convert to the science of animal magnetism. My mind, you see, was *en rapport* with hers. Indeed she says so herself, for she could not otherwise explain the sudden inspiration which caused her to plan this trimming. M. de Fleury wanted me to have these jewels set anew; but I would not allow them to be touched, — this old-fashioned setting is so remarkable, so unique. Probably there is not another like it to be found in Paris : *that* is always vantage ground gained over one's jewel-wearing adversaries."

The marchioness, once launched upon her favorite stream of talk, would have sailed on interminably, had not the announcement of new guests floated her upon another current.

"I hope the spasms are going over, my dear," said the Marquis de Merrivale, who was really distressed by Bertha's supposed illness. "It was very clever to divert observation by talking about dresses and jewels; but the truffles did the mischief. I knew well enough what was the matter with you."

"No — no; it was those jewels," replied Bertha, who had not yet recovered her self-possession. "Those diamonds and emeralds were Madeleine's!"

"Madeleine's!" ejaculated Maurice, who had approached her on witnessing her unaccountable agitation. "Good heavens! is it possible?"

"Yes, they were Madeleine's, — they were her mother's jewels and had been in her family for generations. Madeleine showed them to me only a few nights before she left the Château de Gramont. I am sure of them. I would have recognized them anywhere."

"Then at last — at last, oh thank God — we shall trace her! She must have sold those jewels for her support. We must learn from whence Madame de Fleury purchased them," returned Maurice, with a voice trembling with exultation.

"Madame de Fleury said they were a *cadeau* from the marquis," replied Bertha. "Come, let us find him, — let us ask him at once."

Bertha rose with animation and took her uncle's arm.

"Where are you going, my dear? Pray do not excite yourself again," pleaded her solicitous guardian. "Pray keep cool. Dinner must shortly be served, and you will not be in a fit state to do justice to the sumptuous repast which I have no doubt awaits us, — some of those novel inventions, perhaps, which you were so anxious to taste. I see people are not scrupulously punctual in Paris, — it is ten minutes after the time. Possibly we are waiting for some guest who has not sufficient good taste to remember that viands may be overdone through his culpability."

"I must speak to M. de Fleury," said Bertha. "Let us get nearer to him, that I may seize the first opportunity when he ceases talking to that pompous-looking old gentleman who has the left breast of his coat covered with decorations."

"Well, well, take it quietly — keep cool — don't get your blood into a ferment, — that's all I ask."

Her uncle led her across the room, accompanied by Maurice.

Diplomat and courtier were inscribed on every line of the wrinkled countenance of the Marquis de Fleury. He never took a step, or gave a look, or scarcely drew a breath, by which he had not some object to accomplish, some interest to promote. An oppressive suavity of manner, an exaggerated politeness encased him in an impenetrable armor, and prevented the real man from ever being reached beneath this smooth surface. Impulses he had none. The slightest motions of his wiry frame were studied. When he walked, he slid along as though he could not be guilty of so positive an action as that of planting his feet firmly upon what might prove "delicate ground." When he bowed, a contraction of sinews worthy of an *acrobat* allowed his head to obtain an unnatural inclination, suggestive of a complimentary deference which humbled itself to the dust and kissed the garment's hem. Straightforwardness in word, thought, or action was to him as incomprehensible as it was impossible. He was a great general, ever standing on the political or social battle-field; skilful manœuvres were the glory of his existence, and flattery the magical weapon never laid aside by which he gained his victories.

Madame de Fleury was thirty years his junior. He had purposely selected a young, pretty, harmless, well-dressed doll, as the being best suited to further his ends in the great world. He admired her sincerely. She reached the exact mental stature and standard which he looked upon as perfection in womanhood, and her absolute despotism in ruling the modes and creeds of the *beau monde* were to him the highest proof of her superiority over the rest of her sex.

Though he was engaged in a conversation with the emperor's grand chamberlain, which seemed deeply interesting to both parties, M. de Fleury broke off instantly when Bertha, with her uncle and Maurice, approached.

"You are so radiant to night, Mademoiselle de Merrivale," remarked the courtier, "that all eyes are fixed upon you. It is cruel of you to dazzle the vision of so many admirers!"

Bertha, without paying the slightest attention to these fulsome words, replied, "Will you pardon me, M. de Fleury, if I ask an impertinent question?"

"How could any question from such sovereign lips become other than a condescension? The queen of beauty commands in advance a reply to the most difficult problem which she can propound."

Bertha, with an impatient toss of her head, as though the buzz of this nonsensical verbiage stung her ears, plunged at once into the subject.

"That set of diamonds and emeralds which Madame de Fleury wears to-night were presented to her by you. Will you have the goodness to tell me from whence you procured them?"

For M. de Fleury to have given a direct answer, even in relation to such an apparent trifle, would have been contrary to his nature; besides, it was one of his rules not to impart information without learning for what object it was sought.

"You admire them?" he replied, evasively. "I am delighted, I am charmed with your approval of my taste. I shall think more highly of it forever after. The setting of the jewels is old-fashioned; but Madame de Fleury found it so novel that I could not prevail upon her to have it modernized."

"But you have not told me how the jewels came into your possession."

"Oh, very naturally, very naturally, lovely lady! They were not a fairy gift; they became mine by the very prosaic transaction of purchase."

Maurice could restrain himself no longer.

"My cousin is particularly desirous of learning through what source you obtained them. She has an important reason for her inquiry."

This explanation only placed the marquis more upon his guard.

"Ah, your captivating cousin thinks they look as though they had a history? Yes, yes; jewels of that kind generally have. Does the design strike you as remarkable, Mademoiselle de Merrivale?"

"Very remarkable,—and I have seen it before. I could not forget it. I wished to know"—

Dinner was announced at that moment, and the Duke de Montauban came forward and offered his arm to Bertha.

M. de Fleury, with lavish apologies for the interruption of a conversation which he pronounced delightful, begged the Marquis de Merrivale to give his arm to Madame de Fleury, named to Maurice a young lady whom he would have the goodness to conduct, glided about the room to give similar instructions to other gentlemen, and, selecting an elderly lady, who was evidently a person of distinction, led the way to the dining-room.

Maurice stood still, looking perplexed and abstracted, and quite forgetting that he had any ceremonious duty to perform. Ronald, who from the time he had watched beside the viscount's sick-bed had not relinquished his friendly *surveillance*, noticed his absence of mind, and, as he passed him, whispered,—

"My dear fellow, what is the matter? You are dreaming again. Rouse yourself! Some young lady must be waiting for your arm."

"Ronald," exclaimed Maurice, "something very singular has happened. Madame de Fleury is wearing Madeleine's family jewels!"

"Bravo! That is cheering news, indeed! You will certainly be able to trace her now,—never fear! But you must get through this dinner first; so pray collect your scattered senses as expeditiously as possible."

Elated by these words of encouragement, and the hilarious tone in which they were uttered, Maurice shook off his musing mood, and proffered his arm to the niece of Madame de Fleury, whom he now remembered that the marquis had desired him to conduct.

During the dinner this young lady pronounced the handsome cavalier, who had been assigned to her, tantalizingly *distrait*, and secretly wished that the artistic *maître d'hôtel* of her aunt had decorated the table with a less novel and attractive central ornament; for it seemed to her that the eyes of Maurice were constantly turned upon the miniature cherry-tree, of forced hot-house growth, that rose from a mossy mound in the centre of the festive board. The diminutive tree was covered with superb fruit, and girdled in by a circle of Liliputian grape-vines, each separate vine trained upon a golden rod, and heavily laden with luscious grapes, bunches of the clearest amber alternating with the deepest purple and richest crimson. Among the mosses of the mound were scattered the rarest products of the most opposite seasons; those of the present season being too natural to pamper the artificial tastes of luxury. Truly, the arrangement was a charming exemplification of nature made subservient to art; but was it this magnet to which the eyes of Maurice were so irresistibly attracted? He chanced to be seated where his view of the hostess was partially intercepted by the hot-house wonder, and he was seeking in vain to catch a glimpse of those jewels which had been Madeleine's.

Bertha was placed nearer the marchioness, and the Duke de Montauban could not help noticing that her gaze was frequently fixed upon his sister; but being one of those men who are thoroughly convinced that what the French term "*chiffons*" is the most important interest of a woman's life, he consoled himself with the reflection that Mademoiselle de Merrivale was deeply engrossed by a contemplation of Madame de Fleury's elaborate toilet, and that her absent manner had this very feminine, reasonable, and altogether to be tolerated apology.

When Madame de Fleury and her guests swept back into the drawing-room, Monsieur de Fleury and the grand chamberlain were again closely engaged in some political battle. Maurice, after waiting impatiently for a favorable moment when he might come between the wordy belligerents, whispered to Ronald, —

"I am tortured to death! I shall never get an opportunity to ask the marquis about those jewels. My cousin was questioning him on the subject when dinner was announced; but he seemed to treat her inquiries as of so little importance that she was quite baffled in obtaining information."

"Why not attack him in a straightforward manner?" answered the positive young American. "Walk up to him and ask plainly for a few moments' private conversation. Give him the reason of your inquiries, and demand an answer. Bring him to the point without any fancy fencing about the subject."

"I fear it will look very strange," replied Maurice, hesitating.

"What matter? Are you afraid of *looking strange* when you have a worthy object to accomplish? The information you need is of more importance than mere looks. It thoroughly amazes me to see the awe in which a genuine Parisian is held by the dread of appearing singular! One would imagine that all originality was felony, and that to catch the same key-note of voice, to move with the exact motion, and tread in the precise footprints in which every one else speaks, moves, walks, was the only evidence of honesty. What is a man's individuality worth, if it is to be trodden out in the treadmill tramp of senseless conventionality?"

Maurice glanced at his friend admiringly. He had observed on more than one occasion that although Ronald was thoroughly versed in all the nicest rules of etiquette, he had a way of breaking through them at his pleasure, and always so gracefully that his waiving of ceremony could never be set down to ignorance or ill-breeding.

The viscount literally, and without delay, followed his friend's advice, and soon succeeded in drawing M. de Fleury aside.

"Permit me to explain to you Mademoiselle de Merrivale's anxiety about those jewels," said Maurice. " You have, perhaps, heard the name of Mademoiselle Madeleine de Gramont, my cousin on my father's side. Some six weeks ago she suddenly left the Château de Gramont, and has not communicated with her family since. Those jewels were hers. She must have sold them. We are exceedingly anxious to discover her present residence and induce her to return to my grandmother's protection. If you could inform me from whence the jewels came, it would facilitate my search."

The marquis had no definite motive for concealment beyond the dictates of his habitual caution. This explanation satisfied him in regard to the reasons which prompted inquiry; and being desirous of getting rid of Maurice, and of resuming the conversation he had interrupted, replied, with an assumption of cordiality, —

"It gives me great pleasure to be the medium of rendering the slightest service to your illustrious family. Those diamonds were brought to me by the Jew Henriques, from whom I now and then make purchases. I did not inquire in what manner they came into his possession; but, not intending to be cheated as to their precise worth, I had them taken to Kramer, in the Rue Neuve St. Augustin, and a value placed upon them. I paid Henriques the price those trustworthy jewellers suggested, instead of the exorbitant one he demanded. This is all the information I am able to afford you on the subject."

" May I beg you to favor me with the address of this Henriques ? "

" Certainly, certainly, with pleasure ; but I warn you that
you will not get much out of him. He is the closest Israelite
imaginable; and a golden ointment is the only ' *open sesame* ' to
his lips."

M. de Fleury wrote Henriques' street and number on his card,
and handed it to Maurice.

Meantime Gaston de Bois, in spite of the pertinacious attentions of the Duke de Montauban, had approached Bertha, and
would have drawn her into conversation had she not exultingly
communicated to him the discovery she had made concerning
Madeleine's jewels. Was it the sudden mention of that name
which threw M. de Bois into a state of almost uncontrollable agitation? Why did he flush, and stammer, and try to change the
subject, and, stumbling with suppressed groans over his words,
as though they had been sharp rocks, talk such unmitigated nonsense? Why did he so soon steal away from Bertha's side?
Why did he not approach her again for the rest of the evening?
Could it be that her first suspicion was right, and that he loved
Madeleine? If not, why should her name again have caused
him such unaccountable emotion?

CHAPTER XV.

THE EMBROIDERED HANDKERCHIEF.

MAURICE lost no time, the next morning, in seeking out the
crafty old Jew. Henriques was a vender of jewels that came into
his hands through private sources. There was considerable risk
in his traffic ; for it was just possible some of the precious stones
transferred to him might have been acquired in a manner not
strictly legal. Perhaps it was not part of his policy to acquaint
himself with the history of gems which he bought at a bargain
and reaped an enormous profit in selling; for, when Maurice
endeavored to extract some information concerning the diamonds
purchased by the Marquis de Fleury, the Jew protested entire
ignorance in regard to their prior ownership ; stating that they
were brought to him by one of his *confrères*, of whom he asked no

questions, — that he had purchased them at a ruinous price, and resold them to the marquis without a centime's benefit: a very generous proceeding on his part, he asserted ; adding, with a ludicrous assumption of importance, that he highly esteemed the marquis, and now and then allowed himself the gratification of favoring him in business transactions.

" But the name of the person from whom your friend received the jewels is certainly on his books, and, however numerous the hands through which they may have passed, they can be traced back to their original owner," observed Maurice.

" Not so easily, monsieur, not so easily. Purchaser has nothing to do with original owner. Jewels worth something, or jewels worth nothing, — that's the point ; names of parties holding the articles of no consequence."

" But you certainly inquire from what source the jewels offered you proceed ? "

" Never make impertinent inquiries, — never : would drive away customers. If monsieur has any jewels for sale, shall be happy to look at them ; disposed to deal in the most liberal manner with monsieur."

" Thank you. My object is simply to discover a friend to whom the jewels you sold to the Marquis de Fleury once belonged. It is indispensable that I should learn through whose hands they came into your possession."

" Ah ! " said the cunning Jew, placing his skinny finger on one side of his hooked nose, as if reflecting ; then glancing at Maurice out of the corners of his searching eyes, he asked, " Party would like to be discovered ?.— or would said party prefer to remain under the rose ? "

" Possibly the latter."

" Just so ; that gives interest to the enterprise. But when party objects to being traced, difficulties spring up ; takes time to overcome them ; always a certain cost."

" If you mean that I shall offer you compensation for your trouble, I am ready to make any in my power : name your price."

" Price ? price ? not to be named so hastily ; depends upon time consumed, amount of labor, obstacles party concerned may throw in the way. Other parties will have to be employed to seek out party who presented himself with the jewels ; renumeration requisite to induce communicativeness ; may turn out party had the jewels from another party, who obtained them from another ; shall have to track each party's steps backward to party who was the original possessor."

13 *

"Take your own course. I am unskilled in these affairs," answered Maurice, frankly ; "all I ask is that you learn for me *where* the lady whose family jewels passed through your hands now resides. Name the cost of your undertaking."

The wily Jew fastened his keen, speculative eyes upon his anticipated prey, as he replied, slowly, " Cost? — can't say to a certainty ; thousand francs do to begin."

He heard the faint sigh, of which Maurice was himself unconscious, and drew a correct inference.

From the hour that the viscount had been made aware of the true state of Count Tristan's finances, he had reduced all his own expenses, allowed himself no luxuries, no indulgencies, nothing but the barest necessities, that his father's narrow resources might not be drained through a son's lavishness. The young nobleman had not at that moment a hundred francs at his own command. He had no alternative but to apply to Count Tristan for the sum required by the Jew.

" My means are very limited," returned Maurice, with a great waste of candor. " I must beg you to deal with me as liberally as possible. The amount you demand I hope to obtain and bring you in a few days. In the meantime you will commence your inquiries."

" Assuredly, — just so ; commence putting matters in train at once ; possibly may have some clew between thumb and finger when monsieur returns with the money ; nothing to be done without golden keys : unlock all doors ; carry one into hidden depths of the earth. Shall be obliged to advance funds to pay partiest employed. Have the goodness to write your name in this book."

Maurice wrote down his name and address, and took his leave, once more elated by the belief that he was on the eve of discovering Madeleine's retreat.

The letter to his father written and dispatched, he sought Bertha, and gave her full particulars of his interview with the Jew, delicately forbearing to mention the compensation he expected.

Bertha, as sanguine of success as her cousin, was gayly discussing probabilities, when the Marquis de Merrivale entered.

" Young heads laid together to plot mischief, I wager ! " remarked the nobleman, jocosely ; for he was in a capital humor, having just partaken of an epicurean *dejeuner à la fourchette* at the celebrated " Madrid's."

We are talking about our Cousin Madeleine. Maurice has a

new plan for prosecuting his search," said Bertha. "Ah, dear Madeleine! Why did she forsake us so strangely? How could she have had the heart to cause us so much sorrow?"

"My dear child, it was probably her *liver* not her *heart* that was in fault. Her heart, I dare say, performed its grave duties properly, and should not be aspersed; some bilious derangement was no doubt at the bottom of her singular conduct. The greatest eccentricities may all be traced back to *bile* as their origin. Regulate the bile and you regulate the brain from which mental vagaries proceed. If some judicious friend had administered to your cousin Madeleine a little salutary medicine, and forced her to diet for a few days, she would have acted more reasonably. Talking of diet, that was a princely dinner the Marquis de Fleury set before us. He is really a very able and estimable member of society, — understands good living to perfection. I cordially reciprocate his wish that a lasting bond of union should exist between us. His brother-in-law, the young Duke de Montauban, is enchanted with my little niece. I say nothing: arrange between yourselves; but, by all means, marry into a family which knows how to value a good cook; take a young man who has had his taste sufficiently cultivated to distinguish of what ingredients a sauce is composed. Don't despise a blessing that may be enjoyed three hundred and sixty-five times every year, — that's my advice."

Bertha had not attached any importance to the attentions of the young duke; but her manner of receiving this suggestion, — the

> "half disdain
> Perched on the pouted blossom of her lip," —

convinced Maurice that, if she favored any suitor, her inclinations did not turn towards the duke.

"The Duke de Montauban is not ill-looking," Maurice remarked, to decoy her into some more open expression; "and he is sufficiently agreeable, — do you not think so?"

"I never thought about him," she replied, somewhat petulantly. "If I chance to look at him I never think of any one but his tailor and his hairdresser, without whom I verily believe he would have no tangible existence."

"An accomplished tailor and a skilful *coiffure* are all very well in their way," observed her uncle; "but a scientific *cook* is the grand necessity of a man's life, — a daily need, — the trebly repeated need of each day; and the education of a cook should commence in the cradle. If this point received the attention which it deserves from sanitarians, there would be fewer digestive organs out of order, and consequently fewer police reports, and a vast diminution of eccentric degradation, and moping madness and suicide, and horrors in general."

Bertha and Maurice did not dispute this sweeping assertion; for they knew it would entail upon them the necessity of encountering a battalion of arguments, which the marquis delighted to call into action to defend the ground upon which he took up his favorite position.

Count Tristan's reply to Maurice, enclosing a check for the thousand francs, was received a few days later. Maurice returned to the Jew with the money. The latter rejoiced him by vaguely hinting that there was a prospect of successful operation; but the matter would occupy time. The viscount would be good enough to call again in a week.

Maurice was too unsuspicious and too unskilled in transactions of this nature to doubt that the Jew was dealing with him in good faith. Instead of a week, he returned the next morning, and repeated his visits regularly every day. The Jew diligently fanned his hopes, assuring him that old Henriques was not to be baffled, though the parties through whose hands the jewels had passed were almost unapproachable. Very soon the merciless Israelite notified the young nobleman that further funds would be requisite, and Maurice writhed under the cruel compulsion which forced him to make a second application to his father.

Bertha had been a fortnight in Paris when the anniversary of her birthday, which for the first time had been forgotten, was in a singular manner recalled to her mind. A small package had been received for her at her uncle's residence in Bordeaux, and had been promptly forwarded to Paris. The outer cover was directed in the handwriting of her uncle's *concierge;* on the inner, a request, that if Mademoiselle de Merrivale were absent the parcel might be immediately forwarded to her, was written in familiar characters. Bertha had no sooner caught sight of them than she cried out, —

"Madeleine! It is the handwriting of Madeleine!"

She tore open the paper with trembling hands. There was no note, — not a single written word, — but before her lay a handkerchief of the finest texture, and embroidered with the marvellous skill which belonged alone to those "fairy fingers" she had so often watched.

Vainly might we attempt to convey even a faint idea of her

tumultuous rapture, — of the tears of ecstasy, the hysterical laughter, the dancing delight, with which she greeted her uncle and Maurice, who entered a few moments after the package was received. She kissed the handkerchief moistened with her tears, waved it exultingly over her head, kissed it again, and wept over it again, while the marquis and her cousin stood looking at her in speechless astonishment.

"Madeleine! Madeleine! it is from Madeleine!" at last she found voice to ejaculate. "See, that is her handwriting," pointing to the paper cover; "and this is her work; her 'fairy fingers' send me a token on my birthday. I am seventeen to-day, and no one has remembered it but Madeleine. She thinks of me still; she never forgets any one; she has not forgotten me!"

Maurice caught up the paper in which the handkerchief had been enveloped, and with throbbing pulses eagerly examined the handwriting.

"See, Maurice," Bertha continued, joyfully, "in the corner she has embroidered my name, surrounded by a wreath of for-get-me-nots, — for *she* does not forget. The crest of the de Merrivales is in the opposite corner; and this, — why this looks like the bracelet I gave her on her last birthday. How wonderfully she has imitated the knot of pearls that fastened the golden band! And this corner, Maurice, look, — this is in remembrance of you, — of your birthday token to her. Do you not see the design is a brooch, and the device a dove carrying an olive-branch in its mouth, and the word 'Pax' embroidered beneath?"

Maurice looked, struggling to repress the emotion that almost unmanned him. Pointing to the stamp upon the envelope which had contained the handkerchief, he said, —

"It is postmarked Dresden."

"Dresden? Dresden? Can Madeleine be in Dresden?" returned Bertha. "Ah, uncle, can we not go there at once? We shall certainly find her. Yes, — we must go. I am tired of Paris, — let us start to-morrow."

"Dresden, my dear!" cried her uncle, in a tone of unmitigated disgust. "Why, the barbarians would feed us upon *sour kraut*, and give us pudding before meat! Go to Dresden? Impossible! Not to be thought of! Paris was a wise move, — we have enjoyed the living amazingly; but trust ourselves to those tasteless German cooks? We should be poisoned in a couple of days. Keep cool, my dear, or you will make yourself ill by getting into such a violent state of excitement just after breakfast. How do you suppose the important process of digestion can progress favorably if your blood is agitated in this turbulent manner?"

Bertha was about to answer almost wrathfully, but Maurice interrupted her.

" *I* will go, Bertha. Madeleine must be in Dresden. At last she has sent us a token of her existence, a token of remembrance, thank Heaven!"

" Go! go! go at once!" was Bertha's energetic injunction.

Maurice pressed her hand tightly, and bowing to the marquis, without attempting to utter another syllable, took his leave, carrying with him the envelope which bore Madeleine's handwriting.

After having his passport *viséd*, he returned to his apartment to make rapid preparations for starting that evening. Very soon Gaston de Bois entered, evidently in a state of ill-concealed perturbation.

" Mademoiselle Bertha tells me you are going to Dresden."

" Yes, to seek my cousin. Look at the post-stamp upon that envelope. Madeleine is in Dresden."

" How can you be sure of that?" asked Gaston.

" She writes from Dresden; can anything be clearer?" returned Maurice, confidently.

" It is not clear to me that she is there. I wish I could persuade you against taking this jour — our — ourney."

" That is out of the question, Gaston; so spare yourself the trouble of the attempt."

" But the journey will be use — use — useless," persisted M. de Bois.

" How can you know that?" inquired Maurice, quickly.

" I think so; it is my impression, my conviction."

" It is not mine, and nothing can prevent my making the experiment," answered Maurice, decidedly.

Gaston looked as thoroughly vexed as though he were responsible for the rash actions of his friend; but he knew that Maurice was inflexible where Madeleine was concerned, and that all entreaties would be thrown away unless he could sustain them by some potent reason; and *that* it was not in his power to proffer. He made no further opposition, but remained fidgeting about the room in the most distracting manner, hindering the preparations of Maurice, stumbling over articles scattered on the floor, now and then stammering out a broken, unintelligible phrase, and altogether seeming wretchedly uncomfortable, yet unwilling to leave until he saw the obstinate traveller in the *fiacre* which drove him to the railway station.

CHAPTER XVI.

A VOICE FROM THE LOST ONE.

A few days after the departure of Maurice for Dresden, the Duke de Montauban made a formal proposal for the hand of Mademoiselle de Merrivale. French etiquette not allowing a suitor the privilege of addressing the lady of his love, except through some kindred or friendly medium, his pretensions were of course made known to Bertha by her uncle. She received the communication with a fretful tapping of her little foot, and a toss of her gamboling, golden ringlets, which bore witness to her undisguised vexation and saucy disdain. The uncompromising manner in which she declined the proposed honor, threw her guardian, who had strengthened himself to enact the part of Cupid's messenger, by a somewhat liberal repast, into a state of astonishment which threatened alarming disturbance to his laboring digestive functions.

"Really, my dear, you speak so abruptly that you make me feel quite dyspeptic. What possible objection can you have to the young duke?"

"A very slight one, according to the creed which governs matrimonial alliances in our enlightened land," returned Bertha, pouting through her sarcasm. "My objection is simply that he is not an object of the slightest interest to me."

"But the match is such a suitable one that interest will come after it is consummated," answered her uncle.

"I do not intend to marry upon *faith*," retorted Bertha; then she broke out petulantly, "In a word, uncle, I do not intend to marry a man who is so insipid that I could not even quarrel with him; whom I could not think of seriously enough to take the trouble to dislike; to whom I am so thoroughly indifferent that for me he has no existence out of my immediate sight."

"There, there; keep cool, my dear. Nobody intends to force you to marry him. I did not know that it was necessary to be able to dislike a man, and to have a capacity for quarrelling with him, to fit him for the position of a husband. A very unwholesome doctrine. Emotion is particularly prejudicial to the animal economy. I thought the cultivated taste which the de Fleurys so evidently possess might have some weight with you. That dinner they gave us was unsurpassable, and" —

" If I am to marry to secure myself superlatively good dinners, I had better unite myself to an accomplished cook at once," replied Bertha, demurely.

" That's very tart, my dear. All acids disagree with me, and your acidulated observations are giving me unpleasant premonitory symptoms."

Bertha noticed that the *bon vivant* had in reality began to puff and pant as though he were suffering from an incipient nightmare. Being so thoroughly habituated to his idiosyncrasy that she had learned to regard it leniently, she made an effort to recover her good humor, and answered, —

" I know my kind uncle will not render me uncomfortable by pressing this subject; but, in the most courteous manner, will let the Duke de Montauban understand that I do not intend to marry at present."

" Make you uncomfortable," rejoined the marquis, struggling for breath; " of course, I would not for the world! Do you take me for an old brute? And I have just made arrangements to drive you to the *Bois de Boulogne* and dine at Madrid's this evening. A pretty state you would be in to do justice to a dinner which promises to place in jeopardy the laurels even of M. de Fleury's cook."

" We will strike a bargain," returned Bertha, with her wonted gayety. " If you will agree not to mention the Duke de Montauban, I will agree to do justice to the dinner at Madrid's."

" I am content; we will drop the duke and discuss the dinner."

The attentions of Madame de Fleury's brother to the heiress had been too marked and open for his suit and its rejection to remain a secret. Gaston de Bois heard Bertha's refusal commented upon, and there was a buzz in his ears of idle speculations concerning the origin of her caprice. Was it some blissful, internal suggestion, which diffused such a glow of happiness over his expressive countenance when he next saw Bertha? Was it some hitherto uncertain ground of encouragement made sure beneath his feet, which so wondrously loosened his tongue from its dire bondage? Was it some aerial hope, taking tangible shape, which imparted such an air of ease and elation to his demeanor? Gaston stammered less every day, — his impediment disappearing as his self-possession increased. On this occasion he was only conscious of a slight difficulty in utterance to rejoice at its existence, for it rendered delightfully apparent Bertha's thoughtfulness in catching up words upon which he hesitated, and concluding sentences he commenced, as though she read their meaning in his eyes. Gaston had not seen her in so buoyant a mood since they parted at the Château de Gramont. But the tide of her exuberant gayety suddenly ebbed when she noticed the look of pain with which he involuntarily responded to one of her chance questions. She had asked if he thought it probable Maurice would find Madeleine in Dresden. Again that singular expression on his countenance; again that sudden change of color at Madeleine's name; again that involuntary starting from his seat, with a return of the olden habit which placed fragile furniture in danger! Was it the remembrance that Madeleine was lost to them which occasioned M. de Bois's sudden depression? Was it an overwhelming sense of doubt concerning the result of Maurice's mission, which made his response to Bertha's inquiry so vague, his sentences so disjointed? Once more Bertha asked herself whether he were not, after all, the lover Madeleine had refused to mention. Yet, if this were the case, how could Gaston have appeared so much less anxious and less concerned at her flight than Maurice, who loved her with unquestionable ardor? Why had M. de Bois aided so little in the search for her present habitation? The young girl could not reconcile such apparent contradictions, and while she sat perplexing herself by futile efforts to unravel these mysteries, M. de Bois was equally puzzled to rightly interpret her silence and abstraction.

The interview which, at its opening, had been as bright as a spring morning, closed with sudden April shadows; and there was an April mingling of smiles and tears upon Bertha's countenance when she retired to her chamber, after M. de Bois's departure, and pondered over his strange expression when her cousin was mentioned. Why, if Madeleine was his choice, was his manner toward herself so full of tenderness? Why was it that she never glanced at him without finding his eyes fastened upon her face? Why had he so much power to draw her irresistibly towards him? Why did his step set her heart throbbing so tumultuously? Why did his coming cause her such a thrill of delight, and his departure leave such a sense of solitude? — a void that no one else filled, a pain that no other presence soothed.

Meantime Maurice had reached Dresden and was searching for Madeleine, almost in the same vague, unreasonable manner that he had sought her in Paris. But the mad course upon which he had again started, and which might have once more unbalanced his mind, met with a sudden check. The day after his arrival in Dresden he received a note, which ran thus : —

14

"Madeleine is not in Dresden. She entreats Maurice to discontinue a search which must prove fruitless. Should the day ever come, as she prays it may, when her place of refuge can become known to him, no effort of his will be required for its discovery. Will not Maurice accept the pains of the inevitable present and wait for the consolations the future may bring forth with the hope and patience which must sustain her until that blessed period shall arrive?"

Maurice was almost stupefied as he read these lines. He crushed the paper in his nervous fingers to be certain that it was tangible; he compared the writing with the one upon the envelope which he had taken from Bertha. If that were Madeleine's hand, so was this. He looked for a postmark; there was none; the letter had been brought by a private messenger, and yet Madeleine was not in Dresden! How could this be? That, in some mysterious manner, she became acquainted with his movements was unquestionable. Her thoughts then were turned to him, — her invisible presence followed him. It was some joy, at least, to know that he lived in her memory.

Maurice, without a moment's hesitation, without letting his own personal suffering weigh in the balance of decision, without allowing his mind to dwell upon the probabilities of tracing Madeleine through this new clew, resolved to comply with her request.

When he returned to Paris and placed her letter in Bertha's hands, and told her his determination, she impetuously urged him not to be guided by their cousin's wishes. She pleaded that Madeleine was sacrificing herself from a mistaking sense of duty; that, if her place of abode could only be revealed, Bertha's own supplications might influence her to abandon her present project, and to accept the home which Bertha, with the full consent of her uncle, could offer.

Maurice listened not unmoved, but unshaken, in his selected course. He felt that a woman of Madeleine's dignity of character, — a woman of her calm judgment, — a woman who could look with such steady, tearless eyes upon life's realties, — a woman who would not have trodden in flowery ways though every pressure of her foot crushed out some delicious aroma to perfume her life, if the "stern lawgiver, duty," summoned her to a flinty road, and pointed to a glorious goal beyond, — such a woman, having deliberately chosen her path, having tested her strength to walk therein, having pronounced that strength all-sufficient, deserved the tribute of confidence, and an even blind respect to her mandates. Besides, compliance with her wishes was a species of voiceless, wordless communication with her; it was sending her a message through some unknown and mysterious channel.

Maurice presented this in its most vivid colors before Bertha's eyes; but in vain. She was too wayward, too unreasonable, too full of passionate yearning for the presence of Madeleine, too sensible of an innate weakness that longed to lean upon Madeleine's strength, to see the justice and wisdom of the conclusion to which Maurice had arrived.

As soon as their painful interview was closed by the entrance of the marquis, Maurice sought the old Jew and ordered him to prosecute his search no further. Henriques, who had already extracted a considerable sum from the young nobleman, and looked upon the transaction as a safe investment calculated to yield a certain profit for some months to come, was very unwilling to relinquish his promised gain. He assured the viscount that he had lately received information of the greatest importance; the party to whom the jewels had originally belonged had at last been tracked; the undertaking was on the very eve of success. To abandon it was a refusal to grasp the prize almost within their clutch. Whether the cunning Jew spoke the truth, or fiction, mattered little; for Maurice, in spite of these alluring representations, did not allow himself to be tempted to violate Madeleine's express command. He had, as it were, accepted his fate, and cast away the arms with which men war with so-called "destiny;" struggle and rebellion were over. To "*wait*" in patience was all that remained.

But what was to be done with his existence? In the plenitude of youthful health and strength, was his life to ebb away, like an unreplenished stream, flowing into nothingness? His days became more and more wearisome; the hours hung more and more heavily upon his hands; the feet of time sounded with iron tramp in his ears, yet never appeared to move onward.

"In his eyes a cloud and burthen lay;" a shadowy sorrow dropped its pall of darkness over his mind and obscured his perception of all awakening, quickening inspirations; a smouldering fire within him withered up every vernal shoot of impulse and turned all the spring-time foliage of thought and fancy sere. His voice, his look, his mien, betrayed that an ever-living woe encompassed him with gloom.

Ronald fruitlessly strove to rouse him from this state of supine despondency. The active employment, the all-engrossing interest which would have medicined his unslumbering sorrow, were remedial agents denied by his father's unwise decree. As a substitute, though of less potency, Ronald strove to inspire him with his own strong love for literature. The young American had a passion for books which were the reflex of great minds. His quick hearkening to the voices breathing from their pages, and made prophetic by some sudden experience ; the ready plummet with which he sounded their depths of reasoning ; the sentient hand with which he plucked out their truths and planted them in his own rich memory, to grow like trees filled with singing-birds : these had rendered his communings with master-spirits one of the noblest and most strengthening influences of his life. What wonder, when literature was so bounteously distributed over his native land that it made itself vocal beneath every hedge, — enriched the humblest cottage with a library, — found its way, in the inexpensive guise of magazines, a welcome visitant at every fireside, — poured out its treasures at the feet of rich and poor, liberally as the liberal sunshine, freely as the free air ?

Maurice, educated in a different atmosphere, at the same age as Ronald, was a stranger to the companionship of written minds, save those to which his college studies had formally presented him ; and his dark unrest rendered it difficult for him to follow his friend into the teeming Golconda of literature, and to gather the gems spread to his hands. And when, at last, Ronald's enthusiasm proved contagious and kindled Maurice to seek out some great author's charm, it too often chanced that he stumbled upon passages that irritated him, and increased his moody discontent. We instance one of these occasions as illustrative of many others.

Ronald, whose busy brush had been brought to a stand-still by an unusually dark day, when he returned to his apartments, found his friend reading Bulwer's "Caxtons." Maurice was leaning with both elbows upon the table, his fingers plunged through his disordered hair, his brows almost fiercely contracted, and his wan face bent over the volume before him.

"I found some grand pictures in that book," remarked the young artist. "Which are you contemplating?"

"No pictures. I have not your eye for pictures," answered Maurice, with something more than a touch of impatience. "I am moved, haunted, tormented by truths which have more power than all the ideal pictures pen ever drew, or brush ever painted. You place me here before your library, you lure me to read, and every book I open utters words that make my compulsory mode of existence a reproach, a disgrace, a misery to me. Read this, for instance : 'Life is a drama, not a monologue. A drama is derived from a Greek word which signifies *to do*. Every actor in the drama has something to do which helps on the progress of the whole, — that is the object for which the author created him. *Do your part* and let the *Great Play* go on!' *Do? do?*" continued Maurice, in an excited tone as he finished the quotation ; "it is a torment worthy of a place in Dante's Inferno to know that there is nothing one is permitted to *do !* I too am an actor in the Great Drama ; but I have no part to play save that of lay figure, motionless and voiceless ; yet, unhappy, not being deprived of sensibility, I am goaded to desperation by inward taunting because I can do nothing."

" The play is not ended yet," answered Ronald, with as much cheerfulness as he could command, for his friend's depression affected his sympathetic nature. " We may not comprehend our *rôles* in the beginning ; we may have to study long before we can thoroughly conceive, then idealize, then act them."

"I could bear that mine should be a sad, if it were only an active one," returned Maurice, again fixing his eyes upon the book.

Ronald could make no reply to a sentiment so thoroughly in accordance with his own views. He constantly pondered upon the possibilities through which his friend might be freed from the shackles that bound him to the effeminate serfdom of idleness ; but the magic that could unrivet those fetters had not yet been revealed. Still he was sometimes stirred by a mysterious prescience that they would be loosened, and through his instrumentality.

Ronald's nature was essentially practical without being prosaic. The rich ore of poetry, inseparable from all exquisitely fine organizations, lay beneath the daily current of his life, like golden veins in the bed of a stream, shining through the crystal waters that bore the most commonplace objects on their tide. He thoroughly accepted that interpretation of the Ideal which calls it a " divine halo with which the Creator had encircled the world of reality ; " but while he instinctively lifted all he loved into supernal regions and contemplated them in the glorious spirit-light that heightens all beauty, he lost sight of none of the stern actualities of their existence. His imagination had fashioned a hero out of Maurice, and he had thrown his person in heroic guise upon canvas ; yet he clearly beheld and mourned

14 *

over the morbid tendency that was weakening his mind and threatened to render his character and his life equally unheroic.

Only a few days after the conversation we have just narrated, when Maurice entered Ronald's sitting-room he found the student with an open letter in his hand. As he lifted his eloquent, brown eyes from the paper a glittering moisture beaded their darkly fringed lashes, and an expression of ineffable tenderness looked out from their lustrous depths. The letter was from his mother, — one of those messengers of deep affection which transported him into her presence, placed him, as he had so often sat in his petted boyhood, at her feet, to listen to her holy teachings, and be thrilled to the very centre of his being by her words of love. During his three years of separation, at a period when the expanding mind is most impressible, these letters, weekly received, had surrounded him with a heavenly aura which seemed breathed out through a mother's ceaseless prayers, and had kept his life pure, his spirit strong, his heart uplifted ; had preserved him from being hurried by the wild, ungoverned impulses of youth, rendered more infectuous by the volcanic fires of genius, into actions for which he might blush hereafter.

It was one of the undefined, unspoken sources of sympathy between Ronald and Maurice, that the guarding hand of *woman*, influencing them from a distance, preserved the bloom, the freshness, the pristine purity of both their souls, even in the polluted atmosphere of a city where immorality is an accepted evil. Maurice, who had never known a mother's hallowing affection, gained his strength through his early attachment to a maiden whom no man could love without being ennobled thereby ; and Ronald, whose heart had never yet awakened to the first pulse of tenderness which drew him towards one he would have claimed as a bride, owed his powers of resistance to as strong, as passionate devotion to a mother who united in her person all the most glorious attributes of womanhood, and whose idolizing love for her child was tempered by wisdom which placed his spiritual progress above all other gain. While he was struggling to win laurels in art's arena, she strove to bind upon his brow a crown whose gems were heavenly truths, — a crown the pure in spirit alone could wear.

Blessed the son who has such a mother! Safe and blessed! His foot shall tread upon the serpent that lies hidden beneath the tempting flowers in his path, ere the reptile can sting him ; his hand shall resolutely put away the cup of pleasure from his lips when there is poison in the chalice ; he shall walk through the fire of evil lusts unscathed!. No laurel that wreaths his brow shall render it too feverish, or too proud, to lie upon that mother's bosom with the glad, all-confiding, satisfied sense which made its joy when it lay there in guileless boyhood. That mother's love shall smooth for him the rough ways of earth, and place in his hand the golden key that opens heaven.

As Maurice took his seat beside Ronald, the latter, hastily sweeping his handkerchief across his eyes, said with a vehement intonation, —

"I have come to a sudden determination! I am going back to America. The trip is nothing, — ten days over and ten back, — a mere trifle! I can spend a couple of months with my parents and be back in time for autumn work. Instead of sending my picture, which is nearly completed, I will present it in person."

Maurice sighed as he answered, "They will be proud of your work! Happy are they who have work to do, and who do it faithfully!"

"That is a sentiment worthy of an American," rejoined Ronald; "indeed, you have unconsciously stolen it from one of our most distinguished American writers, who says, 'To have something to do and *to do it* is the best appointment for us all.'* The extent to which I have insensibly Americanized you is very evident. A thought has just struck me: you are weary and melancholy, and seem to grow much paler and thinner every day. It will revive and strengthen you to accompany me. Come, let us go together!"

"Let us fly to the moon!" answered Maurice, half scornfully. "Ronald, *why* do you always forget that although we have lived precisely the same number of years, and I may be said to have lived so much longer than you, if we count time by sorrows that make long the days, — though we have both passed our twenty-first anniversary, you, as an American, have obtained your majority, and are a free agent, while the law of France renders me still a minor for four years? You know I cannot stir without my father's consent; and, of course, that is unattainable."

"Unattainable if you choose to imagine that it is, and will not seek for it," answered Ronald, rebukingly. "The wisest poet that ever penned his inspiration, says, —

> . 'Our doubts are traitors
> And make us lose the good we oft might win
> By fearing to attempt!'

Do not let your traitorous doubts frighten you from the trial."

* Hillard's "Italy."

Maurice smiled away his rising irritability, and replied, " I think, Ronald, your mind is so full of poetic arrows that one could not take a step, or lift a finger, or draw a breath, without your being able to hit him with a verse."

" A verse may hit him who a sermon flies! " retorted Ronald, laughingly. " And a man is easy to hit who sits down with folded hands, like him of whom my rhythmic shaft has just made a target. But, to speak seriously, do you wonder that true thoughts, beautiful thoughts, which have been thrown into the music of verse, keep their haunting echoes in some stronghold of memory, and surge up to the lips when a stirring incident causes the gates of the mind to vibrate ? Why, the very proof of the poet's genuine inspiration, his chiefest triumph lies in this, that he speaks a familiar truth, a common word of hope, a little word of comfort, a simple word of warning, with such potency that it strikes deeper into the soul than any other adjuration can reach ; it defies us to forget ; it takes the sound of a prophecy, and thrills our hearts and governs our actions in spite of ourselves. So much in defence of my poetic memories. Now be generous enough to admit that poetry is usually mingled with a large proportion of prosaic common sense which resolves itself into action. My scoffed-at poetry interprets itself into this matter-of-fact prose : unless you have the courage, the energy to ask your father's consent to your accompanying me to America, you will not get it ; and if you ask you *may* get it ; and if you accompany me it may profit you. Come, — what say you ? I shall be ready to start next week."

" So soon ? ejaculated Maurice, who, often as he had witnessed the promptitude with which the young American moved, could not yet familiarize himself with his national rapidity of action and decision.

" You call it *soon* ? Why, if I had said day after to-morrow it might have been termed *soon ;* but it seems to me a week is time enough to prepare for a journey around the world. Come, you have half an hour before the post closes, — dash off your letter and let it go at once."

As he spoke, he cleared his writing-table of the books and papers by which it was encumbered, and placed a chair for Maurice. The latter, who was always carried onward by the rushing current of his friend's strong will, wrote, on the spur of the moment, a letter more calculated to impress his father than any deliberately studied epistle. The restless and gloomy state of mind under which Maurice labored, revealed itself in this impulsive effusion with a force which might not have found its way into a calmer communication.

The frequent applications for money which Maurice had been compelled to make, that he might meet the demands of the old Jew, were not without their influence in preparing Count Triston to look favorably upon his son's solicitation. The count imagined that the sums so constantly demanded were squandered in the manner habitual to gay young men in Paris. He had experienced much difficulty in complying with his son's last request, and became painfully aware that it would not much longer be in his power to supply him at the same extravagant rate. As a natural consequence, he hailed the proposition to travel, which might break off any unfortunate connections, or *liaisons*, he might have formed in Paris, and without their aid, divert his troubled mind. Then, the present would be a favorable opportunity for Maurice to visit his estate in Maryland, and to learn something further of that railway company which seemed of late to have suspended its operations.

Maurice was not less astounded than overjoyed upon receiving his father's prompt and unconditional consent to his proposed trip. He at once carried the letter to Bertha. She was too generous to oppose a step which promised to be advantageous to her cousin, yet she could not contemplate their inevitable separation without sincere sorrow.

" I wish I were going with you ! " she sighed. " It seems to me everybody is going to America. Have you not heard that the Marquis de Fleury has just received the appointment of ambassador to the United States? I wish my uncle would let me travel to some foreign country. I am weary of this Parisian, ball-going life."

" Has Monsieur de Fleury received his appointment at last? I had not heard of it. Who told you ? " inquired Maurice.

" M. de Bois, this very morning."

" Gaston goes with him, I presume ? "

" Yes, he said so."

" That is an unexpected pleasure, — that is really delightful ! " exclaimed Maurice, enthusiastically.

Bertha did not reply ; but she certainly looked inclined to pout, and as though she had no very distinct perception of the delight in question.

In a few days Maurice and Ronald were on the great ocean.

A fortnight later the Marquis and Marchioness de Fleury, and the secretary of the former, M. de Bois, were also on their way to the New World.

Bertha worried her uncle by her sad face, listless manner, and low spirits, to say nothing of her loss of appetite (to his thinking the most important feature of her *malaise*), until he was convinced that she had lost all interest in Paris, and that her sadness would be increased by a longer sojourn in the gay capital. When she admitted this, he kindly inquired if she desired to travel.

" Yes, *very much,*" was her reply.

Whither would she go ? To Italy ? To England ? To Russia ?

" No, — to America ! "

America ! — land of savages ! — land of Pawnees and Choctaws ! — land where cooking must be in its crude infancy ! Her uncle would not listen to such a barbarous proposition ; and, finding that he could obtain no other answer from his wilful and incomprehensible ward, he carried her back to Bordeaux, consoling himself with the reflection that although the visit to Paris had not been permanently advantageous to his niece, the culinary knowledge acquired by Lucien was a full compensation.

CHAPTER XVII.

" CHIFFONS."

" CHIFFONS ! " " *talking chiffons !* " " *writing chiffons !* " — will any one have the goodness to furnish us with a literal yet lucid interpretation of this enigmatical form of speech so incessantly employed in the Parisian *beau monde* ? Among the translatable words of the French language, — among the expressive terms which cannot be rendered by equally significant expressions in our own more copious tongue, — among the phraseology invented to convey ideas which the phrases themselves certainly do not suggest, — the common application of this curt little word " *chiffons* " holds a distinguished place. Look for " *chiffons* " in the dictionary, and you will see it simply defined as " *rags ;* " yet " *chiffons* " represent the very opposite of rags feminine, and conjure up a multitudinous army of feminine fashions, fripperies, fancies, follies, indispensable aids and adjuncts of the feminine toilet.

We have headed this chapter " *chiffons*," and given an imperfect definition of the term, as a sign-post of warning to masculine readers, — a hint that this is a chapter to be lightly skimmed, or altogether skipped, for it unavoidably treats of " *chiffons*," which the necessities of the narrative will not allow us to suppress.

The Marquis de Fleury had been appointed ambassador from the court of Napoleon the Third to the United States of America.

Madame de Fleury's state of mind, in spite of the consolation afforded by a number of strikingly original costumes, which she innocently flattered herself would prove very effective during a sea-voyage, was deplorable. Terror inspired by the perils of the deep was only surpassed by intense grief excited by her compulsory banishment to a land where, she imagined, the invading feet of modiste and mantua-maker had not trodden out all resemblance to the original Eden; a land where the women probably attired themselves with a leaning to antediluvian simplicity, or in accordance with strong-minded proclivities, and the men were, doubtless, too much engrossed by politics and business to be capable of appreciating the most elaborate toilet that could be fashioned to captivate their eyes; a land, in short, where taste was yet unborn, and where it was ignorantly believed that the chief object of apparel was to perform, on a more extensive scale, the use of primitive fig-leaves and furs.

To prevent her from falling into the clutches of American barbarians, Madame de Fleury secured two French maids as a *body-guard*. Into the hands of one, skilled in the intricate mysteries of hair-dressing, her head was unreservedly consigned; the other, versed in more varied arts, had entire charge of the rest of her person. But these *aides-de-camp* of the toilet were deemed insufficient for the guardianship of her charms. The moment her sentence of exile was pronounced, she had summoned the incomparable Vignon to her presence, and piteously painted the difficulties which must beset her path when she was remorselessly torn from within reach of the creative fingers of the artist *couturière*. Vignon had unanticipated comfort in store: the most accomplished of her assistants, — one who had exhibited a skill in design and execution positively marvellous, — had several times expressed a strong inclination to establish herself in America, and would gladly make her *debut* in the New World under the patronage of the marchioness. This information threw

17 *

Madame de Fleury into such ecstasies that all the waves of the
Atlantic, which had been ruthlessly tossing their wrecks about
her brain, were suddenly stilled, and she declared that Mademoiselle Melanie must make her preparations to sail in the same
steamer; for the knowledge that she was on board would render
the voyage endurable. The marchioness complacently added that
she felt so much strengthened by these tidings, that she could
now look forward to meeting, with becoming fortitude, the trials
incident upon her residence among a semi-civilized nation.

We need hardly relate how soon, after reaching Washington,
the fair Parisian discovered that civilization had made astound-
ing progress if it might be estimated by the deference paid to
"*chiffons;*" nor need we portray her astonishment at finding
that American women "*of fashion*" were not merely close copy-
ists of extreme French modes, but that they exaggerated even
the most extravagant, and hunted after the newest styles with
the national energy which their countrywomen of a nobler class
expended upon nobler objects; and were more ready to deform
or ignore nature, and swear allegiance to the despotic rule of the
Crinoline Sovereign, than any Parisian belle under the sun.

Madame de Fleury's royal sway over the empire of "*chiffons*"
was soon as thoroughly established in Washington as it had been
in Paris. Dress, or head-dress, bodice, bonnet, mantle, gaiter,
glove, worn by her, multiplied itself in important imitations, and
every feminine chrysalis sent forth its ballroom butterfly in a
livery to match. Whatever style, shape, color, she adopted, however extraordinary, became the rage for that season, and disappeared from sight, totally banished by her regal command, at the
inauguration of the next.

At one period no skirt could sweep the pavement, or lie in rich
folds at the bottom of a carriage, unadorned by an imposing
flounce that almost covered the robe; a little later, the one sober
flounce was driven into obscurity by twenty coquettish small
ones; and these were displaced by primly puffed bands; which
gave way to fanciful "keys" running up the sides of the dress
(where they seemed to have no possible right); and those vanished when double skirts commenced their brief reign; to be de-
throned by a severe-looking quilted ruffle marching around the
hem of the dress and up the centre to the throat; and this grave
adornment suddenly found its place usurped by an inundation of
fantastic trimmings, jet, bugles, *passementerie*, velvet or lace.
So much for skirts!

Then the bodices: — *now* nothing was to be seen but the

"square cut" which revealed the fine busts of beauties in the days of Charles II., — now graceful folds *a cœur* sentimentally ruled the day, — now infant waists became a passion, and the most maternal forms aped the juvenility borrowed from their babies. Then for sleeves: at one time they were wide and long and cumbrous, forbidding every trace of the most rounded member beneath; then they took the form of antique drapery, disclosing the arm almost nude, save for the transparent lace of the undersleeve, — then the close, tight fit of the Quaker left all but a distorted outline to the imagination.

And bonnets: at one moment the tiniest bird's-nest of a hat, embowered in feathers and buried in lace, was perched on the back of the head, reminding one of Punch's suggestion that it could be more conveniently carried upon a salver by a domestic walking behind; a little later, the only bonnet admissible closed around the face like a cap, laces and feathers had disappeared, a few tastefully disposed knots of ribbon, or a single flower, were the only adornments: but hardly had Good Sense nodded approvingly at the graceful simplicity with which heads were covered, when, lo! the bonnets shot up like bright-hued coal-scuttles, over which a basket of buds and blossoms had been suddenly upset, and went through a variety of fantastic transformations wholly indescribable.

So with other articles of attire. Mantles that had established for themselves a natural and convenient length suddenly grew down to the hem of the dress; basques, high in favor, were routed by Zouave jackets; girdles were at one moment drawn down with tight pressure until they barely surmounted the hips, the next were allowed to take an almost natural round (as far as their fitting locality went), and next were put wholly to flight by pointed Swiss belts, with enormous bows, and long, flowing ends, — while these, in turn, were chased from the field by picturesque scarfs.

Then as regards the disposition of that native veil of unsurpassable beauty which adorns the head of woman: now, all locks were braided low at the back of the head, almost lying upon the neck; now they surmounted the crown and rose in stories higher and higher; now they sprang into a pair of wings from either side of the temples; now they were clustered in a tuft of disorderly curls above the brow; now smoothed and bandolined close to the face and knotted with an air of quiet simplicity behind the ears.

Whichever of these modes the Parisian queen of "*chiffons*"

rendered graceful in her own person, every fair one, with the
slightest aspiration to *style*, strengthened her claims to be thought
fashionable by scrupulously assuming.   What wonder that Mademoiselle Melanie, prime minister to the absolute sovereign, could
scarcely receive the crowd of clients that thronged her doors?

She hired a spacious mansion, near the capitol, and furnished
it with consummate taste. She combined the vocation of mantua-
maker with that of milliner, and supplied all the materials she
employed from an assortment of her own selection.   This was
one secret of her astonishing success, for it gave her control over
the entire apparel of her customers.   Regarding herself as responsible for the *tout ensemble* of each toilet that issued from her
hands, and her reputation as at stake if any defective touch
marred the general result of her adorning, she exerted a thoroughly despotic sway over those whom she undertook to dress,
and refused, in the most positive, yet most courteous manner, to
allow them to follow the dictates of their own faulty fancies. As
a skilful artist examines a picture in the best light, that all its
beauties may be revealed, she placed each one of her subjects in
the most favorable aspect, studied her closely, searched out every
fine point which might be heightened, and pondered over every
defect which might be concealed. She had the rare gift of knowing how to embellish nature, how to bring forth all the capacities
of a face and form, and how to modify the fashion of the day to
the requirements of the wearer, instead of slavishly following an
arbitrary mode, and thereby sacrificing all individuality of beauty.
Dress became high art in her hands. Wondrously harmonious
were the effects produced. Blondes looked softer and purer than
ever before, without becoming insipid; brunettes grew more
piquante and brilliant; nondescripts gained force and character;
pallid faces caught a reflection of rose tints; too ruddy complex-
ions were toned down by paling colors, and sallow skins found
their ochre hue mysteriously neutralized. Angular shapes were
draped so gracefully that unsymmetrical sharpness disappeared;
too ample forms exchanged their air of uncouth corpulence for a
well-defined roundness; low statures seemed to spring up to a
nobler altitude, and women of masculine height sunk into feminine proportions.   In short, Mademoiselle Melanie was not a
mantua-maker, or milliner,—she was the genius of taste, the artful embodier of poetry in outward adorning.

Her own person was strikingly attractive; but the severest
simplicity characterized her attire. Her manners, though affable,
were exceedingly reserved; without any apparent effort, she re-

pressed the familiarity of the vulgar, and rebuked the patronizing airs of the assuming, winning instinctive deference even from the ill-bred.

By her workwomen she was almost worshipped. Young herself, she impressed them with the sense that notwithstanding her lack of advantage over them in point of years, her superior skill and knowledge entitled her to be their head. She sympathized with their griefs, inquired into their needs, sometimes ignored their short-comings, but never their sufferings, and took care that the thread which helped fashion a lady's robe should not be drawn with such weary and overworked hands that, in the language of Hood, it sewed a shroud at the same moment.

She was seldom seen in the streets; and, when her duties called her, she went forth closely veiled. But her distinguished air, the simple elegance of her apparel, and the dignified grace of her movements could not escape admiration.

She soon found a carriage of her own indispensable, and selected an unostentatious equipage; but allowed herself the indulgence of a pair of superb horses, because she chanced to be an appreciating judge of those noble animals: a rather unusual knowledge for a *couturiere.*

She seldom walked or drove alone. She was usually accompanied by one of her assistants, a young Massachusetts girl, with whom she had been thrown into accidental communication shortly after her arrival in the United States.

The history of Ruth Thornton is one every day repeated, but not less touching because so far from rare. Born and bred in affluence which emanated from the daily exertions of her father, his death left his widow and three orphan daughters destitute. The eldest early assumed the burdens of wifehood and maternity. Ruth was the second child. A girl of high spirit, she quickly laid aside all false pride, and earnestly sought to earn the bread of those she loved by the labor of her fair young hands, until then strangers to toil. But where was remunerative occupation to be found? Needy womanhood so closely crowded the few open avenues of industry that it seemed as though there was no room for another foot to gain a hold, another hand to struggle. To become a teacher, or governess, was Ruth's first, most natural endeavor; but, month after month, she sought in vain for a situation. She possessed a remarkable voice and very decided musical talent. The idea of the concert-room next suggested itself; but her naturally fine organ lacked the long cultivation that could alone fit her to embark upon the career of a singer. Her mind then turned to the stage; but, setting aside the difficulty of obtaining engagements, even to fill some position in the lowest ranks of the profession, she had no means, no time, to go through a long course of requisite study, or to procure herself the costly wardrobe indispensable to such a profession. She pondered upon the possibility of entering that most noble institution, the New York School of Design for Women. Here was meet work, hope-fanning, life-saving work for feminine hands: engraving on wood or steel; coloring plates for illustrated works; sketching designs for fashions to be used in magazines, or patterns for carpets, calicoes, paper-hangings, etc. But, on inquiry, she learned that a year's study would be needful before she could hope to gain a modest livelihood through the medium of the simplest of these pursuits. From whence, in the meantime, could her mother, her sister, and herself derive their support? Next, she resolved to resort to her needle; yet how small was the likelihood of keeping it employed! and how poor the pittance it could earn as an humble seamstress! True, she might learn a trade; but how was she to exist meantime?

She stood erect in the midst of this desert of difficulties, perplexed but undismayed, and still believing in, and steadfastly seeking for, the work allotted to such weak hands as hers.

There is something magnetic in unflagging energy, and untiring hope; they mysteriously attract to themselves the materials which they most need. By a seeming accident, Ruth heard that an assistant housekeeper was required at the Fifth Avenue Hotel in New York. Her high-born relatives learned with horror that one of their kin, the daughter of a gentleman who had held an honorable position in their community, contemplated filling this menial position. But, in spite of their disapproval, Ruth presented herself as an applicant for the post, and though her youth (for she was hardly twenty) was an objection, her services were accepted; and she entered forthwith upon her lowly duties.

We need not dwell upon the manifold and humiliating trials to which she was subjected, — trials to which the loveliness of her person largely contributed. Like a true American maiden, well-disciplined, self-reliant, and of strong principles, she found protection within herself, and bade defiance to dangers which might have proved fatal to one whose early training had been less productive of strength.

It was while Ruth was meekly discharging these humble duties that she became acquainted with Mademoiselle Melanie.

On arriving in New York, Madame de Fleury had taken up her residence for a few days at the Fifth Avenue Hotel, and, as though she feared to lose sight of Mademoiselle Melanie, requested her to do the same. A severe indisposition, which caused the latter to seek feminine aid, threw her in communication with the housekeeper of the hotel and her young assistant. Mademoiselle Melanie quickly became interested in the sweet, pale, patient face hovering about her bed, and did not fail to note the air of refinement which seemed at variance with her position. In less than four and twenty hours the young French *couturière* had learned the history of the young American housekeeper, and resolved, if she prospered in America, to remove this lovely girl from her present perilous position to one less exposed.

Six months later Ruth received a letter from Washington making her an offer to become one of the assistants of Mademoiselle Melanie, and gratefully accepted the proposal. Mademoiselle Melanie found her young *employée's* health too delicate for an exhausting apprenticeship to the needle, and employed Ruth in copying and coloring sketches of costumes which the accomplished *couturière* herself designed. As she became more and more conversant with the noble character of her *protégée* the spontaneous attachment she had conceived for her grew stronger, and Ruth Thornton became her constant companion.

CHAPTER XVIII.

MAURICE.

ON their arrival in America Ronald took Maurice to his southern home, where he was received with a cordial hospitality that strengthened and confirmed the tie of brotherhood between the young men.

We will not attempt to portray the meeting between Ronald and his parents,— a meeting so full of joy that its throbs quickened into the pulse of pain, as though clay-compassed hearts were hardly large enough to endure the ecstasy of such a reunion. Nor will we dwell upon the proud elation with which Ronald's first ambitious attempt in art was contemplated by his

parents. Their praises might simply have testified that love ap-
preciates; the hand that wrought might have sanctified even a
feeble work to their sight; but colder judgments pronounced
Ronald's initiatory achievement a pledge of power, and all the
more decisive because the execution of the youthful hand obviously had not kept pace with the strong conception of the fervid
brain.

We pass on to the effect produced upon Maurice by his sojourn in Ronald's transatlantic home.

Many a pang did the youthful Frenchman endure as he
noted the thorough and genial understanding which seemed to
exist between the southern youth and his father. Maurice was
amazed by Mr. Walton's unfailing recognition that his son was a
responsible being; by the confidence he reposed in him; by
the unequivocal manner in which he placed him upon a footing of
equality, even while guiding him by his counsels, — counsels offered as the results of a larger experience, yet never so compul-
sorily urged as to check his son's freedom of decision. Maurice,
marked, too, the earnest interest with which Mr. Walton entered into all Ronald's projects, albeit some of them appeared
too wild and high-reaching to be easy of accomplishment;
beheld how readily the paternal hand was stretched out to soften
the ordeals through which the neophyte must inevitably pass,
and was moved by the touching frankness with which the noble-
minded parent repeatedly congratulated himself that he had not
permitted his own predilections to force Ronald into a field of
action repugnant to his tastes.

When Maurice instinctively compared this liberal, high-toned
father's mode of influencing his son with the tyrannous control of
the haughty count, and contrasted Ronald's untrammeled position
with his own state of dependent nonentity, he felt that unstrug-
gling submission to the cruel decree which doomed him to waste
those fresh, strong, aspiring years of his life in hopeless idleness
was a weakness rather than a virtue.

He was only spared from passing a judgment upon his father,
more correct than filial, by throwing the blame of his conduct
upon the shackling customs, and false opinions, and arbitrary
laws of his native land. He could not but be forcibly struck by
the wide dissimilarity between the usages and views of life
which distinguished the two nations. In America, he saw men,
self-made and self-educated, at an age when young Frenchmen
have scarcely begun to be aware that they have any independent existence, rising to prominent and honorable positions, taking

a bold part in public affairs, and asserting by their achievements the maturity of their brains. He saw men, who had been forced by circumstances to commence their lives of toil and self-support at fifteen and eighteen, a few years later not only gaining their own livelihood, but contributing to the maintenance of their families, and laying the foundation of future fortune. He saw artistic tastes, literary talents, professional, legislative, and military abilities, brought to opulent fruition in men but a few years his senior; and though every one seemed to work at high pressure, every one appeared to live rapidly, crowding each day with actions, still men *lived*, lived *consciously*, planting along the pathway of their pilgrimage the landmarks of positive deeds; and they sowed, and reaped, and rejoiced in their harvests, and if some of them grew old faster than their European brethren, their age was at least enriched by varied memories, vast experiences, manifold mental gains, that testified to the value of their lives.

And was it imperative, Maurice asked himself, that the accident of noble blood should paralyze a man's volition, and that the bearing of a noble name should render his life inertly ignoble? He recognized that, in the seeming curse which condemned man to "work," God had hidden the richest blessing, even as he buried golden veins in the dark bosom of the earth. "Labor was privilege," and gave its sweetest flavor to the daily cup of life.

As for Ronald, though he loved his country with the enthusiasm which characterized all his affections, he had never been fully cognizant of the advantages it possessed over the land in which he had lately sojourned until he saw them through the eyes of Maurice.

Nothing is more true than that *we can render no service to another by which we are not served ourselves,* served spiritually, therefore *actually*, and in the highest sense; and not merely in his new appreciation of the land of his birth, but in numerous other ways, Ronald was the unconscious gainer by the helpful influence he exerted over his friend. The youthful Mentor confirmed himself in grand and vital truths while imparting them to Maurice; his own noble resolves were quickened into activity while he sought to infuse them into the mind of another; his own spirit acquired strength while he was endeavoring to render his companion strong of soul. Ronald's character was perhaps more affluent and expansive, had more force and fixedness of purpose, than that of Maurice, yet it derived fresh vigor from the less hopeful, less confident nature upon which it acted.

Though Maurice owed much to the young art-student, he soon owed more to that gentle but potent hand by which Ronald had been moulded, refined, and spiritualized. Ronald's mother opened wide her large heart and her loving arms to take in the motherless youth thrown by an apparent accident within her sphere.

Mrs. Walton was one of those beings to whom life is a poem, read it in sorrow or gladness, read it whatever way you will, because all things to her mind had a divine significance ; she knew that nothing had either its *end* or *origin* here, and felt that the very day-dreams and aspirations of impulsive youth descended by influx from those supernal regions in which all *causes* exist, though we darkly behold them through *effects* ultimated upon our earthly plane. Her eyes were never bent upon the ground, to search out stumbling-blocks of doubt, but looked up Godward until the heavens grew less distant, and earth's perplexing mysteries were solved; and daily joys and daily pains only acquired importance through their bearing upon the joys and pains of eternity ; and celestial light, flowing through her pure thoughts, reflected its mellow glory upon her humblest surroundings, and tinged them with ineffable beauty.

Maurice, who had been so deeply impressed by Ronald's attributes and aims, quickly recognized the fountain-head from whence flowed the living waters he had drank, and, humbly bending to quaff at the same stream, became conscious that his whole being was vitalized and renewed. The great ends of existence, for the first time, became apparent to him ; and as he learned to look upon the present and temporal as only of moment through their effect upon the future and eternal, — as he renounced a senseless belief in the very names of *chance* and *accident*, and yielded to the conviction that the simplest as the gravest occurrences all tend to lay some stone in the great architectural edifice which every man is building for his own dwelling-place in the hereafter, — his trials, by some wondrous transmutation, wore a holy aspect, and gently into his unfolding spirit stole the comforting assurance that those very trials might be the fittest, the strongest, the *appointed* instruments to hew out the pathway he panted to tread, and carve for him a future which could never have been wrought by such tools as the velvety hands of prosperity hold in their feeble grasp.

The morbid melancholy into which Maurice had fallen, and which deepened with his vain pondering over the mysterious fate of Madeleine, rolled from his spirit before the breath of hope, — hope breathed through sunshine, from the lips of a woman whose sympathetic voice, tender looks, and quick comprehension of his emotions insensibly melted away reserve, and drew out all his confidence. He could talk to Mrs. Walton of Madeleine with an absence of *reticence,* an unchecked gush of feeling, which would not have been possible when he conversed with Ronald, or with any one but a woman, *and such a woman.*

Far from advising him, as a worldly-wise counsellor would have done, to struggle against a passion which did not promise to prove fortunate, she bade him cherish the image of the one he so ardently loved with perfect trust, that if that woman were indeed his *other self,* — that *separate half* which makes man's full complement, — he would, in spite of all adverse circumstances, be drawn to her, by mysterious and invisible cords, until their union was consummated.

Mrs. Walton entertained the not irrational belief that as " either sex alone is *half* itself," and " each fulfils defects in each," there was created for every male soul some feminine spirit, whose heart was capable of responding to the finest pulses of his; one who could meet his largest requirements; one who could alone render his being perfect, his true manhood complete; one whom he might never meet on earth, and yet who lived for him. This great truth (for as such he accepted it) was a glorious revelation to Maurice. He cast out the remembrance that Madeleine had said she loved another, or only recalled her declaration to feel certain that she had mistaken her own heart, or that he had misconstrued the language she had used. She became more vividly present than ever to his mind, and the constant thought that now confidently and happily wound itself about her seemed to him to annihilate material distances and bring their spirits into close communion.

Maurice passed two delightful months beneath the hospitable roof of Mr. and Mrs. Walton. The period which Ronald had allowed himself for a holiday drew to a close. The sense of unoccupied power had begun to render him restless, and it was with elation which might have appeared tinctured with ingratitude by those who did not comprehend the mysterious workings of his untranquil ambition, that he prepared for his return to that foreign land where he could enjoy advantages for the prosecution of his art-studies unattainable in a young country.

When Maurice embarked for America with Ronald, it was understood that they were to return to Europe together; but one morning, when the latter casually announced his intention of securing their passage on board of a steamer about to sail from New York, Maurice turned to him and said abruptly, —

"Ronald, one berth will be sufficient."

"My dear fellow, what do you mean?" inquired Ronald, only half surprised.

"It is impossible for me," replied Maurice, "to return to my life of indolence and *supposed gayety.* A snake might more easily crawl back into his cast-off skin. I have breathed this free, exhilarating, vitalizing atmosphere, and the convention-laden air of Paris would stifle me. I have written to my father and announced that I propose remaining in Charleston. That is not all: he forbade my studying law in Paris, because his sapient Breton neighbors would have been scandalized by a viscount's taking so sensible a step; but possibly I may prepare myself for the bar at this distance, without subjecting my father to the annoyance of their disapproval. The period required for study is shorter, and I shall have a wider field in which to practise. I cannot be prepared to enter upon the duties of my profession much before the time when, according to the laws of France, I shall reach my majority; meanwhile I study, we will say, *for amusement.* I study as other men hunt, fish, boat, skate. What do you think of my plan?"

Ronald grasped him warmly by the hand.

"It is just what I expected of you, Maurice! When we first met, and I was so strongly attracted to you, an internal prescience whispered that you had within you the very qualities which are asserting their existence to-day."

"They might have been *in* me, Ronald," answered Maurice with emotion; "but I fear they would never have been brought *out* but for your agency. I never can be grateful enough that we have been thrown together! I never can sum up the good you have done me! I stood in such great need of just the influence you and your mother" — The voice of Maurice trembled, and he was unable to proceed.

Ronald broke the somewhat embarrassing silence by saying, —

"In short, you have come to the conclusion that my mother is right in her faith, and whatever we actually need for our spiritual advancement is invariably sent, if we will but preserve ourselves in a state of reception. All that you still lack will be supplied in the same way, if you can but believe."

"*I do believe,*" answered Maurice, in a tone of greater solemnity than the occasion seemed to demand; but there was a world of meaning in those three words. We should be obliged to employ many if we attempted to express a tithe of what he had recently learned to *believe* through the instrumentality of a noble thinker.

A week later, Ronald folded his mother to his throbbing heart, and tenderly bade her adieu ; but, without feeling that he should be parted from her by their material separation. Strange to say, his farewell to his father and Maurice was shadowed by a nearer approach to sadness and a more definite sense of sundering. Possibly their spirits had less power than his mother's to annihilate space and follow him-whithersoever he went.

Maurice was induced to linger a few days longer as the guest of his new friends, and his presence prevented the void left by the departure of a beloved and only son from being too keenly felt. At the commencement of a new week the young viscount removed to Charleston. That city was only a few miles distant from the residence of Ronald's parents. Mr. Walton had made his visitor acquainted with an eminent lawyer, who consented to receive Maurice de Gramont as a student.

Count Tristan at first violently opposed his son's step, but he could not, with any show of reason, forbid his studying law as a *pastime*. The count's affairs became more and more entangled, and he grew more desirous than ever that his son should contract a wealthy marriage. The hope that Maurice might woo and win one of those numerous heiresses, who, Frenchmen imagine, abound in the Southern El Dorado, alone reconciled the haughty nobleman to his son's sojourn in America.

CHAPTER XIX.

THE ARISTOCRATS IN AMERICA.

WHILE Maurice was applying himself to study with a zeal and sense of enjoyment wholly new to him, Bertha was passing through various stages of ennui, and testing the patience, or rather the digestive powers, of that sorely discomforted *bon vivant*, her uncle. Day after day she grew more capricious, unreasonable, unmanageable.

The distressed marquis came to the conclusion that his disturbed animal economy could only be restored by an amicable separation from his niece. But in vain he bestowed his smiles, and his *dinners*, upon the multitudinous suitors by whom the young heiress was besieged; her autocratic decree condemned him to the cruel duty of closing the sumptuous repasts by the *dessert* of a dismissal to each lover in turn, without extending to any the faintest hope that his sentence might be reversed. Finally the marquis became a confirmed dyspeptic; the joy of his life was quenched when his appetite failed, beyond the resuscitating influence of *absenthe* and other fashionable stimulants; the glory of his festive board had departed, and he was haunted by the conviction that the unnatural conduct of his niece would bring his whitening hairs, through sorrow and indigestion, to the grave.

A small but dearly prized respite from his trials was granted him when Bertha paid her yearly visit, of four months, to her relatives in Brittany. Her stay, however, was never extended beyond the wonted period, for she found her sojourn at the Château de Gramont unmitigatedly dull. The reception of letters from Maurice, addressed to his father, alone relieved the tediousness of the hours; but these welcome messengers were infrequent, brief, and somewhat cold. They left Bertha so unsatisfied that before the close of the first year of her cousin's absence she opened a correspondence with him herself. The initiative letter was suggested by pleasant tidings, which she hastened to send. It was written immediately after the eighteenth anniversary of her birthday, and communicated the agreeable intelligence that upon that day she had again received a token of remembrance from their beloved Madeleine.

A yearly gift, bearing the impress of those "fairy fingers," was the only sign Madeleine gave that she lived and remembered.

Three years passed on, and upon each birthday, wherever Bertha chanced to be, in Bordeaux, in Paris, in Brittany, a small parcel was mysteriously left with the *concierge* of the house where she was residing. The package was always addressed in Madeleine's handwriting, and contained some exquisite piece of needle-work, but no letter, and it bore no mark of post or express. It was invariably delivered by private hand. At least, it rendered certain the consolatory facts, not only that Bertha was unforgotten, but that Madeleine was cognizant of all her movements.

No sooner had the heiress reached her majority than she prepared to carry into execution a plan which for a long period had been silently forming itself in her mind. Her earnest desire to visit America had been secretly, but systematically, strengthened by Count Tristan. He well knew that the Marquis de Merrivale would never be induced to become her escort; and, what was more likely than that she should seek the countenance and protection of her other relatives?

He played his cards so adroitly that Bertha, without once suspecting his machinations, wrote to him, on the very day that closed her twenty-first year, and invited the countess and himself to accompany her upon an American tour. She took care delicately to make a stipulation that the expenses of the projected trip should devolve upon her. The count concealed his exultation under an air of well-acted reluctance, and required much persuasion before he could be taught to look with favor upon this *unexpected* and *sudden* proposition.

There was no simulation in the dismay, the horror with which Bertha's proposal was greeted by the countess. How was she to breathe in a land where hereditary claims to rank were unknown?—where distinctions of *brains* not *blood* were alone recognized?—where a man might rise to the highest position, as ruler of the realm, though his father chanced to be a mechanic, and his grandfather's existence was untraceable? For a time, Bertha's entreaties and the count's representations were equally impotent; the countess was inexorable. But her son was not to be baffled; he found an avenue through which her heart could be reached, and her resolution undermined. It lay in the suggestion that Bertha's strong inclination to visit America sprang from a desire again to behold Maurice, and that the result of their meeting, after so long a separation, might be in the highest degree felicitous. Bertha, he urged, during the absence of Maurice, had probably learned that he was dearer to her than she imagined; and, if Maurice had reason to believe that she crossed the ocean for the sake of rejoining him, could he remain insensible to such a proof of devotion? The countess bowed her haughty head to a sacrifice which vitally compromised her dignity.

One of the objects of the count's visit to America was to learn something further of the railroad company with which he was connected. For a time its operations had been suspended, owing to a financial crisis,— a sort of periodical American epidemic that, like cholera, sweeps over the land at intervals, making frightful ravage for a season, and departing as mysteriously as it came. The elastic nation, never long prostrate, had risen out of temporary difficulties and depression with a sudden bound, and prosperity walked in the very footprints of the late destroyer.

Mr. Hilson had lately announced to Count Tristan that the

16

railway association was again in full activity, and that the mooted
question of the direction which the road ought to take would, ere
long, be decided. He added that, according to his judgment, the
left road was indubitably the more desirable. Should that road
be chosen, it would pass through the property owned by the Viscount de Gramont. We have already alluded to the immense
difference in the value of the estate which the advent of the railroad would insure.

Bertha had no difficulty in obtaining the Marquis de Merrivale's approval of the contemplated trip.

Early in the spring the party embarked upon one of those
superb steamers that sweep across the ocean like floating cities,
pulsating with multitudinous life.

The passage was so smooth that Bertha thoroughly enjoyed the
strange, new existence, and found such ever-varying beauty in
the gorgeous sunsets, and the resplendent moonlight, that she
even forsook her berth to see "Aurora draw aside her crimson
curtain of the dawn;" in short she was in an appreciating mood
throughout the voyage, and her happy state allowed her to ignore
all the *désagreméns* of the sea. The countess also, as she sat
upon the deck in a comfortable arm-chair, — which she occupied
as though it were a throne, and received the homage of fellow-
passengers, who were obviously struck and awed by her majestic deportment, — pronounced the transit more endurable than
she anticipated.

Maurice had gone to New York to welcome the voyagers, and
when the steamer neared the land he was the first person who
bounded upon the deck. Bertha caught sight of him, and as she
sprang forward and threw herself into his arms, weeping with joy
and heartily returning his warm embrace, the countess and her
son exchanged looks of exultation which showed that they had
not reflected upon the vast distinction between the frank greeting
of brother and sister, and the meeting of possible lovers.

A slight, irrepressible shadow passed over the beaming countenance of Maurice as he turned from Bertha to welcome his
father and grandmother. The cloud flitted by in an instant,
and only betrayed that the past was unforgotten ; while the look
of manly confidence and self-possession, by which it was replaced,
told that the present and the future could not be subject to by-
gone storms.

After the first salutations were over, the countess scanned
Maurice from head to foot, to note what changes had been
wrought by his residence in a country which she held in such

supreme contempt. The slight curl and quivering of the lip, which accompanied her survey, bespoke that it was not entirely satisfactory. In the first place, his apparel displeased her. The care that he had once bestowed upon his toilet betrayed a slight leaning to the side of foppishness ; *now*, his attire gave him the air of a man of business, rather than of mere pleasure. His bearing was more confident than in former days, his movements more rapid, his tone more animated and decisive, his whole manner more energetic. His face was slightly careworn, his brow had lost something of its unruffled smoothness, and the fresh carnation tints had faded out of his complexion ; but the wealth of expression his countenance had gained might atone for heavier losses. In repose, his features wore a shade of habitual sadness ; but that disappeared the moment he spoke, and was rather an air of reflection than of sorrow. Indeed, all gloom had vanished from his spirit soon after his arrival in America. The hope-inspiring ministry of Ronald's mother, first and engrossing study, and ceaseless occupation next, had effectually medicined his growing melancholy. Maurice had not felt himself a homeless exile during his four years' sojourn in a foreign land. The Château de Gramont was less dear to him than the quiet, unpretentious, but affection-brightened home where he was always welcomed as a son.

When his stately grandmother, after so long a separation, once more appeared before him, the cold dignity, repelling hardness, and self-venerating pride of her demeanor struck him all the more painfully because it conjured up, in contrast, a vision of soft humility, — the gentle strength, the intellectual power, the refined tenderness of the lovely woman who realized his ideal of maternity.

It almost seemed as though the countess had some internal perception that Maurice weighed her in the balance of a new judgment, and found her wanting ; for she shrank beneath his gaze, and turned from him with a sense of sickening disappointment.

Bertha, while she was struck by the marked alteration in Maurice, noted the change with undisguised admiration. To *her* eyes he was a thousand times more attractive than ever, and she told him so without a shadow of bashful hesitation.

The young French demoiselle had made up her mind to be charmed with America, and little is required to satisfy those who are determined to be pleased. How much of her enthusiasm was legitimately excited, and how much was the spontaneous kindling of her own bright spirit, we will not attempt to describe. Be it enough to say, that she frequently declared her most sanguine expectations were far surpassed.

The countess, on the other hand, looked through a distorted medium which filled her with disgust. She was horrified at the publicity of hotel-life in New York. She could not tolerate the careless ease of the persons with whom she was thrown into accidental communication, — the confidence with which the very servants ventured to accost her. The absence of awe, the lack of head and knee bending, in her august presence, appeared a tacit insult. She was puzzled to reconcile the freedom with which she was constantly addressed with the great deference paid to her *sex*. While her *rank* was almost ignored, the mere fact of being *a woman* commanded an amount of consideration unsurpassed by the veneration paid to titled womanhood in her own land. Nothing, however, shocked her more than the liberty accorded to young American maidens. She found it impossible to comprehend that, educated as responsible beings, the strict *surveillance* over girlhood's most trivial actions, which is deemed indispensable in France, ceased to be a matter of necessity in America.

Immediately upon his arrival in New York the count had placed himself in communication with Mr. Hilson; and, a few days later, received a letter informing him that at a recent meeting of the managers of the —— —— Railway Association a committee of nine had been chosen to decide upon the most suitable direction of the new road. The committee was to give in its decision at the end of a fortnight. Mr. Hilson regretted to add that he feared the majority were in favor of the road to the *right.* He concluded by suggesting that it might be well for the count to visit Washington, and exert over members of the committee any influence, that he could command, to secure a majority of votes in favor of the road which would prove so advantageous to his son's property.

The count resolved to act at once upon Mr. Hilson's suggestion. When he proposed to his mother and Bertha that they should start the very next day for Washington, the countess, for the first time since her arrival, expressed herself gratified. At the seat of government she would meet the French ambassador and his wife (the Marquis and Marchioness de Fleury), and possibly, in the circle in which they moved, she might encounter foreigners with whom it would not be repugnant to associate

Bertha heard Count Tristan's announcement with such bright gleamings of the eyes, such happy flushings of the cheeks, that the sudden radiance which overspread her countenance set Maurice wondering over the emotions that caused her to so warmly welcome this unanticipated change of locality.

The revery into which he had fallen was broken by his father. The count launched into a discussion upon the management of property in America, then glided into the subject of the Maryland estate, and finally suggested that it would be advisable for his son to grant him a power of attorney which would place him in a situation to act as his representative in any case of emergency. Maurice unhesitatingly expressed his willingness to comply with this request, and the legal instrument was drawn up without delay. Upon receiving the document, the count assured his son that there was no probability that the power would be required, and voluntarily pledged himself not to make use of it without apprising Maurice.

Count Tristan's words and intentions were wholly at variance. His affairs in Brittany had become so frightfully entangled, that it was absolutely necessary for him to be able to command a considerable sum to redeem his credit; and he saw no means by which this desirable end could be obtained, except by a mortgage upon his son's estate. One of his strongest motives in visiting America was to effect this purpose; but he earnestly desired to conceal from Maurice the step he projected, trusting to his own skill in under-hand management for the smoothing away of difficulties before there was a necessity for explanation.

Maurice accompanied the count, his mother, and Bertha to Washington, and there bidding them adieu returned to Charleston.

His preparatory studies being now completed, he was received as junior partner by the gentleman who had initiated him into the mysteries of his profession.

It chanced that Mr. Lorrillard had large possessions in certain iron mines in Pennsylvania, which gave promise of yielding an immense profit. He had conceived a high esteem for the young viscount, and, with a view of promoting his interests, represented to him the advantage of purchasing a few shares, which could at that moment be favorably secured. Maurice had no funds at his command; but Mr. Lorrillard suggested that the viscount could easily procure the ten thousand dollars needful by a mortgage upon his Maryland estate, and even offered to give him a letter to Mr. Emerson, — a personal friend residing in Wash-

16 *

ington, — who, as the estate was wholly unembarrassed, would willingly loan the money upon this security. It was hardly possible for Maurice to have resided so long in America without being slightly bitten by the national mania for speculation, and he gladly accepted the offer of his principal, and retraced his steps to Washington.

CHAPTER XX.

THE INCOGNITA.

MAURICE arrived in Washington without having apprised his father of his purposed visit. Count Tristan received him with ill-concealed embarrassment ; but the young viscount was too ingenuous himself, and therefore too unsuspicious of others, for him to attribute his father's discomposure to any source but surprise at his unexpected appearance. If Maurice noted an absence of pleasure in the count's constrained greeting, he was too much accustomed to the formal and undemonstrative manners of the aristocracy to dwell upon the lack of warmth.

The count had taken up his residence at Brown's hotel. He chanced to be sitting alone when his son was ushered into the drawing-room. The opportunity was a favorable one for Maurice to communicate to his father the object of his visit.

After the first salutations were over, he inquired, rather abruptly, " Have you seen Mr. Hilson? What does he say in regard to the probabilities that the railroad will take the direction which we so much desire ? "

" Our prospects are tolerably good," returned the count ; " but we need to exert ourselves, and, possibly, you may be of service. The committee that has the decision in its hands consists of nine persons. Out of these, four have declared their preference for the road to the right, and are immovable. Our friends, Meredith and Hilson, who are on the committee, vote, of course, for the left road ; then there are two rival bankers, Mr. Gobert and Mr. Gilmer, who are bitterly opposed to each other, and generally vote in opposition one to the other ; we must bring some agency into play which will induce them, for once, to vote alike."

"That seems indispensable; but is it possible?" questioned Maurice.

"I trust so. Mr. Gobert is the banker of the Marquis de Fleury, who exerts unbounded power over him. One word from the marquis, and Gobert's vote is secured. The marquis, as every one is aware, can always be approached through Madame de Fleury. Obtain *her* promise that we shall have Mr. Gobert's vote, and it is ours! The marchioness, I fear, may not have forgiven Bertha's rejection of her brother's suit; but, as both parties are still unmarried and unengaged, if she can only be convinced that Bertha's refusal was mere girlish caprice, and that there is still hope of the young duke's success, she will be ready enough to serve us."

"But is there hope?" inquired Maurice, quite innocently.

The wily schemer replied by a glance half-angry, half-contemptuous; but, without making any other answer, went on.

"The other banker, Mr. Gilmer, I am seeking the means to influence. I have no doubt that I shall find them. The ninth member of the committee is Mr. Rutledge, quite a young man, the only son and heir of a Washington millionnaire. I learn, from M. de Bois, that Rutledge is deeply enamored of the sister of Lord Linden."

"I beg pardon, but you have not yet told me who Lord Linden is; and it is so unusual to hear *lords* mentioned in this country that my ears are quite unattuned to the sound of a title."

Another hasty look from the count might have been interpreted into one of slight disgust. His son was far more Americanized than he could have desired. He went on, with increased haughtiness.

"The English ambassador to the United States married a sister of Lord Linden, and his lordship and a younger sister accompanied them to Washington. Mr. Rutledge aspires to the hand of this young lady, — so says M. de Bois, who is intimately acquainted with her brother. If she can be interested in our plans the vote of Mr. Rutledge is easily secured."

Maurice could not help laughing.

"It is, *in reality*, the votes of *women*, then, that are to determine the direction of this road? I ought hardly to be surprised at *that*; for, if they have feeble voices in other lands, they have very decided ones in America. But how is the young lady in question to be reached?"

"That is what I am pondering upon," resumed his father.

" I shall form some plan, you may be sure; and no time must be wasted in carrying it into execution. I have already ventured to touch upon the subject to Lord Linden, but have not said anything definite. It is a difficult affair to conduct delicately; yet the obtaining of these votes is of such vital importance that we must strain every nerve to secure them."

" Certainly, since it will more than treble the value of the property," observed Maurice, placidly. " By the by, I presume you have had no occasion to use the power of attorney which I gave you? Just at this moment it is very fortunate for me that the estate is wholly unencumbered."

The count grew ashy pale; but Maurice did not observe his change of color, nor mark the hesitating tone in which he replied, " Very fortunate, of course, — very fortunate, indeed ; " and then, looking at his watch, he added, " It is time for your grandmother and Bertha to return. Lord Linden and M. de Bois escorted them to the capitol. You must be impatient to see them."

" In regard to this property, Mr. Lorrillard informs me," resumed Maurice ; but the count interrupted him.

" A visit to Madame de Fleury is now the first step to be taken ; *there* you may be useful; you are such a decided favorite of hers, that your advocacy may be inestimable. Suppose you call at once, and learn at what hour she will receive your grandmother, Bertha, and myself. A visit from you will open the way."

" I will call with pleasure," answered Maurice. " I have a letter from Mr. Lorrillard to his friend Mr. Emerson, which I should like to deliver without delay. It is a matter of business. Mr. Lorrillard thinks that, as my estate is wholly unencumbered " —

" We can talk of that at another time," replied the count, hurriedly. " Suppose you pay your visit to the marchioness at once. It is hardly worth while waiting for the ladies; no one can tell when they may return."

Maurice, though he could not interpret the count's singular manner, could not even remotely divine the meaning of its abruptness and confusion, felt himself checked in his proposed communication. He experienced no uneasiness ; he had not the faintest conception that the count was dealing doubly with him, and that his very first act, on reaching Washington, had been to mortgage the estate of his son for so large amount that, but for the advent of the railroad, upon which he confidently calculated, the mortgage must prove ruinious to the interests of the land-holder.

Had Maurice been aware of this fact, he would not for a moment have contemplated delivering to Mr. Emerson Mr. Lorrillard's letter, in which it was distinctly stated that the property of the viscount was without lien.

Further discussion between the father and son was prevented by the entrance of the countess, accompanied by Lord Linden, and followed by Bertha and Gaston de Bois.

Maurice, as he saluted his grandmother, was gratified to observe that, albeit her air was by no means less stately, it was more satisfied and complacent. Though titled nobility had no native existence in the semi-civilized land, she rejoiced to find that it was sometimes *imported.* She had at last encountered an individual with whom she could associate without derogation. The French, as all the world knows, have a national antipathy towards the English ; but a nobleman, even though he chanced to be an Englishman, was hailed by the Countess de Gramont, upon American soil, as a God-send. Lord Linden was not aware of the compliment implied by the unwonted graciousness of her demeanor, and the tone of *almost* equality in which she addressed him.

Maurice comprehended the altered expression that softened his grandmother's countenance, but was struck and amazed by the wonderful radiance of Bertha's face. Her eyes shone as though a veritable sun lived behind those azure heavens, and almost annihilated their color by its brightness ; her lips were eloquent with a voiceless happiness they did not care to hide, yet could not speak ; the laughing dimples played perpetually about her softly suffused cheeks ; her elastic feet almost danced, so airy was their tread ; about her whole presence there was a buoyant glow that seemed to encompass her with an atmosphere of light and warmth.

She had not attempted to disguise her joy on again meeting Gaston de Bois ; and, though he had paid them repeated visits during their sojourn in Washington, there was always the same deepening of the hue upon Bertha's cheek ; the same flood of sunshine brightening over her face ; the same softening of the tones of her voice ; the same quickened rise and fall of her fair bosom when he approached.

And he, — did he not note these betraying indications of his own power? Did they strike no electric thrill through his rejoicing soul? If they did, he was too much bewildered by a happiness so unexpected to search out calmly the hidden meaning of these precious signs.

The change in the deportment and character of M. de Bois, which we described at its commencement, was now fully confirmed ; and though the blood still sprang too rapidly into his face, and his breathing grew labored with emotion, and his manner, especially in Bertha's presence, was slightly confused, it was the confusion of elation rather than embarrassment. The self-control he had acquired had almost overcome his propensity to stammer, and Bertha was unreasonable enough to half regret that she could no longer finish his sentences, and thus prove how instinctively she divined his thoughts.

Maurice greeted her, as was his cousinly wont after a separation, with a kiss on either cheek ; but, for the first time, she shrank from his touch, and her ingenuous eyes involuntarily glanced toward Gaston, then were quickly cast down ; and the mutinous ringlets that had, as usual, escaped from bondage, were a welcome veil, as they fell over her face.

" Why, little Bertha, has an absence of four years made you forget that we are cousins ? " asked Maurice, in surprise at her manner.

" No — no," she answered, shaking back the curls, and looking up brightly in his face; " and I am rejoiced that you have come to Washington : it is a delightful place ; I am charmed with everything I see."

Did Bertha reflect how much the charm of a locality depends upon our own internal condition? Was she aware that any place, however tame and dull, becomes delightful through the presence of one who creates in us a state receptive of enjoyment?

Maurice expressed his intention of calling upon Madame de Fleury ; Lord Linden and M. de Bois proposed to accompany him. The three gentlemen took their departure together. But soon after they left the hotel, Maurice changed his mind ; and, telling his companions that he had some business to transact which required immediate attention, apologized for leaving them, adding that he would call upon Madame de Fleury an hour later, and hoped he might have the pleasure of meeting them there.

M. de Bois proposed to Lord Linden that they, also, should postpone their visit.

. " As you please," answered his lordship, languidly. " I am perfectly at leisure. I will go wherever you are going, — it does not matter where ; I am indifferent to place."

Lord Linden always *was* at leisure, and always indifferent, and not unfrequently attached himself to Gaston de Bois, and seemed disposed to accompany him wherever he went.

His lordship was one of that vast race of *blasé* young noblemen whose opportunities of enjoyment had never been circumscribed, except by the absence of the capacity to enjoy, and who, as a natural sequence, were continually oppressed with a sense of satiety, enervated by the noonday sunshine of unbroken prosperity, and thoroughly weary of their own existence. When his brother-in-law had been appointed ambassador to America, he had accompanied him to the United States with a vague idea that he would be thrown in contact with warlike tribes of Indians, the aborigines of the soil, whose novel and barbarous usages might afford him some mediocre measure of excitement. We need hardly picture his disappointment.

The ambassadors from foreign courts and their suites were as a matter of course, thrown into constant communication with each other, and the secretary of the French ambassador and the brother-in-law of the English formed an acquaintance which ripened into an approach to intimacy. There was no particular affinity between them, but Lord Linden liked M. de Bois's society because he was a patient listener, and Lord Linden was the opposite to taciturn; and Gaston, though he sometimes, as in the present instance, felt his lordship an encumbrance, had too often been a victim to ennui not to sympathize with a fellow-sufferer.

"Mademoiselle de Merrivale has a remarkably attractive face," said Lord Linden. "I do not particularly fancy blondes; there is too much milk-and-water and crushed rose-leaves in their general make-up; but, if a blonde could, to my eyes, enter the charmed circle of the positively beautiful, I would give her admission."

Gaston, who had fallen into a pleasant revery, was quickly roused by this observation, and exclaimed, with an indignant intonation, "Not admit a *blonde* into the circle of the beautiful? Can anything be lovelier than the countenance you have just looked upon?"

"Yes," replied the nobleman, musing in his turn.

"I think I could show you a face that would make Mademoiselle de Merrivale's sink into the most utter insignificance."

"Is your beauty a Washington belle?" inquired Gaston, half-scornfully.

"I do not know, — I do not know anything about her. I merely spoke figuratively when I said *I could show you,* — for I certainly could *not,* at this moment; but I allude to the most peerless being that ever captivated the eyes of man. In her, indeed, one could realize the poet's thought, —

"'All beauty compassed in a female form.'"

"And who is this incomparable divinity?" asked Gaston, still with a touch of sarcasm in his voice.

"Who is she? That is more than I know myself. We were thrown together by an accident, — quite an every-day occurrence in this headlong-rushing, pell-mell, neck-breaking land, where the people contemplate railroad catastrophes and steamboat explosions with as cool indifference as though they were a necessary part of a traveller's programme."

"You were thrown in contact with your beauty, then, by a railroad collision, or were blown together through the bursting of a boiler?" remarked Gaston interrogatively, and more because civility seemed to demand the question than because he took any especial interest in the narrative.

"Yes, quite a stirring incident. I felt alive for a month after. I was travelling from New York to Washington, in such a listless and used-up state that, in my desperation, I seriously pondered upon the amount of emotion that could be derived from jumping off the train, at the risk of one's neck. As I was glancing restlessly around, suddenly a face rose before me that riveted my eyes. It was a countenance unlike any I had ever seen. Though features and outline were faultless, in these the least part of its beauty was embodied. There was an eloquence in the rapid transitions of expression that melted one into another; there was a dreamy thoughtfulness in the magnificent hazel eyes. They were not exactly hazel either, — they reminded one of a topaz. I hardly know what name to give to their hue. But it is useless to attempt to describe such a face and form. I might heap epithet upon epithet, and then leave you without the faintest conception of the bewildering loveliness of their possessor."

"You succeeded in becoming acquainted with the lady?" inquired Gaston, now really interested.

"That good fortune was brought about by one of those ill winds, which, for the proverb's sake, must blow good to some one. It could not have been accomplished by any effort of my own, for there was an air of quiet dignity about the lady that no gentleman could have ventured to ruffle by too marked observation, far less by presuming to address even a passing remark. We were about half way between Philadelphia and Baltimore, when suddenly a terrific shock was felt, followed by a dashing of all humanity to one side of the cars, and a great crash. We had run into another train, were thrown off the track, and, in a moment more, upset."

"Since you were longing for excitement," observed Gaston, "this agreeable little variety must have gratified you."

"Yes, it was well enough in its way, not being positively fatal to existence. You may conceive the confusion and the difficulty of getting upon one's feet. How the people scrambled out of the cars I do not exactly know; for a short time I was too much stunned to see anything distinctly. I remember nothing clearly until somebody helped me up, and, in trying to move my left arm, I discovered that it was broken."

"How unfortunate! And you lost sight of the lady?"

"It would have been unfortunate if I *had* lost sight of her; but I did not. The passengers were huddled together in a most primitive inn by the road-side. There I beheld her, moving about, quite unharmed, quieting a child here, assisting a young mother there, doing something helpful everywhere. There chanced to be a surgeon in the cars, who, happily, was uninjured. He saw my predicament, for I was suffering confoundedly, and, upon examining my arm, said that it must be set at once. He called upon several persons to aid him. Some were too much occupied with their own distress; some too bewildered; and some shrank from the task. But, to my supreme joy (it was worth breaking an arm for such a piece of good luck), the lady I just mentioned came forward, and offered her services! She tore my handkerchief and her own into bandages, produced needle and thread from her little travelling reticule, and sewed them together. She assisted the surgeon in the most skilful but the calmest manner. What could I do but express my gratitude? This was the opening to a conversation. We were detained several hours at the inn before a train arrived to take us on our journey. I had always detested these American cars, where all the travellers sit together in pairs; but now I rejoiced over them, for I managed to obtain a seat beside her. We conversed, without pause, during the whole way to Washington; and what propriety and good sense she evinced! Her beauty had deeply impressed me, but her conversation struck me even more. Such elevated thoughts dropped spontaneously from her lips, and so naturally, that she did not seem to be aware that there was anything peculiar about them. It was enough to drive a man distracted; I confess that it did me!"

"She came to Washington then?"

"Yes; and here we were forced to part. I begged that she would allow me the privilege of calling to thank her. In the most suave, lady-like, but resolute manner, — a manner that silenced all pleading, — she declined. But she had inadvertently admitted that she resided in Washington. *That* has kept me here ever since. I have been searching for her these six months."

" And you have never met her again ? "

" No, I have sought her in the highest circles ; for, from her distinguished and even aristocratic air, her exceeding cultivation and good-breeding, I infer that she is a person of standing. It was somewhat singular that a lady of her unmistakable stamp should have been travelling alone ; but that is not unusual in this country. In spite of all my efforts, I have never been able to encounter her again. I examined the strips of the fine cambric handkerchief with which my arm was bound, hoping to find a name. Upon one strip the letter 'M' was daintily embroidered. I have those strips yet carefully preserved."

" Do you think she was an American lady ? "

" No, assuredly not. Though she spoke the English language very purely, and as only a scholar could have conversed, a slight accent betrayed that she was a foreigner; French, or Italian, I imagine. If I could only behold her once again, I should not be so miserably tired of everything and so bored by my own existence. Washington is killingly dull. By the way, the de Fleurys give a grand ball on Monday. I hear that there is great anxiety prevalent in the *beau monde* on the score of invitations. Of course, Mademoiselle de Merrivale will be there. Her face must create a sensation. What a piece of good fortune it would be if I could see it, at this very ball, contrasted with that of my lovely incognita ! *There* is a day-dream for you ! I never attend a ball, or any large assembly, without a vague anticipation of finding her in the crowd. I should like to hear *your* candid opinion if you saw those two faces placed side by side."

The response which Gaston made to this remark, and which expressed certain convictions of his own, was not uttered aloud.

It is one of love's happy prerogatives that the countenance best beloved gains to the lover's eye a charm beyond that with which any other face is endowed, even when he is forced to admit *that* dearest visage is surpassed in point of positive, calculable, tangible beauty.

> " A man may love a woman perfectly,
> And yet by no means ignorantly maintain
> A thousand women have not larger eyes :
> Enough that she alone has looked at him
> With eyes that, large or small, have won his soul."

CHAPTER XXI.

THE CYTHEREA OF FASHION.

MAURICE had so unceremoniously parted from Lord Linden and M. de Bois because he suddenly remembered that Mr. Lorrillard had impressed upon him the necessity of making his arrangements with Mr. Emerson without delay, as the present was a peculiarly favorable moment for purchasing shares in the mines whose iron he hoped to convert to gold.

The viscount presented himself at Mr. Emerson's office, and delivered Mr. Lorrillard's letter. This latter gentleman was held in such high esteem that an introduction of his was certain of meeting with the utmost consideration. Mr. Emerson, after only a brief conversation with Maurice, informed him that he was ready to make the desired loan upon the security offered, and begged that he would call the next morning, when the necessary formalities would at once be gone through.

Gratified by his visit and elated by the prospect of effecting a business transaction of so much importance, never dreaming of the fatal sequence which might be the result, Maurice drove to the residence of the French ambassador. It was not Madame de Fleury's reception-day, but by some mistake he was ushered into her drawing-room. In a few minutes, Lurline, a confidential *femme de chambre*, whom Maurice had often seen in Paris, — a being all fluttering ribbons and alluring smiles and graceful courtesies and coquettish airs, — made her appearance.

"Madame has received the card of monsieur *le vicomte*," she began, with a sugary accent and soft manner, which reminded one strongly of the tones and deportment of her mistress. "Madame would not treat monsieur as a stranger, and therefore sent *me*," — here, with her head on one side, she courtesied again, bewitchingly, — "to say that we have a new valet, — an ignorant fellow, for it is impossible to procure a decent domestic in America, — and this untrained creature has to be drilled into *les usages:* he has forgotten that madame only receives on Saturday. Madame, however, would see *M. le vicomte* at any time that was possible."

"I am delighted to hear you say so," returned Maurice, "for I am very desirous of having the pleasure of paying my respects."

"Madame is preparing for a *matinée,* at the Spanish Embassy. She is just *coiffé,* and monsieur should see what a magnificent head I have made for her. Notwithstanding my success with her head she is at this moment in deep distress: her dress has not yet arrived; we expect it every moment! Madame's agitation is overpowering. She is quite unequal to encountering a disappointment of this crushing nature. She begs monsieur will excuse " —

Before she could finish the sentence, the marchioness herself appeared, wrapped in a delicate, rose-colored *robe-de-chambre,* prodigally adorned with lace and embroidery.

"My dear M. de Gramont, I meant to excuse myself; but as I am forced to wait for that tantalizing dress, a few moments with you, *en attendant,* will divert my thoughts. I had heard from M. de Bois, that the Countess de Gramont and her son, with Mademoiselle de Merrivale, are honoring Washington by their presence; but I was informed that *you* were not here. You see I paid you the compliment of inquiring."

As she spoke, she glanced at the mirror opposite, and arranged the long sprays of feathery flowers that were mingled with her braided tresses.

"I am highly flattered at not being forgotten," replied Maurice. "I only arrived this morning, and hastened to pay my respects."

"And you ought to be very much flattered that I can spare you an instant, at such a critical moment. Here is my toilet for this *matinée* at a dead stand-still, because that tiresome dress has not come. It is one I ordered expressly for the occasion, and, I assure you, it is a perfect triumph of art, — a victory gained over great obstacles. Let me tell you, nothing is more difficult to manage than an appropriate costume for a *matinée.* One's toilet must be a delicate compromise between ball attire and full visiting dress, but Mademoiselle Melanie has hit the *juste milieu,* and succeeded in carrying me through all the perils of Scylla and Charybdis. Oh, dear! oh, dear!" (stamping her tiny slippered foot) "will that dress never come?"

"It must be very trying!" said Maurice, endeavoring to assume a tone of sympathy.

"Trying? it is *killing!* Imagine my state of mind. I cannot go *without* this dress: all my other toilets have been seen more than once in public; and this one was sure to create a sensation, — was planned for this very occasion!"

"I fear my visit is inopportune, and ought to be shortened," replied Maurice, for the agitated manner and troubled look of Madame de Fleury made him feel that he must be an intruder. "I will only remain long enough to know if you will receive my grandmother, my father, and my cousin, Mademoiselle Bertha, to-morrow; they are very"—

"Hush!" cried Madame de Fleury, raising her finger and listening with an eager countenance. "Was that not a ring? Patrick is opening the door. Hush! let me listen! It is the dress,—it must be the dress!" and she made several rapid steps toward the door, but returned to her seat as the servant passed through the entry with empty hands. "This is terrible! I have not my wits about me; I do not know what I am doing or saying!"

"I am truly concerned," observed Maurice, who had risen to depart. "May I tell the Countess de Gramont that you will receive her to-morrow?"

"To-morrow? Yes, certainly. I do not remember any engagement, but I can think of nothing at this moment. If that tormenting dress would only arrive! I fear it will never be here! It is the first time Mademoiselle Melanie ever disappointed me; she is punctuality itself. This waiting is torture, and completely upsets me,—turns my brain; it will throw me into a nervous fever. You, insensible men, cannot feel for such a position; you do not know the importance of a toilet."

"We must be very dull if we do not know how to appreciate those of Madame de Fleury," replied Maurice, bowing courteously. "Pray, do not include me in the catalogue of such sightless individuals. I will bid you adieu until to-morrow, when you will allow me to accompany my grandmother?"

"You are always welcome. Pray tell the countess I shall be charmed to see her, and say the same to that cruel Mademoiselle Bertha,—though I ought not to forgive her treatment of my brother. Say to her that he is yet unconsoled. Good gracious! That dress certainly is not coming! If it were to arrive at this moment I should be obliged to hasten; and to give the *finishing* touches to a toilet in a hurried and discomposed manner is 'to run the risk of spoiling the general effect. What *can* have happened to Mademoiselle Melanie? Hark! is not that some one? Did you not hear a ring? I am not mistaken; some one *did* come in. It is the dress at last!"

The marchioness started up joyfully, with clasped hands, and an expression of deep gratitude. A servant entered with a note; she snatched it petulantly and tossed it into the card-basket unopened.

"How vexatious! Only a note! It is *too* cruel! I shall never, never pardon Mademoiselle Melanie if she disappoints me. But that's easy enough to say, difficult enough to carry into execution. In reality I could not exist without her; and Mademoiselle Melanie knows *that* as well as I do. She is so sought after that her exhibition-rooms are crowded from morning until night. It is now a favor for her to receive any new customers, and I believe she has some thirty or forty work-women in her employment. Of course, you have heard of Mademoiselle Melanie?"

"I have not had that pleasure; she is a mantua-maker, I presume," returned Maurice, repressing a smile.

"I suppose that is what, strictly speaking, we must call her; but she is the very Queen of Taste, the Sovereign of Modistes. She has a genius that is extraordinary, — it is magic, — it is inspiration! A touch of her hand transforms every one who approaches her. What figures she has made for some of these American women! What charms she has developed in them! What an air and grace she has imparted to their whole appearance! She makes the most vulgar look elegant, and the elegant, divine! Another ring. Now Heaven grant it may be the dress at last!"

The marchioness was again disappointed: it was only another note, which shared the fate of the former.

"Oh, I shall not survive this!" she ejaculated, dropping into an arm-chair; "and that horrid little Mrs. Gilmer will triumph in my absence. You know Mrs. Gilmer?"

"I have not that honor," returned Maurice, who, impatient as he was to take his leave, found it impossible to depart while the marchioness chose to detain him.

"She attempts to pass herself off for a belle, and even tries to take precedence of *me*, ignoring all the customs of good society; but, doubtless, the poor thing is actually ignorant of them, and should be pardoned and pitied for her ill-breeding. She is the wife of Gilmer, the rich banker. It is to Mademoiselle Melanie that she is indebted for all her social success. Mademoiselle Melanie positively *created* her, and she never wears anything made by any one else. It is all owing to Mademoiselle Melanie that the men surround her as they do, and try to persuade themselves that she is pretty. Pretty! with her turn-up nose, and colorless hair and eyes. Her husband is immensely rich; and, as wealth rules the day in this country, she takes good care that the depth of his purse shall be known; for that pur-

pose she loads herself with diamonds,— always diamonds. She
has not the least idea of varying her jewels; even Mademoiselle Melanie could not make her comprehend that art. I wonder she does not have a dress contrived of bank-notes! *That*
would be novel, and it would also prove a capital way of an-
nouncing her opulence!"

"A rather dangerous costume!" returned Maurice, laughing.

"At all events it would be original; and, as originality is sure
to produce an effect, the saucy little *parvenue* might afford to
follow my advice, even though it came from an enemy."

Maurice could not help exclaiming with a comical intonation,
— for there was something irresistibly ludicrous in the puny
fierceness of the dressed doll, — "An enemy!"

"Oh, there is no concealment about it!" exclaimed Madame
de Fleury with the air of a Liliputian belligerent. "It is open
warfare; we are at swords' points, and all the world knows our
animosity. And Mrs. Gilmer has the impertinence to pretend
that our *styles* are quite similar, and that the same modes become
us. She even declares that such has been Mademoiselle Melanie's verdict, and from the judgment of Mademoiselle Melanie
nobody dares to appeal."

"This Mademoiselle Melanie is a Parisian, I presume?"
asked Maurice, more because it seemed polite to say something,
than from any interest in the answer to his question.

"Could she be anything else?" replied Madame de Fleury,
with enthusiasm. "Could a being gifted with such wondrous
taste have been born out of Paris? She is a *protegée* of Vignon's; and, when I was exiled, Mademoiselle Melanie came to
America with me. She instantly became known. There is a Mr.
Hilson here, to whom she probably brought letters, for he has
taken the deepest interest in trumpeting her fame. She has created a perfect furor."

"Hilson?" repeated Maurice, musingly. "A gentleman of
that name visited Brittany before I left. I wonder if it can be
the same person."

"Very likely, for he has been abroad. I have heard him mention Brittany. Well, this Mr. Hilson was so infatuated with —
hush! That is a ring!"

While Madame de Fleury listened in breathless expectation,
Lurline opened the door and announced, "The dress of madame
has arrived!"

"Ah! at last! at last! What happiness! I am saved, when

I had almost given up all hope! Monsieur de Gramont, you will excuse me! *Au revoir!*"

Before Maurice could utter his congratulations upon the advent of the dress, she had glided out of the room.

CHAPTER XXII.

MEETING.

THE tangled web Count Tristan had woven for others began to fold its meshes around himself, and to torture him with the dread that he might be caught in his own snare. From the moment Maurice arrived in Washington, — an event the count had not anticipated, — his covert use of the authority entrusted to him was menaced with discovery. To a frank, straightforward character, the very natural alternative would have suggested itself of explaining, and, as far possible, justifying the step just taken; but to a mind so full of guile, so wedded to wily schemes as the count's, a simple, upright course would never have occurred. The fear of exposure threw him into a state of nervous irritability which allowed no rest, and he was compelled to pay the price of deception by plunging deeper into her labyrinths, though every step rendered extrication from the briery mazes more difficult.

On the morrow Maurice accompanied his grandmother, Bertha, and Count Tristan to the residence of the Marchioness de Fleury. Count Tristan's *malaise* evinced itself by his unusually fretful and preoccupied manner, his querulous tone, and a partial forgetfulness of those polite observances of which he was rarely oblivious. He allowed his mother to stand, looking at him in blind amazement, before he remembered to open the door; was very near passing out of the room before her, and scarcely recollected to hand her into the carriage. His abstraction was partially dissipated by her scornful comment upon the contagious influences of a plebeian country; but to recover himself entirely was out of the question.

On reaching the ambassador's mansion, the visitors were disconcerted by the information that Madame de Fleury "*did not receive.*"

"She will receive us!" answered Maurice, recovering himself. "We are here by appointment." And, passing the surprised domestic, he ushered his grandmother into the drawing-room. Bertha and Count Tristan followed.

The servant, with evident hesitation, took the cards that were handed to him, and retired. The door of the *salon* chanced to remain open, and rendered audible a whispered conversation going on in the entry.

"I dare not disturb madame at this moment; she would fly into a terrible rage. You know she never allows her toilet to be interrupted!"

These words, spoken in a female voice, reached the ears of the visitors.

"But the gentleman says it is an *appointment*. What's to be done? What am I to answer?" was the rejoinder in rough male tones.

"You are a blockhead, — you have no management," replied the first voice. "I will arrange the matter without your stupid interference."

Lurline now courtesied herself into the room, and, after bestowing an arch glance of recognition upon the viscount, addressed the countess.

"I am *desolée* to be obliged to inform madame that Madame de Fleury is at this moment so much absorbed by her toilet that I fear I shall have no opportunity of making known the honor of madame's visit. My mistress has made an engagement to go to the capitol to hear some distinguished orator. It is madame's *début* in spring attire this season. Madame's dress, bonnet, and mantle have this moment been sent home. A more delicately fresh toilet *de printemps* cannot be conceived; it will establish the fact that spring has arrived. But madame has not yet essayed her attire and assured herself of its effect. I trust *madame la comtesse* will deem this sufficient apology for not being received."

As she concluded, Lurline simpered and courtesied, and seemed confident that she had gracefully acquitted herself of a difficult duty.

"Not receive us when we are here by invitation?" ejaculated the countess, angrily. "Is Madame de Fleury aware that it is the Countess de Gramont and her family who are calling upon her?"

"There must be some mistake," interposed Maurice; then, turning to the *femme de chambre*, he added, "I beg that you will deliver these cards to the marchioness and bring me an answer."

" How am I to refuse monsieur? " replied Lurline, hesitating, yet softening her unwillingness to comply by a volley of sidelong glances. " Monsieur is not aware that he is placing me in a most delicate position. It is against madame's rules to be disturbed when her toilet is progressing : it requires her concentrated attention, — her whole mind ! Still, if monsieur insists, I will run the risk of madame's displeasure. Monsieur must only be kind enough to wait, and allow me to watch for a favorable moment when I can place these cards before madame."

With a low salutation, and a coquettish movement of the head that set all her ribbons fluttering, the *femme de chambre* made her exit.

" Not receive us ? Make us wait ? " exclaimed the countess, wrathfully; " truly, Madame de Fleury has profited by her sojourn among savages ! This is not to be endured ! Let us depart at once ! "

" My dear mother," began Count Tristan, soothingly, " it will not do to be offended, or to notice the slight, if there be one ; but, I am sure, none is intended. It is absolutely *indispensable* that I should see the countess, and get her to present this letter to the Marquis de Fleury, and also that I should obtain her promise that she will influence him to secure the vote of Mr. Gobert. Pray, be courteous to the marchioness when she makes her appearance, or all is lost."

" What degradation will you demand of me next? How can you suppose it possible that I can be courteous? I tell you I am furious ! "

" But you do not know all that depends upon obtaining these votes. Think of this railroad, — of the vital importance of the direction it takes ! Think of the Maryland property, which is almost all that is left to us "—

" Have I not again and again begged you not to meddle with railroads, — not to occupy yourself with business matters which a nobleman is bound to ignore ? "

" And by obeying you, as far as I could, and only acting in secret, I have nearly ruined myself," answered the count, with growing excitement.

At this moment the loud ringing of a bell was heard, accompanied by the voice of Lurline, speaking in tones of great tribulation.

" Patrick ! Patrick ! do you not hear the bell ? Come here quickly ! What's to be done ? Such a calamity ! It's dreadful ! dreadful ! "

Count Tristan started up, and went to the door to question the *femme de chambre,* fearing that the calamity in question might be of a nature sufficiently serious to prevent the much-desired interview.

Lurline was standing in the hall; she wore her hat and shawl, and was giving directions to a domestic in the most rapid and flurried manner.

"Will Madame de Fleury receive us?" inquired the count, anxiously.

"I told monsieur that I could not promise him, and, now that this misfortune has befallen us, it is thoroughly impossible even to make your presence here known to madame. Who could have anticipated such a *contretems?* Never before has Mademoiselle Melanie allowed a dress to issue from her hands which did not fit *à merveille,* and there are two important alterations to be made in this before it can be worn. Madame is in despair; she will go out of her senses; it will give her a brain fever!"

"Can we not have the pleasure of seeing her for a few moments, when her toilet is completed?" inquired Maurice.

"Ah, there it is! *When* her toilet is completed? Will it be completed in time for her to reach the senate at the hour proposed? Monsieur will pardon me, but I have not a moment to spare."

Turning to Patrick, she added, "I am forced to go out to purchase some ribbons. I have left madame in the hands of Antoinette. Madame is in such a state that one might weep to see her! Take care not to admit any one, except the Countess Orlowski, who accompanies your mistress to the senate. I will be back presently."

The Countess de Gramont rose up majestically.

"Let us depart, my son! Never more will I cross this threshold, — never enter this house where I have been insulted!"

"No insult was intended," replied Count Tristan, nervously. "Even if it were, we are not in a position to be cognizant of insults; we should be forced to ignore them. I cannot leave without entreating the marchioness to deliver this letter to Monsieur de Fleury, herself: it *must* be done, — and *to-day.* There is not an instant to lose."

"And you can stoop so low, — you can demean yourself to such a degree? What a humiliation!"

"Humiliations are not to be taken into consideration where *ruin* stares us in the face!" he answered, violently.

"Is it *so very important?*" inquired Bertha, struck by the count's angry manner.

"Of more importance than I can explain to you!"

"Oh, then let us stay, aunt! We must make allowances for Madame de Fleury's ruling passion. Her toilet first, all the world afterward!"

A carriage just then drove to the door, and attracted the attention of Bertha, who was standing by the open window.

"What magnificent horses! and what a neat equipage! All the appointments in such admirable taste! A lady is descending. I suppose it must be the Countess Orlowski. What a dignified air she has! What a graceful bearing! I wish I could see her face. She must be handsome with such a perfect figure. Yes,—I am right,—it *is* the Countess Orlowski, for the servant has admitted her."

As the lady was passing through the hall, she said to the domestic, "No, you need not announce me; I will go at once to the chamber of Madame de Fleury."

At the sound of that voice, the shriek of joy that broke from Bertha's lips drowned the amazed exclamation of Maurice. In another instant, Bertha's arms were around the stranger, and her kisses were mingled with tears and broken ejaculations, as she embraced her rapturously.

Maurice stood beside them, struggling with emotion that caused his manly frame to vibrate from head to foot, while his dilated eyes appeared spellbound by some familiar apparition which they hardly dared to believe was palpable.

There is a joy which, in its wild excess, paralyzes the faculties, makes dumb the voice, confuses the brain, until ecstasy becomes agony, and all the senses are enveloped in a cloud of doubt. Such was the joy of Maurice as he stood powerless, questioning the blissful reality of the hour, yet in the actual presence of that being who was never a moment absent from his mental vision.

"Madeleine! Madeleine! My own Madeleine! Have we found you at last? Is it really you?" sobbed Bertha, whose tears always flowed easily, but now poured in torrents from their blue heavens.

And Madeleine, as she passionately returned her cousin's embrace, dropped her head upon Bertha's shoulder, and wept also.

"Madeleine!"

At that tremulously tender voice her face was lifted and

turned toward Maurice,—turned for the first time for nearly five long years; and yet, at that moment, he felt as though it had never been turned away.

Bertha involuntarily loosened her arms, and Madeleine extended her hand to Maurice. He clasped it fervently, but his quivering lips gave forth no sound. One irrepressible look of perfect joy from Madeleine's luminous eyes had answered the impassioned gaze of his; one smile of ineffable gratitude played over her sweet lips. For an instant the eyes were raised heavenward, in mute thanksgiving, and then sought the ground, as though they feared to reveal too much; and the smile of transport changed to one of grave serenity, and the wonted quietude of her demeanor returned.

The countess and Count Tristan had both risen in speechless surprise, but had made no attempt to approach Madeleine, whom Bertha now drew into the room.

"Madeleine! I cannot believe that I am not dreaming," cried the latter; "I cannot believe that I have found you!—that it is really you! And you are lovelier than ever! You no longer look pale and careworn; you are happy, my own Madeleine,—you are happy,—are you not? But why have you forgotten us?"

"I have never forgotten—never—never *forgotten!*" faltered Madeleine, in a voice that had a sound of tears, answering to those that glittered in her eyes.

Maurice had not released her hand, and, bending over her, made an effort to speak; but at that moment the stern voice of the countess broke in harshly,—

"How is it that we find you here, Mademoiselle de Gramont? Where have you hidden yourself? What have you done since you fled from my protection?"

"Yes, what have you done?" chimed in Count Tristan. "How is it that we find you descending from a handsome equipage and elegantly attired?"

"I have done nothing for which I shall ever have to blush!" answered Madeleine, with a dignity which awed him into silence.

"It was needless to say *that*, dear Madeleine," cried Maurice, whose powers of utterance had returned when he saw Madeleine about to be assailed. "No one who knows you would *dare to believe* that you ever committed an action that demanded a blush."

Madeleine thanked him with her speaking countenance. Perhaps it was only fancy, but he thought he felt a light, grateful pressure of the hand he held.

18

" But tell us where you have been!" continued Bertha, affectionately. "You look differently, Madeleine, and yet the same; and how this rich attire becomes you! You are no longer poor and dependent then, — are you?"

" I am no longer poor, and no longer dependent!" answered Madeleine, in a tone of honest pride.

" Is it possible?" exclaimed the count and his mother together.

" But how has all this happened?" Bertha ran on. "Oh! I can divine: you are married, — you have made a brilliant marriage."

At those words a suppressed groan, of unutterable anguish, struck on Madeleine's ear; and the hand Maurice held dropped from his grasp.

" Speak! do speak! dear Madeleine!" continued Bertha. " Tell us all your sufferings, — for you must have suffered at first, — and all your joys, since you are happy now. And tell us how you chance to be here, — here in America, as we are; and how it happens that you are calling upon the Marchioness de Fleury, at the same time as ourselves; and why you expect to be received by her, though she will not receive us."

Before Madeleine could reply, and she was evidently collecting herself to speak, Lurline, who had just returned from executing her commission, passed through the hall. The door of the drawing-room stood open; she caught sight of Madeleine, and ran toward her, exclaiming joyfully, —

" Oh, what good fortune! How rejoiced my poor mistress will be! She did not dare to hope for this great kindness! I am so thankful! I will fly to announce to her the good news!"

She hurried away, leaving Madeleine's relatives more than ever amazed by these mysterious words.

Count Tristan was the first to break the silence. Ever keenly alive to his own interest, he saw a great advantage to be gained if he had interpreted the language of the *femme de chambre* rightly.

In an altered tone, a tone of marked consideration, he asked, " You are well acquainted with the Marchioness de Fleury?"

" *Very well!*" replied Madeleine, with an incomprehensible emphasis, while a smile that had a faint touch of satire flitted over her face.

" She receives you?" questioned the count.

" Always," answered Madeleine, smiling again.

" She esteems you?" persisted the count.

"I have every reason to believe that she does."

"And you have influence with her," joined in Bertha, suspecting the count's drift, and feeling desirous of aiding him.

" I think I may venture to say I have."

"Oh, how fortunate!" cried Bertha; "you may be of the greatest service to our cousin, Count Tristan." She took the letter out of his hand, and placing it in Madeleine's, added, " Beg Madame de Fleury to read this letter, and obtain her promise that she will use her influence with the Marquis de Fleury to cause Mr. Gobert, — Gobert, that's his name, is it not ? " appealing to the count, — " to cause Mr. Gobert to vote as herein instructed. See, how well I have explained that matter! I really believe I have an undeveloped talent for business."

" The letter should reach Madame de Fleury this morning. The appeal should be made to the marquis *to-day,* — *this very day!* " urged the count.

"It shall be ! " replied Madeleine, with quiet confidence.

The countess here interposed.

" What, my son, you are willing to solicit the interference of Mademoiselle de Gramont, without knowing how and where she has passed her time, how she has lived since she fled from the Chateau de Gramont? I refuse my consent to such a proceeding."

" Aunt, — madame," returned Madeleine, in a gently pleading voice, "do not deprive me of the pleasure of serving you. Humble and unworthy instrument that I am, leave me that happiness."

"If the marchioness would only grant me a few moments' interview this morning," said Count Tristan, who evidently doubted the strength of Madeleine's advocacy.

"I promise that she *will* grant you an interview this morning," replied Madeleine, interrupting him.

The *femme de chambre* now reëntered and said, " Madame is impatient at this delay ; every moment seems an hour."

" Say that I will be with her immediately," answered Madeleine. She then addressed the count: " Have no fears, — you may depend upon me ; the countess will receive you the moment her toilet is completed."

Madeleine once more embraced Bertha, once more extended her hand to Maurice, who stood bewildered, dismayed, looking half petrified, and passed out of the room.

As soon as she had disappeared, Bertha broke forth joyously, "Well, aunt, what do you think *now* of our Madeleine?

Is not this magic? Is not this a fairy-like *denouement?* She disappears from the Chateau de Gramont as though the earth had opened to swallow her; no trace of her could be discovered for nearly five years, and suddenly she rises up in our very midst, a grand lady, enveloped in a cloud of mystery, and working as many wonders as a veritable witch. She leaves us poor, friendless, dependent; she returns to us rich, powerful, and with influential friends ready to serve those who once protected her. But I think I have found the key to the enigma. Did we not hear strict orders given that none but the Countess Orlowski should be admitted? Well, Madeleine was at once allowed to enter : it follows, beyond doubt, that she is the Countess Orlowski."

This version of Madeleine's position seemed to strike both the countess and her son as not merely possibly, but probably, correct.

"I always thought," returned the count, "that Madeleine was a young person who, in the end "—

His mother finished the sentence, in a tone of pride, "would prove herself worthy of the family to which she belongs."

The loud ringing of the street door-bell attracted the attention of the group assembled in the drawing-room. A well-known voice exchanged a few words with the servant, and Gaston de Bois entered. His manner was unusually perturbed, and he looked around the room as though in search of some one.

The instant he appeared, Bertha exclaimed, "Oh, M. de Bois! M. de Bois! We are all so much rejoiced! Madeleine, our own Madeleine, is found at last! She is here, — here in this very house, at this very moment!"

"I—I—I knew it!" answered M. de Bois, with a mixture of embarrassment and exultation.

"You knew it? How could you have known it?" asked Maurice, eagerly.

"I saw her car—ar—arriage at the door."

"*Her* carriage? She has a carriage of her own, then?" inquired the count.

"Yes, and the most superb horses in Washington."

"You knew, then, that she was here?" cried Maurice, with emotion; "you knew it, and you never told us?"

"I knew it, but I was forbidden to tell you. I hoped you would meet; I felt sure you would. I did not know how or when; but, from the moment you put your foot in this city, I looked for this meeting. I was strongly impelled to bring it

"Of course, you could not break a promise; that explanation is quite satisfactory," remarked Bertha. "I am sure you would have given us a hint but for your promise."

"I almost gave one in spite of it. I found it harder to keep silent than I used to find it to speak; and that was difficult enough."

"But have the goodness to unravel to us this grand mystery," demanded the count. "Madeleine is married — married to Count Orlowski, the Russian ambassador."

"A nobleman of position!" added the countess.

"How did this come about?" inquired the count.

M. de Bois looked stupefied.

"Who — who — said she was married?" he gasped out. "Why do you imagine that she is mar — ar — arried?"

"She is *not* — *not* married then? *Say she is not!*" broke in Maurice, hanging upon the reply as though it were a sentence of life or death.

"No — no — not married at all — not in the least married."

Maurice did not answer, but the sound that issued from his lips almost resembled the sob of hysteric passion.

"Tell us quickly all about her!" besought Bertha, impatiently.

"Yes, speak! speak!" said the countess, imperiously.

"Speak!" echoed the count.

"Gaston, my dear friend, pray speak, — speak quickly!" Maurice besought.

"I wi — is — ish I could! That's just what I wa — an — ant to do! But it's not so easy, you bewil — il — ilder me so with questions. But the time has come when you must know that she has the hon — on — onor — the honor — the honor to be " —

"Go on, go on!" urged Maurice.

"I wish I could! It's not so easy to expla — plai — plain."

The rustling of a silk dress made him turn. The Marchioness de Fleury, in the most captivating spring attire, stood before them.

"Ah! here is Madame de Fleury, and she will tell you herself better than I can," said M. de Bois, apparently much relieved.

The marchioness saluted her guests with excessive cordiality, softly murmured her gratification at their visit, and added apologetically, —

"I must entreat your pardon for allowing you to wait; it

18 *

was not in my power to be be more punctual; a terrible accident — the first of the kind which has ever occurred to me — is my excuse. Do not imagine, my dear viscount," turning to Maurice with a fascinating smile, " that I had forgotten my appointment; but, at the Russian embassy, yesterday, I was prevailed upon to promise that I would be present at the senate to-day to hear the speech of a Vermont orator, a sort of Orson Demosthenes, who has gained great renown by his rude but stirring eloquence. We ladies have been promised admission (which is now and then granted) to the floor of the house, instead of being crammed into the close galleries. It will be a brilliant occasion. I invited the Countess Orlowski to accompany me. If all had gone well I should have been ready to receive your visit before she came."

The brow of the countess smoothed a little as she answered, "I felt confident, madame, that there must have been *some* explanation."

" Ah! I fear you are displeased with me," resumed Madame de Fleury, playfully. " But I will earn my pardon. You will be compelled to forgive me; M. de Fleury meets me at the capitol, and I will deliver this letter of the count's into his hand, and make him promise, blindfold, to consent to any request that it may contain."

" Madame," returned the count, bowing to the ground, " I shall never be able to express my gratitude. You can hardly form a conception of the favor you are conferring upon me. That letter is of the highest importance, and my indebtedness beggars all expression."

" To be frank with you, count," answered Madame de Fleury, " you owe me nothing. You are only indebted to the advocate you chose, — one whom I never refuse, — one to whom I feel under the deepest obligation, especially this morning, — one who is so modest that she can seldom be induced to ask me a favor, or to allow me to serve her. Thus, you see, it is but natural that I should seize with avidity upon this opportunity."

The count looked at his mother triumphantly; and, as the face of the marchioness was turned toward Bertha, he whispered, " Shall I not tell her that Madeleine is our niece?"

The countess seemed disposed to consent, for the words of Madame de Fleury had gratified as much as they astonished her.

The marchioness addressed the Countess de Gramont again. " I trust, madame, that you will allow me to waive ceremony, and take a liberty with you, since it is in the hope of being some

service. I should like to reach the capitol before the oration
commences; and, if this letter must be delivered to M. de
Fleury immediately, my going early will enable me to have a
few moments' conversation with him, which I probably shall not
get after the orator rises. Will you excuse me, if I tear myself
away? And will you give me the pleasure of your company to-
morrow evening? To-morrow is my reception-day, and some of
my friends honor me in the evening. I am *desolée* at this apparent want of courtesy, but I am sure you see the necessity."

The countess bowed her permission to Madame de Fleury's
departure, and the count overwhelmed her with thanks. The
countess would herself have taken leave, but anxiety to learn
something further of Madeleine, caused her to linger.

The marchioness now addressed her valet, who was standing
in the hall waiting orders.

"Patrick, when Madame Orlowski calls, beg her to pardon
my preceding her to the capitol ; say that I will reserve a
seat by my side."

"Then the lady who just visited you was *not* Madame Orlowski?" inquired the count, more puzzled than ever.

"No, indeed ; she is worth a thousand Madame Orlowski's!"

The count's glance at his mother seemed again to ask her permission to allow him to announce that Madeleine was their
relative.

"We felt certain that she was one of the magnates"— began
the count.

The marchioness interrupted him.

"She is better than that; she has all the magnates of the
land — that is the female magnates — at her feet. The foreign
ladies swear by her, rave about her; and, as for the Americans,
they are demented, and would gladly pave her path with gold, —
that being their way of expressing appreciation. Madame Ma-
nesca passes whole mornings with her, — Madame Poniatowski
talks of no one else. She enchants every one, and offends no
one. For myself, I have only one fault to find with her, — I
owe her only one grudge ; if it had not been for her aid, that impertinent little Mrs. Gilmer would not have had such success in
society. If I could succeed in making her close her doors against
Mrs. Gilmer, what a satisfaction it would be! Then, and then
only, should I be content!"

The count could restrain himself no longer.

"We are highly gratified to hear this, madame. It concerns
us more nearly than you are aware ; the lady is not wholly a
stranger to us ; in fact, she — she "—

"Indeed? she was so little known in Paris that you were fortunate in finding her out. I appreciated her there, but I did not know how much actual credit was due to her, for she had not then risen to her present distinction. I confess she is the one person in America without whom I could not exist."

" Is it possible?" exclaimed the countess.

" And I cannot be grateful enough to her," continued the marchioness, " for her visit this morning, for she never goes out, or, so seldom, that I did not dare to expect, to even *hope* for her presence; yet her conscientiousness made her come; she suspected that I was in difficulty, and hastened here."

"It is like her; she was always charming, and so thoughtful for others!" observed the count, as complacently as though this were an opinion he had been in the habit of expressing for years.

" You may well say charming," responded Madame de Fleury; "and what knowledge she possesses of all the requirements, the most subtle refinements of good society! What polished manners she has! What choice language she uses! What poetical expression she gives to her sentiments! I often forget myself when I am talking to her, and fancy that I am communicating with a person of the same standing as myself; and, without knowing what I am doing, I involuntarily treat her as an equal!"

"*An equal?*" Of course, most certainly!" answered the countess, aghast.

The amazement of the count, Maurice, and Bertha, sealed their lips.

"Her taste, her talent, her invention is something almost supernatural," continued the marchioness, enthusiastically; for, now that she was launched upon her favorite theme, she had forgotten her haste. "She sees at a glance all the good points of a figure; she knows how to bring them out strongly; she discovers by intuition what is lacking, and dexterously hides the defects. I have seen her convert the veriest dowdy into an elegant woman. And, when she gets a subject that pleases her, she perfectly revels in her art. Look at this dress for instance, — see by what delicate combinations it announces the spring."

The marchioness was struck with the consternation depicted in the countenances of her visitors.

Bertha was the only one who could command sufficient voice to falter out, "That dress, then" —

"It is her invention," replied the marchioness, triumphantly. "Any one would recognize it in a moment, as coming from the hands of Mademoiselle Melanie. Though she has such wonderful creative fertility, her style is unmistakable. There was never mantua-maker like her!"

"*A mantua-maker! a mantua-maker!*" exclaimed the countess and her son at once, in accents of disgust and indignation.

"Ah, I see you do not like to apply that epithet to her, and you are right. She should not be designated as a mantua-maker, but a great artist, — a true artist, — a fairy, who, with one touch of her wand, can metamorphose and beautify and amaze!"

At that moment, a servant announced that the Countess Orlowski waited in her carriage, and desired him to say that she feared she was late.

"You will excuse me then?" murmured the marchioness. "I must hasten to execute my mission for Mademoiselle Melanie, since it was she who so warmly solicited me to undertake this delicate little transaction, and I would not disappoint her for the world. Pray, do not forget to-morrow evening. *Au revoir.*"

She floated out of the room, leaving the countess and her son speechless with rage and indignation.

Bertha and Maurice stood looking at each other, and then at M. de Bois, the only one who expressed no surprise, but seemed rather more gratified than moved when he beheld the countess sink back in her chair, and apply her bottle of sal volatile to her nose. The shock to her pride had been so terrible, that she appeared to be in danger of fainting.

CHAPTER XXIII.

NOBLE HANDS MADE NOBLER.

AFTER the Marchioness de Fleury had departed, leaving her astonished guests in her drawing-room, M. de Bois was the first to break the silence.

"And you, Mademoiselle Bertha, are you also horrified at this rev — ev — evelation?" he asked.

"I?" answered Bertha, making an effort to collect herself. "No, I can never be horrified by any act of Madeleine's, for she could never be guilty of an action that was unworthy. I am only so much astonished that I feel stunned and confused, just

The countess had now recovered her voice, and said, in a tone trembling with indignation, " It is *infamous!* "

" A degradation we could never have anticipated!" rejoined Count Tristan.

" She has disgraced her family, — disgraced our proud name forever!" responded the countess.

" Do not say that, aunt!" pleaded Bertha. "She has not even used your name, though it is as rightfully hers as yours. Do you not observe that she has only allowed herself to be called by her middle name, and that every one speaks of her as Mademoiselle Melanie?"

Bertha, as she spoke, bent caressingly over her aunt, and took her hand. But the attempt to soften the infuriated aristocrat was futile.

The countess replied, with increasing wrath, " I tell you she has humiliated herself and us to the last degree! She has brought shame upon our heads!"

Gaston de Bois was walking up and down the room, thrusting his fingers through his hair, flinging out his arms spasmodically, and, now and then, giving vent to a muttered ejaculation, which sounded alarmingly emphatic. When he heard these words, he could restrain himself no longer. He came boldly forward, and planting himself directly in front of the countess, unawed by her forbidding manner, exclaimed, —

" No, madame; that I deny! Mademoiselle de Gramont has brought no shame upon her family!"

" She no longer belongs to my family!" retorted the countess. " I disown her henceforward and forever!"

" And you do rightly, my mother," added the count. " We will never acknowledge her, never see her again! Maurice and Bertha, we expect that you will abide by our determination."

Maurice did not reply; he stood leaning against the mantelpiece, lost in thought, his eyes bent down, his head resting upon his hands.

Bertha, however, answered with spirit. " I make no promise of the kind. Nothing could induce me to cast off my dear Madeleine!"

M. de Bois seized her hand, and, involuntarily carrying it to his lips, said, with mingled enthusiasm and veneration, " You are as noble as I thought you were! I knew you would not forsake her!"

Bertha raised her eyes to his face with an expression which thrilled him, as she answered, "You will defend her, M. de

Bois; you, who can perhaps disperse the cloud of mystery by which her life has been enveloped for the last four years. You will tell my aunt how Madeleine has lived, — what she has done. You will tell us *all about her.*"

"That I will, gladly!" replied he. "That is, *if I can.* I never in my life so much desired the pow — ow — ower of spee — ee — eech!"

He broke off, and, in an undertone, gave vent to certain exclamations which indistinctly reached the ears of the countess and Bertha.

Their amazed looks did not escape his notice, and he continued : "Ladies, I ought to ask your pardon; possibly my expressions have sounded to you somewhat profane ; I am under the sad necessity of using very strong language. I cannot loosen my tongue except by the aid of these forcible expletives, and I must — *must* speak ! For I, who have known all Mademoiselle Madeleine's noble impulses, can best explain to you her con — on — onduct."

The last word, which was the only one upon which he stammered, was followed by another emphatic ejaculation.

Bertha, without heeding this interruption, asked, "And have you known where Madeleine was concealed all this time?"

"Yes, mademoiselle, I knew."

"And it was you who assisted her to leave Brittany?"

"It *was* I ! That was about the first good action which brightened my life, and — and — and " — (another muttered oath to assist his articulation) "and I hope it was only a commencement."

"Tell us — tell us everything quickly," prayed Bertha.

"Mademoiselle Madeleine, when she determined to leave the Château de Gramont, — when she resolved to cease to be dependent, — when, in spite of her noble birth, which was to her only an encumbrance, she purposed to gain a livelihood by honest industry, — confided her project to me. And what good she did me in making me feel that I was worthy enough of her esteem to be trusted ! She first committed to my charge her family diamonds, her sole possession, and ordered me to dispose of them " —

"Her diamonds ! those which have been in her family for generations ! What sacrilege !" cried the countess, in accents of horror.

"Pardon me, madame ; it would have been sacrilege, she thought, and so did I, if she had kept them when their sale could have prevented her being the unhappy recipient of the unwilling *charity* of her relatives."

" Go on — go on!" urged Bertha.   " How did she leave the château?   How could she travel ? "

" I obtained her a passport, for it would have been running too great a risk if she had attempted to travel without one.   The passport had to be signed by two witnesses.   Fortunately, two of my friends at Rennes were about to leave the country ; I selected them as witnesses, because they could not be questioned ; I told them the whole story, and bound them to secrecy.   We took out the passport for England to divert pursuit ; but, Mademoiselle Madeleine only went to Paris, and it was not necessary that her passport should be *viséd* if she remained there."

" But the diamonds, — they were those Madame de Fleury wore and which I recognized ! " exclaimed Bertha.

" I made a false step there ; but it was just like me to bungle," continued Gaston.   " I knew that the Jew, Henriques, often had transactions with the Marquis de Fleury.   I took the diamonds to another Jew from whom I concealed my name, and suggested his taking them to Henriques, hinting that the marquis would probably become their purchaser.   The marquis is a *connoisseur* of jewels ; and, as you are aware, at once secured them. The sum realized was sufficient to supply the simple wants of Mademoiselle Madeleine for years.   But this did not satisfy her, — her plan was to work.   When she heard that the diamonds were in M. de Fleury's possession, she embroidered a robe upon which the lilies and shamrock were closely imitated, and took her work to Vignon, Madame de Fleury's dressmaker.   Vignon was amazed at the great skill and taste displayed in the design and execution, and offered to give the embroiderer as much employment as she desired.   Madame de Fleury being the most influential of Vignon's patrons, the dress was exhibited to her.   She was at once struck and charmed by the coincidence that allowed her to become the possessor of a dress upon which the exact design of her new jewels had been imitated.   She asked a thousand questions of Vignon, who gladly monopolized all the credit of inventing this novel pattern.   From that moment Mademoiselle Madeleine's 'fairy fingers' commenced their marvels under the celebrated *couturière's* direction, and Vignon daily congratulated herself upon the mysterious treasure she had discovered.   Mademoiselle Madeleine now determined to remain in Paris incognita. She worked night and day, scarcely allowing herself needful rest ; but, alas ! she worked with a ceaseless heartache, — a heartache on your account, Maurice, for she knew how wildly you were searching for her; and when you fell ill "—

Maurice interrupted him: "It was she who watched beside me at night! I knew it! I have always been convinced of it. Was I not right?"

"I was bound not to tell you, but there can be no need of concealment now. Yes, you *are* right. When the *soeur de bon secours* we had engaged to take care of you during the day, left, and would have been replaced, according to the usual custom, by another to watch through the night, we told her no watcher was needed before morning. Mademoiselle Madeleine made herself a garb resembling that worn by the sisterhood; and, every night, when the good sister we had hired left, Mademoiselle Madeleine took her place. We thought your delirium would prevent your recognizing her."

"Probably it did, at first," returned Maurice; "but, for many nights before I spoke to you, I was conscious, I was sure of her presence."

"When you did speak, I was startled enough," resumed Gaston; "and it was a sad revelation to Mademoiselle Madeleine; for, when your reason was restored, she could not venture any more to come near you."

"Did she go to Dresden? How came my birthday handkerchief to be sent from Dresden?" asked Bertha.

"That was another piece of stupidity of mine. You see what a blockhead I have been. Mademoiselle Madeleine wished to send some token of assurance that she thought of you still; but it was necessary that you should not know she was in Paris. I had the package conveyed to a friend of mine in Dresden, and desired him to remove the envelope and send the parcel to Bordeaux, though you were in Paris at the time. It would not have been prudent to let you suspect that Mademoiselle Madeleine was aware of your sojourn in the metropolis. But, when the postmark induced Maurice to start for Dresden, I saw what a fool I had been. It was just like me to commit some absurdity,—I always do! I could not dissuade Maurice from going to Dresden; but Mademoiselle Madeleine wrote a note which I enclosed to my friend, and desired to have it left at the hotel where Maurice was staying. After that I was more careful not to commit blunders. The other birthday tokens, you received, Mademoiselle Bertha, I always contrived to send you by private hand; thus, there was no postmark to awaken suspicion."

"But how came Madeleine here in America?" inquired Bertha.

19

"When the Marquis de Fleury was appointed ambassador to the United States, Mademoiselle Madeleine learned that Madame de Fleury sorely lamented her hard fate, and mourned over the probability that she would be obliged to have all her dresses sent from Paris. This would be a great inconvenience, for she often liked to have a costume improvised upon the spur of the moment, and completed with fabulous rapidity. Mademoiselle Madeleine had frequently thought of America, and felt that the new country must present a field where she could work more advantageously than in Paris. She desired Vignon to suggest to Madame de Fleury that one of the assistants in her favorite *couturière's* establishment, — the one with whose designs Madame de Fleury was already acquainted, — might be tempted, by the certainty of the marchioness's patronage, to visit America. Madame de Fleury was contented, and immediately proposed that Mademoiselle Melanie should sail in the same steamer. Vignon allowed two of her work-women to accompany her. The sum Mademoiselle Madeleine had realized from her diamonds enabled her to hire a modest house in Washington, and to furnish it tastefully. On her arrival she sent for Mr. Hilson. Perhaps you remember him, Mademoiselle Bertha? He once dined at the Château de Gramont."

Here the count uttered an exclamation of violent displeasure, but M. de Bois went on, —

"He had requested Mademoiselle Madeleine if she ever visited America to let him know. He called upon her at once, and she frankly told him the story of her trials, and the conclusion to which they had forced her. He highly approved of her energy, her zeal, and spirit. She made him promise to keep her rank and name a secret. He brought his wife and daughter to see her, and they became her stanch, admiring, and helpful friends. Through them alone, she would quickly have been drawn into notice; but a more powerful medium to popularity was at work. The sensation produced by Madame de Fleury's toilets caused all Washington to flock to the exhibition-rooms of ' Mademoiselle Melanie,' who was known to be her *couturière.* Soon, it became a favor for 'Mademoiselle Melanie' to receive new customers. She was forced to move to the elegant mansion where she now resides. It is one of the grandest houses in Washington, and Mademoiselle Melanie has only one more payment to make before it becomes her own. The fact is, people have gone crazy about her. Those who seek her merely upon business, when they come into her presence, are impressed with the conviction that she is not merely their equal, but their superior, and treat her with involuntary deference. She is rapidly becoming rich, and she has the glory of knowing that it is through the labor of her own dainty hands, her own 'fairy fingers!'"

"Oh, all she has done was truly noble!" said Bertha, with enthusiasm.

"It was disgraceful!" cried the countess, fiercely. "She might better have starved! She has torn down her glorious escutcheon to replace it by a mantua-maker's sign. She has stooped to make dresses!—to receive customers! Abominable!"

M. de Bois, for a moment forgetting the courtesy due to the rank and years of the countess, replied indignantly, "Madame, did she not make *your* dresses for three years? Have you not been one of her customers? An unprofitable customer? The *profit* was the only difference between what she did at the *Château de Gramont* and what she does in the city of Washington!"

"Sir!" exclaimed the countess, giving him a look of rebuke, which was intended to silence these unpalatable truths.

"You are right, M. de Bois," answered Bertha, not noticing the furious glance of her aunt. "That was a random shaft of yours, but it hits the mark, and strikes me as well as my aunt; yet I thank you for it; I thank you for defending Madeleine; I thank you for befriending her. I shall never forget it—never!"

Bertha frankly stretched out her hand to him; he took it with joyful emotion.

"Whom would she have to defend her if I did not, since her family discard her? Since even an able young lawyer utters not a word to plead her cause?" he added, looking reproachfully at Maurice. "But she shall never lack a defender while I live, for I love her as a sister! I venerate her as a saint. To me she is the type of all that is best and noblest in the world! The type of that which is greater, more valuable than glory, more useful than fame, more *noble* than the blood of countesses and duchesses —*honest labor!*"

Bertha's responsive look spoke her approval.

"And what do I not owe her, myself?" continued M. de Bois. "It was her words, long before her sorrows began, which rendered me conscious of the inert purposelessness of my own existence. It was the effect produced upon me by those words which made me resolve to throw off my sluggish, indolent melancholy and inactivity, and rise up to be one of the world's 'doers,' not '*breathers*' only. The change I feel in myself came through her; even the very power of speaking to you thus freely comes through her, for she encouraged me to conquer my diffidence, she made me despise my weak self-consciousness, and I cannot offer her a sufficient return; no, not if I took up arms against the whole world, her own family included, in her defence! In my presence, no one shall ever asperse her nobility of word, deed, or act!"

Bertha's speaking eyes thanked him and encouraged him again.

In spite of the manifest rage of the countess he went on, —

"But Mademoiselle Madeleine now holds a position which needs no champion. She has made that position herself, by her own energy and industry, and the unimpeachable purity of her conduct. In this land where *labor* is a *virtue*, and the most laborious, when they combine intellect with industry, become the greatest, — in this land it will be no blot upon her noble name, (when she chooses to resume it) that she has linked that name with *work*. She will rather be held up as an example to the daughters of this young country. No one, except Mr. Hilson, not even her zealous patron, and devoted admirer, Madame de Fleury, yet knows her history; but every one feels that she merits reverence, and every one yields her spontaneous veneration. The young women whom she employs idolize her, and she treats them as the kindest and most considerate of sisters might. Some among them belong to excellent families, reduced by circumstances, and she has inspired them with courage to work, even with so humble an instrument as the needle, rather than to accept dependence as inevitable. She is fitting them to follow in her footsteps. If her relatives scorn her for the course she has pursued, she will be fully compensated for their scorn by the world's approval."

All eyes had been riveted upon Gaston, as he spoke, and no one perceived that Madeleine was standing in the room, a few paces from the door. Bertha's exclamation first made the others conscious of her presence.

"Madeleine! we know all! Oh, what you must have suffered! How noble you have been! Madeleine, you are dearer to me than ever, far dearer!"

The tears that ran softly down Madeleine's cheeks were her only answer.

Bertha, as she wiped them away, said, "These are not like the tears you shed that sorrowful day in the *châlet*, that day

when you must have first made up your mind to leave us. Do
you remember how you wept then? Those were tears of agony!
You have never wept such tears since,—have you, Madeleine?"

"No, never!"

"I could not then comprehend what moved you so terribly;
but, at this moment, I understand all your sensations. Now that
we have met again there must be no more tears. You know
that I am of age now; I am mistress of my own fortune; and
you and I must part no more! You must come and share what
is mine. You must have done with work, Madeleine."

"That cannot be, my good, generous Bertha; my day of work
has not yet closed."

"Bertha!" exclaimed the countess, who, until then, had stood
trembling with anger, and unable to command her voice. "Bertha, have you quite forgotten yourself? Remember that you are
under my guardianship, and I forbid your having any association
with Mademoiselle de Gramont."

Madeleine advanced with calm dignity towards the countess,
and said quietly, —

"Madame — aunt" —

The countess interrupted her imperiously.

"Aunt! Do you *dare* to address *me* by that title? *You* — a
dressmaker! When you forgot your noble birth, and lowered
yourself to the working-classes, making yourself one with
them, — when you demeaned yourself to gain your bread by
your needle, bread which should have choked a de Gramont
to eat, — you should also have forgotten your relationship to
me, never to remember it again!"

"If I did not forget it, madame," answered Madeleine, with calm
self-respect, "I was at least careful that my condition should not
become known to you. I strove to act as though I had been dead
to you, that my existence might not cause you mortification. I
could not guard against the accident which has thrown us together once more, but for the last time, as far as my will is
concerned."

"This meeting was not Mademoiselle Madeleine's fault," cried
M. de Bois, coming to the rescue. "It was my folly, — another
blunder of mine! I was dolt enough to think that you had only
to see her for all to be well; and, instead of warning Mademoiselle Madeleine that you were in Washington, I kept from her
a knowledge which would have prevented your encountering each
other. It was all my imprudence, my miscalculation! I see
my error since it has subjected her to insult; and yet what I

did," continued he more passionately, and regarding Maurice, as he spoke, " was for the sake of one who " —

Madeleine, seized with a sudden dread of the manner in which he might conclude this sentence, broke in abruptly, —

" Were I not indebted to you, M. de Bois, for so many kindnesses, I might reproach you now ; but it was well for me to learn this lesson ; it was well for me to be certain that my aunt would discard me because I preferred honest industry to cold charity."

" Discard you ? " rejoined the countess, furiously. " Could you doubt that I would discard you ? Henceforth the tie of blood between us is dissolved ; you are no relative of mine! I forbid you to make known that we have ever met. I forbid my family to hold any intercourse with you. I appeal to my son to say if this is not the just retribution which your conduct has brought upon you ! "

The count answered with deliberation, as though he was pondering some possibility in his wily mind ; as if some idea had occurred to him which prevented his fully sharing in his mother's wrath, or, rather, which tempered the expression of his displeasure, —

" Madeleine's situation has rendered this the most proper and natural course open to us. She could not expect to be formally recognized. She could not suppose it possible, however much consideration we might entertain for her personally, that the Countess de Gramont and her family should allow it to be known that one of their kin is a dressmaker ! Madeleine is too reasonable not to see the impropriety (to use a mild word) there would be even in such a suggestion."

" I see it very plainly," answered Madeleine, not unmoved by the count's manner, which was so much gentler than his mother's, and not suspecting the motive which induced him to assume this conciliatory tone.

The count resumed : " We wish Madeleine well, in spite of her present degraded position. If circumstances should prolong our stay in Washington, or in America, — and it is very possible they may do so, — we will only request her to remove to California or Australia, or some distant region, where she may live in desirable obscurity, and not run the risk of being brought into even *accidental* contact with us."

" No, — no ! " exclaimed Bertha, vehemently. " We shall not lose her again, — we must not ! *You* may all discard her, but *I* will not ! I will always acknowledge her, and I must see her !

She is dearer to me than ever; I will not be separated from her ! "

Did Bertha see the look of admiration with which M. de Bois contemplated her as she uttered these words ?

The countess asked in an imperious tone, —

" Bertha, have you wholly forgotten yourself? I will never permit this intercourse, — I forbid it ! If *you* are willing to brave my displeasure, I presume Madeleine, ungrateful as she has proved herself to be, for the protection I granted her during three years, will not so wholly forget her debt as to disregard my command."

How often Madeleine had been reminded of that debt which her services at the Château de Gramont had cancelled a hundred times over !

Before she could respond to her aunt's remark, Bertha went on, —

" You do not comprehend my plan, aunt. Madeleine, of course, must give up her present occupation ; there is no need of her pursuing it ; I am rich enough for both. She shall live with me and share my fortune. Madeleine, you will not refuse me this? For nearly five years I have mourned over our separation, and wasted my life in the vain hope of seeing you again. You would be ashamed of me if you knew in what a weak, frivolous, idle manner, I have passed my days, while you were working so unceasingly, and with such grand results. I shall never learn to make good use of my hours except under your guidance. Long before I reached my majority I looked forward gladly to the time when I should be a free agent and could share my *fortune* with you. My aunt knows that I communicated my intention to her before you left the Château de Gramont. And now, Madeleine, my own best Madeleine, — you will let the dream of my life become a reality, — will you not? Say yes, I implore you ! "

Bertha had spoken with such genuine warmth and hearty earnestness that a colder nature than Madeleine's must have been melted. She folded the generous girl tenderly and silently in her arms, and, after a pause, which the countenance of her aunt made her aware that the proud lady was on the eve of breaking, answered, sadly, —

" It was worth suffering all I endured, Bertha, to have your friendship tested through this fiery ordeal, and to know that your heart cannot be divided by circumstances from mine. But your too liberal offer I cannot accept ; the path I have marked out I must pursue until I reach the goal which I am nearing. An incompleteness in the execution of my deliberate plans would render me more miserable than I am to-day in being cast off by my own family."

"Do not speak such cruel words," returned Bertha. "They do not cast you off; that is, *I* do not, and never will; and I am sure " —

She turned to look at Maurice, who had stood silent through the whole scene, leaning upon the mantel-piece, his head still resting on his hand, and his eyes fixed upon Madeleine. His mind was too full of conflicting emotions for him to speak; above all other images rose that of the being whom Madeleine had declared she loved. Did she love him still? Was he here? Did he know her condition? Was M. de Bois, whom she had entrusted with her secret, — M. de Bois, who had protected and aided her, — the object of her preference? Maurice could not answer these torturing questions, and the happiness of once more beholding the one whom he had so long fruitlessly sought, made him feel as though he were passing through a strange, wild dream, which, but for *one doubt*, would have been full of ecstasy.

When Bertha appealed to him by her look, he could no longer remain silent.

"You are right, Bertha; Madeleine is to me all that she ever was. I am as proud of her as I have ever been; more proud I could not be! *To renounce her would be as impossible as it has ever been.*"

Madeleine, who had appeared so firm and composed up to that moment, trembled violently; her heart seemed to cease its pulsations; a cold tremor ran through her veins; a mist floated before her eyes; exquisite happiness became exquisite pain! She turned, as though about to leave the room, but her feet faltered. In a second, M. de Bois was at her side, and gave her his arm; she took it almost unconsciously. The voice of her aunt restored her as suddenly as a dash of ice-water could have done."

"Your father's commands and mine, then, Maurice, are to have no weight. We order you to renounce all intercourse with this person, whom we no longer acknowledge as a relative, and you unhesitatingly declare to her, in our very presence, that you disregard our wishes. This, it seems, is the first effect of Mademoiselle de Gramont's renewed influence, which we have before now found so pernicious."

"Do not fear, madame," answered Madeleine; "I will not permit " —

"Make no rash promise, Madeleine,"—interrupted Maurice. "My father's wishes and my grandmother's must ever have weight with me; but when I honestly differ from them in opinion, I trust there is no disrespect in my saying so. Blindly to obey their commands would be to abnegate free agency and self-responsibility."

"I have not forgotten," said the countess, freezingly, "that the first disrespect towards me of which you were guilty was originated by Mademoiselle de Gramont. I perceive that she is again about to create a family feud, and separate father and son, grandmother and grandchild. All her noble sentiments and heroic acting have ever this end in view. During the period that she concealed herself from us she has evidently never lost sight of this great aim of her existence, and has closely calculated events, and bided her time that she might manœuvre with additional power and certainty. She has not disgraced us enough; she is planning the total downfall of our noble house, no matter whom it buries in the ruins. It is not sufficient that we have to blush for the *dressmaker*, who would exchange the device graven upon her ancestral arms for that of a scissors and thimble; but she is laboring to bring her disgrace nearer and fasten it more permanently upon us."

M. de Bois, who felt that Madeleine was clinging to his arm, as though her strength was failing, answered for her, —

"The daughter of the Duke de Gramont has not become less noble, madame, through her noble industry. She has not brought to her own, or any other cheek, a blush of genuine shame. I, who have watched over her from the hour that she left the Château de Gramont, claim the proud privilege of giving this testimony. No duchess has the right to hold her head higher than the Duke de Gramont's orphan daughter."

Before any one could reply, he led Madeleine from the room, and out of the house. The movement which Maurice and Bertha, at the same moment, made to follow her was arrested by the countess. Before they had recovered themselves, Madeleine was seated in her carriage, and had driven away. M. de Bois was walking rapidly to his hotel.

CHAPTER XXIV.

FEMININE BELLIGERENTS.

MADELEINE's residence was one of the most superb mansions in Washington: a spacious house, built of white stone, and located within a few minutes' walk of the capitol. She was in the habit of seeking the beautiful capitol-grounds every fine morning, before the busy city was astir, accompanied by Ruth Thornton. The matinal hour devoted to this refreshing walk was to both maidens the calmest and happiest of the twenty-four. In that peaceful hour they gained strength to encounter the petty vexations and *désagrément* incident to the at once humble and important vocation they had adopted.

Buried deep in Madeleine's heart there was ever a sadness that could not be shaken off, but she turned the sunny side of her existence toward others, and kept the shadow of her great sorrow for herself alone; therefore her mien was ever tranquil, even cheerful. Possibly, she suffered less than many whose griefs were not so heavy, because her meek, uncomplaining spirit tempered the bleak wind that blew over her bowed head, and rounded the sharp stones that would have cut her feet on their pilgrimage, had they stepped less softly. Thus she carried within herself the magic that drew from waspish circumstance its sharpest sting.

The morning after Madeleine's rencontre with her relatives, a group of young women were sitting busily employed around a large table in Mademoiselle Melanie's workroom.

Mademoiselle Victorine, the forewoman, and Mademoiselle Clemence, her chief assistant, were the only foreigners. They had been in Vignon's employment, and had accompanied Madeleine to America. The other workwomen Madeleine had selected herself. Many of them were young girls, well born, and bred in luxury, who had been compelled by sudden reverses to earn a livelihood. Madeleine often wondered how so many of this class had been thrown in her way. In reality, the class is a frightfully numerous one, and she had an intuitive faculty of discovering those of whom it was composed. Not only did her instinctive sympathy attract her toward them, but Mr. Hilson, who was an active philanthropist, had been largely instrumental in pointing out young women who aspired to become self-helpers. Made-

leine took an affectionate interest in teaching them a trade which
almost rose to the dignity of a profession in her hands. She became their friend, adviser, and comforter, and thus experienced
the delicious consolation of creating happiness for others after her
own happiness had received its death-blow.

The room in which the busy needle-women were sitting, was
the farthest of a suite of apartments opening into each other, on
the second story. These apartments were somewhat lavishly
furnished, but in the strictest good taste, and the eye was
charmed by a profusion of choice plants blossoming in orna-
mental flower-vases, placed upon brackets on the wall; or of
orchids floating in pendant luxuriance from baskets attached to
the ceiling. Then, Madeleine had not forgotten the picturesque
use so often made of the ivy in her native land, and had trained
the obedient parasite to embower windows, or climb around
frames of mirrors, until the gilt background gave but a golden
glimmer through the dark-green network of leaves.

Each room was also supplied either with portfolios containing
rare engravings, with musical instruments, or a library.

Rich dresses were displayed upon skeleton frames in one
apartment; mantles and out-of-door wrappings were exhibited in
another; bonnets and head-dresses were exposed to admiring
view in a third.

Near the window, not far from the table which was surrounded
by the sewing-women, stood a smaller table where Ruth was engaged, coloring designs for costumes.

The gossip of the Washington *beau monde*, very naturally furnished a theme for the lively tongues of the needle-women.
They picked up all the interesting items of fashionable news that
dropped from the lips of the many lady loungers who amused
themselves by spending their mornings at Mademoiselle Melanie's exhibition-rooms, giving orders for dresses, bonnets, etc.,
examining new styles of apparel, discussing the most becoming
modes, or idly chattering with acquaintances who visited Mademoiselle Melanie upon the same important mission as themselves.

Mademoiselle Victorine generally led the conversation at the
working-table, or, rather, she usually monopolized it. It was
a source of great exultation to her if she happened to have a
piece of news to communicate; and this now chanced to be the
case.

"Something very important is to take place in this house,
probably this very day!" she began, with a consequential air.

"If Mademoiselle Melanie has a fault, it is that she makes no confidants; and I think I am fully entitled to her confidence. I should like to know what she could have done without *me?*"

"What, indeed?" exclaimed several voices, for every one was anxious to propitiate the forewoman by bestowing upon her the flattery which was essential to keep her in an equable state of mind.

"When we think of the marvels," continued Mademoiselle Victorine, "that issue from these walls; the splendid figures that go forth into the world out of our creative hands, — figures, which, could they be seen when they rise in the morning, would not be recognizable, — we have cause for self-congratulation. And Mademoiselle Melanie gets all the credit for these metamorphoses; though, we all know, she does *nothing* herself; that is, she merely forms a plan, makes a sketch, selects certain colors, and that is *all!* The execution, the real work, is mine — *mine!* I appeal to you, young ladies, to say if it is not *mine?*"

"Yes, certainly," said Abby, one of the younger girls; "but without Mademoiselle Melanie's sketch, without her ideas, her taste, what would " —

"There — there; you talk too fast, Mademoiselle Abby; you are always chattering. I say that without *me* Mademoiselle Melanie would never have attained her present elevated position; without *me* this establishment would never have been what it now is, — a very California of dressmaking. And, in a little more than four years, what a fortune Mademoiselle Melanie has accumulated! That brings me back to the point from which I started. Does any one know what is to happen shortly?" she inquired, with an air of elation at being the only repository of a valuable secret.

"No — no — what is it?" asked numerous voices.

"Well, Mademoiselle Ruth, do you say nothing?" inquired the triumphant forewoman. "Are you not anxious to know?"

Ruth, without lifting her head from the sketch she was coloring, answered, "Yes, certainly, unless it should be something with which Mademoiselle Malanie does not desire us to be acquainted."

"Oh, hear the little saint!" returned Victorine. "She does

Mademoiselle Victorine concluded with a violent shake of the brocade she was trimming.

"But did you learn this from good authority?" asked Esther, a slender, pale-faced girl.

"The very best. I heard Mrs. Hilson say so to some ladies whom she brought to introduce here; and you know Mr. Hilson transacts all business matters for Mademoiselle Melanie. Mrs. Hilson told her friends that Mademoiselle Melanie's establishment was a perfect mint and fairly coined money. When I heard this assertion I said to myself, ' How little people understand that without *me* Mademoiselle Melanie would never have founded an establishment that was compared to a mint — never !' Yet *she* gets all the credit."

"But you see " — began Esther.

Victorine interrupted her.

"What a chatterbox you are, Mademoiselle Esther ! You will never get on with that work if you talk so much. Those festoons want spirit and grace; you must recommence them, or the dress will be a failure, I warn you ! For whom is it ? I have forgotten."

"It is Mrs. Gilmer's, and she expects to wear it at the grand ball to be given by the Marchioness de Fleury."

"She will be mistaken !" said Victorine. "I know that she will not be invited. The marchioness hates her; Mrs. Gilmer is the only rival whom Madame de Fleury takes the trouble to detest; and it makes me indignant to see a lady of her superlative fascinations annoyed by this little upstart American. One must admit that Mrs. Gilmer is very pretty; her figure scarcely needs help, and she is so vivacious, and has so much *aplomb*, so much dash, that the notice she attracts renders her alarmingly ambitious. Still, for her to dare to contrast herself with the French ambassadress is intolerable presumption, and I rejoice that she will get no invitation to the ball."

"How do you know that she will not be invited?" asked Esther.

"How do I know all that I *do* know? It is odd to notice with what perfect lack of reserve the ladies who visit us talk. They chatter away just as if they thought we were human working-machines, without ears, or brains, or memories. This singular hallucination makes it not difficult to become acquainted with certain secrets of fashionable life which one *clique* would not make known to another *clique* for the world."

"But this tittle-tattle "— Esther began.

20

" Chût, chût," cried the forewoman. " How you chatter, Mademoiselle Esther; one cannot hear one's self speak for you ! Somebody has just entered the exhibition *salon ;* who is it ? Mrs. Gilmer, as I'm alive ! M. de Bois is with her ; she has come to try on her dress, I suppose. She may spare herself the pains, for she will not wear it at Madame de Fleury's ball."

Ruth, whose duty it was to receive visitors, and to summon Victorine, if they had orders to give, rose and entered the adjoining apartment.

Mrs. Gilmer was one of those light-headed and light-hearted women, who float upon the topmost and frothiest wave of society, herself a glittering bubble. To win admiration was the chief object of her life. The breath of flattery wafted her upward toward her heaven, — that rapturous state which was heaven to her. To be the *belle* of every reunion where she appeared was a triumph she could not forego ; and there were no arts to which she would not stoop to obtain this victory. Madame de Fleury was a woman of the same stamp, but with all the polish, grace, and refined coquetry which the social atmosphere of Paris imparts ; and though she had far less personal beauty than Mrs. Gilmer, — less mind, less wit, — her capacity for using all the charms she possessed gave her vast advantage over the fair-featured young American.

When Ruth entered the *salon,* Mrs. Gilmer was too much interested in her conversation with M. de Bois to notice her, and continued talking with as much freedom as though she was not present.

" I have set my heart upon it ! " said she, " and I tell you I *must* receive an invitation to this ball. Madame de Fleury positively *shall not* exclude me. I have already set in motion a number of influential pulleys, and I am not apt to fail when I make an earnest attempt."

" I am quite aware of that," answered M. de Bois, gallantly.

" Oh, what a love of a dress ! What an exquisite design ! " exclaimed Mrs. Gilmer, stopping delighted before a robe which had been commenced, but was thrown over one of the manikins, with a sketch of the completed costume attached to the skirt. " The blending of those pale shades of green and that embroidery of golden wheat, with a scarlet poppy here and there, — the effect is superb ! Then the style, as this sketch shows, is perfectly novel. I am enchanted ! Miss Ruth, I must have that dress ! *At any price,* I must have it ! "

" It is to go to New Orleans, madame," replied Ruth. "It was ordered by Mrs. Senator la Motte, and is to be worn at some grand wedding."

" No matter — I tell you *I must have it !* Where is Mademoiselle Victorine ? "

Ruth summoned the forewoman. Victorine advanced very deliberately, and her bearing had a touch of patronage and condescension.

Mrs. Gilmer pleaded hard for the possession of the dress ; but Mademoiselle Victorine appeared to take the greatest satisfaction in making her understand that its becoming hers was an impossibility. The more earnestly Mrs. Gilmer prayed, the more inflexible became the forewoman. As for *repeating* a design which had been invented for one particular person, *that*, she asserted, was against all rules of art. The original design might be feebly, imperfectly copied by other mantua-makers, but its duplicate could not be sent forth from an establishment of the standing of Mademoiselle Melanie's.

Mrs. Gilmer, whose white brow was knitted with something very like a frown, remarked that she would talk to Mademoiselle Melanie on the subject, by and by.

" Mademoiselle Melanie does not usually reverse *my* decisions," replied the piqued forewoman, with an extravagant show of dignity.

" We shall see ! " retorted Mrs. Gilmer. " Now let me choose a head-dress for the opera to-night ; something original. What can you invent for me ? "

" Really," answered Victorine, who was not a little irate at the suggestion that there *could* be any appeal from her verdict ; " I do not feel inspired at this moment ; I am quite dull ; nothing occurs to me out of the usual line."

" Oh! you *must* think! " pleaded the volatile lady. " Invent me something never before seen ; something with flowers will do; but let me have *impossible* flowers, — flowers which have no existence, and which I shall not behold upon every one's else head. Price is no object; my husband never refuses me anything ! Especially," she added in a lower tone, to M. de Bois, " when he is *jealous ;* and I find it very useful, absolutely *necessary*, to begin the season by exciting a series of Othello pangs through which he becomes manageable. I feed the jealous flame all winter, and add fresh fuel in the spring, when I wish to indulge in various extravagances."

" A very diplomatic arrangement," remarked M. de Bois.

" What a bonnet ! What a beauty of a bonnet ! what deliciously adjusted lace! How was it ever made to fall in such folds, over that bunch of moss roses; peeping out of those quivering leaves, touched with dew-drops?"

"That bonnet belongs to *Madame de Fleury*," said Victorine, with a malicious emphasis.

" Ah, indeed!" returned Mrs. Gilmer, changing color. " I wonder what would become of Madame de Fleury were it not for her toilets! If she were despoiled of her gay plumage, a very insipid, commonplace looking personage would remain. I must say, it is rather singular," she continued, growing warm in spite of herself, " but if I ever happen to look at anything particularly worth noticing, I am *always told* it is for *Madame de Fleury!* Is Mademoiselle Melanie in her drawing-room? Is she accessible at this moment?"

" She has just come in; Mademoiselle Ruth will conduct you to her," answered Victorine, with an offended air.

" M. de Bois, I will be back soon," said Mrs. Gilmer to her escort. " There are books in abundance in yonder library, — rather an extraordinary piece of furniture for a dressmaker's *salon*, but, Mademoiselle Melanie has so much tact, she foresaw that they might be useful on some occasions."

Mrs. Gilmer followed Ruth to Madeleine's own apartments, which were on the first floor. Victorine returned to the room where the sewing-women were at work. Gaston selected a book and seated himself in a comfortable arm-chair.

He had hardly opened the volume when the Marchioness de Fleury entered, accompanied by Lord Linden.

As she descended from the carriage she had found his lordship promenading up and down before the house. He was overjoyed at this unlooked-for opportunity to obtain admission.

Madame de Fleury saluted Gaston with one of her most gracious smiles.

Victorine, catching sight of the marchioness, hurried forward, saying to Ruth, —

" Do not trouble yourself, Mademoiselle Ruth, I will have the honor of attending upon Madame de Fleury."

" That is right, Mademoiselle Victorine; but I am going to intrude into your *atelier* of mysteries, and see what *chef d'œuvres* you have in progress."

Judging from Madame de Fleury's tone, one might easily have supposed that she alluded to pictures or statues, and was about reverently to enter the studio of some mighty genius, and wonder over his achievements in marble or on canvas. The apartment she invaded was one which visitors were not usually invited, or expected, to enter.

The gentlemen were left together.

"I am in luck!" said Lord Linden in an unusually animated tone. "My dear M. de Bois, I am the happiest of men! I have encountered my unknown beauty at last! She passed me in a private carriage, which stopped here and was dismissed. I saw her enter this house not a quarter of an hour ago. She did not perceive me, and had disappeared before I could accost her; but I determined to keep watch until she made her exit, and then either to renew my acquaintance or to follow her home and learn where she lived. She shall not give me the slip again."

"Are you sure you have not made some mistake? I do not think there is any lady here, at this moment, except Mrs. Gilmer, whom I accompanied."

"I am perfectly certain I could not be mistaken. I shall make some excuse for remaining here; I will select a shawl or mantle for my sister, who is one of this celebrated Mademoiselle Melanie's customers, and who will not be displeased at such an unprecedented attention."

Before M. de Bois could reply, the marchioness returned with Victorine.

"And you say my dress for this evening will be done in an hour? That is delightful! I am impatient to test its effects. I am half inclined to wait until it is finished, and take it home with me."

"It shall be completed *within* the hour; I am occupied upon it *myself*," answered Victorine, with a fawning manner, very different from that by which the banker's wife had been kept in subjection.

"What an original idea!" cried Madame de Fleury, pausing before the uncompleted dress which had attracted the admiration of Mrs. Gilmer. "What an exquisite conception! Those blades of golden wheat and those scarlet poppies make the most perfect trimming for these ravishing shades of green; just the colors that become me most. That dress is a triumph, Mademoiselle Victorine!"

"The design is Mademoiselle Melanie's, but the *cut*, the *execution*, they are *mine*," said the forewoman, complacently.

"And for whom is the dress intended? But I need hardly ask, — I am determined that it shall be *mine*."

"It was to be sent to New Orleans to Madame la Motte, wife of the distinguished senator. But, I beg to assure madame that

20 *

she cannot judge of this attire; it is nothing now. In a few days, when it is completed, then madame will be able to see that we have surpassed ourselves in that dress."

"You have, indeed!" ejaculated Madame de Fleury, with fervor. "But I claim it. You must invent something else for Madame la Motte. Mademoiselle Melanie surely will not refuse me."

"If the decision depended upon *me*, the dress would assuredly become Madame de Fleury's; although the design has been sent to Madame la Motte, and has met with her approbation; but Mademoiselle Melanie is so frightfully conscientious, she would not disappoint a customer, or break her word, or give a design promised one person to another for a kingdom. She is quite immovable, obstinately unreasonable on these points."

"But I *must* have that dress," persisted the marchioness. "I cannot be happy without it! I will implore Mademoiselle Melanie; she will drive me to despair should she refuse."

"Mrs. Gilmer saw it a few moments ago, and was so enchanted that she did her utmost to make me promise that the dress should be hers."

"*Hers*, indeed! That impertinent little *parvenue!*" replied Madame de Fleury. "I would never forgive Mademoiselle Melanie if she consented to anything of the kind. I suppose the banker's wife imagines this delicate green would tone down her milk-maid complexion. But she shall not try the experiment."

At this moment Mrs. Gilmer herself reëntered. The marchioness pretended not to be aware of her presence, and, turning to the dress in question, remarked, —

"Yes, this dress *must* be one of the twelve that I shall order to take with me to Maryland. Twelve will suffice for one week. I hear Mr. Meredith's estate could bear comparison with our European country residences; the toilets of his guests should do honor to their host." She went on, addressing herself to Gaston. "There are but thirty guests invited, and I hear that great indignation is felt by *certain persons* who are not included in the number."

Madame de Fleury's shaft was directed towards Mrs. Gilmer, who was writhing with vexation, at not forming one of the select party.

Mrs. Gilmer heard, and bit her lips with suppressed rage.

"Twelve dresses!" cried Lord Linden. "Twelve new dresses for seven days?"

"Quite a moderate supply; but I could not possibly get through

the week with less," answered Madame de Fleury, serenely.
" You are invited of course ? "

Lord Linden replied in the affirmative.

" And you, M. de Bois ? " inquired the marchioness innocently,
though she was quite aware that he would repeat his lordship's
answer, for she had been consulted in regard to the guests whom
it would gratify her to meet.

Mrs. Gilmer, who was choking with vexation, sought revenge
in one of those petty manœuvres which women of the world thoroughly understand. She paused, in the most natural manner,
before the hat which she had just extolled, and which she had
been informed was designed for Madame de Fleury, and said
aloud, —

" What a pretty bonnet ! Admirably suited to hide the defects of an uncertain complexion, and hair of no color, neither
light nor dark. It is not too gay or coquettish either; just the
thing for a woman of thirty, who has begun to fade."

" I beg pardon, madame, it is intended for Madame de Fleury,"
answered Victorine, reprovingly, and not immediately comprehending the intentional spite of Mrs. Gilmer's remark.

" Indeed ! " returned the latter, still speaking as though she
had no suspicion of the presence of the marchioness ; " will it not
be rather *young* for her ? It seems to me that these colors are a
little too bright for a person of *her age.*"

" Madame de Fleury is present, and may overhear you,"
whispered Victorine, warningly. •

" Ah, indeed ! I did not perceive her ; much obliged to you
for telling me, for she conceals her age so well that I would not
mortify her by letting her suppose that I am aware of her advanced years," continued the malicious little lady in a very
audible tone.

Madame de Fleury was, in reality, but twenty-five, and particularly sensitive on the subject of her age, or rather of her
youth. She expected to be taken for twenty-two at the most,
and had been furious when Mrs. Gilmer talked of her bonnet as
suitable to a person of thirty ; but when her spiteful rival had the
audacity to suggest that Madame de Fleury had even passed that
decisive period, she could scarcely contain her rage. By a sudden impulse she turned and faced the speaker. Both ladies
made a profound courtesy, with countenances expressive of mortal
hatred.

Lord Linden could not help whispering to Gaston, " Feminine
belligerents ! Those courtesies were exchanged after the manner

that men exchange blows. It is very strange," he continued, looking about. " I do not see my fair incognita, though she certainly entered here. I fancy the marchioness intends to depart ; I prefer to linger awhile. There are several *salons* yonder; I will steal off quietly and take refuge where I can watch who passes."

Lord Linden had hardly disappeared before the marchioness remarked to Victorine, " You said my dress would be ready in an hour, Mademoiselle Victorine ? I will take a short drive and return in that time. Let Mademoiselle Melanie know that I particularly wish to have an interview with her. I must see her about that unfinished dress which certainly shall not go to New Orleans."

She courtesied once more very profoundly to Mrs. Gilmer and departed, quite forgetting Lord Linden, who was well pleased not to be missed.

" Mademoiselle Melanie will not be so unjust as to let Madame de Fleury have that dress after refusing it to me," observed Mrs. Gilmer tartly. " If she is, I *never more* " —

The threat was nipped in the bud, for she well knew no one could replace the sovereign modiste, and that the loss of Mrs. Gilmer's custom would not in the least affect Mademoiselle Melanie, who daily refused a crowd of applicants.

Recovering herself, the banker's wife concluded by saying, " Madame de Fleury is to return in an hour ; very well ; I will call somewhat later to learn Mademoiselle Melanie's decision. If the dress is not mine it certainly must not be Madame de Fleury's. We shall see if Mademoiselle Melanie's boasted justice is found wanting, or if she acts up to her professions."

M. de Bois conducted Mrs. Gilmer to her carriage, and returned to the *salon;* for he had an especial reason for desiring to see Madeleine ; but, having called during the hours which she scrupulously devoted to her vocation, he did not feel at liberty to intrude in her private apartments.

CHAPTER XXV.

THE MESSAGE.

SHORTLY after M. de Bois returned to the exhibition *salons*, Madeline entered the workroom. Gaston could see her moving about among the young girls, distributing sketches, making smiling comments upon the occupation of this one and that; pointing out defects or praising execution. Every face seemed to brighten when it was turned toward her, and every countenance wore an unmistakable expression of affection. We might, perhaps, except that of Mademoiselle Victorine, whose high opinion of her own abilities made her somewhat jealous of Madeleine's supremacy. Yet,'even she experienced an involuntary reverence for the head of the establishment, though golden dreams of some day leaping into her place were ever floating through the Frenchwoman's plotting brain.

Beside the table where Ruth was painting, Madeleine made the longest pause. She seemed disposed to converse with her young favorite ; and Ruth smiled so gratefully that M. de Bois was half reconciled to the delay, though he had an important reason for wishing to exchange a few words with Madeleine as soon as possible. The interval before she passed out of the room to return to her boudoir appeared sufficiently tedious. Gaston followed her and said, —

" Will you grant me a few moments, or are you very busy this morning ? "

" Busy always," replied Madeleine, extending her hand to welcome him ; " but seldom *too* busy to lack time for my best friend. Will you come to my own little sanctum ? "

The room to which Gaston followed her offered a striking contrast, in point of furniture, to those which they had just left. Madeleine's boudoir, though it had an air of inviting comfort, was adorned with almost rigid simplicity. The only approach to luxury was a tiny conservatory, she had caused to be built, rendered visible by glass doors.

Madeleine took her seat before a small rosewood table, and with a pencil in her hand, and a piece of drawing-paper before her, said, " You will not mind my sketching as we talk. I have an idea floating through my head, and I want to throw it off on paper ; I can listen and answer, just as well, with my fingers occupied."

Well might Gaston contemplate her in silent and wondering admiration. Neither her countenance nor her manner betrayed any trace of the suffering she must have endured on the day previous. She seemed to have completely banished its recollection from her thoughts. M. de Bois was fearful of touching upon the subject, it seemed so wholly to have vanished from her mind; yet his errand compelled him.

"What courage, what perseverance you possess, Mademoiselle Madeleine! It is incredible, — inexplicable," he said, at last, as he watched the delicate fingers moving over the paper.

"There you err," answered Madeleine, brightly. "It is, at least, very *explicable*, for it is in working that I find my strength, my inspiration, my consolation! It was *work, incessant work*, which sustained me when I determined to take a step from which my weaker, frailer part shrank. A step which utter wretchedness first suggested to me; which seemed terribly galling, oppressively revolting; which I ventured upon with inconceivable pain. Yet, as you have seen, I was enabled, in time, to look upon that step with resignation; I afterwards contemplated it with pride; I now regard it with positive pleasure. This could never have been had I not resolved to resist all temptation to brood over grief, and turned to work as a refuge from sorrow."

"And it is really true, then, that you, a lady of noble birth, dropping from so high a sphere into one not merely humble, but laborious, find your vocation a pleasure at last."

"It is most true," said Madeleine lifting her beautiful eyes, with such a radiant expression that the genuineness of her reply could not be doubted. "When one has, for years, lived upon the bare suffrage of others, no matter how dear, — when one has had no home except that which was granted through courtesy, compassion, charity, — you cannot conceive how delicious it is to dream of independence, of a home of one's own! And this sweet dream has become reality to me more speedily and more surely than my most sanguine hopes dared to anticipate. Think, in what a rapid, an almost miraculous manner my undertaking has prospered; by what magic my former life (that of an aristocratic lady who employed herself a little, but without decided results) has been exchanged for the delights of a life of active use, bringing forth golden fruition! In a word, how suddenly my poverty has been turned to wealth, — at all events, to the certain promise of opulence. And the most delightful sense of all is the internal satisfaction of knowing that I have done this *myself*, unaided; save, indeed, by the kindness, the counsel, the invisible protection of such a friend as you are, and such a friend as Mr. Hilson has proved."

"We have done nothing — but watch and admire."

"Nothing?" answered Madeleine, with gentle reproach. "Who helped me carry out all my projects? When a man's hand was needed, who stretched out his? but always with such prudence and delicacy that I could not be compromised. How helpless I should have been in Paris without you! And how many mistakes might I not have committed in America without Mr. Hilson's aid! Little did he think, when he dined at the Château de Gramont, with a noble family, and asked one of its members to promise that if she ever visited America she would apprise him of her presence there, — little could he imagine how soon she would make a home in his native land, and of what inestimable aid his friendship would be to her."

"He has been truly serviceable," answered Gaston. "His advice was always good, and in nothing better than in deciding you to take this house, which you, at first thought too magnificent; he was wise, also, in persuading you to furnish it so luxuriously. He comprehended, better than you or I did, that a certain amount of pomp and show would make a desirable impression upon the inhabitants even of a republican country."

"Yes, I have cause to thank him for that counsel. And when I reflect that this house, which I at first thought too splendid, will soon become my own, I can hardly believe my good fortune. To-day, or to-morrow, I am to make the last payment of ten thousand dollars, and the house will be mine, clear of all incumbrance. I have the money ready, and probably before night it will be paid. This very morning, when I returned home, as I entered the door, I could not but pause suddenly, and say to myself, ' Is this no dream? Have I a home of my own, at last? Will this elegant mansion to-day become mine, and through the toil of ' " —

" ' Fairy fingers,' " interrupted Gaston.

"Something magical, I am inclined to admit," returned Madeleine, gayly. "But had it not been for the earnest counsels of Mr. Hilson, I should never have felt justified in living in my present style; he convinced me that the money I expended in surrounding myself with all the elegances of life was laid out at interest; and I suppose he is right; these elegances have perhaps drawn the rich to my door."

"What was it that drew the poor?" asked Gaston. "You have tried to keep your charities as secret from me as your noble

birth was kept from others, but accident has made me acquainted
with more than you are aware. I know with what liberal hands
you have succored the needy."

"Those who have endured the sharp sting of poverty themselves may well feel for the poor," replied Madeleine. "And
yet, I do little enough for my poor human sisters and brothers;
but we are gossiping very idly. Did you not say that you particularly wished to speak to me? It was not simply to make
these sage reflections, was it?"

"No; but I shrank from touching upon the subject while you
seemed so serene and happy. I could not bear to recall the
painful interview with your family yesterday, when they —
they — they" —

"When they cast me off! — spurned me as one degraded!
Do not fear to speak out. My aunt is implacable, — I might have
known that she would be, — and Count Tristan is the same."

"What matter? You have no need of their affection. And
yet, the day will come when they will all seek you, and be
proud and glad to claim you. I say it, and I feel it!"

Madeleine shook her head.

"And they did not *all* throw you off. Was not Mademoiselle
Bertha just what she always is? And was not Maurice, — though
he appeared to be so completely overwhelmed that he could not
command his voice, — was he not the same as ever?"

"*Was* he the same, think you?" asked Madeleine, eagerly.

"Yes, I am sure of it; and I come here to-day as his messenger, — or, rather, as the herald of his coming."

Madeleine trembled, in spite of herself. The thought of beholding Maurice once more, of conversing with him, of listening to him, affected her too strongly for her to be able even to
assume indifference.

M. de Bois regarded her with an air of exultation.

"I have judged you rightly, then, and you are unchanged.
Maurice is not less dear to you than" —

Madeleine's hand, appealingly lifted, checked him.

For a few moments she remained silent. When her tranquillity
was somewhat restored, she said slowly, but in an altered tone, —

"You are the messenger of Maurice; what did he request you
to say to me."

"He commissioned me to let you know that he earnestly desired an interview with you, at once, — and alone, — free from
interruption. He entreats you to receive him to-day. I promised, as soon as I could make known to you his petition, that I

would return to him with your answer ; — he awaits it impatiently. What answer shall I give him ? "

" He may come," answered Madeleine, in a tone of suppressed emotion.

" I will tell him that he may be here in an hour ? " said Gaston interrogatively, for he saw the mighty struggle Madeleine was making to control herself, and thoughtfully desired to give her some little time for preparation.

Madeleine bowed her head in acquiescence.

Gaston had too much delicacy to prolong the conversation. He bade her adieu and at once sought Maurice.

CHAPTER XXVI.

MEETING OF LOVERS.

M. DE BOIS lost no time in communicating to Maurice the result of his visit. He found the young viscount awaiting him with torturing impatience. Gaston had scarcely said that Madeleine would receive her cousin in an hour, when Maurice, without heeding the last words, caught up his hat, convulsively grasped his friend's hand, and, without uttering a syllable, hurried forth.

He was acquainted with Madeleine's residence, — he had sought it out the night previous, — and thither he now hastened. He bounded up the street door-steps, but paused a moment as his hand touched the bell. Was he again about to look upon that face which he had sought with such fruitless, but frenzied ardor ? He thought of those days when all creation became a blank because that heaven-lit countenance no longer shone upon him. His brain and heart throbbed and beat at those tumultuous recollections until both seemed mingled in one wild motion.

He comprehended Madeleine's character so well that he knew he should find her tranquil and self-possessed ; and was he about to enter her presence as voiceless and unmanned as during their brief recontre the day previous ?

He turned to descend the steps in the hope of collecting his scattered faculties, by walking awhile, but the very thought of delaying, even for a few moments, an interview for which he had

21

so long pined caused him too sharp anguish for endurance; he seized the bell, and rang with as sudden an impulse as though he feared the mansion before which he stood would vanish away, and he would awake from one of the old dreams by which he had been haunted.

The door opened and he was at once conducted to Madeleine's boudoir.

Madeleine was still sitting before the little table where Gaston de Bois had left her. The sketch she had commenced lay before her, and the pencil beside it; but though she had not moved from her seat, the drawing had not received an additional touch.

As Maurice entered she rose, and advanced toward him, stretching out both her hands. Closely clasping those extended hands, he gazed upon her with an expression of rapture. For a moment, the large, clear windows of her soul opened as naturally and frankly as ever; but his look was so full of unutterable tenderness that over her betraying eyes the lids dropped suddenly, and her face crimsoned, it might be with happiness which she felt bound to conceal.

Madeleine was the first to speak; but the only words she murmured were, "Maurice! — my dear cousin!"

How her accents thrilled him! How they brought back the time when that voice, which made all the music of his existence, was suddenly hushed, and awful silence took its place, leaving the memory of departed tones ever sounding in his aching, longing ears!

"Madeleine! — have I found you at last? Oh, how long we have been lost to each other!"

"*You* have never been lost to *me*," answered Madeleine involuntarily; but the words were hardly spoken when she repented them.

"I know it; M. de Bois kept you informed of my movements. But, ah, Madeleine, how could you be aware of my anguish, and so cruelly refuse a sign by which I might learn that you were near me?"

"I had no alternative. I could not have carried out the project I had formed, and which" — Madeleine paused, and looked around her somewhat proudly, then added, "and which you now see crowned with success, if I had run the risk of your tracing me. You would have opposed my undertaking, — do you not feel that you would? Answer that question, before you reproach me."

"Yes, you are right, Madeleine; I fear I should have opposed your enterprise. And yet, believe me, I honor it, — I honor you all the more on account of that very undertaking. Thank Heaven, I have lived long enough in this land, where men (and women too) have sufficient courage to use their lives, and senseless idlers are the exceptions; to realize that man's work and woman's work are alike glorious; that labor is dignified by the hand that toils; and that you, Madeleine, the daughter of a duke, — you, the duchess-mantua-maker, have reached a higher altitude through that very labor than your birth could ever command."

"Maurice, — my cousin, my dear, dear cousin! — these words compensate me for all my trials and struggles. I hardly dared to dream that I should hear them for your lips. Ah, to-day, — to-day when I am about to accomplish one of the ends for which I have most earnestly toiled, — to-day when I shall become full possessor of this mansion, henceforth a home of my own, — this day will ever be full of precious memories to me; it will be written upon my book of life moistened with the sweetest tears I ever shed, — tears of gratitude and joy."

"You are to purchase this magnificent mansion? Is it possible?" asked Maurice, for the first time looking around him. "How can you have achieved this, Madeleine? You have had some friend who aided you, and" — he paused abruptly.

"I *have* had friends, Maurice, warm and devoted friends," answered Madeleine, simply.

"But," he resumed, and hesitated, "how — how has all this been brought about? Ah, Madeleine, I have not forgotten, I cannot forget the sad revelation you made to me in Brittany. He whom you love, — it is *he*, — *he* who has protected you, who has enjoyed the exquisite happiness of aiding you by his advice, and by his own means perhaps" —

Maurice uttered these words excitedly and almost in a tone of reproach.

"No, Maurice," returned Madeleine, growing ghastly pale, and speaking with an effort which gave her voice a hollow, unnatural sound. "He whom I love has never aided me, — I have received no assistance from him, — I have given him no right to offer any."

"He whom you love!" repeated Maurice with culminating anguish. "Then you love him, — you *do* love him still? Answer me, Madeleine. Do not torture me by suspense! Answer me, — you love him still?"

"*As ever!*" replied Madeleine, and an irrepressible blush chased the ashy whiteness of her cheeks.

" And he is *here*, — here in America, — here in Washington ? "
asked Maurice.

" Yes."

" And you see him? You have seen him perhaps this very
day ? "

" Yes."

" And he loves you, — loves you as much as ever ? "

Madeleine silently bowed her head, but the radiant light that
overspread her countenance answered more unmistakably than
the affirmative action.

" Ah, Madeleine, can you think, can you believe that his love
equals mine? You do not answer; speak, I implore you!
Do you believe that *he* has loved you as *I* love you ? "

Madeleine felt impelled to reply because she deemed it best
for Maurice to be confirmed in his error. In a low, tremulous
tone, and with her eyes swimming in the soft lustre of a half-
formed tear, she murmured, " Yes."

" No! no! It cannot be!" burst forth Maurice. " No woman was ever loved *twice* with such absorbing devotion. You
cannot be to him what you are to me! You cannot have saved
him from all the perils from which you have saved me! Ah,
Madeleine, since you have been selected to fill the place of a
guardian angel to me, why, why was my love rejected? Why
did another rob me of your heart? Why were you willing to
unite your fate to his and not to mine ? "

" Maurice," said Madeleine, regaining some degree of composure, " I shall never forget the noble offer you made me when I
was a desolate outcast; I shall never forget the joy it gave me,
— the gratitude it caused me, — the good it did me, at the very
moment when I was forced, *ay forced* to reject that offer.
But had there been no other barrier could I have consented to
become a burden to you? I, — poor and friendless, — *could* I
have consented to draw down the anger of your family upon
you? *Could* I have consented to separate you from them ? —
to make a lasting feud between you? Say, Maurice, would you
have had me do this ? "

" I would have had you leave me still a hope upon which I
could have existed, until I had fitted myself to enter an honorable profession; until I had a prospect of earning an independence through that profession; until I had the right to say to
you (as I now might, were you but mine in heart), Madeleine,
I have waited patiently, and toiled earnestly, — will you share
my narrow means, my almost poverty? Will you be my

wife? We might have been exiles, so to speak, for we should perhaps have been cast off by our own kindred, and might never have returned to our native land ; but your presence would have made this new country, — this young Hercules of lands, — this land full of sinews, bones and muscle, not yet clothed with rounded symmetry of outward form, but fresh and strong and teeming with promise, a true home to us. Its vast, ever-growing mind would have given new expansion to our own mental faculties. We should have grown spiritually, and reached nobler heights together. If we had griefs to endure, grief itself would have been sweet to me if we drank it from the same cup. All this might have been, Madeleine, if you had loved me as I love you."

Madeleine passed her hand over her eyes as if to shut out some picture of blinding brightness conjured before them by his words ; and, looking up with forced serenity, said, —

" Maurice, though I cannot be your wife, do you refuse to let me take the place of a sister? — a sister who loves you with the most tender affection, — who will rejoice in your joy and share your sorrow, and look upon her own life as brighter if she brightens yours? Since it has been the will of Heaven that we should meet again before the time I proposed arrived, there is no need that we should become strangers to each other. Because I cannot be *all* that you desire, you will not reject such affection as I *can* offer you?"

" Reject it? No, *rejection* has only emanated from your side," he continued bitterly. " I was and am unworthy of your affection, your confidence ; but what you will grant I will thankfully receive, too poor not to feel enriched even by your coldest regard."

" Will you prove that to me, Maurice?"

" Yes; how can I do so?"

" By promising that you will never have a sorrow which you do not confide to me ; by promising that you will never doubt my ready sympathy ; more yet, — by giving me an invaluable privilege, — one which will make me proud indeed. Do not be offended, Maurice; but — but — should you ever need means to carry out any enterprise (and you know, in this land, how many offer themselves), I would claim the privilege of being your banker, and joining in your undertaking as freely as if I were indeed your sister."

" You, Madeleine? Can you imagine that I could force myself to consent to this? You are already rich then?"

"I am becoming rich, — I have laid the foundation of wealth. But tell me that you do not reject my sisterly regard, my devotion" —

"Would he whom you love permit this devotion?"

"Yes," answered Madeleine, smiling gravely.

"It would not render him wretched? It would not exasperate him?" questioned Maurice.

"No."

"He is not jealous, then?"

"Yes, I fear he is, — very jealous; but not of *you.*"

"And yet, he has cause," returned Maurice, with violence which he could not control; "more cause than I trust he has of being jealous of any other man; and there may be, *must* be other men who aspire to love you. Your position, Madeleine, must expose you, at times, to impertinence; you must need protection."

"I have a talisman within which protects me ever," answered Madeleine.

"Ah, I know, — the love you bear *him*, my rival! Let us not speak of him. I cannot endure it; let us ever banish him from our conversation."

"I did not mean to make you suffer," said Madeleine, soothingly.

Before he could reply, Victorine entered with a mysterious air. Her countenance intimated that she had a matter of the utmost importance upon her mind.

Habituated to some of the little, pleasant, and *supposed to be* harmless customs of her own country, she could not comprehend that Mademoiselle Melanie appeared to have no lovers, that she entertained no gentleman in particular. M. de Bois was so openly her *friend* that mystery never attached itself to his visits. Mr. Hilson was a frequent visitor, but he was a married man, whose wife and daughters were among the most zealous of Mademoiselle Melanie's patrons. Victorine was always on the *qui vive* for the accession of a lover, as a necessary appendage to one in Mademoiselle Melanie's position; and, at this moment, she felt as though she had a clew to some intrigue.

Instead of speaking in an audible tone, she approached Madeleine, and glancing dubiously at Maurice, said, in a whisper, "Mademoiselle, I have something to communicate."

"What is it?" asked Madeleine, without the slightest embarrassment.

"A gentleman desires to see Mademoiselle Melanie immediately, and *in private*," whispered Victorine. "He particularly said *in private*, and, evidently he is very desirous of not being seen. He was quite confused when that stupid valet ushered him into the exhibition-rooms; but fortunately, I came to his assistance. He was so anxious to escape observation that he *would* follow me downstairs; I therefore ushered him into Mademoiselle's private drawing-room."

" Did you not ask his name?" inquired Madeleine, quietly.

" He would not give his name, mademoiselle. He said I must deliver you this note when no one was by, or slip it in your hand unperceived."

She spoke in a whisper, and gave the note with her back turned to Maurice, probably supposing that he was not aware of its delivery. Madeleine broke the seal quite openly. At the first line, however, she changed color, and was visibly disturbed. Victorine, who was watching her closely, exulted in secret. Maurice perceived Madeleine's agitation with surprise and pain. A suspicion that the letter was from his rival could not be escaped.

" What is it?" he asked, impulsively.

" I cannot tell you," replied Madeleine, hastily refolding the letter.

" Can you not tell me from whom this letter comes?"

" No — no!" she replied with unusual vehemence.

" Alas! I know too well," returned Maurice sadly. "But why should you be agitated and troubled by what he says? What right has he to give you pain?"

" You must leave me — leave me at once!" cried Madeleine, nervously.

Victorine was enchanted; the plot thickened! Here was a mystery, and she held the clew to it! It was very plain that Mademoiselle Melanie did not wish these two gentlemen to meet.

" Victorine, you will conduct monsieur" — said Madeleine. " I do not wish him to leave by the front entrance; you will conduct him through the garden."

There was a private entrance into the street through the large garden at the back of the house; but this was the first time that Victorine had ever received an order to show any visitor out by that way, and she felt she was beginning to be admitted to Mademoiselle Melanie's confidence, — an honor for which she had long sighed.

Maurice was about to remonstrate, but Madeleine said to him, imploringly, " Can you not trust me? Will you not

consent to my wishes, and trust to their being explained some
future day?"

Maurice, though tormented by the keenest pangs of jealousy,
could not resist this appeal.

"I trust you ever, Madeleine," he replied, taking up his hat.
"When may I see you again?"

"When you choose; you are always welcome; but go now.
Show monsieur *through the garden*, Victorine."

Victorine smiled a mysterious assent. Maurice followed her
out of the room, but Madeleine's intention was unexpectedly frustrated.

The visitor whom Victorine had ushered into the drawing-
room had followed her unnoticed to the small entry which led
into Madeleine's boudoir. The forewoman and Maurice had
only taken a few steps when they encountered him.

Maurice exclaimed in astonishment, "Good heavens, my
father!"

"You here, Maurice," returned the count in a severe tone.

"Are you not here, my father?"

"That is different," answered the count, hiding his annoyance
beneath a frigid air. "You heard what your grandmother said.
She would be indignant if she knew of this visit, and you must
be aware that it does not meet with *my* approval."

"Have I reason to think so when I find you here also?" replied Maurice, in a manly tone.

"I come as the head of the family, and to talk upon a family
matter of great importance. I do not, however, wish that my
visit here should be known to any one. You understand me, —
it is not to be mentioned."

"Be assured I shall not mention it," said Maurice, bowing
and moving onward.

As the gentlemen had met, Victorine concluded there was now
no need of showing the way through the garden entrance. She
opened the door of the boudoir to admit Count Tristan, and then
led the way to the entrance from the street. Maurice did not
comprehend why Madeleine's orders were disregarded; for he
never suspected that his father was the writer of the note.

At the sound of a footstep on the stair, the viscount raised
his head, and caught sight of a gentleman who had commenced
descending, but suddenly turned back, as though he also did not
wish to be seen. He could not, however, disappear before
Maurice had recognized Lord Linden.

Why should Lord Linden have so rapidly retreated when he

thought he might be seen? Could this languid, *blasé* nobleman be the man Madeleine loved? Could she have been acquainted with him in France? When could their acquaintance have commenced? Why had she never mentioned him? It was very singular.

Maurice left the house he had entered with such joyous sensations, sadly and slowly. Madeleine was found at last, yet Madeleine was again lost to him!

CHAPTER XXVII.

COUNT TRISTAN'S POLICY.

WHEN Count Tristan was ushered into Madeleine's presence, he was received, not perhaps with warmth, but with marked courtesy. Nothing in her greeting betrayed that his past conduct was remembered, and yet nothing in her manner indicated that their relationship was unforgotten. Her demeanor was simply that which would have been natural and appropriate in receiving, beneath her own roof, one who was almost a stranger.

The count had been completely disconcerted by the unexpected meeting with his son; his wily smoothness was too much ruffled for him to couch his first words in polite language; he could not forbear saying, —

"I entertained the hope that my visit would be private; it is very unfortunate that I encountered Maurice; it will give him cause to think that I am opposed to his grandmother's course." He smoothed over this slip of the tongue by adding, "And, certainly, so I am! I disapprove of her excessive rigor; her conduct toward you does not meet with my full sanction."

It was the unintentional expression of Madeleine's countenance, perhaps, which made Count Tristan remember that his own conduct had strongly resembled that of his mother. But his auditor spoke no word; she was too kind to utter her thoughts, and too frank to say what she did not think.

The count went on, —

"I could not yield to my strong impulse yesterday, and defend you; it would not have done; my mother would only have been exasperated. I was forced apparently to agree with her.

mother,' which is never to be forgotten,

The sacred title of 'mother,' which is never to be forgotten, compelled me to yield her this respect, — a respect due alike to her years and to her position. But, now that we are alone, I may tell you how pained, how grieved I was at the occurrences of yesterday."

"I no longer think of them," replied Madeleine.

"As I said," continued the count, "when you left us so mysteriously in Brittany, however troubled we might have been at your sudden step, however anxious about your welfare, it was useless to be indignant, since you thought your course the right one, and you were ever conscientiousness personified; besides it should always be taken into consideration that, come what might, you are still our relation; the ties of blood are indissoluble. I said to my mother, 'It can never be forgotten that Madeleine is your niece.'"

"I would have had her forget it," replied Madeleine. "I preserved my incognita, and kept at a distance from you all that you might not be wounded by the remembrance."

"But be sure, Madeleine, that I, for one, cannot forget our relationship, nor cease to treat you as my niece."

Madeleine could not but be touched by this unexpected declaration. She answered, gratefully, "It is more than I ask, yet I thank you."

"Yes," returned the count, "and to prove to you how far I am from looking down upon you, — how much I honor your position, and how highly I esteem you, — how thoroughly I comprehend your character, and the readiness with which you always serve others, — I come here to-day to ask a favor at your hands."

"Is it possible?" exclaimed Madeleine, delightedly. "You make me truly happy. Can I, indeed, serve you? You could scarcely have spoken words that had more power to gladden me."

"That is precisely what I imagined," answered the count, complacently. "Now let me explain the matter. You have often heard me speak of the property left to Maurice by his uncle. It is now almost our sole possession. Its value depends upon the railroad which may or may not run through that portion of the country. A committee of nine persons has been selected to decide whether this road shall run to the right or left. If they choose the road to the right, the property of Maurice will not be benefited, and — and — and — I cannot enter into particulars, but — but — it is almost valueless. If they choose the left road, the value of the estate will be so much increased that it will yield us, — that is, will yield my son something very handsome. Of this committee, Mr. Hilson and Mr. Meredith will vote for the left road, and, through the influence of Madame de Fleury, for which I am indebted to you, M. de Fleury's banker, Mr. Gobert, will also vote for the left: that secures us three votes."

"How glad I am that I was able to accomplish something to serve you!" said Madeleine.

"There is much more, I trust, that you will be able to accomplish. The votes of Mr. Gilmer and Mr. Rutledge must be gained, — the only two which it seems possible to obtain; for the other gentlemen are inflexible in their decision. Mrs. Gilmer is one of your customers. I hear that she raves about you; if that is the case, you can do anything with her, and *she* will manage her *husband*. Have you no mode of winning her over to our side?"

Madeleine pondered a moment, then answered gayly, —

"Yes, I have at my command one method that is certain, — *perfectly certain*. Mrs. Gilmer is very desirous of receiving an invitation to Madame de Fleury's ball. The marchioness has left her out on purpose. Mrs. Gilmer has made numerous efforts, but, thus far, unsuccessful ones, to obtain this invitation; if I could secure it for her she would gladly repay me by inducing her husband to vote as you desire."

"Bravo! Bravo! we shall succeed; for you can surely obtain the invitation. Madame de Fleury herself said that she was enchanted at the opportunity of obliging you, — that she could not do too much to show her great consideration."

"Yes; but you can scarcely comprehend the difficulty of persuading her to consent to invite Mrs. Gilmer. She mortally detests her, and I could offer few petitions which she would be less likely to grant. Still, I will use strong arguments, — powerful inducements. I will endeavor to think of some temptation which she cannot resist."

"That is just what I believed you would do, my dear Madeleine," said the count, taking her hand.

Madeleine withdrew it, though not too abruptly. The contact gave her, magnetically, as it were, a painful impression.

"But how," she asked, "is Mr. Rutledge to be reached?"

"Through you, — through *you* again, my kind, good Madeleine," answered the count, hilariously.

"Through *me?* I do not know him except by name. He is a bachelor; therefore there is no wife who can be induced to become a mediator."

" No, there is no wife, to be sure, but there is a lady-love whom he hopes to make his wife, and she, also, is one of your patrons ; it is the sister of Lord Linden ; you might solicit her, or you might obtain her influence through his lordship."

" Through his lordship? That is not possible," replied Madeleine, decisively.

" Surely it may be," remarked the count, " since you are acquainted with him, and I have faith in your powers of persuasion."

Madeleine looked very much astonished as she answered, " What has made you imagine that I have any acquaintance with Lord Linden ? "

" I saw him upstairs in one of your *salons,* sitting in a comfortable arm-chair, as though he were very much at home, reading a book."

Madeleine looked confounded.

" Lord Linden ? "

" Yes ; you will therefore admit that it was quite natural for me to suppose that he had the *entrée* here ? "

" I did not know that he was in the house ! " returned Madeleine, ingenuously. " He has never been here before to my knowledge. I once was thrown in contact with him in travelling from New York to Washington. The cars met with an accident and he broke his arm ; I, being unhurt, was of some little assistance ; but I have never seen him since."

" Then it is a most fortunate chance," resumed Count Tristan, " that brings him here. Through him you can influence his sister, — through her the vote of Mr. Rutledge will be secured, and these two votes gained ; the road to the left will be chosen, and for this I shall be wholly your debtor. Truly, Madeleine, you are the fairy Maurice used to call you in old times ; for you have the power, the gift of working wonders, and you always *had !* "

" Cousin Tristan," — began Madeleine, seriously, then paused ; " do you allow me still to call you so ? "

" Yes, — yes, undoubtedly ; and especially when we are alone. Call me *cousin,* certainly ; but what did you wish to say ? "

" You must find some other advocate as far as Mr. Rutledge is concerned. I fear I have not sufficient influence with Lady Augusta Linden to make this request, or to induce her to grant it, or to prevent her thinking the petition itself an impertinence."

"That does not matter; you can manage the affair through Lord Linden, and the opportunity presents itself this very moment, since he is here, — here under your own roof."

"I cannot see him, — I particularly desire not to see him; there are reasons which must prevent my asking any favor at his hands. It is totally out of my power to do what you desire."

"But it is of the greatest importance, Madeleine; this opportunity must not be thrown away. What would Maurice think if he believed that you refused to serve him at such a critical moment?"

"Maurice, if he knew all which I could tell him, would be the first to forbid my appealing to Lord Linden. I pray you to seek some other means of influencing Mr. Rutledge; he cannot be reached through me."

"I have no other!" cried the count, with desperate energy. "My sole dependence is upon you. And, Madeleine, this is not the mere question of gain : more than I dare confide to you depends upon the decision of that committee."

Madeleine made no response, but her manner plainly manifested that she was not prepared to retract what she had said.

"Madeleine," continued the count, with ill-disguised anger, and feeling that he had no alternative but to make a confession which humbled him to the dust, "this property was held in trust by me; my difficulties, my embarrassments, have been overwhelming : they have brought me to the verge of absolute ruin. A man may be placed in positions where he is forced into actions from which he would otherwise shrink; this was my case. I obtained from Maurice a power of attorney which he thinks I have never used, — but — but — impelled by my troubles, and without his knowledge, I have been induced, — women cannot understand business matters ; it was a course that could not be avoided, — I have been forced to compromise the interest of Maurice ; I have been compelled to mortgage his estate so heavily that it is valueless unless this road augments its present worth. Do you not see what is at stake? Will you not exert yourself to save me, to save Maurice from the mortification of knowing that I have committed an action which might be misconstrued, — which might be condemned, — might be considered," — the count paused, overcome with shame.

Madeleine hesitated ; for the sake of Maurice she could endure to be misunderstood, — she could submit to place herself in a position which humbled and compromised her.

The count saw that her resolution was shaken, and he did not lose his advantage.

" Remember that Maurice is beginning life ; he has imbibed the sanguine spirit of the land in which he has lately lived. What a sudden and crushing blow to him will be the revelation that awaits him ! Can *you* bear to contemplate its effect? *I* cannot. Answer, Madeleine ; he has suffered much, much for *your* sake : will you, will you make him suffer more ? "

" No ! " answered Madeleine, firmly. " Come what may, I will see Lord Linden, and obtain his influence with his sister *if I can.*"

" There spoke the Madeleine of other days ! "

Madeleine interrupted him : " Spare me your praises ; I do not deserve them. If Lord Linden is here, as you say, I will see him at once."

" That is right; you are prompt as ever. I will take my leave. It may not be well for him to see me here. Success to you, Madeleine ! But you always command success. It is a condition of your existence."

The count withdrew, and Madeleine, with a sad countenance, only waited until the street door closed upon him, to keep her promise and seek Lord Linden.

CHAPTER XXVIII.

LORD LINDEN'S DISCOVERY.

Lord Linden, who had resolved not to leave the house until he had discovered his incognita, waited with laudable patience, closely scanning every lady who passed through the adjoining apartments. His position did not command a view of the work-room. An hour passed, and he began to get puzzled. The non-appearance of the lady who had entered the house was inexplicable, unless she resided there. His perplexity was momentarily increasing, when he saw Count Tristan in conversation with the forewoman. They left the apartment together. It then occurred to Lord Linden that there might be other exhibition-rooms in the lower story, and he had better reconnoitre.

He had made up his mind to do this, and was descending the stair, when he caught sight of Maurice de Gramont and involuntarily retreated. What was Count Tristan doing here? What brought his son here? Neither of the gentlemen were accompanied by ladies. He returned to his former station, uncertain what step to take next. Just then, Victorine passed through the apartment on her way to the workroom. He accosted her and inquired if there were exhibition rooms on the lower floor. She informed him that the first story was reserved by Mademoiselle Melanie for her own use.

Lord Linden returned to his arm-chair, and had just made up his mind that the lady of whom he was in search had visited Mademoiselle Melanie in her own apartments and left the house again, when he was startled, astounded, and overjoyed by the sight of the very being he sought, tranquilly approaching him.

Madeleine looked serious, even sad; for she had consented to stoop to an action which mortified her deeply.

Lord Linden was so thoroughly amazed at her sudden appearance that he could not move, — could not collect himself to address her.

She courtesied, and said, with grave sweetness, —

"I was only informed a few moments ago of your presence here, my Lord."

Lord Linden rose and stammered out, "Is it possible? Do I really behold you? This morning I saw you enter this house. I gained my admission as Madame de Fleury's escort, and lingered in the hope of seeing you after she left."

Lord Linden did not know how to proceed. He had expected to encounter his incognita wearing her hat and mantle. He had supposed that her visit to the residence of the celebrated *couturière* was to make some purchase. To behold her so apparently at home bewildered him.

Madeleine perfectly comprehended his perplexity, and, with the utmost composure, attempted to clear away the mist from his mind by saying, —

"I beg pardon; I was not aware that you accompanied Madame de Fleury. As I have the honor of numbering Lady Augusta Linden, your lordship's sister, among my customers, I thought" —

"Customers? Your customers? You, then, are " —

"Mademoiselle Melanie, the mantua-maker," answered Madeleine with an unfaltering voice.

"*You?* Can it be?"

Pointing in the direction of the workroom, she answered with a half-smile, "Yonder are a number of witnesses who can testify to my identity."

Lord Linden, trying to conceal the shock he had received, and gazing upon her with admiration, exclaimed, in an impassioned tone, —

"Ever since I first met you, when you were returning from " —

"From New York," broke in Madeleine, "where I went to choose silks and velvets and other feminine paraphernalia for the use of my customers."

Lord Linden was again discomfited. After a moment he went on, —

"I have sought you everywhere. I was certain I should find you in the first drawing-rooms in Washington."

"You find me in a *salon* which a great many ladies visit before they enter those drawing-rooms."

"It is incredible!"

"To me it seems very comprehensible," answered Madeleine stoically.

He looked into her lovely countenance and continued, with increasing fervor, —

"I have never ceased to think of you. No other woman has had power to efface your image. Having known you, without ever suspecting who and what you are " —

Madeleine interrupted him.

"Now that you are aware *who* I am and *what* I am, my lord, it becomes easier to dissipate any illusion which owes its origin to a mystery with which you were pleased to surround me."

"To *exchange* my illusions, perhaps, for others, more captivating, more poetic," resumed the nobleman.

"Do you talk of poetry, my lord, to a mantua-maker?"

"Say, rather, to one who, in spite of her vocation, inspires me with the most absolute veneration. I swear to you — But no, my actions, not my words, must prove my admiration. You shall find me ever at your command. I shall count it the greatest happiness of my life to devote myself to your service."

"My lord, you tempt me to put your words to the test."

"Do so, I pray you. It is what I most desire."

"By a singular chance," said Madeleine, "one of those marvellous coincidences which sometimes occur in real life, but which look like fiction when they are related in books, an opportunity presents itself that may enable you to prove the sincerity of your protestations. You must understand that I am a woman of business. But that is easily comprehended, as I am a woman who toils for her daily bread. I take great interest in the decision of the committee of a certain railroad company, one of the members of which I desire to influence."

Lord Linden looked stupefied, and almost as if he thought Madeleine were making a jest of him. But her grave manner contradicted that suggestion.

She went on as tranquilly as before, —

"They are to decide, at their next meeting, whether a certain railroad shall take the direction to the right or left. I desire that the left road should be chosen."

Lord Linden still regarded her as though he were too completely astounded to make any comment.

"Certain members of the committee will, I am aware, vote for the left road. I wish to secure the vote of Mr. Rutledge."

"Mr. Rutledge!" exclaimed Lord Linden. "I know him well."

"He is the warm admirer of Lady Augusta Linden," observed Madeleine. "It is even reported that he aspires to her hand."

Lord Linden showed plainly that he was astonished to find one in Madeleine's position so conversant with the affairs both of the business world and the *beau monde*.

Madeleine proceeded, —

"If any influence can be used with Mr. Rutledge to induce him to vote for the left road, it will cause me gratification, I cannot explain of what nature. You have spoken, my lord, of desiring to serve me. I have very frankly pointed out in what manner it was possible that you might confer a favor upon me. If I could enter into full particulars, this request would lose its singularity. As that cannot be done, I can only entertain the hope that you will believe it has an interpretation which I should not blush to reveal."

"That I feel, — of that I am certain," returned the nobleman, earnestly. "No one could look at you and doubt the nobility of your actions and motives. I am almost hardy enough to venture to promise Mr. Rutledge's vote. Will you permit me to return here after I have spoken with him, and report to you the result of my advocacy?"

Before Madeleine could reply, Mrs. Gilmer entered the adjoining room.

Madeleine rose, and, courtesying to her visitor, said, —

22 *

" Your lordship will excuse me; my duty requires that I
should leave you and attend to this lady."

She glided out of the room, but Lord Linden continued to
watch her, as though he could not force his eyes away.

It was some time before he made his exit.

Mrs. Gilmer was looking very much depressed. She had begun to believe that it was very possible she would receive no
invitation to Madame de Fleury's ball.

" Ah, Mademoiselle Melanie," said she, as Madeleine entered;
" you will sympathize with me. I have never had such a mortification before. I knew Madame de Fleury's enmity, but I could
not believe her so cruel, so *inhuman.* She is thoroughly de-
void of feeling, and has determined to leave me out of her invitations. I actually induced the Russian ambassadress, with whom
she is very intimate, to intercede for me. I have just seen Madame Orlowski, and she tells me Madame de Fleury refused point
blank. She resisted Madame Orlowski's most urgent entreaties,
and will not yield to any one; I have no longer any hope. I
shall be excluded from this ball, of which all Washington is talking. How am I to survive such a slight ? "

" It, however, may still be possible," said Madeleine, smilingly,
" to obtain you an invitation."

" You think so? You really think so?" cried Mrs. Gilmer,
in joyful surprise. " Do not raise my hopes to the highest pitch
to cast them down again unless you want to make me ill for a
month. Who could have the power to obtain me an invitation
after the Russian ambassadress has been refused? "

" It sounds very presumptuous to say so, but *I* may have."

" *You?* My dear Mademoiselle Melanie,—*you?* I can well
believe it. Madame de Fleury adores you; she owes all her
success to you. Oh, I know it, well enough, though you may
pretend to be ignorant of what you have done for her. And you
seriously think you can get me this invitation? You will positively make the effort? "

" I will use my best endeavors, and I am pretty sure I shall
succeed; but it is to be the return for a favor which I desire you
to grant me."

" A favor? You can ask none that I will not grant in return
for this invitation," replied Mrs. Gilmer, eagerly.

Madeleine could scarcely repress a smile, tinged with a slightly
scornful expression.

" You American ladies are said to be all-powerful with your husbands; you, no doubt, have great influence with Mr. Gilmer? "

"I fancy I have," said Mrs. Gilmer, tossing her graceful head. " I arrange matters so as to have him in my power. I know his weak points, and I make it a rule to play upon them until I obtain everything I desire. Just at this moment, he is in a particularly favorable state : he is frantically jealous ; though, between ourselves, I never give him real cause. I only excite his jealousy to use it as a valuable weapon against himself. Tell me quickly what favor you desire."

"Mr. Gilmer is a member of a committee which is to decide upon the course a certain railroad is to take. I wish to secure his vote for the left road."

" How odd ! What difference can it make to you ? "

" It would occupy too much time to explain that, and might not interest you. The important question is, can he be induced to vote for this left road ? "

" I dare say ; I do not doubt it, — that is, if you are really in earnest, and can promise me my invitation to the ball in exchange for his vote."

" The one depends upon the other," replied Madeleine. " I had the good fortune to secure the vote of Mr. Gobert, the banker of Monsieur de Fleury, and " —

" Mr. Gobert votes for the left road ? Ah, that increases the difficulty. My husband makes a point of never voting as he does, — never ! It is enough that Mr. Gobert votes one way for him to vote the other."

" That is singular ; they are both bankers, and I thought they were friends."

" It is because they are both bankers that they are the bitterest enemies. Talk of the jealousies of women, of artists, of men of genius, of nations ! Those are nothing to the jealousy of these rival capitalists, who are engaged in a perpetual strife to excel each other. If Mr. Gobert gives a ball that costs two thousand dollars, Mr. Gilmer gives one that costs four thousand. If Mr. Gobert builds a superb house, Mr. Gilmer builds a palace. It is a steeple-chase of vanity, in which the conqueror has for the only price of his victory the delight of seeing his rival conquered."

" Then you find the difficulty of reconciling Mr. Gilmer to vote for the left road beyond your skill ? "

" No, — no, — I do not say *that*. I do not admit *that*, by any means. But Mr. Gobert is a great obstacle."

" But one which the pleasure of attending this ball will enable you to surmount ? "

" Yes, I trust so. There is a way, — there is a sacrifice I can make ; and I will not hesitate for such an object. My husband detests, without the slightest cause, a gentleman who visits me frequently: now, if I promised not to receive this ob- noxious, but very delightful individual (whom I care nothing about), I think Mr. Gilmer, in return, would be willing, for once, to cast his vote on the same side as his enemy. It would need some such grave inducement, some such unquestionable sacrifice on my part."

" That sacrifice may also be a prudent action," observed Madeleine.

" Oh, I do not know about that," replied the thoughtless woman of fashion ; " a woman is expected to have admirers ; they only render her more valuable in the eyes of her husband. I should not consent to offend this devoted friend without some strong incentive. But to insure being present at Madame de Fleury's ball, I would agree to anything. So, it is a bargain : if I obtain you my husband's vote, you obtain me this invitation?"

" That is our compact," answered Madeleine.

" Agreed. I shall return home with a light heart ; you have cheered me wonderfully ; I am inclined to be so amiable to all the world, my husband included, that all the world and my hus- band are your debtors. When shall I receive the good news that you have conquered Madame de Fleury ? "

" At whatever time you think you will be prepared to send me the intelligence that you have vanquished Mr. Gilmer."

" That will be this evening, before my husband goes to his club."

" By this evening, then, I will have procured you the invitation."

" Remember, I depend upon you. Good-morning."

" Mrs. Gilmer departed in high good-humor, leaving Made- leine reflecting with regret upon the tools which harsh circum- stance seemed to force her to use.

CHAPTER XXIX.

A CONTEST.

WHEN Mrs. Gilmer took her leave, Madeleine returned to the seclusion of her own boudoir, having first given orders that she should be apprised when Madame de Fleury made her ap-

Madeleine was unnerved by the agitating incidents of the morning. There are days into which emotions which might fill years are crowded. It was long since she had felt oppressed by such a sense of lassitude and melancholy. Her interview with Maurice had stirred all the tenderest chords of her spirit, yet left them vibrating sadly. The mysterious visit of Count Tristan had perplexed her mind with ominous forebodings. She could scarcely be said to have seen through his machinations, yet she had an instinctive disbelief in his sincerity, and the uprightness of his motives, — a disbelief which she vainly tried to conceal from herself. More painful still had been her conversation with Lord Linden ; she could not fail to perceive that he assumed the attitude of a lover, and she felt humbled at having *apparently allowed*, or rather *ignored*, such a position. Lastly, her late *bargaining scene* with Mrs. Gilmer had disturbed Madeleine's sense of delicacy; and a similar scene remained to be enacted with Madame de Fleury.

Madeleine involuntarily rubbed her eyes, as though she were trying to wake from a confused dream. She could not believe that she had really entangled herself in this web of plotting, and at the bidding of Count Tristan! She feared that she had acted too impulsively, — that she had made unwarrantable use of her power. Then she remembered the look of deep distress upon Count Tristan's face as he made his half confidences; she recalled his assurances that without her interposition Maurice would not only be ruined, but that disgrace must attach itself to his father's name. She had promised her aid, had half gained the victory, and must not retreat now when the only portion of her work which remained to be accomplished consisted in compelling a fashionable puppet to send an invitation to a rival whom she detested. There was nothing objectionable in the act itself ; yet Madeleine, during these calm reflections, shrank from the part she was playing, and revolted against being mingled up with stratagems, however innocent.

This revery was broken by the announcement that Madame de Fleury had arrived, and was at that moment trying on her dress.

When Madeleine entered the apartment, Madame de Fleury was standing before a mirror, evidently admiring her new costume, and in great good-humor. She turned to Madeleine gayly, and said, —

"Mademoiselle Melanie, this dress is perfection! This corsage sets off my figure beautifully! And what exquisite apologies for sleeves you have invented! My arm is one of my best

points, and the tinier the sleeve the better. Then the looping
of this lace dress through these miniature chaplets of wild roses
is very original; the whole effect is wonderfully airy and poetic.
This is one of your great triumphs; you have really surpassed
yourself."

As she spoke, she turned around and around, complacently
contemplating her reflected image from various points of view.

"I am particularly gratified at having pleased you, madam,"
said Madeleine, with more gravity than was usual to her when
she accosted her light-brained customers.

Madame de Fleury, without noticing her serious mien, commenced disrobing. Victorine folded up the dress and placed it in
a *carton.*

"I mean to take the dress with me," said the marchioness.
" Mademoiselle Victorine, have the goodness to desire my servant to place that *carton* in the carriage."

As Victorine prepared to obey, Madeleine motioned her to
desist, and said, " Not yet; leave the dress for a few moments.
You may retire."

The forewoman reluctantly left the room, looking puzzled, curious, and indignant.

" What? Is some alteration needful?" asked Madame de
Fleury. " Have you some fresh inspiration? Has a new idea
that will improve the dress suddenly struck you?"

Without replying to these questions, Madeleine looked earnestly at the marchioness, who was now resuming her bonnet,
and asked, —

" You are, then, satisfied with my work, madame?"

" Satisfied? that is a cold word. I am transported!"

" And if," continued Madeleine, " for that dress I should require a price " —

" Oh, whatever you please," replied the marchioness, lightly.
" Take me prisoner, gag me, plunder me, what you will, I shall
not complain: the dress is worth it ; and we have never had any
discussion in regard to prices."

" But the price in question is not one that can be paid with
money; the price I place upon this dress is the granting of a
favor, — a favor most precious to me."

" A favor? you have only to speak. Do you want an office
for a friend? A recommendation for some ambitious com-
patriot to the emperor? A pardon for some exiled transgres-
sor? Anything possible to the wife of the French ambassador
is at your service; you have but to speak."

" My petition is somewhat easier to grant; for I only ask a few words from you in writing."

As she said this, Madeleine opened a desk, and placed upon it a sheet of note-paper, a gold pen, and an inkstand. Then she paused, and said, hesitatingly, —

" Yet, though I ask but these few written words, in full compensation for that dress, the materials of which as well as the work being mine, I fear to make my petition known, for I feel that it will cost you much to comply with my wishes."

" Nonsense! speak plainly," said Madame de Fleury, smoothing her ribbons with caressing touches.

" I would solicit an invitation to your ball for one of your acquaintances who, as yet, has received none, and who chances to be one of my customers."

" Is that all? We are enacting much ado about nothing," said the marchioness, seating herself smilingly at the desk. " You shall have the invitation, modest and mysterious petitioner. What name shall I write?"

" Mrs." — Madeleine faltered.

" Go on," cried the marchioness, who had commenced her note with the usual formula.

" Mrs. Gilmer!" responded Madeleine.

Madame de Fleury threw down the pen and started up.

" Mrs. Gilmer! Invite Mrs. Gilmer to a ball from which I have purposely excluded her? Invite her when I have the satisfaction of knowing that she is dying of mortification because she cannot get an invitation? — when I have steeled myself against the solicitations of Madame Orlowski? Never! I would rather bear the weight of all the years which she impertinently added to my age."

Madeleine, who was fully prepared for this burst, said, very quietly, and approaching the marchioness, —

" Madame, it is not long since you assured me that it would be a positive happiness to be able to render me a service."

" And I mean it. I would gladly serve you, but not by inviting Mrs. Gilmer to my ball: that is a little too much to demand."

" But this is the service I most need; a service for which I would be deeply grateful, — for which I could never sufficiently thank you, — which would attach me to you as nothing in the past has ever done."

" The offer of your gratitude and the promise of your attachment are, certainly, very touching," said Madame de Fleury, with a scornful petulance which she had never before evinced toward Madeleine ; " but I beg leave to decline the indebtedness. You have forced me to remember, for the first time, that when a lady in my station deals with a person in your sphere, it is possible to be *too* kind, *too* condescending, *too* ready to forget necessary distinctions, and thus to draw upon one's self the consequences of that forgetfulness. You have given me a lesson, mademoiselle, by which I shall profit : in future I shall remember the distance between us."

She walked toward the work-room and called Victorine, who immediately responded to the summons.

Pointing to the *carton*, the indignant lady gave the order, " Have that dress placed in my carriage."

" No ! " said Madeleine, addressing Victorine, commandingly. " Let the dress remain where it is."

" What do you mean, mademoiselle ? " asked the marchioness, in angry astonishment.

" That dress is still mine ! " answered Madeleine.

" Yours ? "

" It is mine, and we will each keep that which belongs to us, — *you* the privilege of your rank ; I, the results of my labor, however humble."

" Do I understand you rightly ? Have you the hardihood to say " —

Madeleine interrupted her, —

" That I refuse to part with that dress for gold, or for any compensation you can offer, except the one already named, — an invitation for Mrs. Gilmer to your ball."

" She shall never have one ! I have said it, and nothing can change my resolution."

" Nor mine ! We are in the same position, madame, in spite of the *difference of our stations*," answered Madeleine, with cold sarcasm. " Nothing can change my resolution."

" But the dress is mine ! " cried Madame de Fleury. " I will prove that it is mine ; but we will settle that question afterward. Meantime, I order you, Mademoiselle Victorine, to have that dress placed in my carriage."

" I order you not to touch it ! " said Madeleine.

Madame de Fleury now became so much exasperated that she seemed to be on the point of seizing the dress and carrying it off in her arms.

Madeleine perceived her intention, and, suddenly lifting the dress out of the *carton*, rolled it up rapidly, for the materials were light.

" I prove to whom the dress belongs, madame, by disposing of it *thus !* "

And with the most perfect tranquillity, she flung the disputed prize into the fire ! It was burning brightly, for the day was cool, though spring had commenced.

The marchioness, for a moment, was stunned; but, as the flames caught the lace, she cried out, "Save it ! save it ! It is burning ! What an infamous action ! What a crime ! It has killed me ! "

She dropped upon the sofa, and was seized with one of those hysterical paroxysms which French women designate as an *attaque de nerfs.*

Victorine, with a great display of distress, flew to the sufferer, loosened the strings of the bonnet which she was recklessly crushing, — held a bottle of sal volatile to her nose (for the Frenchwoman was always prepared for similar pleasant excitements, and carried a vial in her pocket), and commenced rubbing the lady's hand with great energy.

" Save, — save the dress ! Do not let it burn ! " Madame de Fleury gasped out between her sobs.

" The dress is beyond saving, madame," replied Madeleine ; " it no longer exists."

At this moment the marchioness suddenly recovered.

" And you have destroyed it ? You have destroyed a toilet which would have made me talked of for a week ! It is abominable, — it is disgraceful, — it is *criminal !* "

Madame de Fleury always used the strongest terms where matters of the toilet, the most important interests of her life, were in question.

" What am I to wear this evening ? What is to become of me ? "

The marchioness wrung her hands, and wept in genuine tribulation. She sunk back again upon the sofa, as though prostrated by her crushing sorrow.

Madeleine allowed the grief of the fine lady to expend itself in incoherent lamentations, and then said, in an icy tone, —

" Madame, do you desire to appear to-night in a dress which far surpasses the one I have destroyed ? "

The marchioness was sobbing so violently that she could only answer by a movement of the head.

" Do you desire to wear a dress which has been refused to others ? — a dress which Mrs. Gilmer used every argument to induce me to finish for her, but in vain ? — a dress which I would

23

even have refused *you,* with whose wishes I have ever been ready
to comply ? ”

“ What — what dress ? What do you mean ? ”

“ I refer to the dress the design of which you so much admired
this morning, — the dress which is to be sent to New Orleans
for Madame la Motte.”

“ But that dress is not finished ; it is hardly commenced ;
only the embroidery is completed. Mademoiselle Victorine told
me it could not be done under three days.”

“ It shall be finished for *you,* if you so please, before it is time
for you to dress for this evening’s assembly.”

“ But that cannot be ; it is not possible ; it is four o’clock
now ; it would be a miracle ! ”

“ Not quite,” returned Madeleine, quietly. “ In past days I
was said to have the fingers of a fairy, and you shall admit
that magical power remains to me. I repeat, the dress shall be
completed, if you desire it, to-night.”

“ But you have sent the design to Madame la Motte, who has
approved of it, and, I hear, you are bound not to furnish a duplicate to any one.”

“ True, I must run the risk of losing the confidence of a patron
for the first time in my life. I will tell Madame la Motte the
truth, and furnish her with another equally elaborate dress, — not
a very easy matter, as it must leave here in three days by express,
and a new design must not only be planned, but executed, within
that time. I may lose Madame de la Motte’s patronage, — her
esteem ; but that will be the price I pay for the favor I seek at
your hands.”

“ The favor ! ” repeated the marchioness, abstractedly.

In her bewilderment and grief caused by the destruction of the
dress, she had forgotten, for the moment, all that had just taken
place.

Madeleine pointed to the note which the marchioness had commenced, and said, —

“ The invitation for Mrs. Gilmer.”

“ Ah ! Mrs. Gilmer ! ” cried Madame de Fleury, as though
she had been stung by the name.

“ As you remarked, it is four o’clock,” continued Madeleine ;
“ the dress ought to be at your house by half past nine ; there is
scarcely time for any one who only *pretends* to be a fairy to accomplish the work. Four o’clock : it *is* just possible that I
have promised too much, — that is, if we lose many minutes.
Have you decided to write me the invitation ? ”

"You do not give me time for reflection," said Madame de Fleury, hesitating.

"You scarcely give *me* time," returned Madeleine, "to perform what I have promised; the moments are precious."

"You are sure the dress can be completed if — if I give you this invitation?"

"Yes, madame, if it be given *at once*. See," pointing to the clock, "five minutes have flown already, and in every moment we are to do the work of an hour. There is the pen."

Madame de Fleury took it reluctantly.

"That detestable Mrs. Gilmer will triumph so much!"

"You triumph in having obtained the dress that was refused to her, and has been refused to many others. But time flies, and I shall not be able, with all the magical aid for which I am given credit, to keep my word. Victorine, while Madame de Fleury is writing, apprise the young ladies to put by, as rapidly as possible, all other work, and be ready to take in hand that which I will give them directly. We want our whole force; let me find every one prepared to aid."

Victorine left the room to execute these orders.

Madame de Fleury seated herself and dipped the pen in ink.

"If you knew what it costs me to consent," she began.

"If I did *not* know," rejoined Madeleine, "I should not have offered to make a sacrifice of so much importance. A few moments more and it will be too late to decide, — your consent will be of no avail."

"Ah, that is true," cried Madame de Fleury, writing rapidly.

She left the note unfolded on the desk, and, as she rose, said in a tone of ludicrously mingled petulance and elation, "You have conquered! But I shall have my dress!"

"Be sure of it!" answered Madeleine.

Victorine now announced that all other work had been laid aside, and the young ladies awaited Mademoiselle Melanie's commands.

"Go — go — go! or you will be too late!" urged Madame de Fleury, hurrying away.

Madeleine hastened to the work-room, and distributed portions of the dress to different needle-women. After giving a number of minute directions, and making known that she would return in a couple of hours to see what progress was made, she retired to write to Mrs. Gilmer.

CHAPTER XXX.

BERTHA.

IF Madeleine had been asked which of her relatives would first have sought her after the unexpected *rencontre* at Madame de Fleury's, she would have answered, " Bertha," — Bertha, whose devotion had been so unflagging, so open, so daring. But on the day which succeeded that stormy interview, Count Tristan and Maurice had visited Madeleine, yet Bertha remained absent; another day passed, and still she came not.

The Countess de Gramont had resolved, at least, to postpone a meeting she might not be able wholly to prevent. She formed her plans so dexterously that Bertha was chained to her side, fretting through the tedious hours, yet powerless to secure a moment's freedom.

Exasperation caused Bertha sleepless nights; and on the third morning she rose with the sun, summoned her maid, sent for a carriage, and was on her way to Madeleine's residence some three hours before it was likely that the slumbers of the countess would be broken.

Madeleine was preparing for her matinal walk, when her cousin was announced.

After the first joyous greetings were over, Bertha said, with tender delight, —

" And now that I have found you, my own Madeleine, I mean to come to see you every day."

Madeleine shook her head sadly. " Madame de Gramont will never permit that."

" How can she help it if I choose to order all my dresses made here? The choice and discussion of becoming attire shall occupy as much of my time as it does of Madame de Fleury's. I mean to become her rival and almost ruin myself in splendid toilets, — that is, unless you accept my proposition."

" What proposition, Bertha?"

" To give up your — your — your — What shall I call it? Your *occupation*, — your *vocation*, — I have a great mind to say your ' *trade*,' that the word may shock you. Live with me; travel with me; go where I go. Will you not consent?"

" No," answered Madeleine, gently, but resolutely.

" Do not decide hastily. You cannot know how much I need

you, Madeleine. Your counsels were indispensable to me even
in days when I had no secret to confide : now — now " —

" Now you *have* a secret? Is it indeed so? "

Bertha nodded, paused awhile, then went on abruptly, —

" I have been pestered to death by men who aspired to my
hand, and my uncle declares there is no possibility of my finding
peace until I make some choice."

" And you intend to secure peace upon his terms? Possibly
among those who aspired to your hand there is one who has discovered the entrance to your heart."

" Among those who have aspired, — ah, there is the difficulty !
Among those there is none."

" Then you love one who has never aspired? "

" I fear so," answered Bertha, ingenuously, and yet blushing
deeply.

Madeleine looked troubled ; she had long entertained a pleasant hope which she saw about to vanish.

" And you have loved him, — how long ? " she asked, gravely.

" Oh, a very short time ; only since day before yesterday,"
replied Bertha.

This answer added to Madeleine's discomposure. There was
no hope for Gaston de Bois.

" Why do you look so sorrowful? " inquired Bertha, noticing
her cousin's expression.

" I am thinking of one who has loved you long, with such devotion, with such self-abnegation, with such an ardent desire to
become worthy of you, that I could not but sigh over his disappointment. But this sudden affection of yours may not be very
deep."

" Ah, but it *is !* And as for suddenness, when I say I have
only loved him since day before yesterday, I mean that I only
then discovered how much I cared for him."

" And how came you to know that he was dear to you? "

" You will be very much shocked when I answer that question ; but you always said I was eccentric. I first felt that I loved
him when I saw him getting into a great rage, and when I positively fancied that I caught the sound of a horrible oath, which
he uttered in an undertone ! "

" That *is* original ! I never before heard of a young lady
being inspired by love for a young man when he was angry, or
when he was profane."

" Ah, but he was angry in a good cause," returned Bertha,
earnestly. " It was righteous indignation, and it was the vio-

lence with which he defended one whom I love, that won my
heart completely."

"Whom did he defend?" asked Madeleine, unsuspiciously.

"*You,* — *you,* my own, best Madeleine, and for *that* I loved
him. It was so wonderful, knowing how constitutionally diffident
he is, to see him so courageous. And when I remembered how
he used to hesitate and stammer, it seemed marvellous to hear
him talk on with an ease, a fluency, a fervor truly eloquent. I
never ask to listen to finer oratory. My aunt, in spite of her indignation, was confounded into silence. Count Tristan could not
say a word, and Maurice looked as though amazement alone
kept him from throwing himself in his friend's arms, and I fear
I almost felt like doing the same."

"It was Gaston de Bois, then?" cried Madeleine, with sudden
transport.

"Yes. Who else could it be? And he was so comical at the
same time that he was so pathetic! At first I almost felt like
laughing at his odd gesticulations. And then he talked so nobly,
so grandly, that I felt like weeping; and you know it is my nature to laugh and to cry in spite of myself. I have made up my
mind that I could never love anybody who could not make me
do both *at once,* just as he did, in such a comically pathetic manner."

"How shall I thank you? Gaston de Bois is my best, my
truest, friend!" said Madeleine, rapturously.

"I know *that* well enough! Once I feared he might be the
mysterious individual whom you loved; but he said himself that
you were a sister to him; and I almost leapt for joy at those
words. A sister never fills the *whole* of a man's heart, — does
she?"

"Not such a heart as Gaston de Bois'. He will tell you himself who occupies the sovereign place in that heart when he
knows that he may speak."

"But how is he to know? You must promise me not to tell
him, not to give him even the faintest hint, of what I have
communicate. Promise me that you will not."

"I promise. But you forget how diffident M. de Bois is,
how distrustful of his own merits. He will not easily believe that you *can* think of him. And, meantime, you" —

"Will suffer. Yes, I know it; but I should suffer more if I
were guilty of an unmaidenly action. So you will keep your
promise?"

"I will keep it faithfully."

It was time for the cousins to part. Bertha returned to the hotel with a lighter heart, because she had transferred its weighty secret to another's keeping. But Madeleine's joy was mingled with forebodings that Gaston de Bois would not suspect his own happiness for a long, sad period, if ever.

When she went forth, it was long past the hour usually devoted to her walk. The capitol grounds were gay with promenaders. Madeleine and Ruth attracted more attention than was agreeable, and, after a short ramble, turned homeward.

As they passed out of the gates, the first person they met was Gaston de Bois. He bowed, hesitated, seemed half inclined to walk on without speaking, but changed his mind and joined them.

It was long since Madeleine had seen him apparently so ill at ease or so distressed. She smiled as she reflected how quickly three little words (which she, alas! was forbidden to speak) would change that perturbed look to one of ineffable happiness.

For a few moments he walked moodily by her side, replying at random to her casual remarks. It chanced that Ruth was not conversant with the French language, and Madeleine, struck by his abstracted air, inquired in that tongue whether he had any cause for vexation.

Gaston answered, vaguely, that he was troubled; he did not himself know with how much real cause. A moment after, he mentioned her interview with Count Tristan, and, stammering a little in his old fashion, asked whether she would deem it a great liberty if he desired to know the object of the count's visit.

A moment's reflection convinced Madeleine that M. de Bois would not have made this inquiry out of sheer, causeless curiosity; and she made known to him the count's request concerning the votes which she was to exert herself to obtain. Gaston caught eagerly at her words, and exclaimed, —

"Valueless? Are you sure Count Tristan said the property of Maurice would be valueless but for the advent of this railroad?"

"Yes," replied Madeleine; "I am quite sure that such was his assertion. But why do you ask? What has happened? Nothing to compromise Maurice?"

"I do not yet definitely know; but, if it be what I suspect, what I fear, it will compromise him wofully."

"Pray be explicit," said Madeleine, becoming alarmed. "Tell me what you positively know, and what you fear. Remember, Maurice is my cousin."

" Would he were more! But that wish now is vain. In a word, then, I have no faith in Count Tristan. I believe him capable of unscrupulous actions which might ruin his son. At the club, last night, a group of gentlemen chanced to be conversing near me. The name of Maurice de Gramont attracted my attention. A Mr. Emerson asserted that he had just made a discovery which convinced him that the Viscount de Gramont was a young man regardless of honor; and added that he intended, without delay, to commence legal proceedings against him. As soon as I could control my indignation, I informed Mr. Emerson that the Viscount de Gramont was my friend, and I could not allow his name to be used with disrespect without demanding an explanation."

" And he gave you one? " inquired Madeleine, greatly agitated.

" He did not give me one. At first he was inclined to treat my request cavalierly. But, upon my persisting, he replied that neither place nor time served to discuss a business matter; adding that he would be at his office on the morrow, at twelve o'clock, and, if I chose to call at that hour, the whole matter would be made known to me; remarking, significantly, that he had no intention of keeping the transaction from the public."

" What could he mean? "

" *That* I can only surmise. But a few hours will make all clear."

" To gain a few hours' time may be of the utmost importance," answered Madeleine. " Try to see Mr. Emerson *at once.* Learn the meaning of his words, and return to me with the intelligence."

" Ah, Mademoiselle Madeleine, you are always so prompt! I should have lingered until twelve without " —

" Go! Go at once, and come back to me quickly! You have said enough to awaken a horrible suspicion. I do not dare to let my mind dwell upon the frightful possibility that suggests itself."

M. de Bois bade her good-morning as precipitately as she could desire, and hastened upon his mission.

When Madeleine reached her home she said to Ruth, " I am unfit for my usual duties to-day. Ruth, I have long intended that you should occupy a more active and prominent position in this establishment. Do you not feel yourself competent to do so? "

Ruth returned affectionately, —

" I have studied diligently under your tuition; sometimes I fancy that I have almost mastered some of the rules, and fathomed some of the mysteries, of your art."

" To-day, then," rejoined Madeleine, " I mean that you shall wholly take my place. I have faith in your ability."

Ruth retired, well pleased at the confidence reposed in her; and Madeleine entered her boudoir to await, with a sense of dread which she could ill repress, the return of Gaston de Bois.

The clock had just struck twelve when he was announced. One glance at his pale face hardly left Madeleine courage to ask,—

" What has happened?"

"The worst, the very worst that I deemed possible, and I have been able to accomplish nothing. I feel like a brute to bring you these ill tidings a single hour before you are compelled to know them."

" Do not keep me in suspense !" urged Madeleine.

M. de Bois went on, " Maurice obtained a loan of ten thousand dollars from Mr. Emerson. The security given was upon this Maryland property, which Maurice declared to be free of all mortgage ; and, no doubt, he thought it was so."

" And, alas! it is not ?"

" So far from clear that Mr. Emerson yesterday learned the estate was mortgaged to its full value. Count Tristan, who held in his hands a power of attorney, has doubtless made use of the instrument without his son's knowledge."

" Did you not explain this to Mr. Emerson in defence of Maurice ?"

"Assuredly; but Mr. Emerson received my assertion with open incredulity. He is determined to write to Maurice and inform him of his discovery, and also to commence legal proceedings at once."

" Should these ten thousand dollars be paid into the hands of Mr. Emerson, would they not prevent his sending the threatened letter to Maurice, or taking any other steps?" inquired Madeleine, eagerly.

" Undoubtedly; but how are we to command ten thousand dollars ?"

Madeleine smiled an inexpressibly happy smile, opened her desk, took out a paper, and said, —

" I had arranged to make the last payment upon this house yesterday ; the sum due was ten thousand dollars : by some mistake, the person who was to receive this money did not keep his appointment. He will, doubtless, be here to-day. A few hours later, I might no longer have had these funds under my own control. See how fortunate it is that I urged you to act promptly!"

"Mademoiselle Madeleine, what — what do you intend to do?"

"Is not my intention plain and simple enough? Here is a check for ten thousand dollars; draw the money at once, and place it in Mr. Emerson's hands."

"But the payment for your house?"

"Cannot be made. We have no time for further discussion."

"Mademoiselle Madeleine, you are "—

"Very impatient and very imperative when I issue orders that I intend to have obeyed? Admitted. You need not waste time in summing up the catalogue of my imperfections."

Gaston took the check and was preparing to depart, when Madeleine delayed him.

"Mr. Emerson must not know that these funds are furnished by me. What an endless theme for gossip and speculation would be afforded by the very suggestion that the fashionable mantua-maker came to the assistance of the young nobleman! Let Mr. Emerson understand that this money is paid by one of Maurice's relatives. That will be sufficient."

"Good," returned Gaston; "and if he should conclude that it was supplied by Maurice's grandmother, all the better. If I said a relative, and Madame de Gramont were not supposed to be the person, there is no one but Mademoiselle Bertha; and Mr. Emerson might infer — I mean, it would be natural to suppose"—

"You are right. We must guard against such a false step. Surely, no name at all is necessary; but I leave the matter to your discretion; pray hasten."

Without further discussion, Gaston set out to execute his agreeable mission. He reached Mr. Emerson's office too late to stop the threatened letter; it had already been despatched.

The young viscount was sitting in his father's drawing-room, at the hotel, musing upon the mournful singularity of his own fate, and the mystery that still enveloped Madeleine, when this letter was placed in his hands. He was, at first, too completely wonder-struck to experience a high degree of indignation. He thought he must have mistaken the meaning of what he read. But no; the words were plain enough; the accusation plain enough; the threat of legal proceedings to be instituted against him plain enough. Still, he was too much amazed to be able to give credence to the communication. He seized his hat, with the intention of hurrying to Mr. Emerson, and demanding an explanation. As he opened the door, his father entered.

"What has disturbed you so much?" asked Count Tristan, noticing his son's disordered mien.

"Nothing that will prove of consequence," returned Maurice, glancing over the open letter. "There is some vexatious mistake which will easily be explained away. And yet, the language of this letter is grossly insulting."

The count's secret guilt kept him in a constant state of torturing fear, and he now vainly endeavored to conceal his alarm.

He gasped out, "That letter — let me see it!"

Before Maurice could hand the letter, it was eagerly snatched by the count. His face grew livid as he read, — his white lips were tightly compressed, — but could not shut in the sound of a convulsive groan.

Maurice, not suspecting the true cause of his father's agitation, went on, —

"The language is rude; the accusation is made in the most unmannerly style, and as if its justice were beyond doubt; but business men, in this country, are usually abrupt, and, when they are annoyed, not too courteous; one must get accustomed to their manner. My dear father, do not let this mistake affect you too deeply; it will easily be rectified. But, first, let me explain the transaction."

The count dropped his head without speaking, but again the sound of a half-suppressed groan was audible.

"An opportunity offered," continued Maurice, "for the advantageous employment of ten thousand dollars. Mr. Lorrillard suggested my raising the money through Mr. Emerson, on the security of the Maryland estate."

The count staggered and sank into a chair. The hour of discovery then had arrived, — there was no escape! Like those hopeless culprits before the eternal judgment-seat, he could have cried out to the mountains to fall upon him and hide him.

Maurice was too much alarmed by his father's appearance to go on. The death-like pallor of his face had given place to a purple hue; his veins seemed swollen; his blood-shot eyes appeared to be starting from their sockets; his stalwart frame shivered from head to foot; he clutched the table as though for support, and his head dropped heavily upon it.

"My dear father," exclaimed Maurice, "do not let the mistake move you thus. I will go to Mr. Emerson at once " —

The count's face was lifted for an instant, as he cried in a tone of intense agony, "No, no! Not for the world!"

His head fell again ; he could not bear the unsuspicious gaze of the son whom he had wronged, and in whose presence he sat, a self-condemned criminal.

"Surely it is the fitting course," replied Maurice. "I will make him retract his words."

"Impossible!" was all the count could ejaculate, still with bowed head.

"But I will prove it very possible!" returned Maurice, in a tone of determination. "Mr. Emerson cannot use such language with impunity. Though he threatens that the affair shall be made public, he cannot act so rashly as to carry out that menace, and upon a mere surmise of some kind. If there is any *publicity*, he shall publicly retract."

"Impossible! Impossible!" the count groaned forth again.

"That will soon be decided," answered Maurice, moving toward the door.

The count started up.

"Stay! do not go yet! You do not know what you are doing! Stay! I forbid you to go!"

Maurice had such thorough confidence in his father's probity, that his suspicions were not aroused even by this vehement language. He only imagined that the very suggestion of a dishonorable action associated with his son's name affected Count Tristan thus powerfully.

"But it is absolutely necessary that immediate notice should be taken of this letter," argued Maurice. "If I had been guilty of the act of which I have been accused, I could never have lifted my head again, and I feel degraded by the very suspicion. Do not detain me, I entreat you."

"There is something you must hear before you go!" the count whispered hoarsely.

For the first time an indefinable dread stole into the mind of Maurice. He put down his hat, and, approaching his father, could only echo the words, —

"Something I must hear?"

"You should have consulted me," the count continued, speaking with great effort.

"True, and I meant to do so, had I not been prevented. But the transaction was simple enough. My estate is unmortgaged. I had given you a power of attorney, but I knew that it had not been used; you told me so yourself, scarcely an hour before I requested Mr. Emerson to make me this loan."

"No — no, — I did not say *that* ; — you misunderstood me, —

I did not say *that*, — I never said *that!* You only *inferred* it! I could not be answerable for your *inferences,*" returned the count, in the tone of a man defending himself.

" Great heavens! What does this mean? " exclaimed Maurice " I cannot have misunderstood you? You cannot have used the power of attorney? "

The count was silent, but the shame and confusion depicted upon his countenance were a fearful answer.

It was some minutes before Maurice could rally sufficiently to take a clear view of his own position. His first impulse caused him to turn to his father in an excess of rage; but the broken, contrite, abject demeanor of the latter silenced the angry reproaches that were bursting from his son's lips.

The count was the first to break the silence.

He said, in a pleading, exculpatory tone, —

" There was no other way; matters had gone terribly wrong with me in Brittany; we were reduced to worse than poverty; I was frightfully entangled; nothing remained but a mortgage upon your property."

" What Mr. Emerson writes me in this letter is true, then? " was all Maurice could utter; but his tone pierced his father as deeply as the sharpest reproaches.

The count assented.

Maurice, unable longer to control himself, broke forth, " And I shall not only be forced to endure the blighting suspicion of being guilty myself, but I must bear the terrible certainty that my father is so ! "

The count only murmured in broken accents, " Oh, if the committee should select the left road ! "

Maurice caught eagerly at the faint hope, and after a few moments' reflection, replied in a voice which, in spite of its coldness, was not without a touch of pity, —

" I must see Mr. Emerson, and make an effort to postpone his present intentions until the decision is made."

" It will be against us ! " cried the count, vehemently. " Mr. Rutledge has made up his mind to vote for the road to the right; that one vote would have saved us ! But we are too unfortunate ; there is no longer a chance left ! "

Maurice went forth without replying.

24

CHAPTER XXXI.

A SURPRISE.

THE severe mental suffering that he endured during the half hour that was occupied in walking from Brown's hotel to the office of Mr. Emerson, may easily be conceived. On reaching that gentleman's place of business, Maurice learned that he was not within, but would probably return immediately. The young viscount was painfully conscious that the clerks answered his inquiries with a pointedly cold brevity. He saw them glance at each other, and one of them shrugged his shoulders, and gave a low whistle as Maurice seated himself to wait. The blood mounted to his face at this indignity, and rage took the place of mortification; but he could only nerve himself to endure with assumed composure the scorn he so little deserved. It was half an hour before Mr. Emerson entered.

"The business which brings me here is so important that I took the liberty of waiting," said Maurice, rising.

Mr. Emerson answered, stiffly, —

"Have the goodness to walk into my private apartment."

Maurice obeyed.

Mr. Emerson was one of those reserved men who never choose the initiative in any transaction. He motioned Maurice to take a chair, then seated himself in the attitude of a listener.

"I am placed in a position which renders explanation very difficult," commenced the viscount.

Mr. Emerson assented by a half bow, but did not in any manner assist the speaker.

"Nothing could have astonished me more than the letter I have just received from you," continued Maurice.

Mr. Emerson lifted his eyebrows a little incredulously, and crossed his legs, but still played the auditor only.

Maurice, galled by his supercilious manner, said, in a tone of irritation of which he repented a moment afterward, "I presume that you had no doubt that my conduct justified your letter?"

"None," replied Mr. Emerson, with quiet severity.

"You were wrong, you did me the greatest injustice," cried Maurice, "and yet unless you can credit this fact upon my bare assertion I have no means of convincing you."

Mr. Emerson smiled sarcastically.

"You do not seem to me desirous, sir, of learning in what

" You are right," returned Mr. Emerson ; " I do not see that it is a matter which further concerns me."

" But it concerns my honor " — began Maurice, angrily.

He was checked by another contemptuous smile from Mr. Emerson.

" I see, sir, you are not disposed to allow me to defend myself, or to encourage me to enter into any explanation."

" I have said that the matter no longer concerns me."

" Then I will not occupy your time with a vain attempt to change your opinion of me, but will proceed at once to the request I have to make."

" I shall feel obliged by your doing so," said Mr. Emerson, in a manner which intimated that he wished to close the interview.

" All I ask," proceeded Maurice, " is that you will take no further steps until " —

" I have no further steps to take," interrupted Mr. Emerson, frigidly.

Maurice looked puzzled, but, imagining that Mr. Emerson did not choose to understand him, he added, " I mean, in plain language, that you will not make the affair public, and that you will not institute legal proceedings until " —

" The repayment of the money loaned, obviated the necessity for legal proceedings," returned Mr. Emerson, in the same cold manner.

" The *repayment?* " exclaimed Maurice, in amazement ; " what *repayment?* what money ? "

" The ten thousand dollars loaned to you by me, *somewhat rashly,* and without examining a security which proved to be valueless."

In spite of Maurice's astonishment at this unexpected communication, the arrow of this reproach did not miss its mark, but he only said, —

" Am I to understand that these ten thousand dollars have been repaid ? "

" They were repaid about an hour ago."

" Repaid ? Who could have repaid them ? How is it possible ? " Maurice uttered these words to himself rather then addressed them to Mr. Emerson.

But the latter answered briefly, " The Countess de Gramont."

" My grandmother ? Impossible ! It was not in her power ; she knew nothing of the transaction."

Mr. Emerson continued, without noticing this assertion, —

"A quarter of an hour ago I despatched a clerk to Brown's hotel, with a receipt for the money."

"My grandmother!" repeated Maurice, musingly, and unable to credit the possibility of her interference.

"You will find the information I have given you correct," said Mr. Emerson, rising.

The hint was too marked to remain unnoticed by Maurice, in spite of his bewilderment, and he also rose.

"If I had been aware of this fact I should not have trespassed upon your time, sir; for, it is not difficult to perceive that you have formed an opinion of my character which cannot readily be altered."

"I judge men by their actions rather than by their words and manners: a very homely rule, sir, but one which is not subject to change at my time of life."

The bow which closed this sentence was too pointedly a parting salutation to be mistaken. Maurice returned it, and, without another word, went forth. He hurried to Brown's hotel in the hope of unravelling the mystery.

Meantime, the Countess de Gramont had been thrown, by the reception of Mr. Emerson's letter, into a state of excitement almost equal to that of Maurice. Over and over again she read the few lines acknowledging the sum of ten thousand dollars sent by her, and the information that the legal proceedings about to be instituted against the Viscount de Gramont would be arrested.

The letter was in English; thus her difficulty in comprehending its contents was increased, and, though she was tolerably conversant with the language, she imagined that she must have misunderstood the words before her.

The countess requested Bertha to read and translate the letter.

"Aunt," cried Bertha, "what is this about ten thousand dollars? You cannot have sent this gentleman ten thousand dollars, and yet he makes you a formal acknowledgment that the money has been received. There must be some error."

"The error itself is an impertinence," returned the lady. "Does this low person imagine that the Countess de Gramont meddles with business matters? — with the sending of money and the receiving of receipts?"

At that moment Maurice entered, and his grandmother, taking the letter from Bertha, and placing it in his hand, accosted him with no little asperity of tone.

"What is the meaning of this?"

He glanced over the letter hurriedly and replied, "It is of you that I should ask that question, my grandmother, and I must also ask how I am to thank you for making me so deeply your debtor, and at a moment when, for the first time in my life, my honor was implicated!"

"Your *honor* implicated? *Your honor? The honor of a de Gramont?* What do you mean?"

"Had you not, in some inexplicable manner, become aware of my position, and paid those ten thousand dollars with such liberality and promptitude, I should have been — I cannot bear the thought! The very remembrance of the position from which I have been extricated cuts me to the soul."

"Are you mad, Maurice?" demanded the countess. "*I* pay ten thousand dollars for you? What do I know about money?"

"Then the money was not sent to Mr. Emerson by you?" inquired Maurice, more bewildered than ever.

"Mr. Emerson? Who is Mr. Emerson? I never heard of the person."

Maurice turned to Bertha. The idea at once suggested itself that she had used her aunt's name to conceal her own generosity.

"And you, Bertha, — do you also disclaim all knowledge of the transaction?"

"Yes, I only wish I *had* known."

"It was not you, then?" replied Maurice, more and more astonished. "Who could it have been? I have no intimate friend in Washington but Gaston de Bois, and he has not the power to do me this service."

"Was he aware of the circumstances which made you need this sum?" asked Bertha.

"He certainly knew something of the transaction, but I do not think" —

"That is enough!" she replied, joyfully. "If he knew anything about it, I know from whom the money came. There is but one person who could have sent it; and that is Madeleine!"

"Madeleine?"

"Yes, Madeleine, — our own, generous Madeleine," returned Bertha. "M. de Bois is her trusted friend and counsellor."

The Countess de Gramont rose up majestically, white with rage.

"But what *right* has she, the mantua-maker, the tradeswoman, to make use of *my* name? How did she dare even to al-

low it to be suspected that I had ever come in contact with a
person who has so demeaned herself? It is unpardonable audacity!"

"You little know the full value of the service she has rendered me!" exclaimed Maurice, unheeding his grandmother's
anger.

"A service which you must not and shall not stoop to accept.
Never will I consent to that," returned the countess, fiercely.
"Would you profit by her ignoble labor? Has your residence
in this plebeian land bowed you as low as that?"

"If," replied Maurice, "it be a blow to my pride to be forced
to accept her aid (for it has been tendered in a manner which
cannot now be declined), it is a blow which has lifted me up,
not bowed me down. It has made me feel that a great spirit
which humbles itself and bends meekly to circumstance and
does not regard any toil, nearest to its hand, as too lowly, — that
spirit has truest cause for pride, since it earns the privilege of
serving others. You have yet to learn that Madeleine's timely
assistance has saved, not me alone, but our whole family from
disgrace, — ay, positive *disgrace!* If you would know more on
that subject, I refer you to my father. For myself, I will seek
Madeleine and discover whether she has indeed made me so
greatly her debtor."

The countess would have detained him; but Maurice was
gone before she could speak.

He had alluded to his father as involved in this mysterious affair, which the countess was now tremblingly desirous of solv-
ing. She sought Count Tristan. He was in the drawing-room,
where Maurice had left him. He sat beside the table, — his
hands clinched, his head bowed, his face rigid in its expression
of stony despair. He looked like a man who awaited the sentence of death.

The entrance of the countess scarcely roused him; nor did he
hear, or rather heed, her first address. But when she placed
the letter, received from Mr. Emerson, in his hand, and asked
him if he knew what it meant, he sprang from his seat with a
sudden burst of half-frantic joy.

"Who has done this?" he almost shrieked out.

"Who indeed?" returned his mother. "It has been suggested that it may be one of the evidences of Madeleine's presumption. I can scarcely credit it. I can scarcely believe she
would have the audacity to use my name, or occupy herself with
the affairs of my family. Yet there is no one else" —

" It is like her! It is she! And may Heaven bless her for it!" cried the count, stirred by a sudden impulse of genuine gratitude. "I must have confirmation! I must go to her at once!"

" Yes, go to her," replied his mother ; "but let it be to inform her that we disdain her bounty; that we are astonished at her temerity in offering it; and that we hope never to hear from her again."

Count Tristan had left the room before his mother had finished speaking, — an act of disrespect of which he had never before been guilty. Exasperated by his manner even more than by that of Maurice, and dreading the result of their interview with Madeleine, the countess resolved herself to take a step which would make her niece conscious of her true position and of the light in which her presumption was viewed by her aunt. She determined to follow her son to Madeleine's residence and to give her a lesson, in the presence of the count and Maurice, which would be the last he would ever need.

She had rung the bell to order a carriage, when Bertha entered. Learning her destination and its object, Bertha expressed her intention of accompanying her; and to this the countess could not object.

CHAPTER XXXII.

THE NOBLEMAN AND MANTUA-MAKER.

As we are already aware, Madeleine absolved herself from her usual duties for one day, and made Ruth her representative in the working department. In spite of Madeleine's habitual self-control, she experienced some slight stirrings of irritation when Victorine, who deemed herself a privileged person, intruded upon her privacy.

" Pardon, mademoiselle," began the consequential forewoman. " I should not have ventured to disturb you, but there is a matter of importance to be settled. Madame Orlowski has come in person to order six ball-dresses ; and she is not satisfied to decide upon the varieties of style that will most become her without consulting Mademoiselle Melanie herself. She insisted upon my bringing you this message."

"You have done wrong," answered Madeleine, somewhat less gently than was her wont.

"But in a case of such great importance" — began Victorine, flushing angrily.

Madeleine interrupted her with a slight touch of sarcasm in her tone: "It is, no doubt, inconceivable to you that my mind should be occupied with matters of even *greater* importance than six ball dresses for one lady. Still, I must be tyrannical enough to request you to believe so, and not to allow me to be molested again. At all events," she added, her good-humor returning, "I venture to hope that I have not often subjected you to tyranny or caprice."

"No, no, certainly not," responded Victorine, a little mollified. "And since it was *so obvious* that mademoiselle had *something upon her mind*, I have exerted myself as much as possible to prevent her being annoyed."

"Thank you; have the goodness to send Robert here."

This order was so pointedly a dismissal that the forewoman had no excuse to linger. She left the room thoroughly convinced that Mademoiselle Melanie was in love, — in love at last! The house would soon be gayer; Mademoiselle Melanie would leave the business more in her forewoman's hands; the pleasant change so long desired was coming about; but she could not rest until she discovered the object of Mademoiselle Melanie's attachment. One thing was certain: there was romance and mystery about the whole affair, and this lent zest to the Frenchwoman's enjoyment.

Victorine not only summoned Robert, but stole after him on tiptoe to the door of Madeleine's boudoir to hear what order was given. She distinctly caught these words :—

"You will admit no one but the Count de Gramont and M. Maurice de Gramont."

"The Count de Gramont and his son!" said Victorine to herself, as she hurried back to her satins and velvets; "Oh, this is decidedly getting interesting, — Mademoiselle Melanie aims high, — and, in spite of her prudence and propriety, she — well, well, we shall see! It's always still water that runs deepest. The Count de Gramont and his son! Dear me, Mademoiselle Melanie would do better if she made me her *confidante* at once."

Victorine, as she excused Mademoiselle Melanie to the Countess Orlowski, could not help dropping a hint that Mademoiselle Melanie might not in future be so wholly at the command of her customers, — she would receive more visitors of her own, — there were noblemen from her own country who were to have free access.

When Madame Orlowski departed and the forewoman returned to the work-room, these inuendoes were repeated, and caused no little excitement among the group of young women, who revered Madeleine almost as though she were a patron saint, and they the most devout Catholics. Ruth was highly indignant; but to have admonished the circulator of the intelligence, by even the faintest reproach, would have been to make matters worse, and to induce Mademoiselle Victorine to defend her rash assertions by still rasher ones.

Madeleine was not destined to enjoy the uninterrupted solitude she so much desired, for Robert had scarcely received his orders to admit no one, when he returned to the boudoir with a card in his hand. He presented it with hesitation in spite of the large bribe he had received.

" His lordship insisted upon my taking his card to Mademoiselle," he said apologetically.

" You should not have transgressed my orders," answered Madeleine, with some show of impatience. " I have given you the names of the only persons whom you were to admit to-day."

"I understand *that*, mademoiselle, but his lordship would not be denied, and said that he called upon a matter of the greatest importance, and that he knew Mademoiselle Melanie would see him."

Madeleine could not, after this, refuse to allow Lord Linden to enter; he no doubt brought her some information concerning the vote which she had charged him to obtain.

Lord Linden's countenance, which usually wore a moody, discontented expression, was bright with expectation, as he entered Madeleine's presence.

" You will pardon," he began, " my refusing to accept your servant's denial; I based my hopes of forgiveness upon the good tidings which I bring. My advocacy, or rather my sister's (but that is *entre nous*), has not been used in vain with Mr. Rutledge; he had definitely made up his mind to cast his vote differently, but his gallantry could not withstand a fair lady's solicitation; — he is too thoroughly an American for *that*, and you may depend upon his vote."

" I am more deeply grateful to you than you can imagine! I thank you heartily!" exclaimed Madeleine, extending her hand with impulsive frankness, but the action was checked almost as quickly as made. For a moment she had forgotten the difference of station which she wished him to believe existed between them.

"Do not withdraw your hand," he pleaded, making an attempt to imprison that hand in his own. But he had the good taste instantly to abandon his intention when he saw Madeleine's reluctance. "As you will; I am more than satisfied by the assurance that I have a claim upon your gratitude."

"You have, indeed, my lord; I am truly grateful."

"I will only ask in return," commenced his lordship, "that you will listen to me for a few moments; that you will allow me to tell you what is in my mind, — my heart."

Madeleine saw that the evil hour could not be escaped, or postponed, and she answered with calm dignity which would have awed a man less under the dominion of passion, "You are at liberty to speak, my lord; yet what is there of *importance* which your lordship can have to say to the *mantua-maker* ?"

Lord Linden, at first, found it difficult to avail himself of the privilege so frigidly given; but he soon collected himself.

"The mantua-maker? How little that title seems to belong to you! The proudest, the noblest lady could not have inspired me with the respect, the veneration I feel for you."

"*Respect* is peculiarly grateful to one in my position;" answered Madeleine pointedly.

This answer seemed to suggest that he might be forgetful of the respect due to her, and confused him for a moment; but such an opportunity as the present was not to be lost. He went on with renewed animation.

"From the first moment that I met you, — from the moment when, during that memorable journey, you shone forth as the guardian angel of all the suffering — and especially mine " —

Madeleine tried to restrain him again, by saying, with a forced smile, —

"*An angelic mantua-maker!* You have a great faculty of *idealizing,* my lord. I believe the extent of my services to you consisted in the sacrifice of an old pocket-handkerchief, torn into strips for a bandage, and the use of my own especial implement, a needle, with which the bandages were sewed."

"I have those strips yet," replied the nobleman with ardor. "I shall never part with them, — they are invaluable to me; for, from the moment we met, I loved you!"

Madeleine was about to answer, but he frustrated her intention and went on, —

" You were lost to me for six months, yet I could not forget you. I sought you unceasingly, and thought to find you in the society of — of — of those who are not, in reality, your superiors — not your equals even ; I found you at last — but let me pass that over ; since I have had the happiness of seeing you again, every moment has increased my admiration, — my devotion."

Madeleine would have interrupted him, but was again prevented.

" If I had not the misfortune to be a nobleman, if I were not accountable to my family for the connection I formed, I would say to you, ' Will you honor me by becoming my wife ? ' Never have I met a woman who united in a higher degree all the attributes which are most beautiful in my eyes, — all that man could desire in a companion, — all the charms of person, intellect, soul ! "

Madeleine took advantage of a moment's pause, for his lordship found it sufficiently difficult to proceed, and replied, with glacial dignity, —

" Were all your compliments as merited as you perhaps persuade yourself to imagine them to be, they would not alter the fact, my lord, that *you* are a nobleman and *I* a dress-maker."

" True," replied Lord Linden, undaunted by her chilling demeanor ; " and it is not easy to break the iron bonds of conventionality. But, if the difference of our rank prevents my enjoying the triumph of presenting such a woman to the world as my wife, it does not prevent my renouncing the whole world for her, — it does not prevent my devoting my life to her, — my sharing with her some happy seclusion where I can forget everything except my vow to be hers only."

This time Madeleine allowed him to conclude without word or movement. She sat with her eyes fastened upon the ground, and though a bright, crimson spot burned on either cheek, her manner was as calm as though the offer just made her were full of honor. When it was unmistakable that he had finished speaking and awaited her answer, she said, in a firm voice, the mild serenity of which could not fail to penetrate the breast of the man who had just insulted her, —

" In other words, my lord, you have in the most delicate phrases in which infamy can be couched, — in phrases that are as flowers to hide the serpent beneath them, given me to understand that were I of your own rank you would address me as a man of honor might, and expect me to listen to you ; but, as I am but a mantua-maker and you are a nobleman, you offer me *dishonor* in place of honor, and expect that I shall accept it as befitting my position."

"You use harsh language, my dear Mademoiselle Melanie, — language that " —

"That clearly expresses your meaning, and therefore sounds harshly. I am accustomed to speak plainly myself, and to strip of their flowery *entourage* the sentiments to which I listen. It may be an ungraceful habit, but it is a safe one. I am persuaded that if vice were always called by its true name, shame, misery, and ruin would darken fewer lives."

"Your candor is one of your greatest charms," said Lord Linden, who was deeply impressed by her singular and open treatment of a proposition which it had cost him a struggle to make.

"I am glad that you approve of my frankness, for I must be franker still. When I asked you a favor I was impelled by motives which may perhaps be explained to you hereafter; I was exceedingly unwilling to make the request which you so promptly accorded, — but the strength of those motives urged me to set aside prudence and reserve. I will not pretend to conceal that I feared you might be placed upon a footing of less restraint through the performance of the service I solicited at your hands, and that you might make your visits more frequent than I should be inclined to permit, — but I did not dream that the price you set upon the performance of this act of kindness was the privilege of offering me an insult."

"An insult? You do not imagine — you cannot suppose that I had any such intention?"

"You have spoken too plainly, my lord, to leave anything to my *imagination;* possibly, however, you may be acquainted with some fine phrase, unknown to me, in which you would couch what I have plainly styled, and as plainly comprehend to be an insult. Your advocacy with Mr. Rutledge has brought about a result which will benefit one who — who — who has the strongest claims upon me, and, under ordinary circumstances, I should have been your debtor. As it is, you and I are quits! The privilege of insulting me will suffice you! And now, my lord, you will excuse me, if, being a woman who earns her livelihood and whose time is valuable, I bring this interview to a close."

Madeleine, as she spoke, rose and courtesied, and would have passed out of the room; but Lord Linden, forgetting himself for a moment, prevented her exit by springing between her and

"You will not leave me without, at least, one word of pardon?"

"I have said we were quits. You demanded a price for the service you rendered me; I have paid it by listening for the first time to language which, had I a father, or a brother, could not have been addressed to me with impunity; I have neither."

"Let me, at least, vindicate myself. You do not know to what lengths passion will drive a man."

"You are right, I never knew until now; I have learned to-day. Allow me to pass without the necessity of ringing for a servant."

"First you must hear me," exclaimed Lord Linden, almost beside himself at the prospect of her leaving him in anger, and closing her doors henceforward against him. "I know how contemptible I must seem in your eyes. I read it in your countenance; I have no excuse to offer, except the plea that my love for you overleapt the bounds of all discretion."

"I ask for no excuse," answered Madeleine, freezingly.

"I only plead for forgiveness; I only entreat that you will forget the error of which I have been guilty, that you will allow me to see you again; that you will permit me to endeavor to reinstate myself in your esteem."

"My lord, our intercourse is at an end. The service you have rendered me it is no longer in my power to refuse, but you have received its full equivalent. I can spare no more time in the discussion of this subject. Once more, I request you to let me pass without forcing me to ring the bell."

"I obey you, but on condition that I may return, if it be but once more. Promise to grant me one more interview, and I leave you on the instant; I implore you not to refuse."

He approached her, and before Madeleine was even aware of his intention, seized her hand.

The door opened; M. Maurice de Gramont was announced just as Madeleine snatched away the hand Lord Linden had taken, but not before the action had been noticed by Maurice.

He paused at the sight of the nobleman, but Madeleine relieved and rejoiced by the presence of her cousin, unreflectingly hastened toward, and greeted him with a beaming face.

Lord Linden's astonishment was eloquently portrayed upon his countenance. His hostess, recovering her presence of mind, turned to the nobleman, and bowing as courteously as though she had no cause for indignation, wished him good-morning. Her tone seemed to imply that he was taking his leave when

25

Maurice entered.   Lord Linden had no alternative but to withdraw.

Maurice, whose heart was swelling with deep gratitude, with
increased tenderness, with exalted admiration, experienced, at
the sight of Lord Linden, a sickening revulsion of feeling.

This nobleman, then, was received by Madeleine in her own
especial apartment, the doors of which were only opened to her
particular friends ; he was alone with her, and his unusually agitated manner betrayed that he had been conversing upon some
subject of the deepest interest.   Madeleine, too, looked paler
than usual, and the troubled expression which had displaced the
wonted placidity of her countenance was, doubtless, owing to this
unanticipated interruption.

As Lord Linden made his exit, he glanced at Maurice at once
haughtily and inquiringly.   What was this young man, of his
lordship's own rank, doing here, in the boudoir of the mantua-
maker?   What claim had he to admission?   Must he not be
upon an intimate footing? for, had not Madeleine extended her
hand to him without reserve, and as though she were greeting
one who was far from a stranger?

" A lover ! " exclaimed Lord Linden to himself as he closed
the door ; " a rival to whom she listens in spite of her bewitching prudery.   It is incomprehensible! and yet it has inspired
me with new courage ; I will not leave him an undisputed
field."

He had approached the street-door when he reflected that
something might be learned from Mademoiselle Melanie's *employées.*   He turned back and went upstairs to the exhibition
rooms.

Ruth Thornton received him ; and, at his request, displayed
shawls, mantles, scarfs innumerable.   He had desired to see
these articles on the plea of making a selection for his sister.
Hardly looking at them, he purchased one of the most extravagant, while making an attempt to lure Ruth into conversation.
She replied simply and politely, but appeared to be only interested in her occupation, and quite to ignore the occasional gallantry of his remarks.   He was on the point of desisting, when
Victorine, who had been attending to customers in another
apartment, chanced to look into this room, saw Lord Linden,
recognized him as the gentleman with whom she had noticed
Mademoiselle Melanie earnestly conversing on the day previous,
and at once came forward as though to assist Ruth.   The latter
had been rendered very uncomfortable by the deportment of his

lordship, and was only too glad to retire, leaving the forewoman alone with Lord Linden.

The nobleman added so largely to his purchase that Lady Augusta's astonishment must be greatly excited by the number of shawls and scarfs which her brother deemed it possible for a lady to bring into use during a season.

As may be supposed, it was not difficult to lure the lively Frenchwoman into talking of the head of the establishment; and she very speedily gratified Lord Linden by communicating as much of Mademoiselle Melanie's history as she herself knew. But had Mademoiselle Melanie lovers? Or was her vestal-like demeanor genuine? This was difficult and delicate ground to tread upon; yet his lordship was too much in earnest not to venture a step or two.

The wily Victorine now assumed a mysterious air, for she entertained a suspicion that the gentleman did not make inquiries without being deeply interested in the answers. It would be impossible to relate precisely *what* she said. Her confidences were given more by inuendoes and arch glances and knowing shakes of the head, which suggest so much, because they leave so much to the imagination. Lord Linden received the impression that Mademoiselle Melanie, though much admired by the opposite sex, had conducted herself with exemplary decorum *until lately;* but, of late, certain mysterious proceedings had become known to the forewoman of which she did not wish to speak too unreservedly.

The handsome black lace shawl which Lord Linden begged Victorine to accept delighted her to a point which won further confidence; for, while folding it up with caressing touches, and thanking the donor with that grace which belongs to her nation, she admitted that there was a certain M. de Gramont who was enamored of Mademoiselle Melanie, and for whom the latter had evinced a marked preference, though Mademoiselle Melanie evidently wished to act with all possible discretion, and keep his attentions from the eyes of the public.

Be it understood, that with Victorine's lax ideas of morality, keeping an *affaire de cœur* from the eyes of the public was all that was necessary to preserve the honor of a woman who chose to indulge in a *liaison.*

Lord Linden had no alternative but to believe that Mademoiselle Melanie, in spite of her air of exquisite purity, and the chaste dignity which characterized all her words and actions, was, after all, not inaccessible. It was (he reflected) as much out of the question for the Viscount de Gramont to marry a mantua-maker as it was for Lord Linden to marry her; as a natural sequence, their intentions must be the same; and it remained to be proved which would be the successful lover.

He quitted the house enraged with himself for having been deceived; indignant with Madeleine for her successful acting; furious with Maurice, because he looked upon him as a rival; determined to seize an early opportunity of quarrelling with him, and resolved to find some pretext to gain admission to Mademoiselle Melanie's presence through the aid of her obliging forewoman.

Let us return to Maurice, whom we left in Madeleine's boudoir. When the door had closed upon Lord Linden, he said, in a wounded tone, —

" I thought only especial friends were admitted to this sanctum of yours. I did not know, Madeleine, that you were acquainted with Lord Linden."

" He came to bring *Mademoiselle Melanie* an important piece of information; and one which concerns you, Maurice."

Maurice was exasperated, rather than soothed, by this intelligence, and answered, hastily, —

" I am sorry for it. He belongs to a class of men whom I hold in supreme contempt; — a *blasé* idler, whose chief occupation in life is to kill time. Madeleine, forgive me! What a brute I am to speak so harshly when I come to thank you! But the sight of that senseless *roué* in your boudoir, and apparently upon a familiar footing, has made an idiot of me. I will not pay you so bad a compliment as to suggest that *he* is the mysterious lover whom you have refused to name. But why is he here to-day? Why did I see him here yesterday? Why did he, yesterday, when he caught sight of me, suddenly disappear, as though desirous of eluding observation? "

" Maurice, if there be true affection between us," said Madeleine, gently, and laying her delicate white hand upon his, " if there be true, *cousinly* affection between us, we should trust each other wholly, and *in spite of appearances.* Though it is easy for me to explain *why* I admitted Lord Linden to a private interview, it may not always be equally easy to give you explanations; and we may bring great future sorrow upon each other if either give entertainment to a doubt."

" No, Madeleine, I can never doubt that all you do is well and wisely done. Would that I had no cause to doubt your affection for me; no cause to be distracted by jealousy when I see any other man allowed privileges which I long to claim as mine alone! But how is it possible to love you, and not to be hourly tormented by the position in which I am placed? Since you have rejected me as a lover, could I even be known to the world as your cousin, I might, at least, have the joy of protecting you. Must that, too, be denied me?"

"Yes, Maurice. Do you not know how important it is that our relationship should remain undivulged, unsuspected?"

"No; I cannot see the importance! I cannot submit to such an interdiction! Let my grandmother and my father say what they will, I am not bound to yield to so unnatural a request!"

"You will yield to it as my petition, Maurice. Think of it as a favor, a sacrifice I ask of you. If you refuse me, I shall believe that you feel I have no right to ask favors."

"No right?" There you touch me deeply! Madeleine, I am here to-day to learn whether you have not laid me under the deepest obligation — whether it was not by you " —

Madeleine, though she was not a little discomposed by learning that her recent interference in his behalf was suspected, had presence of mind left to endeavor to divert his thoughts. She interrupted him by saying, in a lively tone, —

"I have made several vain attempts to explain Lord Linden's presence here, and you will not permit me to do so, though his visit concerns yourself. Have you no curiosity? I am half inclined to punish you for your indifference."

Before Maurice could reply, Count Tristan de Gramont was announced.

"It is *you* whom I have to thank, — you, good, generous, noble Madeleine, I am sure it is!" said he, excitedly. "It is your hand which has saved me and my son from the precipice over which we were suspended! I could scarcely credit the good news."

"If you talk of good news," replied Madeleine, "I have some to give you which I have just received from Lord Linden. Mr. Rutledge has promised his vote for the left road."

The count looked at her as though he could not trust his ears; then he said, in a tremulous voice that broke into a childish sob, "It is all wonder! You are the Fairy they called you, the magician, — the — the — the " —

Robert opened the door and announced the Countess de Gramont and Mademoiselle de Merrivale.

CHAPTER XXXIII.

MADAME DE GRAMONT.

The countess entered the room casting disdainful glances around her.

Madeleine, who could not suspect the object of her visit, accosted her in astonishment.

"You, madame, beneath my roof; this is an unhoped-for condescension!"

"Do not imagine that I come to be classed among your customers, and order my dresses of you," returned the countess, disdainfully, and waving Madeleine off as the latter advanced toward her.

Bertha felt strongly inclined to quote from a former remark of Gaston de Bois, and retort, "You have done that already, and the transaction was not particularly profitable," but she restrained herself.

"Nor do I come," continued the imperious lady, "as one who stoops to be your visitor! I came to rebuke impertinence, and to demand by what right you have dared to make use of my name as a cloak to give respectability to *charities* forced upon your poor relations."

Madeleine was silent.

"Then the aid which came to me at such an opportune moment *was* yours, Madeleine?" said Maurice. "It was you who saved me from worse than ruin?"

Still no answer from Madeleine's quivering lips.

"Do not force her to say, — do not force her to acknowledge her own goodness and liberality," said Bertha, "we all know that it *was* she, and she will not deny it. Does not her silence speak for her?"

"You thought, perhaps," resumed the countess, even more angrily than before, "that because my son has flown in the face of my wishes, and has mingled himself up with business matters, and because Maurice has chosen to degrade himself by entering a profession, — you thought that you might take the liberty of coming to his assistance, in some temporary difficulty, and might also be pardoned the insolence of using my name; but I resent the impertinence: I will not permit it to pass uncorrected! I will write to the person whom you have deceived

and let him know that the name of the Countess de Gramont
has been used without her authority. I shall also inquire at
whose suggestion he ventured to address an epistle to me."

"No need of that, madame," said M. de Bois, who had entered
the room in time to hear this burst of indignation. "*I*, alone,
am to blame for the liberty of using your name. Knowing
how desirous Mademoiselle de Gramont was to conceal her relationship to your family, I suggested that the money indispensable to her cousin should be sent in such a manner that
it might be supposed to come from you. I also took the responsibility of suggesting to Mr. Emerson that it would be well
to send a line to you, enclosing a receipt for the sum paid into
his hands by me ; one of my motives was to insure that the news
of its payment would at once reach Maurice."

"You presumed unwarrantably, sir," replied the countess.
"You presumed almost as much as did Mademoiselle de Gramont, in supposing that she could use the money acquired in
a manner so degrading to our *noble house* for the benefit of my
grandson."

"That money, madame," rejoined M. de Bois, warmly, "has
saved the honor of your *noble house !* I will leave you to learn
of Count Tristan how it was imperilled, and how it would have
been sullied but for Mademoiselle Madeleine's timely aid."

"It has been *sullied,*" began the countess.

"Not by Mademoiselle de Gramont," returned M. de Bois.
"Once more, I tell you that she has saved your escutcheon from
a stain which could never have been effaced. And for this act
you spurn her, you scorn her generosity ; you tell her she is not
worthy of rendering you a service, instead of bowing down before
her as you, — as we all might well do, in reverence and admiration ; thanking Heaven that such a woman has been placed
in the world, as a glorious example to her own sex, and an inspiration to ours. The burden of her nobility has not crushed
the noble instincts of her heart, or paralyzed her noble hands.
But you do not know all yet ; you owe her another debt " —

"Another debt ? " Count Tristan was the first to exclaim.

"Yes," continued M. de Bois, in a tone of pride, "through her
influence, the influence of the duchess-mantua-maker, the votes
you could never otherwise have secured have been obtained ;
the committee met an hour ago, and the road to the left, which
you so much desired, has been decided upon, and this, this too,
you owe to Mademoiselle Madeleine's exertions."

Neither Maurice nor Count Tristan was allowed to speak, for
M. de Bois went on without pause, —

"And do you deem *this*, *too*, madame, an impertinence, a presumption, a crime, upon the part of your niece? Do you say that this is a favor which you desire to reject? Happily it is not in your power! And now, after she has been cast off, despised, and denounced by you and your son, you are bound to come to her with thanks, if not to implore her pardon."

"Sir," answered the countess, "you have forgotten yourself in a manner which astonishes me, and must astonish all who hear you; and henceforth, I beg you to understand"—

Bertha prevented the sentence of banishment, which the countess was about to pronounce against M. de Bois, from being completed, by saying, abruptly,—

"You will readily understand, M. de Bois, that we are so much surprised that astonishment deprives us of fitting words."

Maurice now turned to Madeleine and said, with the emotion of a genuinely manly nature which is not ashamed to receive a benefit,—

"To owe you so much is not oppressive to me, Madeleine. There is no being on earth, man or woman, to whom I would so willingly be indebted. I know the happiness it confers upon you to be able to do what you have done. I know your thankfulness is greater even than mine; though how great that is, even you cannot"—

"What, Maurice!" broke in the countess; are you so thoroughly without pride or self-respect that you talk of accepting the bounty of Mademoiselle de Gramont? You consent to receive this charity doled out by the hands of a *mantua-maker*?"

Maurice grew livid with suppressed anger at this new insult, because it was levelled at Madeleine, rather than at himself.

"My grandmother, when you are calmer, and when I myself am calmer, I will speak to you on this subject."

"How pale you look, Madeleine!" cried Bertha, suddenly. Surely you are ill!"

These words caused Maurice and M. de Bois to spring to the side of Madeleine. Her strength had been over-taxed by the emotions of the last few days, and it suddenly gave way. It was by a strong effort of volition that she prevented herself from fainting. Maurice, who had caught her in his arms, placed her tenderly in a chair, and for a moment her beautiful head fell upon his shoulder; but she struggled against the insensibility which was stealing over her, and feebly waved her hand in the direction of a small table upon which stood a tumbler and a carafe of water. M. de Bois poured some water into the glass and would have held it to her lips; but Maurice took the tumbler from him, and, as Madeleine drank, the delight of ministering to her overcame his alarm at her indisposition, and sent shivering through his frame a thrill of almost rapture.

In a few moments she lifted her eyes over which the lids had drooped heavily, and, trying to smile, sat up and made an effort to speak; but the pale lips moved without sound, and her countenance still wore a ghastly hue.

"Are you better, my own dear Madeleine? What can I do for you?" asked Bertha, who was kneeling in front of her.

Madeleine murmured faintly, —

"I would like to be left alone, dear. Forgive me for sending you away. I shall soon be better when I am alone."

"Impossible, Madeleine!" cried Maurice, his arm still about her waist. "You will not ask *me* to leave you."

Perhaps she only at that moment became conscious of the supporting arm; for she gently drew herself away, and the palest rose began to tinge her ashy cheek; but it deepened into a sudden crimson flush, as she saw the eyes of the countess angrily fixed upon her.

"Yes, Maurice, do not refuse me. I am better, — I am quite well." And she rose up, forcing her limbs to obey her will. Then, leaning on Bertha's shoulder, whispered, "I entreat you, dear, to make them go, — make them *all* go; I cannot bear more at this moment. Spare me, if you love me!"

"O Madeleine, how can you?" began Bertha.

But M. de Bois, who had perfect reliance in Madeleine's judgment, felt certain that she herself knew what was best for her, and said, —

"Mademoiselle de Gramont will be better alone. If she will allow me, I will apprise Miss Thornton of her indisposition, and we will take our leave."

Madeleine smiled assent, and sank into her seat; for her limbs were faltering.

M. de Bois could not have uttered words better calculated to induce the countess to take her leave. She had no desire to be found in the boudoir of the mantua-maker by any of Madeleine's friends. She said, commandingly, —

"Bertha — Maurice — I desire you to accompany my son and myself. Mademoiselle de Gramont, though my errand here is not fully accomplished, I wish you good morning."

Neither Bertha nor Maurice showed the slightest disposition to obey the order of the countess, but Madeleine said, pleadingly, —

" Go — go — I pray you ! You cannot help me so much as by going."

They both began to remonstrate ; but she checked them by the pressure of her trembling fingers, for each held one of her hands, and said, pleadingly, —

" Do not speak to me now, — another time, — when you will ; but not *now*."

There was something so beseeching in her voice that it was impossible to resist its appeal. Bertha embraced her in silence ; Maurice pressed the hand that lay in his to his lips ; and both followed the countess out of the room.

Count Tristan took the hand Maurice had relinquished, and, giving a glance at the retreating figure of the countess, commenced speaking ; but Madeleine interrupted him with, —

" Another time, I beg. Leave me now."

Just then Gaston de Bois entered, accompanied by Ruth, and, reading Madeleine's wishes in her eyes, placed his arm through that of the count, and conducted him out of the room, closing the door behind him.

CHAPTER XXXIV.

HALF THE WOOER.

Count Tristan was about to hand Bertha into the carriage which the countess had entered, when the young girl paused, with her tiny foot upon the step. She shrank from a discussion with her aunt who was in a high state of indignation. Madame de Gramont's wrath was not only directed against Gaston de Bois, but she was exasperated by Bertha's interference just when the haughty lady had been on the point of making him feel that he would no longer be ranked among the number of her friends and welcome visitors. While Bertha's foot still rested upon the step, she glanced over her shoulder and saw Gaston standing beside Maurice. Her decision was made. She looked into the carriage and said, —

" You will have the kindness to excuse me from accompanying you, aunt ; I will take advantage of the beautiful day and walk

Having uttered these words, she drew back quickly and tripped away before the answer of the countess could reach her. Maurice walked on one side of her, and what was more natural than that Gaston should occupy the place on the other side?

For a brief space all three pursued their way in silence, then Bertha made an effort to converse. Maurice answered in mono-syllables and those were followed by deep sighs. Gaston seemed to be hardly more master of language, though his taciturnity had a different origin; it was occasioned by the unexpected delight of finding himself walking beside Bertha, who constantly lifted her sweet face inquiringly to his, as though to ask why he had no words.

Maurice was in a perplexed state of mind which caused him a nervous longing for entire seclusion. Even sympathy, sympathy from those who were as dear to him as Bertha and Gaston, jarred upon his highly-strung nerves.

All at once, he stopped and said, —

"Gaston, I will leave you to conduct Bertha home; I fancy you will not object to the trust," and trying to simulate a smile, he walked away.

Gaston, left alone with Bertha, quickly regained his power of speech. They were passing the Capitol; how lovely the grounds looked in their spring attire! The day, too, was de-licious. The opportunity of seeing Bertha alone was a happi-ness that might not soon return.

"These grounds are Mademoiselle Madeleine's favorite prom-enade," remarked M. de Bois. "Have you ever seen them?"

Bertha made no reply, but she moved toward the gate and they entered. A short silence ensued, then she said abruptly, "What an heroic character is Madeleine's!"

"A character," returned Gaston, tenderly, "which exerts a holy influence upon all with whom she is thrown in contact, and works more good, teaches more truth by the example of a pa-tient, noble, holy life than could be taught by a thousand ser-mons from the most eloquent lips." He paused, and then con-tinued in a tone of deep feeling, "*I* may well say so! I shud-der to think what a weak, useless, self-centred being I should have been but for her agency."

"You seem far happier," replied Bertha, smiling archly, "than you did in Brittany! And this change was wrought by"—

"Mademoiselle Madeleine! It was she who made me feel that we are all too ready with our peevish outcries against the beautiful world in which we have been placed; too ready to complain that all is sadness and sorrow and disappointment, when the gloom exists *within* ourselves, not *without* us; it is from ourselves the misty darkness springs; it is we ourselves who have lost, or who have never possessed, the secret of being happy, and we exclaim that there is no happiness on the face of the globe! It is we ourselves who are '*flat, stale,* and *unprofitable,*' not our neighbors; though we are sure to charge them with the dulness and insipidity for which we, alone, are responsible."

Bertha answered, "One secret of Madeleine's cheerfulness is her unquenchable *hope.* Even in her saddest moments, the light of hope never appeared to be extinguished. It shone about her almost like a visible halo, and illumined all her present and her future. Have you not remarked the strength of this characteristic?"

"That I have!" he replied with warmth. "And it forced upon my conviction the truth of the poet's words that '*hope* and *wisdom* are akin'; that it is always wise to hope, and the most wise, because those who have most faith, ever hope most. She taught me to hope when I was plunged in the depths of despair!"

Bertha blushed suddenly, as though those fervently-uttered words had awakened some suggestion which could not be framed into language.

"This seat is shady and retired, and commands a fine view of the garden," remarked Gaston, pausing. There was an invitation in his accents.

Bertha, half unconsciously seated herself, and Gaston did the same. Then came another pause, a longer one than before; it was broken by Bertha, who exclaimed, —

"You defended Madeleine nobly and courageously! and how I thanked you!"

"I only did her justice, or, rather, I did her far less than justice," returned Gaston.

"Yet few men would have dared to say what you did in my aunt's presence."

"Could any man who had known Mademoiselle Madeleine as intimately as I have had the honor of knowing her, through these four last painful years of her life, could any man who had learned to reverence her as I reverence her, have said less?"

"But my aunt, by her towering pride, awes people out of what they *ought* to do, and what they *want* to do; at least, she does *me;* and therefore, — therefore I honored you all the more when I saw you had the courage to tell her harsh truths, while pleading Madeleine's cause so eloquently."

Gaston was much moved by these unanticipated and warmly uttered commendations. He tried to speak, but once again relapsed into his old habit of stammering.

"Your praises are most pre — pre — pre " —

Bertha finished his sentence as in by-gone days. " Precious, are they indeed? I am glad! I am truly glad that they are precious."

M. de Bois, notwithstanding the happiness communicated by this frank declaration, could make no reply. What *could* he answer? And what right had he to give too delightful an interpretation to the chance expressions of the lovely being who sat there before him, uttering words in her ingenuous simplicity, which would have inspired a bolder, more self-confident man, with the certainty that she regarded him with partial eyes.

His gaze was riveted upon the ground, and so was hers. Neither spoke. How long they would have sat thus, each looking for some movement to be made by the other, is problematical. The double reverie was broken by a well-known voice, which cried out, —

" Ah, M. de Bois, you are the very man I wanted to see. Good-morning, Mademoiselle de Merrivale."

Lord Linden and his sister, Lady Augusta, stood before them. M. de Bois instantly rose, and Bertha invited Lady Augusta to take the vacant place. Lord Linden had already seized Gaston's arm, and drawn him aside.

" My dear fellow," began the nobleman, " Do you know that I have been vainly seeking you for a couple of days! I am in a most awkward predicament; but I suppress particulars to make a long story short; in a word, I have discovered the fair unknown! I expected, — you know what sort of woman I expected to find."

" Perfectly," answered Gaston, laughing, " a walking angel, minus the traditional wings. I remember your description. Perhaps the lady grows more earthly upon a better acquaintance ? "

"No, not by any means. I found her more enchanting than ever ; but hang it, unless you had seen her, you could not comprehend how I could have made such a confounded mistake. This lovely being is — is — is — don't prepare to laugh. I shall be tempted to knock you down if you do, for really my feelings are so much interested that I could not bear even a friend's ridicule."

" Well, go on," urged M. de Bois. " The lady in question is, — not an angel, unless it be a fallen one; that I understand; good; then *what* is she? "

" A *mantua-maker!*" exclaimed Lord Linden, in accents of deep mortification.

Well might he have been startled by the change that came over Gaston's countenance ; the merriment by which it had been lighted up suddenly vanished; he looked aghast, astounded, and his features worked as though with ill-suppressed rage.

" I see you are amazed: I thought you would be! You did not take me for such a greenhorn! But, in spite of her trade, — her *profession*, as it is considerately called in this country, — she is the most peerless creature ; any man might have been duped."

" And her name?" inquired Gaston, in an agitated voice, though he hardly needed the confirmation to his fears contained in Lord Linden's answer.

" Mademoiselle Melanie!"

" Good heavens! how unfortunate!" exclaimed Gaston, not knowing what he was saying.

" Unfortunate," repeated Lord Linden; " you may well say *that*. But as marrying her is out of the question, there may possibly be an alternative " —

" *What* alternative? *What do you mean?*" demanded Gaston, turning upon him fiercely.

" It does not strike me that my meaning is so difficult to divine," replied the other, lightly. " When a woman is not in a position to become the wife of a man who has fallen desperately in love with her, there is only one thing else that he will very naturally seek to " —

" Forbear, my lord! I cannot listen to such language," cried Gaston, angrily. " You could not insult a pure woman, no matter in what station you found her, by such a suggestion. I will not believe you capable of such baseness."

Lord Linden looked at him in questioning amazement ; then answered, somewhat scornfully, —

" Really, I was not aware that instances of the kind were so rare, or that your punctilious morality would be so terribly shocked by an every-day occurrence. If the lovely creature herself consents to my proposition, I consider that the arrangement will be a very fair one."

" Consents?" echoed Gaston, lashed into fury. " Do you know of whom you are speaking? This Mademoiselle Melanie is one of the noblest, — that is to say, one of the most noble-minded, and one of the most chaste of women."

" You have heard of her then? Perhaps seen her?" inquired Lord Linden, eagerly. " As for her vaunted chastity,

that is neither here nor there, — that *may* or *may not* be ficti-
tious. I have heard from the best authority that she receives
the private visits of titled admirers, whose attentions can hardly
be of a nature very different from mine. You see, it is fair game,
and if I succeed " —

" For Heaven's sake stop ! " said Gaston, losing all control of
his temper. Then reflecting that this very energy in defending
her might compromise Madeleine, he said, more calmly, " I beg
your lordship to pause before you insult Mademoiselle Melanie.
I know something of her history. She bears an unblemished
name ; she has a highly sensitive, a most delicate and refined
nature. Could she deem it possible that any man entertained
toward her such sentiments as those to which you have just
given utterance, it would almost kill her."

Lord Linden's lips curled sarcastically, but he did not feel
disposed to communicate how completely Mademoiselle Melanie
was already aware of those sentiments. He now essayed to put
an end to the conversation by saying, —

" I shall bear your remarks in mind ; though the accounts we
have heard of the fair mantua-maker differ materially."

" Who has dared to slander her ? " demanded Gaston, with an
air which seemed to assert his right to ask the question.

" I have not said that she has been slandered. I see we are
not likely to understand each other ; let us join the ladies."

As he spoke, he walked toward Lady Augusta and Bertha.
His sister rose and made her adieu.

When Lord Linden and Lady Augusta had passed on, Gaston
was surprised to see that Bertha did not appear desirous of returning to the hotel. She sat still, and, when he approached her,
drew her dress slightly aside, as though to make room for him
to resume his seat. Could he do otherwise than comply ? She
sat with her head bent down. The shining ringlets falling in
rich, golden showers, partly concealed her face. She was tracing letters upon the gravel-walk with her parasol. Gaston was
too much moved by his painful conversation with Lord Linden
to start any indifferent topic ; and Bertha's manner, so different
from her usual frank, lively bearing, made it still more difficult
for him to know how to accost her.

At last, without raising her eyes, she said, " You and Lord
Linden were having a very animated discussion. At one time
I began to be afraid that you were quarrelling."

" We certainly never differed more. I doubt if we shall
ever be friends again."

This assertion was uttered so earnestly that Bertha involuntarily looked up into Gaston's face. It was flushed by his recent anger, and the expression of his countenance betokened perplexity mingled with vexation.

What woman ever saw the man she loved out of temper without seeking to pour oil upon the troubled waters, even at the risk of being charged with her sex's constitutional curiosity ? for an attempt to soothe includes a desire to fathom the secret cause of annoyance. If there be women who are not stirred by impulses of this kind they are cast in moulds the very opposite to that of Bertha.

She said, in a soft and winning tone, " Has he done you wrong ? "

" He has grossly wronged one whom I esteem more highly, perhaps, than any woman, — any being living," answered Gaston, firing up at the recollection of Lord Linden's insinuations ; then he corrected himself. " I should have said any — any oth — oth — other — but " —

" It was a woman — a lady, then, whom he wronged ? " inquired Bertha, betraying redoubled interest at this inadvertent admission.

Gaston perceived that he had said too much ; but, in adding nothing more, he did not extricate himself from the difficulty. His silence could only be interpreted into an affirmative.

" And one whom you esteem more highly than all others ? " persisted Bertha. " Whom do you esteem so highly as Madeleine ? Surely it could not have been Madeleine ? Lord Linden did not speak disrespectfully of Madeleine ? "

Gaston had gone too far for concealment. " He spoke of Mademoiselle Melanie, the mantua-maker ; but I warrant I have silenced him ! "

" Madeleine is very happy in the possession of such a true friend as you are ! one upon whom she can always lean, — always depend, — one who can never fail her ! Yes, she is very, very happy ! When I heard you defending her before my aunt, I said to myself, ' Oh that I had such a friend ! ' "

Would not Gaston de Bois have been the dullest of mortals if those words had failed to infuse a sudden courage into his heart ?

He replied with impetuous ardor, " Would — would that you could be induced to accept the same friend as your own ! Would that he might dare to hope that some day, however distant, you would grant him a nearer, dearer title ! Would that he might believe such a joy possible ! "

Bertha spoke no word, made no movement, but sat with her eyes bent on the ground. Her manner emboldened Gaston to seize her hand; she did not withdraw it from his clasp; then he comprehended his joy, and poured out the history of his long-concealed passion with a tender eloquence of which he never imagined himself capable.

If, when he awoke that morning from a dream in which Bertha's lovely countenance was vividly pictured, some prophetic voice had whispered that ere the sun went down he would have uttered such language, and she have listened to it, he would not have believed the verification of that delightful prediction within the bounds of possibility. Yet, when the happy pair left the capitol grounds to return to the hotel, Gaston walked by the side of his betrothed bride.

It is true that the wealthy heiress had lured on her self-distrusting lover to make a declaration which he had not contemplated; but who will charge her with unmaidenly conduct? The most modest of women are daily doing, unaware, what Bertha did somewhat more consciously. Shakespeare, who read the hearts of women with the penetrating eyes of a seer, and who never painted a heroine who was not the type of a class, pictured no rare or imaginary order of being in his beauteous Desdemona,—

> "A maiden never bold,
> Of spirit so still and quiet that her motion
> Blushed at herself,"—

who was yet "*half the wooer.*" And there is no lack of men who can testify (in spite of the feminine denial which we anticipate) that they owe their happiness (or misery) to some gentle, timid girl who was nevertheless "*half the wooer.*"

CHAPTER XXXV.

A REVELATION.

BERTHA was too happy as she walked toward the hotel, to dread the rebukes which she had good reason to anticipate from the countess. For a young lady to traverse the streets alone with a gentleman, however intimate a friend, was, according to the strict rules of French etiquette, a gross breach of propriety. And, though the escort of a gentleman was deemed allowable in the purer and less conventional society of the land in which they were sojourning, Bertha knew that her supercilious aunt considered all customs barbarous but those of her refined native country.

The countess was sitting in her drawing-room, evidently in a state of high excitement, when Bertha and Gaston entered. Count Tristan appeared to be endeavoring to palliate his recent conduct by a series of contradictory statements, and a garbled explanation of the events which had placed Maurice in a dubious position; but his mother had sufficient shrewdness to detect that his object was to deceive, not to enlighten her.

The appearance of Bertha and Gaston gave inexpressible relief to the count, and his satisfaction betrayed itself in a singularly unnatural and childish manner. He kissed Bertha on both cheeks as though he had not seen her for a long period, asked her how she did, shook hands warmly with Gaston as if they had not parted a couple of hours before, offered them chairs, put his arm about Bertha, and drew her to him, as though he were making her his shield against some imaginary assailant.

"What is the meaning of this prolonged absence, Bertha?" demanded the countess, without appearing to notice M. de Bois. "Where have you been? Why did you not return immediately? Where is Maurice?"

"The day was so fine," answered Bertha, trying to speak with some show of dignity and composure, but failing lamentably, "that I thought I would enjoy a walk in the capitol grounds. We met Lady Augusta and Lord Linden. Maurice did not return with us."

"Are you aware of the singular impropriety of your behavior, Mademoiselle de Merrivale? Is it possible that a niece of mine can have become so perfectly regardless of all the rules of decorum?"

"Will you excuse me for the present, aunt?" interrupted Bertha, retreating toward the door in a rather cowardly fashion. "I leave M. de Bois to — M. de Bois wishes to " —

Gaston had risen and opened the door for her to pass, with as much self-possession as though bashfulness had not been the tormenting evil genius of his existence. His look reassured her, and, without finishing her sentence, she disappeared.

The countess rose with even more than her wonted stateliness, and was about to follow her niece; but M. de Bois, pretending not to perceive her intention, closed the door and said, —

"There is a communication which I desire to have the honor of making to Madame de Gramont and Count Tristan."

"You can make no communication to which I feel disposed to listen," answered the countess haughtily, and advancing toward the door.

"I regret to hear the aunt of Mademoiselle de Merrivale say so, as I have this morning ventured to solicit the hand of that young lady in marriage, and have received a favorable answer to my suit, as well as permission to request the approval of her relatives."

The countess sank into the nearest chair. She knew that her consent was a mere form, and that Bertha could dispose of her hand in freedom.

Count Tristan, still speaking in a confused, incoherent manner, exclaimed, —

"Bless my soul! How astonishing! The game's up, and Maurice has lost his chance! Bertha's fortune is to go out of the family! It's very puzzling. How did it all come about? De Bois, you sly fellow, you lucky dog, I never suspected you. Managed matters quietly, eh? Should never have thought you were the man to succeed with a pretty girl."

"Really," returned Gaston good-humoredly, "I am almost as astonished as you are by Mademoiselle de Merrivale's prefer-ence. Let me hope that the Countess de Gramont and yourself will render my happiness complete by approving of Madem-oiselle Bertha's choice."

"Of course, of course; there's nothing else to be done; we have lost our trump card, but there's no use of confessing it! Very glad to welcome you as a relative, sir; very happy indeed; everything shall be as Mademoiselle de Merrivale desires."

Count Tristan uttered these disjointed sentences, in the flurried, bewildered manner which had marked his conduct since Gaston entered. A stranger might easily have imagined that the count was under the influence of delirium; for his face was scar-let his eyes shone with lurid brightness, his muscles twitched, his hands trembled nervously, and he was, to all appearance, not thoroughly conscious of what he was doing.

His mother's look of rebuke was entirely lost upon him, and he rattled on with an air of assumed hilarity which was painfully absurd.

Gaston was disinclined to give the disdainful lady an opportu-

nity of expressing her opposition to his suit, and, pretending to
interpret her silence favorably, he took his hat, and said, "I
thank you for the cordial manner in which my proposition has
been received; I hope to have the pleasure of visiting Mademoiselle de Merrivale this evening; I wish you a good-morning."

The door had closed upon him before the countess had recovered herself sufficiently to reply.

That evening, before paying his proposed visit to Bertha, M.
de Bois sought Madeleine, to make her a participator in the happiness which she had so truly predicted would, one day, be his.
He also purposed, if possible, to put her on her guard against the
advances of Lord Linden. At the door he encountered Maurice,
who with unaffected warmth, congratulated him upon his be-
trothal.

When the servant answered their ring, both gentlemen were
denied admission. Mademoiselle Melanie was not well, and had
retired.

"Are you going back to the hotel?" asked Gaston, as they
left the door.

"No, not until late. I hardly know what I shall do with
myself; I may go to the reading-rooms."

As their roads were different, they parted, and Maurice, not
being able to select any better place of refuge, took his way to
the reading-rooms most frequented by gentlemen of the metropolis. He was fortunate in finding an apartment vacant. He
sat down by the table, took up a newspaper, though the words
before him might have been printed in an unknown tongue, for
any sense they conveyed.

He had been sitting about half an hour, musing sadly, when
Lord Linden sauntered through the rooms. The instant he observed Maurice, he advanced toward him, and unceremoniously
took a seat at the same table. This was just the opportunity
which the *piqued* nobleman had desired. Maurice returned his
salutation politely, but with an occupied air which seemed to forbid conversation. But Lord Linden was not to be baffled. He
opened a periodical, and, after listlessly turning the leaves, closed
it, and, leaning over the table in the direction of Maurice, said,
with a sarcastic intonation, —

"I hope you had an agreeable visit, M. de Gramont."

Maurice looked up in surprise.

"I beg pardon, — I do not comprehend. To what visit do you
allude?"

"When we last met," returned Lord Linden, in the same offensive manner, "I left you in charming company; the lovely mantua-maker, you know!—the very queen of sirens!"

Maurice flushed crimson and half started from his chair, then sat down again, making a strong effort to control himself, as he answered coldly, "I am at a loss to comprehend the meaning of the language in which you are pleased to indulge."

"'Pon my life, that's going too far; especially as I feel not a little aggrieved that your inopportune entrance cut short my visit. And you seemed to be a decided favorite. Deuced lucky! for she is the handsomest woman in Washington. Come, be frank enough to confess that you think so, and I'll admit that I think her the most beautiful woman upon the face of the globe."

"My frankness," returned Maurice, sharply, "forces me to confess that this conversation is particularly distasteful to me. The lady in question"—

Lord Linden interrupted him with a light laugh. "Lady? Oh! I see you adopt the customs and phraseology of the country in which you live; and *here*, a mantua-maker is, of course, a lady; just as a respectable boot-black is, in common parlance, an accomplished gentleman."

"My lord,"—began Maurice, angrily; but Lord Linden would not permit him to continue.

"Oh, don't be offended; I suppose you are a naturalized foreigner; you are quite right to accept the manners of the country you adopt; it is the true diplomatic dodge. And, besides, I admit that the *lady* in question might anywhere be mistaken for a thorough lady. She has all the points which betoken the high-bred dame. I'll not quarrel with the term you use! All I ask is fair play, and that you will not attempt to monopolize the field."

"Lord Linden," replied Maurice, unable to endure this impertinence any longer, "once more I beg to inform you that you are using language to which I cannot listen. I will not permit any man to speak of that lady in the manner which you have chosen to employ. I shall consider it a personal insult if you persist."

"Indeed! Have matters gone so far? Really, I did not suspect that the ground was already occupied, and that the *lady* whose mantua-making and millinery are the admiration of all Washington, had a protector by whom her less favored acquaintances must expect to be taken to task."

These words were spoken in a tone sufficiently caustic to render their meaning unmistakable.

"She has protectors, my lord,— legal protectors,— who are ready to prove their right to defend her," replied Maurice, with severity, and rising as he spoke.

All considerations of prudence,— the wishes of Madeleine and of his family,— were forgotten at the moment: she was insulted, and he was there to defend her; that was all he remembered.

Lord Linden, though he could not but be struck by the tone and manner of the viscount, echoed the words, "The right?"

"Yes, the *right*, as well as the *might*. Mademoiselle Melanie, the mantua-maker, is in reality Mademoiselle Madeleine Melanie de Gramont, the daughter of the late Duke de Gramont, and the second cousin of my father, Count Tristan de Gramont."

"Good heavens! of what gross stupidity I have been guilty! How shall I ever obtain your pardon?"

Without answering this question, Maurice went on.

"You have forced me to betray a secret which my cousin earnestly desired to keep; but it is time that her family should refuse their countenance to this farce of concealment. I, for one, will not be a party to it any longer. I will never consent to calling her, or hearing her called, by any but her true title, and I do not care how soon that is proclaimed to the world."

"M. de Gramont," said Lord Linden, whose embarrassment was mingled with undisguised joy, "I am overwhelmed with shame, and I beg that you will forget what I have said. My apology is based upon the error under which I was laboring. I make it very humbly, very gladly, and trust the Viscount de Gramont will accept it generously. Without being able to conceive the circumstances which have placed a noble lady in a position which has caused me to fall into so grave a mistake, I shall only be too proud, too thankful, to make the one reparation in my power,"—

Lord Linden had not finished speaking, but Maurice was disinclined to hear any more or to prolong the interview, and said, frigidly, "I am bound to accept your apology; but your lordship can hardly expect that I can find it easy to forget that my cousin, Mademoiselle de Gramont, has been regarded by you in an unworthy light. Good-evening."

Feigning not to see Lord Linden's outstretched hand, and disregarding his attempt to exculpate himself further, Maurice walked out of the reading-room, leaving the nobleman too much elated by the discovery of Madeleine's rank to experience a natural indignation at her cousin's cavalier treatment.

CHAPTER XXXVI.

THE SUITOR.

LORD LINDEN, when the Viscount de Gramont abruptly left him, returned to his lodgings, and, in spite of the lateness of the hour, wrote to Madeleine, implored her pardon for the presumption into which he had been lured by his ignorance of her rank, and formally solicited her hand. That night the happy nobleman's dreams, when he could sleep, and his waking thoughts when he courted slumber in vain, had an auroral tinge hitherto unknown. As soon as the sound of busy feet, traversing the corridor, announced that the much-desired morning had at last arrived, he rang his bell, gave his letter into the hands of a sleepy domestic, and ordered it to be delivered immediately.

What was the next step which propriety demanded? To see Mademoiselle de Gramont's relatives, to make known his suit to them, and to solicit their approval.

He considered himself fortunate in finding both Madame de Gramont and Count Tristan at home. The former received him with as much cordiality as her constitutional stiffness permitted, but the latter appeared to be in a half-lethargic state; he scarcely rose to welcome his visitor, spoke feebly and indistinctly, and, as he sank back in his seat, leaned his flushed face upon his hands.

"My visit is somewhat early," remarked Lord Linden, "but I was impatient to see you, for I came to speak of your niece, Mademoiselle de Gramont."

The count looked up eagerly.

Madame de Gramont replied before her son could speak, "The person whom you designate as my niece has forfeited all right to that title, and is not recognized by her family."

"I nevertheless venture to hope," returned the nobleman with marked suavity, "that, under existing circumstances, the alienation will only be temporary."

The countess broke out angrily: "The impertinence of this young person exceeds all bounds! She gave us to understand that she possessed, at least, the modesty to hide her real name, and had no desire to disgrace her family by proclaiming that it was borne by a person in her degraded condition; but this, it seems, is only another evidence of her duplicity and covert manœuvring; she has taken care that your lordship should become acquainted with a relationship which we can never cease to deplore."

"You do her wrong," replied Lord Linden, with becoming spirit; "I regret to say she so scrupulously concealed her rank that I was led into a great error, — one for which I now desire amply to atone. It was from M. Maurice de Gramont that I learned the true name of the so-called Mademoiselle Melanie."

"Maurice!" cried the countess and her son together.

"I received the information from him last evening," said Lord Linden, "and I have now come to solicit the hand of Mademoiselle de Gramont in marriage."

The suggestion that Madeleine could thus magically be raised out of her present humiliating condition, and that all her short-comings might be covered by the broad cloak of a title, took such delightful possession of the haughty lady's mind that there was no room even for surprise. While Count Tristan was vehemently shaking hands with Lord Linden, and stammering out broken and unintelligible sentences, his mother said gravely, —

"We consider your lordship, in all respects, an acceptable *parti* for a member of our family. I have ever entertained for Mademoiselle de Gramont the strongest affection, in spite of her lamentable eccentricities. But these I would prefer to forget."

"Yes, that's it! That's the trump card now! — forget, — forget all about it!" cried Count Tristan, hilariously. He had recovered his power of utterance, yet spoke like a man partially intoxicated. "Let the past be forgotten, bury it deep; never dig it up! There are circumstances which had better not be mentioned. I myself have been mixed up with the affair; of course, I was an innocent party; I beg you to believe so. It's all right — quite right — quite right!"

Though it was so evident that Count Tristan's mind was wandering, — at all events, that there was no connection in his ideas, — his mother could not stoop to admit any such possibility, and said sternly, —

"My son, your language strikes me as singular. Lord Linden, of course, comprehends that he has our consent to his union with Mademoiselle de Gramont; but we also wish him to understand we expect him to remove his wife to his own country, or some other land where her history will not be known. Upon this condition we will pardon our relative's vagaries, and give our sanction to her nuptials."

Lord Linden was not a man who could, with any complacency, consent to have conditions enforced upon him by the family of the lady whom he selected as his wife; his pride was quite as great as theirs; but before he had obtained Madeleine's consent to his suit, it was politic to preserve the favor of those who could influence her decision.

Turning to Count Tristan, he observed, "I sent a letter to Mademoiselle de Gramont this morning, and I hope to be honored by an answer during the day. Would it be asking too much if I begged that you would see the lady, and inform her of the flattering reception which Madame de Gramont and yourself have given my proposals?"

"I will go at once," replied Count Tristan. "An open visit, of course; no need of concealment now! Where's my hat? What has become of it? It's got a trick lately of getting out of the way."

Count Tristan, though his hat stood on the table before him, tottered across the room, looking about in a weak, flurried way. His mother was not willing to attribute his singularly helpless, troubled, and childish demeanor, to the perturbed state of his brain, and said severely, though addressing her words to Lord Linden, —

"Count Tristan's gratification at the intelligence you have communicated, and his desire to serve your lordship, appear to have somewhat bewildered him. He was always very much attached to Mademoiselle de Gramont."

"Attached to her? Certainly! *Certainly!*" replied the count. "Though she did not always think so! I was devotedly attached to her when she imagined quite the contrary! This is my hat, I believe."

He took up Lord Linden's.

"I beg pardon, — *that*, I think is mine," replied his lordship; and then, indicating the one upon the table which Count Tristan apparently did not see, asked, "Is not this yours?"

"I suppose so; it cannot be any one's else; there are only two of us. I wish you a good-morning."

With a forced, unnatural laugh, he left the room.

Count Tristan's deportment, in general, was almost as calm and stately as that of his august mother; though it was only a weak reflex of hers; accordingly the change in his demeanor surprised Lord Linden unpleasantly; but he took leave of the countess without endeavoring to solve an enigma to which he had no clew.

CHAPTER XXXVII.

A SHOCK.

COUNT TRISTAN, on reaching Madeleine's residence was ushered into her boudoir. He found her reclining upon the sofa, with a book in her hand. She had not entirely recovered from her indisposition, and wisely thought that one of the most effectual modes of battling against illness was to divert the mind : an invaluable medicine, too little in vogue among the suffering, yet calculated to produce marvellous amelioration of physical pain. As all *matter* exists from, and is influenced by, spiritual causes, the happy workings of this mental ministry are very comprehensible. Madeleine invariably found medicinal and restorative properties in the pages of an interesting and healthful-toned volume which would draw her out of the contemplation of her own ailments. She had trained herself, when the prostration of her faculties or other circumstances rendered it impossible for her to read, to lie still and reflect upon all the blessings that were accorded to her, to count them over, one by one, and *compel* herself to estimate each at its full value. In this manner she successfully counteracted the depression and unrest that attend bodily disease, and often succeeded in lifting her mind so far above its disordered mortal medium that she was hardly conscious of suffering, which was nevertheless very real. Sceptical reader ! you smile in doubt, and think that if Madeleine's wisdom and patience could accomplish this feat, she was a rare instance of womanhood. Try her experiment faithfully and then decide !

Madeleine only partially rose when Count Tristan entered.

" My dear niece, — my dearest Madeleine, — I hope you are not ill ? "

Although the count spoke with an air of exaggerated affection, his manner was far more self-possessed than when he left the hotel. The fresh air had revived him. Madeleine was not struck by any singularity in his deportment.

" Not exactly ill, yet not quite well," she answered, without pretending to respond to his oppressive tenderness ; "and I was trying to forget myself."

" That was always your way, Madeleine ; you are always forgetting yourself and remembering others. I always said so. I always appreciated your beautiful traits. The time has come when your whole family will appreciate them, and rejoice that you are restored to us. My mother is in a very different frame of mind to day; you must forget all that took place yesterday. You must forgive the past, and accept the hand of reconciliation which she extends to you."

"Is it possible that the Countess de Gramont has charged you to say this for her?"

"This, and a great deal more. She opens her arms to you; hereafter you two are to be as mother and daughter."

Count Tristan spoke with so much earnestness, that probably he had succeeded in believing his own liberally invented statements.

"It seems very strange," returned Madeleine; "yet I thank the countess for her unlooked-for cordiality. I do not know what good angel has opened her heart to me; but I am grateful if she will give me a place there."

"The good angel in question was Lord Linden," answered the count, quite seriously. "His lordship called this morning. I left him with my mother."

"Lord Linden?"

"Yes, it was at his suggestion that I hastened here; not that I thought any influence of mine was needed; but just now it is well to keep in with every one, and you must oblige me by permitting Lord Linden to imagine that it was through my advocacy you were induced to look favorably upon his suit."

"That is impossible."

"Not at all; a mere suggestion in your letter will have the desired effect. You have not answered Lord Linden's letter yet, — have you."

"No, — I intend to reply this morning, and " —

"That's right! You will grant me this favor, I know you will! Say that *after having conversed with me*, you accept the offer of his hand."

"I mean to decline it in the most definite manner."

"Decline?" cried Count Tristan, breathing hard, while his face rapidly changed color; for at one moment it was overspread with a death-like pallor, and then suddenly grew purple. "Decline? Such a thing is not to be thought of; you are jesting?"

"I was never more serious in my life."

"But you will think better of the matter; you will listen to reason; you will reverse your decision," pleaded the count, his nervous incoherence and confusion increasing as he grew more and more agitated. "It's for the honor of the family to say ' yes,

and therefore 'yes' is the proper *answer*, — eh, I
joke any more, my dear ; it troubles me ; it gives
bing and heavy weight in my brain.   All's righ

Count Tristan lay back in his chair, and con
though his words were no longer comprehensib

Madeleine now began to be alarmed, and, :
said kindly, " Can I give you anything?   Y
Let me order you a glass of wine."

He stared at her with vacant, glassy eyes, wh
and twitched without giving forth any distinct s
up his arms in appeal ; they dropped suddenly,
giant's invisible hand, and his head fell forward

Madeleine, greatly terrified, spoke to him
shook him gently by the shoulder, to rouse hi
his head ; the face she succeeded in turning
frightfully distorted ; white foam oozed froi
eyes were suffused with blood.   She had nev
person in a fit, but instinct told her the nature (

Her violent ringing of the bell quickly bro
her assistance, and she ordered Robert to sum
with the utmost haste.

This distinguished physician pronounced the
and, after applying those remedies which recc
science have proved most efficacious, ordered i
undressed and put to bed.

Madeleine's own chamber was prepared for
The attack was of brief duration, and he re
violence soon after the physician arrived, l
hausted and insensible.

Another critical case required Dr. Bayard
tendance, and after giving Madeleine minute d
his leave, saying that he would return in a coup

Then Madeleine, who had been engrossed by
promptly ministering to the sufferer, remembere
family should at once be made aware of his co
frightful shock the countess would receive wl
her son's state !   And Maurice and Bertha,— v
greatly alarmed?   How could intelligence of
most gently communicated?   Should Madel
note bearing the tidings might startle his n
Madeleine saw but one alternative, — it was to
break the sorrowful news as delicately as possil
waste a moment in pondering upon the man

haughty countess might receive her, but ordered her carriage, and drove to the hotel, leaving Count Tristan under the charge of Ruth, and Mrs. Lawkins, the housekeeper.

Arrived at her destination, Madeleine ordered her servant to inquire for the Viscount de Gramont. He was not at home. Was Mademoiselle de Merrivale at home? The same reply. Was the Countess de Gramont at home? Madeleine could not help hoping that a negative would again be returned, for she grew sick at heart at the prospect of encountering her aunt alone. The countess was within.

Madeleine's card was requested. She had none. What name should the servant give? Here was another difficulty: she was only known as "*Mademoiselle Melanie;*" she could not make use of her real name; besides, she feared that the countess would deny her admission if made aware who was her visitor. But something must be done. Madame de Gramont had issued orders that prevented any guest from entering her presence without permission. Madeleine asked for a sheet of note-paper, and, with her pencil, hastily wrote, —

"Madeleine entreats the Countess de Gramont to see her for a moment. She has a matter of importance to communicate."

The servant returned almost immediately, and, replacing the note in Madeleine's hand, said, "The Countess de Gramont desires me to say that she is engaged."

"It is absolutely necessary that I should see Madame de Gramont," replied Madeleine. "I will bear the blame of her displeasure if you will show me to her apartment."

"The lady is very rigid, ma'am. I don't dare."

"She will be angry at first, I admit," returned Madeleine; "but her dissatisfaction will not last when she knows upon what errand I have come. I can confidently promise you *that.* Perhaps you will consider this money sufficient compensation for her displeasure, should I prove wrong; and if I am right, you can keep it in payment for having served me."

She handed him a piece of gold, which the man took with so little hesitation it left no doubt upon Madeleine's mind that he was well acquainted with the nature of a bribe.

"I'll do what I can, ma'am, if you will take the blame," replied he.

Madeleine alighted, followed him to the door of the room which he designated as the drawing-room of the countess, and then desired him to retire; he obeyed with well-pleased alacrity.

The young girl had been trembling from agitation until that

27 *

moment; but there was necessity for calmness in executing her mission. She opened the door with a firm hand, and entered the apartment with unfaltering steps.

The countess was sitting with her back turned to the entrance; she did not perceive Madeleine until the latter stood beside her.

Madame de Gramont pushed back her chair with a repellant gesture, and, before her niece could speak, asked indignantly, " What is the meaning of this intrusion? Did you not receive my message, Mademoiselle de Gramont, and understand that I declined to see you? "

" I received it, madame," returned Madeleine, mildly and mournfully; " but I feel sure you will pardon an intrusion I could not avoid when you learn the cause which brings me here."

" I can divine your errand, Mademoiselle de Gramont; you probably imagine that, because I permitted my son to say that your marriage with Lord Linden would, *after a proper interval,* allow me to acknowledge you once more as a relative, your mere acceptance of his lordship's hand entitles you to seize upon any frivolous excuse to force yourself upon my privacy. You are mistaken. I have no intention of recognizing *the mantua-maker,* and I forbid her to make any attempt to hold the most transient intercourse with me. I have already said, I will receive Lady Linden when I meet her in another country, where her history is unknown; but not until then. And now I must request you to retire, or you will compel me to leave my own apartment."

Madeleine had made one or two fruitless attempts to interrupt the countess; but now, as the latter moved toward the door, about to put her threat into execution, the young girl sprang after her and said, beseechingly, —

" I implore you not to go until you hear me! I did not come to speak of myself at all. I came in the hope of sparing you too severe a shock."

" Very generous on your part, but somewhat misjudged, as your unwelcome presence has given me as great a shock as I could well sustain."

" Ah, aunt, — Madame de Gramont, — do not speak so harshly to me! I have scarcely strength or courage left to tell you; I came to speak of — of Count Tristan."

" My son seems to have chosen a somewhat singular messenger, and one who he was well aware would be far from acceptable," returned the countess, wholly unmoved.

" He did not send me ; I came myself; he is not aware of my coming, for — for " —

Madeleine's voice failed her, and the countess took up her words.

" *For* you desired to make me fully sensible of the length to which you carried your audacity. So be it ! I am satisfied ! Mademoiselle de Gramont, for the second time I request you to retire."

" I cannot, until I have told you that Count Tristan is — is not, not quite well; that is, he became indisposed at my house."

" In that case, it would have appeared to me more natural, and certainly more proper, if he had returned to his old residence, and spared me the pain of being apprised of his indisposition by an unwelcome messenger."

" He had no choice, or, rather, I had none. I feared to have the news broken in a manner that might alarm you too much, and therefore I would not even trust myself to write. Count Tristan was seized with, — I mean was taken ill while conversing with me. He is not in a state to return home at present, and I came to beg that his mother or his son will go to him."

" I comprehend you, Mademoiselle de Gramont; you were always politic in the highest degree. You know how to make the best of opportunities. You find my son's temporary indisposition an admirable opportunity to lure his relatives to your house, and to make known to the world your connection with them. Your well-laid, dramatic little plot will fail. Your good acting has not succeeded in alarming me, and I see no reason why Count Tristan de Gramont, in spite of his sudden illness, should not send for a carriage and return to the hotel. By your own confession, the step you have taken is unwarranted; for you admitted that my son was not aware of your intention."

" Because he was too ill to be aware of it, madame," replied Madeleine, with an involuntary accent of reproach.

The cold and cruel conduct of the countess did not render her niece less compassionate, less fearful of wounding; but it inspired her with the resolution, which she had before lacked, to impart the fearful tidings.

" He is too ill to be moved at this moment. I sent for medical aid at once, and everything has been done to restore him."

" *Restore him?* What do you mean ? " almost shrieked the countess, now becoming painfully excited, and struggling against her fears, as though, by disbelieving the calamity which had befallen her son, she could alter the fact. " Why do you try to alarm me in this manner? It is very inconsiderate! very cruel! You do it to revenge yourself upon me! Where is Maurice? Where is Bertha? I must have some one near me on whom I can depend! Why am I left at your mercy?"

"I asked for Maurice and Bertha before I attempted to force my way to you," returned Madeleine. "I was told that neither was at home. Pray do not allow yourself to be so much distressed. I have no doubt that we shall find Count Tristan better."

"*We* shall find! What do you mean by *we* shall find?" sternly demanded the countess, whose grief and alarm did not conquer her pride, though her voice trembled as she asked the question.

"My carriage is at the door: I thought I might venture to propose that you would enter it, and return with me to my house, that no time might be lost." Madeleine said this with quiet dignity.

"*Your* carriage? And you expect me to be seen *with you*, in *your* carriage? I cannot comprehend your object, Mademoiselle de Gramont. What possesses you to try to exasperate me by your insolent propositions?"

"Pardon me; I did not mean to add to your trouble; if my suggestion was injudicious, disregard it. Nothing can be easier than to send for another carriage. Will you allow me to ring the bell for you to do so? And, since you would not wish to be seen in my company, I can leave the house before you."

"And you expect me to follow? You expect that I will order the carriage to drive to the residence of *Mademoiselle Melanie*, the *mantua-maker?*"

"You need only say, 'Drive to —— street, number ——.' My errand here is at an end. I pray you to pardon me, if I have executed it clumsily. My sole intention was to spare you pain, and I almost fear that I have caused you more than I have shielded you from."

Madeleine was retiring, but the countess called her back.

"Stay! You have not told me all yet. What is the matter with my son? Was it a fainting fit? I never knew him guilty of the weakness of fainting."

It was difficult to answer this question without explaining the grave nature of the attack. Madeleine was silent.

"Did you not hear me? Why do you not answer?"

"The doctor did not call it a fainting fit," was Madeleine's vague response. "Yet Count Tristan was in a state of insensibility, and had not spoken when I left him."

" Why did you leave him, then? How could you have been so neglectful?" The countess burst out as though it was a relief to have some one on whom she could vent her wrath. " If he is seriously ill, — so ill as to continue insensible, — you should have remained by his side, and not left him to the improper treatment of strangers : it is abominable, — outrageous!"

" I will gladly hasten back. Pray be composed, madame, and let us hope for a favorable change. I expect to find him better. Before you reach the house, his consciousness may have returned."

Madeleine retired, without waiting for any further comment; for she had an internal conviction that whatever she did or said would be unpleasant to her aunt in her present troubled state.

There was no perceptible alteration in the condition of Count Tristan. Ruth, who was sitting by his side, said he had scarcely stirred. His face still wore a purplish hue, and his glassy, bloodshot eyes, though wide open, were vacant and expressionless. He lay as still as if deprived of sensation and motion.

Madeleine had been at home nearly an hour before she heard the carriage which contained the countess stop at the door. Madame de Gramont, even in a case of such extremity, was not able to complete her arrangements hurriedly.

Madeleine, when she went forth to receive her relative, was much relieved to find her accompanied by Bertha.

Bertha threw herself in Madeleine's arms, whispering, " Is he *very* ill?"

"Yes, I fear so," answered Madeleine, in too low a voice for the countess to hear. Then turning to Madame de Gramont, she inquired, gently, " Do you wish to go to him at once?"

" For what other purpose have I come?" was the ungracious rejoinder.

Madeleine led the way to the apartment, and motioned Ruth to withdraw.

The countess walked up to the bed with a firm step, as though nerving herself to disbelieve that anything serious was the matter.

" My son!" she said, in a voice somewhat choked, but which expressed confidence that he would immediately reply, "My son! why do you not answer me?"

She took his hand; it remained passive in hers; his eyes still stared vacantly. His mother more tightly grasped the hand she held, shook it a little, and called out to him again in a hoarser tone; but there was no answer.

Bertha burst into tears, and knelt down sobbing by the bed.
"Hush!" said the countess, angrily. "You will disturb him.
Why do you cry so? It is nothing serious, — nothing *very* serious;" and she looked around appealingly, her eyes resting, in
spite of herself, upon Madeleine.

"We must hope not," said the latter, now venturing to draw
near. "The doctor will be here again shortly, and, if you would
permit me to advise, I would suggest that Count Tristan should
remain undisturbed."

"I only ask that he will speak to me once!" exclaimed the
countess, in peevish distress. "A *mother* may demand that! Do
you not hear me, my son? Why, why will you not answer?"

Her voice was raised to a high pitch, but it did not seem to
reach the ears of the insensible man.

Voices in the entry attracted Madeleine's attention; the
sound of well-known tones reached her ears, and she hastily left
the room.

The servant was communicating to Maurice the sad event
which had just taken place. Madeleine beckoned her cousin to
follow to her boudoir, and, in a few words, recounted what had
just taken place.

Maurice had listened, too completely awe-stricken for language, until Madeleine rose and asked, "Will you not go to him
now, Maurice?"

Then he ejaculated, "How mysteriously all things are ordered,
Madeleine! Truly you are the ministering angel of our
family!"

As Maurice, with Madeleine, entered the chamber where
Count Tristan lay, the countess experienced a revulsion of feeling at beholding them side by side, and cried out, in a louder
tone than seemed natural in that chamber at such a moment, —

"Maurice! Maurice! I have wanted you so much to advise
me! You see your father's condition: he does not seem to recognize us; but it cannot be anything serious. The great point
is to make arrangements for removing him at once to the hotel.
You must attend to that; I wish no time to be lost."

Maurice was gazing in dumb anguish upon his father's altered
face, and, though no tears moistened his eyes, his frame shook
with emotion far more painful to man than weeping is to woman.

"You will see to his immediate removal," repeated his grandmother, authoritatively, finding that he did not notice her request.

"That cannot be done with safety, I feel certain," answered
Maurice.

" But he cannot remain here," persisted the countess. " He must be taken to the hotel, where I can watch by him."

" You would not have the attempt made at the risk of his life ? " remarked Maurice, with more sternness than he intended.

Madeleine gently interposed.

" Dr. Bayard, the physician who was called in, promised to return in a couple of hours : he must be here shortly : will it not be best to ask his opinion ? And if he says Count Tristan cannot yet be removed with safety, I entreat, madame, that you will allow me to place this suite of apartments at your disposal and his. They are wholly disconnected with the rest of the house, and you can be as private as you desire."

" Do you expect *me* to remain under this roof? *Your roof?* Do you imagine that I will allow my son to remain here, even in his present condition ? Oh, this is too much ! This would be more terrible than all the rest ! I could not humble myself to endure *that !* "

The countess spoke in a perfect agony of mortification.

Madeleine only replied, " There is no necessity for a decision until you have consulted the physician."

Maurice thought it wise to echo her words ; the countess was partially soothed, for the time being, and sat down to await the coming of Dr. Bayard.

CHAPTER XXXVIII.

THE MANTUA-MAKER'S GUESTS.

AROUND Count Tristan's bed were grouped in silence his four nearest of kin, waiting for the physician who was to decide upon the possibility of removal. The countess sat erect and motionless by her son's head. Her countenance wore a look of granite hardness, as though she were fighting her grief with *Spartan*-like determination which would not let her admit, even to herself, that any anguish preyed upon her heart. Maurice sat at the foot of the bed, mournfully watching the spasmodic movements of his stricken father : they were but feeble and few. Madeleine had placed herself upon the other side of the couch. Her instinctive delicacy prompted her to withdraw as far as possible from the countess. Bertha had softly stolen to Madeleine's side, and sat silently clasping her hand, and leaning against her shoulder; for hers was one of those clinging, vine-like natures that ever turn for support to the object nearest and strongest.

This was the disposition of the group when Ruth Thornton entered the room on tiptoe and placed a card in Madeleine's hand.

"Did you tell him what had occurred?" whispered Madeleine.

"I did, and he still begged to see you."

Though Ruth spoke in a low voice, Bertha was so near that she heard her reply, and it caused her, almost unconsciously, to glance at the card.

"Say that I will be with him directly," said Madeleine.

"It is M. de Bois. I will go with you," murmured Bertha, rising at the same time as her cousin.

The countess did not move her eyes, but Maurice turned his head to look after them. Madeleine could never pass from his presence without his experiencing a sense of loss which inflicted a dull pang.

M. de Bois had been ushered into Madeleine's boudoir. He had not anticipated the happiness of seeing Bertha. When she entered, his start and flush of joy, and the gently confident manner in which he took her hand, and drew her toward him, might well have surprised Madeleine; but that surprise was quickly turned to positive amazement, for Bertha's head drooped until its opulent golden curls swept his breast, — and — and — (if we record what ensued be it remembered that constitutionally bashful men, stirred by a sudden impulse, have less control over their emotions than their calmer brothers) — and — in another second, his own head was bent down, and his lips lightly touched her pure brow, just where the fair hair parting ran on either side, in shining waves. Truly was that first kiss

> "The chrism of Love, which Love's own crown
> With sanctifying sweetness did precede."

Gaston's ideas of what amount of tender demonstration punctilious decorum permitted a lover, had finally undergone an alarming modification, through the corrective influence of the social atmosphere he had inhaled during the last few years. In his own land the limited privileges of an accepted suitor do not extend thus far until the day before a wedding-ring encircles the finger of a bride. Is it on this account that the Parisian *Mrs. Grundy*, dreading some irresistible temptation, never allows affianced lovers to be left alone?

Bertha's conceptions of propriety must also have been in a very unsettled state; for, albeit "to her brow the ruby mounted," that first kiss seemed to her to lie there as softly as an invisible gem, and she did not withdraw her head, nor look up reproachfully, nor utter one word of chiding.

Gaston noticed Madeleine's wonder-struck look, and said, "You did not know, then, Mademoiselle Madeleine, how happy I am?"

Then Bertha escaped from the arm that encircled her, and nestling in her cousin's bosom, faltered out, "I was so much troubled about Cousin Tristan that I could not tell you."

"One of my most cherished hopes has become reality!" returned Madeleine, fondly. "M. de Bois knows how much I have wished for this consummation; and I think you have known it, Bertha, ever since you made me a certain confession."

"What? Mademoiselle Bertha confessed to you, and you kept me in ignorance?" cried Gaston, reproachfully.

"I did *as I would be done by*, — an old rule that wears well, and keeps friendships golden."

There was a significance in Madeleine's look comprehended by Gaston. It warned him that any confidence which she had reposed in him must be sacred, even from his betrothed bride.

Dr. Bayard was announced, and Madeleine conducted him to the chamber occupied by her suffering guest, and withdrew.

It strikes us that Madeleine's interpretation of the rules of decorum must also have suffered by her residence in America; for she very coolly left the lovers to themselves, and, passing through the dining-room, walked into the garden.

When she reëntered her boudoir she found Gaston and Bertha conversing as happily as though no sorrow found place upon the earth, or certainly none beneath that roof; but, since the world began, lovers have been pronounced selfishly forgetful of the rest of mankind. We have our doubts, however, whether their being wholly wrapped up in each other deserves so harsh a name as *selfishness*, since that very closeness of union renders souls richer and larger, and gives to each additional power to receive and communicate happiness, while thoroughly selfish people lack the capacity to impart good gifts, and are content with being recipients.

Madeleine had just seated herself opposite to the lovers, and was thinking what a pleasant picture to contemplate were those two radiant countenances, when Maurice entered with the physician.

"I fear, sir, you look upon my father's state as very critical?"

"Very," replied Dr. Bayard, who was a man of such acknowledged ability that he could afford to be frank without being suspected of a desire to magnify the importance of a case under his treatment. "Apoplexy may be produced by various causes, hereditary disposition, high living, or anxiety of mind, or all united. I cannot decide what was the origin of Count Tristan de Gramont's seizure. One side is entirely paralyzed, and the other slightly."

"Can he be removed to his hotel with safety?" inquired Maurice.

"Assuredly not. The risk would be very great. It should not be encountered if there is any possibility of his remaining here for the present."

He looked questioningly toward the mistress of the house.

Madeleine promptly replied, "These apartments are entirely at the service of Count Tristan and his family, if they will honor me by occupying them."

"That is well," returned the doctor. "Let the count remain undisturbed until he is convalescent. I will see him again in the evening."

Dr. Bayard took his leave, and Maurice turned to Madeleine, —

"This is most unfortunate. It is a great burden to be thrown upon you, Madeleine."

She interrupted him quickly. "You could hardly have spoken words less kind, Maurice. If this shock could not have been spared your father, I am thankful that it fell beneath my roof. He will be more quiet here than in a hotel, and can be better tended. If the countess will permit me, I will gladly constitute myself his chief *garde malade*. I have had some experience" —

That inadvertent remark increased the agitation of Maurice, and he answered, in a voice tremulous from the rush of sad recollections, "Who can testify to that better than *I*? Do you think I have forgotten the good *sœur de bon secours* whose movements I used to watch, and whose features, dimly traced by the feeble light of the *veilleuse*, I never ceased to gaze upon, as she moved about my bed?"

Madeleine smiled and sighed at the same moment, and then remarked, perhaps to turn the conversation, —

" But your grandmother, — I fear it will be very difficult to obtain her consent to Count Tristan's remaining under my roof."

" She cannot desire to risk my father's life!" returned Maurice, somewhat angrily. " I may as well tell her what is decided upon, at once."

Madeleine detained him.

" First let me explain to you the arrangements I propose making. If the countess will condescend to remain here, I will have the drawing-room, which opens into the room Count Tristan occupies, made into a bed-chamber for her. The apartment beyond is the dining-room. This little boudoir can be converted into a chamber for you. There is an apartment upstairs which I will occupy; and, as Bertha cannot remain at the hotel alone, I shall be truly happy if she will share my room, or that of the countess."

" Yours! yours!" exclaimed Bertha. " Oh, what a pleasant arrangement! And how quickly and admirably you have settled everything, just as you always used to do; and nobody could ever plan half so well!"

" It will be your turn to play the hostess, and to them all!" cried Gaston. " Who would have believed such a revolution of the great wheel possible! That's what I call *compensation in this world;* for few things, I know, can make you happier; and nothing can strike such a severe blow at the pride of the Countess de Gramont as to find herself the compulsory guest of the relative she has despised and persecuted."

Gaston, in his ardor and desire to see Madeleine avenged, had forgotten the presence of the viscount; but Madeleine's look of reproach and her glance toward her cousin recalled his presence to the mind of her enthusiastic defender.

" I beg pardon, Maurice," said he; " I ought not to have spoken disrespectfully of the countess; that is, while you were by."

" I understand and can pardon you, Gaston. Now I must go to my grandmother and learn what she says; for I can see Madeleine's 'fairy fingers' are impatient to commence their magical preparations for our comfort."

He spoke sadly; though his words were half gay in their import.

Very few minutes elapsed before Maurice returned, accompanied by the countess. She swept into the room, towering as majestically as though she could rise above and conquer all the assailing army of circumstances arrayed against her.

Madeleine made a movement toward the door.

" Remain! I wish to speak to you, Mademoiselle de Gramont," cried the countess in her most icy tone.

" Permit me first to request Miss Thornton to watch beside Count Tristan. He ought not to be left alone."

Madeleine had been more thoughtful of the patient than his mother, and the latter could not detain her.

" Are you positive that your father cannot be moved? I am not convinced that it is out of the question."

The countess addressed these words to Maurice.

" The physician has just declared that the risk would be too great. That question, then, is definitely settled. It only remains for you to say how far you will accept Madeleine's hospitable proposition."

" *Hospitable!* Do not talk of *hospitality* but of *degradation!* What will be said when it is known that Count Tristan de Gramont was sheltered, during his illness, by his *mantua-maker relative!* — his *tradeswoman niece!* There is only one condition upon which I can be forced to consent."

Here Madeleine reëntered, and the countess accosted her.

" Mademoiselle de Gramont, the tide of fortune has, for the moment, set against our ill-fated house, and our humiliation can scarcely be more complete. You are aware that the physician you have employed (and with whom I trust you are not in league) says that my son cannot be removed without danger."

" Yes, madame, and I hope Maurice has communicated the suggestion which I have hesitatingly, but very gladly, made for your accommodation."

" He has done so," replied the countess, with undiminished stateliness. " As for myself, it is asking too much, — it is an impossibility that I should stoop to take up my abode here; but, while my son lies in his present state, which I am told is alarming (though I believe I am misinformed), I, as his mother, should feel bound to visit him though it were in a pest-house. Your offer is declined for myself and Mademoiselle de Merrivale. Maurice gives me to understand that he considers his place to be by his father's side, night and day; therefore for him it will be accepted upon certain conditions; upon these only can I allow my son and grandson to remain beneath your roof."

" Name them, madame. I will promptly, joyfully comply with your wishes if it be in my power to do so."

" You will immediately close your establishment, that none of the transactions of the trade which has sullied your rank may go on within these walls; and you will at once make known to the public your intended nuptials with Lord Linden."

" I never had the remotest intention, madame, of becoming the wife of Lord Linden."

" Has he not offered you his hand ? "

" Yes, and but for the accident which has wholly diverted my thoughts, he would have received a distinct refusal before now."

" What reason can you advance for declining so eligible an offer ? "

" The same I gave at the Chateau de Gramont, nearly five years ago. My affections belong to another."

Madeleine spoke with fervor, as though she experienced a deep joy in thus proclaiming her constancy. Maurice, with a stifled sigh, turned from her, and pretended to be gazing at the flowers in the conservatory.

" And may we, at last, be favored," demanded the countess, scornfully, " with the name of this unknown lover, who has been able to inspire you with such a rare and romantic amount of constancy ? "

" It is one, madame, I cannot now mention with any more propriety than I could have done years ago."

" Then it must be one of which you are ashamed ! But how can I doubt that ? Has he not allowed you to become a trades-woman ? Has not the whole affair been a disgraceful and clan-destine one ? You may well refuse to mention his name ! It can only be one which your family can object to hear."

" You are right in one respect, madame : it is one which they object to hear ; but, as I shall never be the wife of any other man, — yet never, in all probability, the wife of *that one*, — let the subject of marriage be set aside. In regard to closing this establishment, you are hardly aware, madame, what you re-quest. It would not be in my power to close it suddenly, grant-ing that I had the will to do so. I should not merely throw out of employment some fifty struggling women, who are at present occupied here, but would prevent my keeping faith in fulfilling engagements already made. I will not dwell upon the great personal loss that it would be to me. I should be glad to be-lieve you are convinced of the impossibility of my complying with your wishes."

" Do you mean to say that you actually refuse ? "

" I am compelled to do so ; but I will exert myself to render

28 *

your visits private. I will devise some method by which you will be entirely shielded from the view of those who come here on business."

"You presume to think, then, that in spite of your insolent refusal, I will allow my son to remain here?"

Madeleine felt that she could say no more, and looked beseechingly toward Maurice, who exclaimed, —

"My father must remain here, for he cannot be removed. I gladly accept my cousin's kind offer, and will remain to watch beside my father. Bertha and yourself can continue to live at the hotel and visit him as often as you feel inclined."

"Let me go! Let me go! I am suffocating! I stifle in this house!" burst forth the countess, as though she were really choking. "I cannot remain. Bertha, I want you. Maurice, give me your arm, — let me get away quickly."

Maurice reconducted his ·grandmother to the hotel, almost without their exchanging a word by the way. Bertha accompanied them, but she walked behind with Gaston de Bois.

CHAPTER XXXIX.

MINISTRATION.

MAURICE, exasperated as he was at his grandmother's insolence to his cousin, well knew that any attempt to soothe Madame de Gramont, or even to reconcile her to the inevitable, would be fruitless. Her domineering spirit could not bow itself to be governed, even by the pressure of inexorable circumstance; she strove to control events by ignoring their existence, and to break the force of her calamity by encasing herself in an iron mail of resistance, which, she thought, no blows could penetrate. This was her state when she hastened to her own chamber, and was about to lock herself in, under the conviction that she could shut out the phantom of misery which seemed to dog her steps.

"I will return this evening, and let you know how my father progresses," said Maurice, as she was closing the door.

She reopened it without moving her hand from the silver knob. "Then you persist in going back to that house?"

"Would you have me leave my father without a son's care?

I shall remain at Madeleine's while it is necessary for my father to stay there."

Maurice spoke with a decision that admitted no argument.

The countess shut her door, and the sound of the turned key was distinctly audible. How she passed the succeeding hours no one knew; she was not heard to move; she answered no knock; she took no notice of Bertha's petition that her dinner might be brought to her; she was not again seen until the next morning.

There is no proverb truer than the one which suggests that even an ill wind blows some one good. Bertha was the gainer by her aunt's seclusion: she had full liberty, and for a large portion of the time she did not enjoy her freedom *alone*.

Madeleine had been actively employed during the absence of Maurice. Her first step was to send for an upholsterer. Other arrangements followed which quickly converted the drawing-room into a comfortable bed-room. She herself proposed to take such rest as she found needful upon the sofa in her boudoir.

The upholsterer had arrived, and Madeleine had no little difficulty in making him comprehend her plan of completely shutting off the staircase which led to the exhibition and working rooms above, by means of drapery. She had felt bound thus far to consult the countess' desire for privacy. A separate entrance from the street was out of the question, but the draperies were to be disposed in such a manner that the instant Madame de Gramont and her family passed the threshold they were completely secluded.

Madeleine was standing in the hall giving her orders, when Maurice reappeared. Finding her occupied, he passed on to his father's chamber.

It was now six o'clock. Dinner was served for three persons. Madeleine summoned her housekeeper and requested her to watch beside Count Tristan while his son dined.

On entering the count's room Madeleine assured herself that there was no change in the patient's condition, and then said, " Come, Ruth, dinner is served ; come, Maurice, if you assume the office of *garde malade*, I must take care that your strength is not exhausted."

Her cheerfulness dispelled some of the heavy gloom that hung about Maurice, and he rose and followed her. She led the way through the apartment which had been the drawing-room, and pointing to the bed, said, —

" That is for you ; this is your bed-chamber."

"Mine? I do not expect to need a bed; I mean to sit up
with my father."

"Yes, to-night; but not every night," she added, with playful
imperativeness. "I shall not allow *that*, and you see I have
taken the reins into my own hands, and show that a little of
the de Gramont love of rule has descended to me with its
blood."

They entered the dining-room. Maurice was struck by the air
of combined simplicity and elegance which characterized all the
appointments. The dinner, too, was simple, but well-cooked.
Maurice had no appetite at first, but was soon lured to eat, —
everything placed before him appeared so inviting. Then, it was
delightful to see Madeleine sitting quietly opposite to him, looking even lovelier than she did in those happy, happy, by-gone
days in the ancient chateau! Ruth's pretty and pleasant countenance at another time might have been an addition; but we
fear that Maurice at that moment, did not appreciate the presence of a very modest and attractive young girl who reflected
in her own person not a few of Madeleine's virtues. The repast
was of brief duration; but Madeleine was the one who partook
of it most sparingly. She enjoyed so much seeing Maurice eat
that she could not follow his example.

Maurice and Madeleine returned to Count Tristan's apartment together. Soon after, Dr. Bayard paid another visit, but
expressed no opinion. Maurice went back to the hotel to keep
his promise to his grandmother. There was no response when
he knocked at her door; no reply, though he spoke to her, that
she might hear his voice and know who was there.

Bertha and Gaston were sitting together. Albeit the conversation in which they were engaged appeared to be singularly absorbing, the latter said, —

"Do you return immediately to Mademoiselle Madeleine's?
If so, I will accompany you; and, as I suppose you will watch
beside your father, we will sit up together."

Maurice assented and they set forth; that is, as soon as Bertha, who detained them, first upon one plea and then upon
another, would permit.

But when Madeleine learned Gaston's friendly proposition,
she answered, "We shall not need you. Maurice is hardly experienced enough for me to trust him just yet. I intend to
sit up to-night; to-morrow night Maurice must rest, at least part
of the night, and then, M. de Bois, we will be glad to claim you

There was no appeal from Madeleine's decision. She exerted a mild authority which was too potent for argument.

After Gaston departed, Madeleine, for a brief space, left Maurice alone with his father. When she stole back to her place at the head of the bed, she was attired in a white cambric wrapper, lightly girded at the waist; a blue shawl of some soft material fell in graceful folds about her form. She had entered with such a soundless step, that when Maurice saw her sitting before him, he started, and his breath grew labored, as though, for a second, he fancied that he gazed upon some unreal shape. The flowing white drapery, and the delicate azure folds of the shawl helped the illusion, which her musical voice would scarcely have dispelled, but for the sense of reality produced by the words she uttered.

"It is just eleven; that is the hour at which the medicine was to be given."

She took up the cup and administered a spoonful of its contents, before Maurice had quite recovered himself.

The silence which followed did not last long. Madeleine began to question Maurice concerning his life in America, his opinions, his experiences, the people he had known and esteemed; and he responded, in subdued tones, by a long narrative of past events.

It was the first time that Maurice had been called upon to watch beside a bed of sickness, and his was one of those vivacious temperaments to which sleep is so indispensable that an overpowering somnolence will fling its charms about the senses, and bear the spirit away captive, even in the soul's most unwilling moments.. Five o'clock had struck when Madeleine perceived that her companion's eyes had grown heavy, and that he was making a desperate struggle to keep them open. With womanly tact she leaned her elbow on the bed, and rested her forehead on her hand, in such a manner that her face was concealed, and thus avoided any further conversation. In less than ten minutes, the sound of clear but regular breathing apprised her that Maurice had fallen asleep.

When she looked up, at first timidly, but soon with security, Maurice was lying back in his arm-chair — his hands were calmly folded together, his head drooped a little to one side, the rich chestnut curls (for his hair had darkened until it no longer resembled Bertha's golden locks) were disordered, and fully revealed his fair, intellectual brow; the pallor of his face rendered more than usually conspicuous the chiselling of his finely-cut features; the calm, half-smiling curve of his handsome mouth gave his whole countenance an expression of placid happiness which it had not worn, of late, in waking hours. Madeleine sat and gazed at him as she could never have gazed when his eyes might have met hers; she gazed until her whole soul flashed into her face; and if Maurice had awakened, and caught but one glimpse of the fervent radiance of that look, he would surely have known her secret.

There is intense fascination to a woman in scanning the face that to her is beyond all others worth perusing, when the soft breath of sleep renders the beloved object unconscious of the eyes bent tenderly upon his features. No check is given to the flood of worshipping love that pours itself out from her soul; then, and perhaps *then only*, in his presence, she allows the tide of pent-up adoration to break down all its natural barriers. However perfect her devotion at other times, there *may*, there always *does* exist a half-involuntary *reticence*, a secret fear that if even her eyes were to betray the whole wealth of her passion, it would not be well with her. Men are constitutionally, unconsciously *ungrateful;* give them abundance of what they covet most and they prize the gift less highly than if its measure were stinted. And women have an instinct that warns them not to be too lavish. Those women who love most fervently, most deeply, most *internally,* seldom frame the full strength of that love into words, or manifest it in looks even; that is, in the waking presence of the one who holds their entire being captive.

Maurice slept on, though the streets had long since become noisy, and door-bells were ringing, and there was a sound of hammering in the entry (the upholsterer at work), and steps could be distinguished passing up and down the stair.

Madeleine, who at one period of her life had been used to night vigils, hardly felt fatigued; but she knew that she must hoard her strength if she would have it last to meet prolonged requirements. She touched Maurice softly; but he was not aroused until she had made several efforts to break his slumber. He looked about him in bewilderment, and then at the white-robed figure before him as though it were an apparition.

"It is I, and no ghost," said Madeleine. "The morning has come; go and lie down for a couple of hours to refresh yourself, — I will do the same. Mrs. Lawkins will stay with your father."

"Have I really been asleep?" asked Maurice, in a tone of

mortiffcation. "Asleep, while you were waking? What a stupid brute I am!"

"Have brutes easy consciences? for that is said to be man's best lullaby. You must consider yourself still subject to my orders. Go and lie down. You shall be called to breakfast at nine o'clock; that will give you two hours' rest. As for me, I shall fall asleep in a few moments."

Maurice yielded.

Madeleine did *not* fall asleep quite as soon as she predicted; but, after a time, she sank into a refreshing slumber. At nine o'clock the ringing of the alarum she had taken the precaution to set, awoke her. She stole to Maurice's door, but had to knock several times before she could arouse him; he was again enjoying that blessing which he had lately professed to despise.

"What is it? Who is there?" he cried out, at last.

"It is I, Madeleine. Nine o'clock has just struck. We will breakfast as soon as you are ready to come into the dining-room."

She returned to her boudoir and made a hasty toilet, substituting, for her simple white wrapper, another, somewhat richly embroidered, and trimmed with pale blue ribbons. We reluctantly venture upon the suggestion, for it would indicate a decided weakness, quite unworthy of Madeleine's good sense; but there is just a possibility that she remembered she was to breakfast once more with her lover, and her artistic eye selected the most becoming morning-dress in her possession.

Ruth had breakfasted some hours before; Madeleine and Maurice sat down to table alone. In spite of the grief which lay in the depths of both their hearts, it must be avowed that both experienced a sense of calm felicity which made them shrink from contemplating the past, or looking forward to the future; the delicious *present* was all sufficient. Maurice wondered at himself, — was almost angry with himself, — and then he looked across the table and wondered no longer.

Madeleine was less astonished at her own pleasant emotions. Partly through discipline, and partly through temperament, she always caught up all the sunshine of the passing hour, even though she did not lose sight of the clouds that lay in the distant horizon. And how often the present beams had pierced their way through thick darkness to reach her!

"Come and tell me what you think of my invention," said she, as they rose from the table and opened the door which led into the hall.

The upholsterer had already completed his work. A crimson drapery was suspended from the ceiling to the ground, along the whole length of the entry, and entirely shut out the staircase. At the street door this drapery was so skilfully arranged that a person visiting the apartments on the first floor could, at once, pass out of sight.

"Will not these curtains render this portion of the house quite secluded? I hope they will make your grandmother feel less aversion to coming here."

"What resources you have, Madeleine! And how kindly you employ your fertile ingenuity! *Who* would have thought of such an arrangement?"

"Why *any one* who took the trouble to sit down and think about the matter at all! Possibly some people might not have been in the habit of exercising their ingenuity enough to do that; but *any one* who took the trouble to reflect how the desired object could be accomplished would have seen the difficulties melt away."

"Under the touch of ' Fairy Fingers,' " returned Maurice, admiringly.

"Ah, that is an old superstition of yours which you have not quite outlived. Will you not go to your grandmother now? She may be expecting you, and must be anxious for news."

"She showed great anxiety last night," replied Maurice, bitterly.

"Maurice, we have no right to judge her! Unless we ourselves have experienced her sensations, we cannot even comprehend her state. Speak to her this morning as though you had parted in all affection yesterday; and bring her here, if you can. For her own sake try to bring her."

Shortly after Maurice left, Madeleine received another letter from Lord Linden. Finding that she did not reply to the first, he had called upon her twice on the day previous; but, greatly to his mortification, had been denied. Later in the day, his wounded vanity was somewhat soothed by learning the calamity which had befallen Count Tristan, at Madeleine's house; though his lordship could hardly deem even such an event sufficient excuse for her tardiness in replying to a letter of so much importance. In reality, Madeleine had entirely forgotten her suitor and his letter. She glanced hastily over his second epistle, and, without further delay, wrote a few frigid lines conveying a definite refusal of the proposed honor with which he had followed his proposition of dishonor.

It is needless to describe Lord Linden's emotions when this response reached him. Madeleine's language was so cuttingly cold, yet so full of dignity, that he could only curse the rash blindness which could have permitted him to make dishonorable advances to such a woman. He ordered his trunk to be packed, and left Washington by that afternoon's train.

Bertha had not seen Madame de Gramont from the time she locked herself in her chamber until the breakfast hour, next day. The maid Mademoiselle de Merrivale brought with her from Paris was in the habit of attending the countess as punctiliously as she did her own mistress; but her services were, for the first time, dispensed with on the night previous. Bertha was oppressed by a vaguely uncomfortable sensation when she entered the room where breakfast awaited her, and found the apartment vacant. In a few moments the countess entered.

How frightfully old she had grown in a single night! Her step, which used to be so firm and measured, was feeble, uncertain, and heavy. Sixty-six years had not bowed her straight shoulders; but now they stooped. The blow of an iron hand had bent them at last! Her features had grown sharp and hard, and the lines looked as though they had been cut to twice their usual depth; the mouth appeared to have fallen, the corners pressing downward; one might have thought that tears had scalded away the lustre and dimmed the vision of the dark eyes that yesterday flashed with such steel-like brilliancy. The soft, white locks, that were usually arranged with so much skill, hung partially uncurled, and scarcely smoothed about her face, adding to the desolation of her whole appearance.

Bertha was impressed with greater awe than she had ever experienced toward her aunt in the latter's most imperious moments; yet the young girl mustered courage to advance and embrace her, — more timidly, perhaps, but also more tenderly than was her wont. The countess permitted her own cold lips to sweep Bertha's forehead; but they could hardly be said to press upon it a kiss.

As they sat at table, Bertha, whose tongue had a gift for prattling, could not make an effort to speak. The countess had not tasted food since the light, noonday repast of the day previous, yet she now swallowed her cup of coffee as though it nearly choked her, and tried, in vain, to force down a few morsels of bread. Nothing would have induced her to depart from the custom of her country where coffee and bread are considered all-sufficient for the first meal.

They had returned to the drawing-room when Maurice entered. The countess greeted him with an inclination of the head, but asked no questions.

"My father seems to be in the same state," said he. "There was no change during the night; he does not appear to suffer; but, as yet, he is not conscious."

Madame de Gramont made no reply, but her breast visibly heaved.

"Did you sit up?" asked Bertha. "Are you not very much fatigued? Did Madeleine watch also? Is she not very weary?"

"Not very; nor am I." Then he turned to his grandmother. "Will you come with me to see my father? You will find that every arrangement possible has been made for your privacy."

The lips of the countess curled scornfully, but she rose and passed into her chamber.

"I must make ready also," cried Bertha, flying out of the room. "I am so glad that we are to go."

She returned wearing her bonnet and mantle. It was sometime before the countess reëntered, prepared to depart.

Maurice had ordered a carriage, and they were soon at Madeleine's door.

If the countess noticed the draperies which closed off a portion of the house, she gave no sign of doing so.

Madeleine was sitting beside Count Tristan, but rose to yield her place to his mother. Madame de Gramont only betrayed that she was aware of her niece's presence by a slight movement of the head, while her eyes looked past her toward the passive figure lying on the bed. She took the vacant seat with a sort of frozen quietude, and her limbs seemed to settle themselves rigidly into positions where they remained immovable.

Madeleine at once retired, knowing that her presence must be galling to the proud relative whom circumstance thus forced into contact with her; nor did she reënter the room again while the countess was there. Maurice remained with his father and grandmother, but Bertha stole away to Madeleine's boudoir.

M. de Bois, who had called to inquire after the count, and to know of what service he could be, found the cousins together. Madeleine, whose wealth of energy rendered idleness, when it could be avoided, another name for weariness, had seated herself at her desk, and was making sketches for Ruth to copy. Bertha sat beside her, destroying pencils in her awkward attempt to sharpen them. Madeleine did not desist from her occupation, but Bertha's was quickly at an end.

She and her lover conversed for a while; then Gaston offered to show her Madeleine's conservatory, and then they passed into the garden. What wonder that they found unknown charms in the opening flowers! Was it not a spring morning? And was there not spring in their hearts? Was it not life's blossoming season with them?

At noon luncheon was served; and Madeleine, in remembrance of her guests, had given such especial instructions to Mrs. Lawkins that the luncheon closely resembled the *déjeuner à la fourchette* served at that hour in France. As Bertha was still in the garden, Madeleine passed into the conservatory and called her.

" Will you not go in, Bertha, and see if you can induce the countess to accompany you and Maurice to the dining-room? Say that I will remain with Count Tristan while they take luncheon."

Bertha went on her errand, but quickly returned with Maurice.

" My aunt does not seem disposed to eat."

In reality Bertha had received no answer from the countess. Did Madeleine expect that Madame de Gramont would break bread under her roof? The haughty aristocrat would sooner have perished of hunger.

" Then we will go to table together," replied the hostess, disappointed, in spite of herself. " M. de Bois, you will join us?"

The meal passed off very quietly, but very pleasantly. Bertha and Gaston were happy enough in each other to have thought a repast of bread and cheese a banquet. Maurice could not but be penetrated by the charm of sharing Madeleine's home; and, at table, where she presided with such graceful ease, he never forgot that it was in *her* home he was dwelling. Madeleine herself could not gaze upon the little circle of beloved ones, from whom she had been so long separated, and who were now so singularly drawn around her, without feeling supremely happy. In the midst of sorrow there are often given, to soften and render it endurable, passing flashes of absolute joy.

When they rose from table Maurice returned to his father's chamber. His grandmother still sat erect and statue-like in her chair as though she had not moved.

The hours flew by only too rapidly with Bertha, however they might have dragged in the sick-chamber. M. de Bois, also, must have lost all consciousness of time, for he did not propose to take his departure, and could Madeleine, even by a hint, dismiss him from her own house?

"Past five o'clock," said she, looking up from her drawing. "Bertha, pray ask Maurice to come to me."

When Maurice obeyed the summons, Madeleine remarked, showing him her watch, "You see how late it is; I fear the countess will become exhausted for want of food. It is in vain to hope that she could be induced to dine here; had you not better conduct her home and return?"

"Yes, certainly; it would be the wisest plan; how thoughtful you are!"

"Shall I send for a carriage? I fear she would not enter mine, or I would order that."

"I suppose not; it is wonderful to what cruel and inconsistent length she carries her pride."

"It is not our place, Maurice, to measure its length or analyze its workings. There is Robert in the hall; tell him to call a carriage."

When the carriage arrived, the countess, Bertha and Maurice, drove away together.

CHAPTER XL.

RECOGNITION.

WITH electric rapidity flashed the news through Washington that Mademoiselle Melanie, the fashionable dressmaker, was a lady of rank, — a heroine, — a being hardly inferior to those disguised princesses who figure in popular fairy tales. Numberless romantic stories were fabricated and circulated, and the startling and improbable motives assigned for her incognita bore witness to the fertile imagination of the American public.

It may well be imagined that there was but one all-engrossing theme discussed in the working-rooms of Mademoiselle Melanie's establishment. Mademoiselle Victorine was not a little disgusted when she learned that a secret of such moment had been so successfully concealed from her. But the quick-witted foreigner had too much tact to betray her ignorance by evincing astonishment in the presence of the *employées*, or the patrons of Mademoiselle Melanie. On the contrary, Mademoiselle Victorine gave them to understand that she had all along been the repository of

Mademoiselle de Gramont's secrets, and knew more of her past history and future plans than was yet suspected.

Madeleine's thoughtful kindness prompted her to make a brief explanation to Ruth Thornton, whom she had so long treated as a friend, or younger sister. Ruth was moved and gratified by the unsought confidence; but her genuine, up-looking veneration for Madeleine could not be increased by the knowledge that she was the daughter of the late Duke de Gramont. Madeleine concluded her narrative by saying, —

"One may be very poor, and very dependent, and yet be the daughter of a duke; and even a duke's daughter may find it less irksome to earn her own bread than to eat the bread of charity."

Ruth asked, tremblingly, "But now will all go on as before? Will your noble relatives permit you to continue your present life?"

"My relatives can exert no influence which will turn me from the path I have chosen," replied Madeleine, divining her young *protegée's* thoughts. "While Count Tristan remains in my house, *you* will act as my representative. When he is restored, or, rather, when he is no longer my guest, I shall resume my former duties."

Ruth's sinking heart was lifted up by this assurance, and the cloud that had gathered upon her sweet face passed away, and left it as placid as Madeleine's own. Madeleine's tranquillizing influence over others was one of her most remarkable traits. She was not merely calm and self-possessed herself, but her presence communicated a steadfast, hopeful calmness that was irresistible.

The *beau monde* had decided that as Mademoiselle de Gramont's family had claimed her, she would unhesitatingly abandon her humble occupation, and assume her legitimate position in the social sphere; and great were the lamentations over the noble *coutourière's* supposed abdication of her throne.

The next question to be settled was whether her former patrons should recognize and visit her as an equal, ignoring their previous acquaintance. Madame de Fleury was the first to reply to that query. We will not make ourselves responsible for the assertion that she was prompted by purely disinterested motives, and the unqualified admiration with which Mademoiselle Melanie had long since inspired her. It is *just possible* that other incentives had their weight in her light head, and that believing herself about to be deprived of the inventive genius which had rendered her toilet the glory and delight of her life, she might have determined to preserve Mademoiselle Melanie's friendship that she might secure her advice on all important occasions. Be that as it may, Madame de Fleury immediately left cards for Mademoiselle de Gramont, and her example was followed by the Countess Orlowski, and a host of other ladies, who conscientiously walked in her footsteps.

The morning of the third day after Count Tristan's seizure passed much in the same manner as the second. Maurice conducted his grandmother and Bertha to Madeleine's residence. The countess was as silent, as frigid, as immovable as before. She took the same seat, kept the same unbent position, appeared to be as completely abstracted from what was passing around her, as on the day previous. Madeleine absented herself, and Bertha soon stole to her side. M. de Bois, whose vigils, it appeared, had not fatigued him sufficiently for extra repose to be requisite, joined them at an early hour.

About noon, Maurice hastily entered Madeleine's boudoir and said, " I think there is some change in my father ; his face is much paler and his eyes appear to be wandering about with a faint sign of consciousness ; the motion of his right hand is restored, for he has lifted it several times. Pray come to him, Madeleine."

" I only banished myself in the fear that my presence would not be agreeable to the countess," replied Madeleine. " Do you think it will not now pain her to see me ? "

" I cannot tell, but you *must* come."

Madeleine obeyed.

The countess had risen and was bending over the bed.

" My son ! Tristan, my son ! do you not hear your mother ? " she cried, in a hollow, unnatural voice.

His eyes still gazed restlessly about, with a helpless, hopeless, supplicating look.

" My dear father," said Maurice, taking the hand which the count had again lifted and let fall.

No sign of recognition followed.

" What do you think of his state, Madeleine ? Is he not better ? "

His cousin softly drew near, and taking in her own the hand Maurice had dropped, said, " You know us, Count Tristan, do you not ? "

His eyes, as though drawn by her voice, turned quickly, and fastened themselves upon her face ; his hands made a nervous clutch, his lips moved, but the sounds were thick and indistinct, yet the first syllable of her name was audible to all.

"Do not try to speak," said Madeleine, soothingly; "you have been very ill; you are still weak; do not endeavor to make any exertion."

He continued to look at her beseechingly, and to clasp her hand more and more tightly, — so tightly that it gave her positive pain, and his quivering lips again made a fruitless effort to utter her name.

"Tristan, my son!" exclaimed the countess, motioning Madeleine to move aside.

Madeleine attempted to obey, but could not release her hand from its imprisonment.

Count Tristan did not appear to hear, or rather to recognize the voice of his mother, although she continued to address him in a loud tone, and to beg, almost to command, him to listen to her. Maurice also spoke to him, but without making any impression on his mind. There was no meaning in his gaze when it rested on the faces of either; but his eyes, the instant they fell upon Madeleine's countenance, grew less glassy, more *living*, and through them the darkened soul looked dimly out.

Whatever might have been the internal sufferings of the countess, they did not conquer her stoicism. She resumed her seat, and her lips were again sealed; their close compression and ashy hue alone told that the torture of the mental rack upon which she was stretched had been augmented.

As soon as Madeleine felt the count's hand relaxing its firm grasp, she withdrew hers, though he made a faint attempt to detain her. As she retired from the bed, his eyes followed her, and his lips moved again.

"You are not going, Madeleine?" questioned Maurice. "My father evidently knows you, — wants you near him; you are the only one he recognizes; do not leave us!"

Was that low, stifled sound which reached their ears, in spite of the firmly-compressed lips of the countess, an inward sob or groan?

As Madeleine sat down, Dr. Bayard entered. Maurice related what had passed, and the doctor requested Madeleine to address the patient. That he made an effort to reply was unmistakable. Dr. Bayard then spoke to the count, but without attracting his attention. He desired Maurice to accost him, but no better result ensued. He signified to the countess that she should do the same; but the agony of beholding her son rec-

ognize, cling to one toward whom she entertained the bitterest
enmity, while the voice of his mother — his mother who loved him
with all the strength of her proud nature —was unheeded, became
intolerable. She rose up, not quickly, but with all her wonted
stateliness, and with a firm and measured pace walked out of the
room. She had no definite purpose, — she did not know where she
was going, or where she wished to go, — but she could not abide
the sight forced upon her eyes in that chamber.

"Maurice, attend your grandmother," whispered Madeleine.

Maurice had not thought of stirring, but he rose and opened
the door of the adjoining room.

"Leave me! I would be alone!" said the countess, as he
entered.

He returned to his father's side.

Dr. Bayard was giving his orders to Madeleine. A crisis had
just passed, he said. Count Tristan was better; there was reason
to hope that he would recover. One side was still paralyzed
and there was partial paralysis of the tongue. His mind, too,
was in a torpid state, but might gradually awaken. As Madeleine was the person whom he recognized, it would be well for
her to remain near him and minister to his wants. Madeleine
was more than content.

An hour passed and the countess did not return to her son's
bedside. Maurice, at Madeleine's suggestion, ventured to intrude
upon her. She appeared to be lost in a deep revery, and did
not raise her eyes at his approach.

"I fear you are not well, my grandmother; will you not allow
me to conduct you home?"

"I am *well*," she answered bitterly, "but I will go. My presence is of no use here; my own son ignores it!"

She spoke as though the invalid had refused to recognize
her for the express purpose of adding a fresh insult to those
which an evil fortune, a malicious chance (to use her own expressions), had heaped upon her head.

Without again visiting her son's chamber, she entered the carriage which Maurice had ordered; he took his seat opposite to
her, and neither remembered, until they entered the hotel, that
Bertha was left behind.

"I was thinking so much of my poor father that I quite forgot Bertha," he said, apologetically. "I will return for her at
once."

"Yes, go, go!" was all the countess replied.

CHAPTER LXI.

UNBOWED.

MAURICE did not suspect how Bertha was employed at that moment, and how much his heart would have had cause to rejoice if she proved successful in her undertaking. She was so happy herself in her betrothed that she was possessed by a strong desire to make some effort by which a like felicity might be secured to Madeleine. It had been one of the day-dreams of Bertha's girlhood that she and Madeleine should receive their wedding rings in the same hour. Gaston was entreating his *fiancée* to name a period, even though it might be some months hence (only a few days before, we think, he declared himself content with knowing that he might hope for this crowning joy *at the most distant date*), when he might call her his.

Bertha replied, tantalizingly, " The time depends upon Madeleine, not upon me. She must name the day."

" May she, indeed?" asked M. de Bois, joyfully, for he was convinced that he could influence Madeleine's decision.

" Yes, she will name it in naming the day for her own wedding. I have always intended that we should be married together."

M. de Bois's countenance fell.

" But Mademoiselle Madeleine is not even engaged."

" Is she not? Are you sure?"

" Quite sure," returned Gaston.

" But she loves some one, — does she not?" questioned Bertha, artfully.

" She has said she did," was the cautious response.

" Then, if she loves some one, we have only to find out who it is and bring them together, and get them to understand each other, and help them to fix the day. Would not that be charming?"

" Yes, very," replied M. de Bois; but he sighed as he spoke, remembering how improbable it was that anything of the kind would take place.

Bertha had a suspicion that he must have some knowledge of Madeleine's mysterious lover, and her idea of the perfect confidence that ought to exist not only between husband and wife, but a lover and his betrothed bride, would of itself have been sufficient inducement to make her endeavor to discover the secret.

"You have been near Madeleine all these years that she has been lost to us."

"Yes, happily for *me ;* and if she can only say happily for *her,* I should be proud as well as thankful."

"She does, — I am sure she does say so," responded Bertha, affectionately. "What could she have done without you? It was because you were so much to Madeleine that you became so much to — to — that is so — so — I mean " —

Many a sentence of Gaston's had she finished when his words became entangled through confusion ; it was but a fair return for him to conclude this one of hers, though perhaps he did so in a manner that added to her embarrassment.

Bertha recovered herself, and shook back her curls as though they were in fault. Then looking up archly in Gaston's face she said, —

"And if I wanted an excuse for what I have done, could I have found a better ? "

"Not easily," returned the delighted lover, "and I excuse you for a piece of bad taste which has rendered me the happiest and proudest of men."

"But we were talking of Madeleine," persisted Bertha ; "you know every one whom she knows, — do you not ? "

"What, all her patrons? Heaven forbid ! "

"No, — no, — you are very tantalizing, — I did not mean those. I mean the persons who visit her : you know them all ? "

"Most of them, I believe."

"Then you must be acquainted with this invisible lover of hers ! "

Now was M. de Bois puzzled. Bertha saw the advantage she had gained.

"You must have seen him, — you must know all about him, — and *I must know* also. Not to satisfy my curiosity, — do not imagine *that !* — I am not in the least curious ; but because I want to assist Madeleine. I want to judge whether nothing can be done to bring about her union with him."

"Nothing, — I fear, nothing," replied M. de Bois, sadly.

"Then you *do* know who he is ? There, you have admitted that you did ! "

"Are you laying snares for me, then, sweet Bertha? But I shall not let you exult over my falling into one of these well-laid traps. I only said I feared nothing could be done to bring about Mademoiselle Madeleine's union with any one."

" But you know whom she loves ? "

" She has never told me."

" But you at least *suspect* ? "

" What right have I to *suspect?* And you know I am *dull,* — I did not even suspect *whom* her cousin Bertha loved."

Bertha hung her head for a moment, but quickly returned to the attack.

" Tell me, at least, whom you think Madeleine *prefers.*"

" I have no right to do that, — it would not be fair to Mademoiselle Madeleine, — she would never forgive me ! "

" Ah, then you and I may have secrets from each other? That is the inference I shall draw if you refuse," said Bertha, provokingly.

This was a most distasteful suggestion to Gaston, who had a masculine touch of jealousy in his composition, — just enough to make him desire to monopolize Bertha *entirely.* He was not willing that she should have a thought which she could not communicate to him ; to hide anything from him was to rob him ! Was his an exceptional case, or are men in general as *exigeant?*

" Well, you do not answer ? " Bertha observed.

" I should be grieved if I had not your *whole* confidence, now and ever," he replied.

" So shall I be if I have not yours. Should one exact more than one is willing to give ? Tell me who it is that you suspect Madeleine of loving. Tell me at once ! "

" I cannot, — I have no right ! "

" I think you have no right to withhold the knowledge from me."

" I think so too," answered Gaston, sorely perplexed ; " and yet I must not tell you ! Will you not be generous enough to pity me, and ask me no more ? "

Bertha only pouted at this appeal ; but Gaston must have found some means of soothing her, for, by and by, she said, coquettishly, —

" Of course, I only wanted to know on Madeleine's account and on yours."

" *Mine?* " exclaimed Gaston.

" Yes, *yours ;* because if I had discovered who this lover was, I might have given him some valuable hints, and all might come right very quickly ; as it is, you may have to wait a long time for a bride."

" I ? Why, I am not Mademoiselle Madeleine's lover ! "

" No, but you are very dependent upon him. You cannot en-circle your bride's finger with a wedding-ring until he passes one on the taper finger of his."

" Bertha, that is unreasonable !" remonstrated Gaston.

" All the more womanly! Of course it is unreasonable ; I never laid claim to being *reasonable ;* but, on the other hand, I am obstinate. When Madeleine names the day for her mar-riage she names the day for mine."

" But if she should never marry, and that is possible."

" Then *I never shall!*" said Bertha, with a petulant little air of determination which looked only too real.

M. de Bois had no opportunity at that moment to test the effect of his newly-acquired eloquence, for Maurice entered.

" Bertha, will you believe that I have escorted my grand-mother home and actually forgotten you ? The carriage waits, and I am deputed to see you safely to the hotel."

" Do you suppose I shall accept as an escort one who thought me of too little importance to bear me in mind ? " asked Bertha, who was not wanting in feminine tact, that sixth sense of wom-anhood, which becomes wonderfully quickened when love sharp-ens the faculties.

Gaston joined in ; " My dear fellow, you could scarcely hope to be treated civilly after such a confession. But I will do my utmost to relieve you in this unpleasant predicament. Madem-oiselle Bertha refuses you as an escort — but, as she cannot return alone, I will take your place."

" And you may dismiss your carriage," returned Bertha. " I prefer to walk."

" And you really will not let me accompany you ? " asked Maurice. " What will my grandmother say ? "

" No doubt we shall hear *that* when we reach the hotel," .was the young lady's saucy reply.

But they did *not* hear ; for the countess had closed her door, and did not open it again until she summoned Adolphine to un-dress her.

The watchers beside Count Tristan that night were Madeleine and Maurice. The count was somewhat restless and often muttered unintelligible words ; but he continued to recognize Madeleine and seemed pleased to have her near him. Maurice did not fall asleep again ; he and Madeleine talked, in whispers, the whole night through, with the exception of those brief inter-vals when the count was awake. The themes of conversation were so abundant, so self-increasing, there was always so much which remained untold, that the topics of interest appeared to be inexhaustible.

Madeleine had given orders that Ruth and Mrs. Lawkins should commence their watch at five o'clock; but she could hardly believe that hour had arrived when the housekeeper entered, followed by Ruth. Maurice declared that he was not in the slightest degree fatigued, or sleepy, and did not need rest; but Madeleine, with smiling imperativeness, ordered him to bed; and certainly Maurice, when he obeyed, slept remarkably sound for a man who was not in the least fatigued or sleepy, and who was inclined to battle against sleep because he could not bear to lose the consciousness of being beneath the same roof as the one so long loved, so long and vainly sought; and because it was a joy inexpressible to lie still and think over all the words she had just uttered, and to picture her face until it seemed actually before him. Yet, in spite of this delightful occupation, inexorable sleep would suddenly fling her mantle over his senses, and even refused to grant him the happiness of continuing his blissful dreams in her own realm.

Maurice sought his grandmother the next morning, at the usual hour, and carried her the tidings that Count Tristan moved his limbs more freely, and that he had even spoken several words which could be comprehended. She gave no sign of preparing to accompany her grandson, and, after waiting awhile, he asked, —

"Will you and Bertha be ready soon? It is later than usual."

"I shall not go," replied the countess slowly, and as though it cost her a great effort to force out the words.

Maurice made no remonstrance; he well knew that to endeavor to alter a resolution of hers would be a fruitless attempt.

"And you, Bertha?" he inquired.

Bertha looked toward the countess: "Perhaps you would not like me to leave you?"

"*All leave me!*" she almost groaned out. "Why not you?"

"I will stay with my aunt," replied Bertha, without hesitation.

And she remained all day beside the afflicted, but ever haughty, countess. They did not converse, for the latter rarely spoke, even in answer to Bertha's questions, and Bertha could invent no mode of arousing and amusing her.

M. de Bois, not finding Bertha at Madeleine's, came to the hotel; but his presence was obviously very distasteful to the countess. She did not withdraw, she would have suffered martyrdom (as she did) rather than commit the impropriety of leaving Bertha alone with her lover; but she sat with knitted brows, her stony eyes turned scrutinizingly upon them, listening to and passing judgment upon every word they uttered, and looking a rebuke if Bertha ventured to smile. The icy chill of such a presence rendered Bertha and Gaston so thoroughly uncomfortable, that the young girl, although she was one of those beings who could hardly bear to live out of the sight of those she loved best, felt relieved when Gaston rose and bade her adieu. His visit had been brief, yet it seemed longer than all the combined hours they had passed together during the last three days. The visage of the countess relaxed somewhat after Gaston had gone, but she remained lost in thought without further noticing her niece. Bertha was, at least, spared the nervous unrest produced by those piercing eyes ever upon her.

Unfortunately Bertha's resources for self-diversion were of the most limited description. Hers was a social, a wholly dependent nature; she could not, like Madeleine, create her own amusement, and make her own occupation. She tried to read, but could not fix her attention; she tried to embroider, but quickly threw down her work; she could only wander in and out of the room, now watching at the window as though she expected some one; now sitting down and jumping up again; now turning over books and papers, and looking about for something, she did not know what, until she had thrown the room into complete disorder; and certainly her restless flitting backward and forward would have half distracted any one less absorbed than the countess. During one of Bertha's fits of contemplation at the window, she exclaimed, —

"Here comes Maurice, at last! I thought he would never be here!"

"I think my father is decidedly improving," said Maurice, as he entered. "I feel certain he recognized me to-day, and I thought he attempted to pronounce my name."

A faint light gleamed in the eyes of the countess at these words, but it was quenched by those which followed.

"Madeleine, he always seems to know, and he evidently likes to have her near him. His eyes wander after her when she leaves the room, and to-day, I thought he tried to smile when she returned."

"He is better then; it will soon be possible to move him; he can soon have that care which *should* be most acceptable to every son, and, I trust, has ever been to mine."

The countess made this assertion proudly, in spite of the deep wound she had received through her son's recognition of Madeleine ; she had tried to forget that blow, or to persuade herself that it had not been dealt.

Maurice did not know what answer to make, and remained silent.

"Aunt, you would not think of having cousin Tristan brought here until he is nearly well, — that is, well enough to walk about, — would you?" asked Bertha ; and her accents expressed her disapproval of such an attempt.

"He shall come the very moment that it is possible ! Do you suppose that I would submit to his remaining where he is one instant longer than is absolutely necessary?"

No reply to this declaration was needed or expected. Maurice returned to Madeleine's house with a sense of thankfulness that the count's seizure had taken place where it did.

Gaston and the housekeeper were the watchers beside the count that night, taking the places of Madeleine and Maurice at midnight, — this exchange having now become the established rule for alternate nights.

In spite of the iron-like constitution, and iron-like character of the countess, — in spite of her valiant, her desperate struggles, — her strength began to fail under the pressure of her hidden sorrow. She was unwilling to admit that she was subject to bodily any more than to mental infirmities. She belonged to that rare class described by the poet when he speaks of one who

> "Scarce confesses
> That his blood flows, or that his appetite
> Is more to bread than stone."

And though she had been suffering for days from a low nervous fever, neither her words nor actions gave the slightest indication that she was not in her usual health. But, one morning, when she endeavored to rise, her limbs refused to support her, — her head swam, — it was with difficulty that she poured out a glass of water to cool her parched and burning lips, and she was so fearful of falling (there seemed something positively awful to her in the possibility of *prostration*, perhaps on account of the fall it typified) that she staggered back to bed and there remained.

Neither Bertha's persuasions, nor those of Maurice, could induce her to allow a physician to be summoned. Maurice suggested Dr. Bayard, who was attending Count Tristan, but the countess was even more opposed to him than to any other medical attendant. Was he not aware of her relationship to the *mantua-maker?* Had he not seen Count Tristan recognize that humble and degraded relative when he did not know his own mother? —his own son? No, — she never allowed physicians to approach her; she never had need of them; she had none now, so she affirmed.

Bertha was not particularly well fitted to preside in a sick-room, and her maid, Adolphine, was versed in the arts of the toilet alone. She could have made the most charming cap for an invalid, but would have proved particularly clumsy in smoothing a pillow for the head by which the cap was to be worn. Yet the countess obstinately refused to have a proper attendant engaged. She wanted nothing, she said, except to be left to herself, — not to be disturbed, — not even to be accosted.

The position of Maurice grew far more painful than ever. He could no longer devote himself exclusively to his father. Even though he could, in reality, do nothing for his grandmother, yet he felt bound to pass a portion of the day by her side; for Bertha was too much distressed and too inefficient to be left with no assistance save that of her frivolous maid. Madeleine longed to seek her aunt, and make some few, needful arrangements for her comfort; but she could not doubt that her presence would do more harm than good. All that she could effect was to instruct Maurice, as far as possible, in the requirements of a sick-room, and to have prepared, in her own kitchen, the light food suitable to an invalid, which it would be difficult to obtain in a hotel. Every day delicate broth, beef tea as clear as amber, panada, simple jellies, and choice fruit were sent to Bertha for her aunt, without the knowledge of the countess; indeed, the only nourishment the invalid tasted was provided by the thoughtful Madeleine.

CHAPTER XLII.

DOUBLE CONVALESCENCE.

A FORTNIGHT passed on. At its close the vigorous constitution of the countess, united to her powerful volition, gained a victory over her malady. She had remained unshaken in her resolution not to receive medical advice; she had taken no remedies, — used no precautions; yet the fever had been conquered. Her strength began to return, and she insisted upon leaving her bed, and being dressed, not as befits an invalid, but in her usual precise and *soigné* style. Adolphine timidly suggested that a wrapper would be more comfortable than her ordinary attire, and a morning cap would allow her to repose her head. The countess awed her into silence by remarking:

"I keep my chamber no longer. I shall dress in a manner suitable to the drawing-room."

During the progress of the tedious toilet, it was more than once apparent that she was battling against a sense of faintness; but even this discomfort did not induce her to allow a single pin to be less conscientiously placed, a single curl less carefully smoothed. Adolphine did not dare to betray that she perceived the failure of her mistress' strength, and had not courage to offer her a glass of water. When the folds of her heavy black silk dress were adjusted, her collar and sleeves, of rich lace, arranged, her girdle tightly clasped with a buckle of brilliants which was an heirloom, and her snowy hair ornamented with a Parisian head-dress of mingled lace, velvet, and flowers, she contemplated herself in the mirror as complacently as though she perceived no change in her shrunken, haggard, altered features, and rose up to proceed to the *salon*.

Her first steps were so feeble and uncertain that Adolphine started forward involuntarily, to offer her arm; but a look from her mistress made her draw back, and the tread of the countess grew firmer as she entered the drawing-room. She did not sink into the nearest seat, but crossed the apartment to the arm-chair which she was accustomed to occupy; but she had hardly sat down, before her eyes closed and her head fell back; her face was as white as that of the dead. Adolphine caught up a bottle of cologne; but she stood in such fear of the countess, that without using the restorative she ran to summon Bertha. Bertha approached her aunt in great alarm, but sprinkled the cologne on her face with lavish hands, applied it to her nostrils, and bathed her temples. In a few moments Madame de Gramont opened her eyes and said, —

"A little on my handkerchief, Bertha. Adolphine carelessly forgot to give me any."

Her proud, unconquered spirit would not admit the passing insensibility of its mortal part. There was nothing to be done except for her niece and maid to appear unconscious of the weakness which she herself ignored. Adolphine placed a footstool beneath her mistress' feet and retired. Bertha went to the window and looked out, — a favorite amusement of hers, as we are aware.

The fortnight had been one of severe privation and discipline to her. She had not once seen Madeleine, for she could not have left her aunt, except when Maurice was with her, and the countess would not have permitted her niece to go forth unprotected by Maurice or her maid, and the latter could not be spared. The escort of Bertha's affianced husband Madame de Gramont would have considered highly improper.

Gaston's visits, though he came every day, were brief and unsatisfactory; for the countess, who could not forbid them, (as she felt inclined to do), ordered the large folding-doors which divided her chamber from the drawing-room to be left open, and desired Adolphine to take her work into the latter apartment. Conversation in an ordinary tone was quite audible to the countess, and could not but be heard by Adolphine, who had a tolerable knowledge of English. What lover cares to converse to more than one listener?

Bertha pined for the fresh air, — for a drive in the country, or, better still, a stroll in the capitol grounds with Gaston; but this latter was a happiness almost as far out of her reach as the paradise which she deemed it foreshadowed.

The countess had grown highly irascible during her illness, and as Bertha and her maid were the only ones upon whom she had a chance of venting her spleen, she spared neither. She experienced a sick longing for her native land; she more than ever detested the republican country in which she was sojourning, and she heaped upon Bertha the bitterest reproaches as the instigator of the exile which had been followed by so many calamities. The countess never condescended to remember that her wealthy young relative had liberally borne all expenses since they left the Château de Gramont, where its owners had no longer the means of residing. Of this fact she might be supposed to be ignorant, as she never vouchsafed a thought to *money matters;* it, however, had been made known to her by Count Tristan before she consented to the journey; but the *trivial circumstance* was quickly forgotten.

While Bertha was dreamily looking out of the window, and wondering when she would be freed from this prison-like life, she heard the door open, and turned quickly, hoping to greet the all-brightening presence. It was Robert, Madeleine's servant, who entered bearing a silver salver. Bertha had not supposed that the countess would, without warning, occupy her usual place in the drawing-room, and had not guarded against Robert's being seen. The young girl was so much discomposed that she stood motionless, aghast, expecting some terrible outburst from her aunt. Robert had admitted the countess at each of her compulsory visits to the residence of " Mademoiselle Melanie," and it seemed hardly possible that she would not recognize him again. Bertha ought to have known Madame de Gramont better than to have supposed she would have stooped to bestow glances enough upon a servant of Madeleine's, or, indeed, any servant, to know his features. Robert placed the salver upon the table, and either because he was naturally a silent man, or because the presence of the countess struck him dumb, or because he had no message to deliver that morning, retired without speaking. Bertha looked anxiously at her aunt; the immobility of her features was reassuring.

The salver bore a pitcher of admirably prepared chocolate, made by Madeleine herself, a plate carefully covered with a napkin, containing a delicate species of Normandy cake, to which the countess had been particularly partial in Brittany (Madeleine had remembered the recipe), and a dish of enormous strawberries, served, according to the French custom, with their stems. It occurred to Bertha, for the first time, that perhaps there was a cipher upon Madeleine's plate which would betray from whence it came; she examined a spoon before she ventured to present the tray to her aunt. The silver only bore the letter " M." Bertha, considerably relieved, but still flurried by the peril she had just escaped, placed a small table before Madame de Gramont, then poured out and handed her the chocolate in silence, fearing to provoke some question.

The countess, who was growing faint again, gladly accepted the nourishing beverage, and even ate several cakes. She seemed to enjoy them, for it was long since she had spoken in so pleasant a tone as when she remarked, —

" These cakes remind me of our noble old château; one would hardly suppose that they would be found in America."

Bertha suspected who had made the cakes, and, to draw her aunt's attention away from them, said, —

" What delicious strawberries ! And how fragrant they are ! "

The countess took one by the stem, and dipped it in the sugar, but with a disparaging look. It was large and juicy, and possessed a rich flavor and an aromatic odor which French strawberries can seldom boast; but the countess would not have admitted the superiority even of American fruit over that of her

own country, and after tasting a few of the strawberries returned to the cake which reminded her of her forsaken home.

How fared it with Count Tristan during the fortnight in
which he had not seen his august mother? Under judicious
and tender care, he had steadily, rapidly improved. His mental
faculties had been sufficiently restored for him to recognize
every one around him, but his memory was still clouded, and his
thoughts sadly confused. He had partially recovered his articulation, though his speech continued to be thick and at times
unintelligible. His limbs also had been partly freed from the
thraldom of paralysis, but were still heavy and numb, as though
they had long worn chains. He clung to Madeleine more
eagerly than ever, and seemed to be disturbed and uncomfortable except when she was near him. He had a vague consciousness that she was the medium through which all good
flowed in to him, and often repeated, as he held her hand, —

"You, — you — yes, you, Madeleine, you saved us all! Good
angel — good angel!"

That her ministry in the sick-room was so grateful to the sufferer was not surprising; for a gentle, efficient hand which knows
precisely how to make a pillow yield the best support, — a low,
soft, yet encouraging voice, — a cheerful, yet symathizing face, —
a soundless step, — garments that never rustle, — movements that
make no noise, — are among the chief blessings to an invalid.

The count seemed less happy at the sight of his son; his mind
was haunted by an undefined fear that there was something
Maurice would learn which would make him shrink from his
father, — which would disgrace both; the sufferer had quite forgotten that the discovery he dreaded had already been made.
When he looked at Maurice he often muttered the words, —

"Unincumbered, — no mortgage, — of course it's all right, —
power of attorney untouched, — leave all to me!"

At other times he would plead, in broken sentences, for pardon,
and denounce himself as a villain who had ruined his only son.

It was a somewhat singular coincidence that the very morning
the countess had risen and dressed for the first time for a fortnight, Count Tristan appeared to be so much more restless than

He smiled placidly and gratefully as he looked toward the flowers, and stretched out his hand to Madeleine. She took her place on a low seat, her little sewing-chair, and, unbidden, sang some of the wild, old strains to which he had often listened in the ancient château. The sigh he heaved was one of pleasure, as though his heart felt too full, but not of care. Madeleine sang on, ballad after ballad, for she could not pause while he appeared to be so calmly happy, and her voice only died away as she felt the hand that clasped hers relax its hold, and, looking up, she found that her patient was gently slumbering.

Maurice had sat listening and gazing as one spellbound, but Madeleine roused him by saying, —

"It is long past your usual hour for visiting your grandmother. Had you not better go? I think it likely your father will sleep some time. The change of scene and the fresh air have lulled him into a tranquil slumber."

"And your voice had nothing to do with his rest?" asked Maurice, tenderly.

"Any old crone's would serve as well for a lullaby," she answered, playfully. "Now go, and be sure you find out whether the countess liked the chocolate and those Normandy cakes."

CHAPTER XLIII.

OUTGENERALLED.

MADAME DE GRAMONT welcomed Maurice that morning with more animation than she had evinced during her illness. He did not anticipate finding her in the drawing-room; and was even more surprised to see her not in an invalid's *déshabille*, but dressed for visitors; not reclining, but sitting up almost as stiffly as in the days of her grandeur. He congratulated her upon her convalescence with mingled warmth and astonishment.

"Thank you, I am quite well," she replied; though her colorless lips and wan, sunken face solemnly contradicted the words. "How is your father?" This question was asked apparently with newly-awakened anxiety; for of late she had made no inquiries, but listened in silence to Maurice's daily report, and turned sullenly from him as though he were responsible for its

He now answered in an unusually cheerful tone, —

" My father is better, much better, to-day ; improving fast, I think."

Some of the old triumphant light flashed out of the countess' black eyes as she ejaculated, —

" Thank God ! Then he can be brought here at once ! "

Maurice perceived his mistake too late. He had not foreseen that the countess would have drawn this conclusion from the intelligence just communicated.

" My dear grandmother, you cannot think of desiring to remove my father at present ? "

" Cannot think of it ? What other thought fills my mind night and day ? He *must* be removed from that house. I say *must*, the very instant his life would not be perilled by the attempt. Better that it should have been placed in jeopardy than that he should have remained there thus long."

" We will talk of this when he is more decidedly convalescent," returned Maurice, perceiving that some generalship must be employed to protect his father. " I will let you know how he progresses, and we will make all the necessary arrangements for his change of abode in due season."

The countess was too shrewd not to see through this answer, and she was quite competent to return Maurice's move by generalship of her own ; for, in the battle of life, it is the tactics of womanhood that oftenest win the day. She allowed the conversation to drop ; and Maurice secretly rejoiced at her having, as he supposed, yielded the point. He chatted awhile with Bertha ; then his eyes chanced to fall upon the salver which Madeleine had prepared. It called to mind her request.

" What have you here ? Chocolate ? Did you find it well made ? "

The countess took no notice of the inquiry.

" These are very fine strawberries," persisted Maurice. " Did you enjoy them ? And these cakes," — he tasted one, — " used to be favorites of yours."

The countess checked a rising sigh ; for her aversion to betraying even a passing emotion was insuperable. " They reminded me of Brittany," she said, involuntarily.

" You liked them, then ? They are to your taste ? " questioned her grandson, hoping to be able to tell Madeleine that her labors had been rewarded.

But the countess answered coldly, —

" I find very little in this country, even though the object be

She did not open her lips again until Maurice was taking his leave. Then she said, —

"Has your father's physician been to see him to-day?"

"No; he had not come when I left, though it was past his usual hour.

"Let him know that I wish to see him," ordered the countess.

Had Maurice suspected her object he would not have replied so cordially, —

"I am truly glad that you will accept medical aid at last. You look very feeble."

The countess considered such a suggestion an insult; and drew herself up as she replied, —

"You are mistaken. I am far from feeble. Feebleness does not belong to my race, My strength does not forsake me readily; it will last while I last. Still you may inform your father's physician that I desire to see him."

"I will send him to you at once. You shall certainly see him to-day."

"Thank you."

These two words were spoken dryly by the countess, and with an emphasis which might have struck Maurice and caused him to suspect her intentions and possibly to frustrate them, had he not been so thoroughly convinced that her own state required medical care, and had he not known that her stoical fortitude made it easier for her to suffer than to admit that she *could* suffer.

Maurice found Madeleine where he had left her. The count had just awakened, much refreshed. He was softly stroking her head and saying with the same indistinct utterance, "Good angel! good angel!"

At the sight of Maurice the old troubled look passed again over his face, and he whispered hoarsely, —

"He shall never know. Never, never let him know. It would kill me! kill me!"

Maurice had told Madeleine how much better he had found his grandmother, and was giving her the gratifying intelligence that Madame de Gramont had said the cakes reminded her of Brittany (the highest praise possible for her to bestow on anything), when the doctor entered.

His patient, he said, had made marvellous progress; but that was owing, in a great measure, to admirable nursing; and he nodded approvingly to Madeleine.

"If physicians had only at their disposal a train of well-informed, efficient, conscientious nurses to distribute among their patients, medical services might be of some use in the world ; but, as it is, we might make a new application of the old proverb, that God sends us dinners, and the devil sends us cooks who make the dinners valueless ; a physician gives his orders and prescriptions, and a careless nurse renders them null."

Dr. Bayard was not a man who dealt in compliments, even in a modified form ; he was sagacious, abrupt, straightforward, and at times spoke his mind rather sharply. He had been impressed by Madeleine's unremitting care of his patient, and, in declaring that the count's convalescence was, in a large degree, due to her prudence and vigilance, he simply said what he thought.

"I am glad to see you have removed your charge to this room," he continued. "Change of scene and of air is always good, when practicable. I recommend a short drive to-morrow. I never keep an invalid imprisoned one hour longer than is necessary."

Maurice delivered his grandmother's message ; and Dr. Bayard promised to call upon her before his return home. The claims upon his time, however, were so numerous that it was evening before he reached Brown's hotel. The countess would not, even to herself have admitted that she could be subject to such an unaristocratic sensation as impatience ; but we are unable to hit upon any other word to express the state of unquiet anxiety with which she awaited his coming.

He was announced at last.

At that hour in the day, it was not unnatural for Dr. Bayard to be in a great hurry to get home to his dinner ; and consequently his manners were even more blunt and informal than usual. Without losing a minute, he took a seat in front of the lady whom he supposed to be his patient, looked scrutinizingly into her face and said, —

"Well, and what's the matter? A touch of fever, I suspect. We shall soon bring that under."

Without further ceremony he placed his fingers on her wrist.

The countess drew her hand away, as though something loathsome had dared to pollute her ; and the bright red fever spot on either cheek deepened into the crimson of wrath.

"Sir, I am perfectly well. I did not send for you to ask your advice concerning myself."

Dr. Bayard drew back his chair an inch or two, but made no apology.

"I am the mother of Count Tristan de Gramont whom you

Dr. Bayard bowed.

" I hear that he is much better."

" Much better," was the physician's laconic reply.

" It would no longer be dangerous for him to be removed from his present most unfit abode," the countess asserted rather than interrogated.

Dr. Bayard, in answering the queries of patients, or those of their families, did not follow the practice of physicians in general, but adhered to the exact truth. He replied, " It would not be dangerous, madame, but it would be unwise, — confounded folly, I might say. He is very comfortable where he is, and he has capital care. I do not believe there is such another nurse as Mademoiselle Melanie in Christendom."

If fiery arrows ever flash from human eyes, as some who have felt their wound declare they do, such darts flew fast and thick from the eyes of the countess as she regarded him.

" Sir, it is not a question of nurses. A mother is the fittest person to watch beside her son."

Dr. Bayard differed with her, but did not give her the benefit of his private opinion.

" As Count Tristan is in a state to be removed, I will give orders to have him brought here to-morrow. I suppose it is too late to-night?" observed the countess.

" I have already said that I do not see the necessity of his being moved at all, until he is perfectly restored," persisted the doctor.

" It is enough that I see it!" remarked the countess, frigidly. " I believe my inquiries only extended to asking your medical opinion as to the *danger* not the *propriety* of moving my son."

" Then I have nothing more to say," replied the physician, rising. " I have already stated that his removal, if advisable in other respects, would not be dangerous. Allow me to wish you good-evening."

Though Dr. Bayard's visit had highly irritated Madame de Gramont, exultation prevailed over all other emotions.

Bertha had been present during the interview, and albeit she was filled with grief at the prospect of Madeleine's sorrow and mortification, she had not the moral courage to remonstrate.

The countess was up betimes on the morrow. It may be that her strength had really returned; it may be that excitement supplied its place; but there was no recurrence of the feebleness which she had not been able wholly to conceal on the day previous. Before Bertha was dressed for breakfast her aunt had sent to borrow her writing-desk (having no correspondents, the countess did not travel with one of her own), and Bertha experienced a heart-sickening foreboding at the request. When she entered the drawing-room, Madame de Gramont was writing slowly and elaborately, as though she were preparing some document which was to pass into the hands of critical judges; but she never wrote in any other manner. A hasty, impulsive, dashing off of words and ideas would have lacked dignity. The whole character of the haughty lady might easily have been read in the stiff but elegant hand, the formal and carefully constructed phrases, the icy tenor of her simplest missive.

She folded the note, told Bertha where to find her seal with the de Gramont arms, impressed it carefully upon the melted wax, desired Bertha to ring the bell, and bade her send the note at once to Maurice. The countess could not have stooped to name to the servant the residence of the mantua-maker.

Though Madame de Gramont expected that her command would be instantly obeyed, she was too little used to attend to household matters, or bestow a thought upon the comfort of others, to give any orders concerning her son's room, or even to reflect that additional care in its preparation was needed for an invalid.

Count Tristan had passed the best night with which he had been favored since his attack. He had slept so uninterruptedly that Gaston and Mrs. Lawkins (whose turn it was to replace Madeleine and Maurice) had followed the invalid's example and travelled with him to the kingdom of Morpheus.

In the morning he expressed a desire to rise. The first words he uttered showed that his articulation was clearer. Madeleine had arranged the pillows in his arm-chair and placed it where he could look into the conservatory. He walked into the boudoir supported only by Maurice. There was a rare amount of stamina, a wondrously recuperative power in the de Gramont constitution, as was manifested both by mother and son.

When the count was comfortably seated, Madeleine placed before him a little table with his breakfast so neatly arranged that merely to look at it gave one an appetite. She served him herself, and the tranquil pleasure he felt in receiving what he ate from her hands was unmistakable. His own hands were still weak and numb, and she cut up the delicate broiled chicken, and broke the bread, disposed his napkin carefully, and then steadied the cup of chocolate which he tried to carry to his lips. Maurice stood watching her, just as he always did; for it was difficult for him to remove his eyes from her face when she was present, though, in truth, when she was absent he saw her before him hardly less distinctly.

The trio was thus agreeably occupied when the note of the countess was placed in the hands of Maurice. His consternation vented itself in an irrepressible groan, which made Madeleine and the count look up.

The latter trembled with alarm, and, his haunting fear coming back, he asked, in a terrified tone, —

" What has happened? What do they want? What would they make you believe? No harm of me, — you wont! you wont! Here's Madeleine will make all right ! "

" Do not trouble yourself," said Madeleine, soothingly; " there are no business matters to fret you now."

Her sweet, quieting voice, or the assurance, calmed him, and he repeated once more, for the thousandth time, " Good angel! good angel ! "

" It is a note from my grandmother," said Maurice, biting his lips. " She has seen Dr. Bayard, and insists on carrying out certains views of hers, and she informs me that she has his permission to do so."

Madeleine had not nerved herself against this blow ; it fell heavily upon her ; she could not at once resign the precious privilege of ministering to her afflicted relative ; and she could not hope that the countess would allow her to approach him if he were removed to the hotel.

" Surely she will not be so cruel! It will harm him, — it will retard his recovery."

" I will see her, at once, and try what argument and remonstrance can do," replied Maurice.

And he set forth on his difficult mission.

A moment's reflection convinced Madeleine that if the countess had received the doctor's consent, she would prove inexorable. There was no resource but to submit as patiently as possible. Count Tristan must be reconciled to the change, and to effect that was the task now before her. She tried to break the news gently ; she told him his mother had not seen him of late because she had been ill ; and now, hearing he was so much better, she desired him to return to the hotel that he might be nearer to her.

The count answered peevishly, " No — no, — I'll not go! I'm better here, — better with you, my good angel ! "

" But if Madame de Gramont is determined," said Madeleine, " I have no right, no power to resist her authority."

" Can I not stay? Let me stay ! " he pleaded, pathetically.

" I would be only too thankful if you could ; but you know the wishes of the countess cannot be disregarded."

" I cannot go! It will kill me if I go back! I am better here. I'm safe with you! I'll not go ! "

He seemed so much distressed that Madeleine dismissed the subject by saying, " Maurice has gone to see his grandmother ; we need not torment ourselves until he returns."

The count was easily satisfied, and the remembrance of his trouble soon faded from his mind. Madeleine asked him if she should sing, and he nodded a pleased assent. She could not give voice to any but the saddest melodies, for a sorrowful presentiment that she would never sing to him again, filled her mind. She continued to charm away his cares by the witchery of her accents until Maurice returned. The result of his advocacy was quickly told. The countess was inflexible, and awaited her son.

CHAPTER XLIV.

A CHANGE.

THE strongest heart will sometimes betray that it is over-taxed through the pressure of a sorrow which appears trivial contrasted with the stupendous burdens it has borne un-flinchingly; the firmest spirit is sometimes crushed at last, by the weight of a moral " feather " that breaks the back of endur-ance. Madeleine's courage proved insufficient to encounter calmly this new trial. She could not see that poor, wretched, brain-shattered sufferer, that proud man bowed to the dust, clinging to her with such a strange, perplexed, yet steady grasp, and know that she could no longer tend, amuse, and soothe him ! Her composure was forsaking her, and she could only hurriedly whisper to Maurice, —

" I will pack your father's clothes ; make him comprehend that we have no alternative ; reconcile him if you can. Since he must go, it had better be at once ; the countess is no doubt anxiously expecting him."

She passed into the count's room, gathered together all his wearing apparel, and knelt down beside his trunk. Her heart swelled as though it would burst; she bowed her head upon the trunk she was about to open, and sobbed aloud!

Madeleine's tears were not like Bertha's, — mere summer rain which sprang to her eyes with every passing emotion, and fell in sun-broken showers that freshened and brightened her own spirit. Madeleine seldom wept, and when the tears came, they sprang up from the very depth of her true heart, in a hot, bitter current which was less like the bubbling of a fountain than the lava bursting from a volcano. It is ever thus with powerful, yet self-controlled natures, and Madeleine's equanimity in the midst of trials which would have prostrated others, was not a lack of keen, quick sensibility, but an evidence of the supremacy she had gained by discipline over her passions.

Madeleine wept and wept, forgetting the work before her, the time that was passing, the necessity for action! All the tears that she might have shed during the last few weeks, if it were her nature to weep as most women weep, now rushed forth in one passionate torrent. She did not hear a step approaching; she was hardly conscious of the encircling arm that raised her from the ground, nor was she startled by the voice that said, —

"Madeleine! my own Madeleine! Is it you sobbing thus?"

"I feel *this!* O Maurice, I feel *this!* My aunt has never had power to make me feel so much since that day in the little *chûlet* when my eyes were opened, — when she cast me off, and I stood alone in the world."

"Ah Madeleine, dearest and best beloved, if you had only loved me then, — if I could only have taught you to love me, — you would not have stood alone! I should have battled against every sorrow that could come near you; or, at least, have borne it with you. O Madeleine, why could you not love me?"

For one instant Madeleine was tempted to throw herself in his arms and confess all. The high resolves of years of self-denial were on the verge of being broken in one weak moment; but the very peril, the very temptation calmed her suddenly. She brushed away her tears, and, gently withdrawing the hand Maurice held, said, in broken accents, —

"I have caused you too much pain in other days, Maurice. I should not have added more by allowing you to witness my weakness. Help me to be strong; for you see I have sore need of help."

"All that I can offer, Madeleine, you reject," said Maurice, re-

31 *

proachfully.   "My heart and life are yours, and you fling them from you."

"Maurice, my cousin, my best friend, spare me!   I have no right to listen to this language."

"But the right to hear it from the lips of another," retorted Maurice bitterly.

"Be generous, Maurice.   For pity's sake, do not speak on that subject."

There was so much anguish depicted in Madeleine s face that Maurice was conscience-stricken by the conviction that his rashly selfish words had caused her additional pain.

"This is a poor return, Madeleine, for all the good you have done my father, — all the good you have done me, — you have done us all.   You see what a selfish brute I am!   My very love for you, which should shield you from all suffering, has, through that fatal selfishness, added to your sorrow.   Can you pardon me?"

"When you wrong me, Maurice, I will; but that day has yet to come.   Leave me for a few moments, and I will complete what I have to do here and join you."

Maurice complied, but slowly and reluctantly, and looking back as he left the room.

Madeleine wept no more; she bathed her face and smoothed her disordered hair, and then collected all the articles scattered about, placed them carefully in the trunk, shut it and locked it, looked about to see that nothing was forgotten, ordered her carriage, and with a composed mien entered the little boudoir.

Maurice must have used some potent argument with his father which reconciled him to his change of habitation, or made him comprehend that resistance was useless, for when Robert announced that the carriage was at the door, and Madeleine brought the count's coat to exchange for his dressing-gown, he allowed her to assist him, only repeating the term of affection so often on his lips.

The count was ready, and Madeleine signed to Maurice not to linger.   He gave his arm to his father, and they passed through the entry.   Madeleine preceded them; she opened the street door herself; father and son passed out, but without bidding her adieu.   The steps of the carriage were let down; just as Maurice was assisting his father to ascend them, the count drew back with native politeness and said, —

"Madeleine first."

Madeleine was still standing in the doorway ready to wave her handkerchief as the carriage drove off.

" Come, Madeleine, come! come! We are waiting for you!"
cried the count.

Maurice expostulated in vain; his father insisted that Madeleine should go with them.

"Only get into the carriage, my dear father, while I speak with her."

" Get in before a lady? No — no! We are not backwoodsmen, — are we? Come, Madeleine, come!"

Madeleine saw that argument would not avail with the count; his mind was not sufficiently clear; it only had glimpses of reason which allowed him to comprehend by fits and starts.

Ever quick of decision, she said cheerfully, "Yes, in one moment," and withdrew; but before Maurice had divined her intention, returned, wearing her bonnet and shawl, and sprang into the carriage.

" Drive into the country," was Madeleine's order to the coachman.

Maurice looked at her with inquiring surprise.

" Dr. Bayard said a drive would do your father good. We can first take a short drive, then return, and go to the hotel."

Count Tristan looked happy. The motion of the carriage was agreeable to him, and the fresh air revived him; he gazed eagerly out of the window as though the commonest objects had caught the charm of novelty. His pleasure was of brief duration; for when they had driven about a mile, prudence suggested to Madeleine that it would be well to return before the patient became fatigued. She pulled the check-cord, and herself gave the order, " To Brown's hotel."

Count Tristan paid no attention to the command. The hotel was quickly reached; the carriage stopped; Maurice descended and handed out his father.

" Let me hear good news of you," said Madeleine to Count Tristan, encouragingly, and kept her seat.

Leaning heavily on his son's arm, the count mounted the hotel steps, but he did not comprehend Madeleine's words as an adieu, and turned to speak to her, thinking she was beside him. The coachman was closing the carriage-door preparatory to driving away.

" Madeleine! Madeleine!" cried out the count, stretching his hand imploringly toward her. " Madeleine, come! come!"

Madeleine perceived that Maurice was remonstrating with his father, and trying to lead him on, but that the count would not move, and still cried out, " Come! come!" in a voice of piteous

Curious strangers began to collect; Madeleine knew that if the scene continued even a few moments, a crowd would gather, and all manner of inquiries be made of her coachman, the hotel-keepers, the servants. She leaped out of the carriage, hastened to the count's side, and said, —

"I will go upstairs with you; the assistance of Maurice may not be sufficient; lean on my arm also."

And Count Tristan did lean upon her, for his limbs were too feeble to ascend a long flight without difficulty.

The door of the countess' *salon* was but a few paces from the top of the stair. Madeleine paused, took the count's hand affectionately in hers, and pressed it several times to her lips, saying, —

"Now I must bid you adieu. It would not be agreeable to the countess to see me. She would think my coming with you impertinent. You will not force me to bear the pain of seeing her displeasure? Bid me adieu and let me go!"

The count, easily swayed by her persuasive voice, and inspired with a vague dread of his mother's anger, kissed her forehead, and did not remonstrate, but stood still and watched her gliding swiftly down the stairs.

Maurice had whispered to her, "I will be with you as soon as possible, Madeleine. Be brave, for my sake!"

The countess had only betrayed her anxious expectancy by changing her usual seat to one where she could watch the door, and by looking up eagerly every time it opened. When, at last, Maurice entered, supporting Count Tristan, there was a gleam of mingled joy and triumph in his mother's eye. It was doubtful whether the triumph of having compelled obedience to her commands, and of having wrested her son from Madeleine, did not surpass the joy she experienced in beholding that son once again.

From her greeting, a stranger would hardly have imagined that when she saw him last his life was in imminent peril, and that she had rushed from his presence overcome by grief and mortification. She now received him as though she had cheated herself into the belief that she was doing the honors in her ancestral château, and that his brief absence had no graver origin than some ordinary pleasure party.

"Welcome, my son, welcome!" said she, kissing him on either cheek. "We have missed you greatly; you are thrice welcome for this brief separation."

Count Tristan returned her salutation, but looked strangely

uncomfortable, as though the atmosphere oppressed and chilled him.

"Dear cousin Tristan, I am so glad to see you better; you will soon be quite well again," said Bertha, embracing him far more warmly than his mother had done.

The countess made no allusion to his illness; she preferred wholly to forget the past.

Maurice led his father to an arm-chair, and asked Bertha to bring a pillow. Under Madeleine's tuition Maurice had become quite expert in promoting an invalid's comfort, and yet he now failed to arrange the pillow satisfactorily. Perhaps his father's chair was not easy, or the one to which he was accustomed was more commodious, or Maurice was more clumsy than usual; for though Bertha also lent her aid, the count kept repeating, fretfully,—

"It's not right,—it does not support my shoulders! You can't do it! Leave it alone! Leave it alone!"

They desisted, and sat down beside him.

The countess had no faculty of starting conversation, and Bertha's merry tongue had of late lost its volubility; she had so often irritated her aunt by her remarks that she had become afraid to speak. Maurice was too sad to be otherwise than taciturn. Thus the reunited little family sat in solemn silence. Count Tristan looked around him drearily for a while, and then having for a moment lost recollection of what had just taken place, exclaimed disconsolately,—

"Where is Madeleine?"

These unfortunate words roused the countess. She rose up as loftily as in her proudest, most unchastened days, and approaching him, asked, in a rebuking voice,—

"For *whom* do you inquire, my son? Am I to understand that a mother's presence is not all-sufficient for her own child? Is not hers the place by his side? If that place has been, for a season, usurped, should he not rejoice that she to whom it legitimately belongs occupies it once more?"

The count looked awed, and did not attempt to reply. Maurice perceived that he must exert himself to shield his father from as much discomfort as could be warded off, and inquired, without directly addressing either the countess or Bertha,—

"Is my father's room prepared for him? But I suppose that it is. His drive must have fatigued him, and I think he would like to retire."

The countess disclaimed any knowledge of the state of the

apartment, signifying that she was not in the habit of occupying herself with matters of this nature. Bertha was equally ignorant, but said she would go and see. Maurice prevented her by going himself.

The room looked as though it had not been entered since the day when he had packed up his father's clothes to move them to Madeleine's, and that was more than a fortnight ago. There was some delay in getting a chambermaid; servants are always busy, yet never to be had in an American hotel; after several ineffectual attempts, he obtained the services of an Irish girl; and he induced Adolphine to lend her aid, that the room might be aired, swept, and put in order more rapidly. Adolphine was rather a hinderance to the bustling Irish help, for a Parisian lady's-maid knows one especial business, and knows nothing else, however simple; she is an instrument that plays but one tune, and she boasts of her *speciality* as a virtue. In something more than an hour Adolphine announced that the apartment of *M. le Comte* was in readiness.

Count Tristan was very willing to retire, and after Maurice had played the valet without assistance, his father seemed disposed to sleep, and Maurice closed the blinds and sat down quietly until he perceived that the invalid had fallen into a deep slumber. Henceforth he was to watch beside him, when watching was needed, alone! Those blessed nights, shorter and sweeter than the happiest dreams, when he had sat in the pale light, with that beautiful face beaming opposite to him, — that soft voice sounding melodiously in his ears, — they were gone, never to return!

At that very moment Madeleine herself was haunted by the same reflections. When she drove home alone, and reëntered her house, how desolate and dreary it appeared! How empty and lonely seemed those apartments so lately occupied by the ones nearest of kin and dearest to her heart! She wandered through the rooms, up and down, up and down, with restless feet, pondering upon the singular events of the last few weeks; she had not before had leisure to dwell upon them. Was it indeed true that her roof had sheltered Count Tristan de Gramont? — Count Tristan de Gramont, whose persecutions in other days, had driven her from his own roof, and whose hatred had embittered and blighted her life? And had he learned to depend upon her? to love her? To talk to her, even when his mind wandered, of *gratitude*, as though that emotion was ever uppermost in her presence? And Maurice, her dear cousin, — Maurice, the beloved of her soul, who must never know that he was all in all to her, — had he been her guest for more than two weeks? And had she been permitted the joy of promoting his comfort in a thousand little, unnoted, womanly ways? Had he sat at her table? Had they watched together, night and day, by his father's bed? — talking through the night hours, unwearied when the morning broke, unwilling to welcome the first rays of the sun, because their sweet, inexhaustible converse came to an end? Had they shared the happiness of ameliorating Count Tristan's melancholy state, and seeing him daily improve? And now it was all over,: she must resume her old course of life, her temporarily laid aside labors! To muse too long upon departed happiness would unfit her for those. Even the sad joy of recollection was denied her.

She sent for Mrs. Lawkins and directed everything to be restored to its usual order. The draperies in the entry were to be taken down; — no, let them remain; Madeleine had been accustomed to see that portion of the house divided from the rest; let them stay. In passing through the drawing-room she noticed Maurice's trunk, which he had not thought of packing. Though it gave her many a pang, because she was forced to realize more keenly that he was surely gone, it was also with a sense of pleasure that she collected together the articles belonging to him and packed them carefully. Hers was a nature peculiarly susceptible to the pure delight of serving, aiding, sparing trouble to those whom she loved. The meanest household drudgery, the severest labor, the most prosaic making and mending, would have gained a charm and been idealized into pleasures, if they contributed to the well-being of those dear to to her; but, when performed for the one more precious than all others, they became positive joys.

She left Mrs. Lawkins busied in the arrangement of the apartments, and went upstairs to the workroom, which she had not entered for nearly three weeks. She had not seen any of her *employées*, except Ruth and Mademoiselle Victorine, since they all had learned her rank. Her unexpected appearance created a great commotion. No one but Ruth had expected to behold her in that apartment again. The women all rose respectfully; but an unwonted restraint checked the expression of gratification which her presence ever imparted. Madeleine smilingly bade them to be seated; then passed around the table and spoke to every needle-woman in turn, inquiring after the personal health of each, or asking questions about her family, — for she knew the histories of all; and then learning particulars concerning the work that had been done, and the work in hand.

The obsequiousness of Mademoiselle Victorine was perfectly overwhelming, yet she experienced no little disappointment. She had made up her mind that since Mademoiselle Melanie was known to be Mademoiselle de Gramont, she would never again be able to appear among her workwomen, even to superintend their labors, and a large portion of the resigned power must be delegated to the accomplished forewoman. Ruth Thornton, Madeleine's favorite, as Victorine considered her, was in the way; but what were a French woman's wits worth if they could not devise some method of removing a dangerous rival?

Madeleine lingered long enough to be *au courant* to the present state of affairs, and she found that the business of the establishment had so much increased during her seclusion, that every day, a host of orders had to be declined. This overwhelming influx of patronage was partially attributable to the reports circulated concerning Mademoiselle Melanie's romantic history, and also to the strong desire of the public (a democratic public) to secure the honor of procuring habiliments from the establishment of a dress-maker whose father was a duke.

Madeleine had taken a seat near Ruth, and was listening to Mademoiselle Victorine's *histories* and suggestions, when Robert made known that Monsieur Maurice de Gramont begged to see Mademoiselle Melanie.

Maurice had left his father as soon as he slept; he was impatient to return to Madeleine. He was tortured by the remembrance of her burst of grief, and her bitter words. The forced composure by which they were succeeded could not hide from him the deep wound she had received. Though the period which had elapsed since his father was conducted from Madeleine's house was so brief, the rooms, grown familiar to Maurice, already wore a different aspect; he actually felt hurt that Madeleine could have made the change thus rapidly. Men are so unreasonable! Maurice resembled his sex in that particular. Then, too, he found his trunk packed, and he knew by whose hand that duty had been performed. Doubtless, he was grateful? Not in the least! It seemed to him that Madeleine was in too much haste to remove the last vestige of his sojourn near her. When she entered the drawing-room he was standing contemplating the neatly filled trunk, and was cruel enough to say, —

"You used your *old magic* to make ready for us, Madeleine,

and you have used it again to efface all our footprints here. I can hardly persuade myself that I occupied this room."

Madeleine felt the implied reproach; but without answering the unmerited rebuke, she asked, "Is your father doing well?"

"He is sleeping at this moment; but it is very evident that he is going to have a sorrowful time; he will miss you so much; and my grandmother is as cold and hard as though her illness had petrified her more completely than ever."

That was another observation to which Madeleine could find no reply. Without essaying to make an appropriate answer, she said, "It will never do to let the whole burden of nursing your father devolve on you, Maurice; you will be broken down. May I plan for you? You need an experienced *garde malade*. It would be difficult, at short notice, to procure any so reliable, and so well versed in the duties of a nurse as Mrs. Lawkins. Then, too, your father is accustomed to see her near him; and a familiar face will be more welcome than a stranger's. Do you think it would be wrong to engage her without your grandmother's knowing that she had been in my employment?"

"I have no scruples on that head," returned Maurice; "but there are others which I cannot readily get over. She is your house-keeper, and I have heard you say she was very valuable to you. I know that it is exceedingly difficult to obtain good domestics in this country; you cannot replace her at once. How can you spare her?"

"Easily, — easily; do not talk of that. I will speak to her and she will go to you to-morrow morning. Meantime, I advise you to inform the countess that a nurse is coming. One charge more: you father is so much better that instead of wearing yourself out by sitting up with him, it would be wiser to have a sofa, upon which you could take rest, placed beside his bed. M. de Bois will gladly take his turn in watching, but after a few nights, I think Count Tristan will need no one but Mrs. Lawkins."

"Ah, Madeleine" —

Madeleine interrupted him. "One word about the delicacies which you cannot readily procure in a hotel, and which it would deprive me of a great happiness if I could not send. As the countess is now up, and might see and recognize Robert, I will order him to deliver the salver to the waiter who attends upon your rooms. Would it not be advisable to say a few words to this man to prevent any inadvertent remark in the presence of your grandmother?"

" Well thought of. How do you keep your wits so thoroughly about you, Madeleine? How do you manage to remember everything that should be remembered, and at the right moment?"

"If I do, — though I am not disposed to admit that such is the case, — it is simply through the habit of taking the trouble to *think at all*, to reflect quietly upon what would be best, what is most needed, — a very simple process."

"And, like a great many other simple but important processes, *rare* just because it *is so simple*," remarked Maurice, with great justice.

During this conversation Maurice and Madeleine had been standing where she found him on entering the room; but he had not resolution to tear himself quickly away, and said, —

"Let me sit a little while in your boudoir, and talk to you, Madeleine. *I* have not been able to reconcile myself so quickly to my own change of abode as you seem to have done to our departure from yours."

Was it not surprising that such a noble-minded man as Maurice could make an observation so ungracious, so ungenerous, and one which in his heart he knew was so unjust, to the woman he loved? Yet it would be difficult to find a lover who is incapable of doing the same. Why is it that men, even the best, are at times stirred by an irresistible prompting, themselves, to wound the being whom they would shield from all harm dealt by others with chivalric devotion? Let a woman commit the slightest action that can, by ingenious torturing, be interpreted into a moment's want of consideration for the feelings of her lover, and all his admiration, his tenderness, his reverence, will not prevent his being cruel enough to stab her with some passing word that strikes as sharply as a dagger.

"You think me a true philosopher, then?" replied Madeleine, gravely. But she added, in a lower and less firm tone, while a soft humility filled her mild eyes, "Do you think *I am reconciled*, Maurice?"

"Do you not think I am a heartless, senseless brute to have grieved you? Do not look so sorrowful! You make me hate myself! Ah, you did well not to trust your happiness to my keeping; I was not a fit guardian."

It was far harder for Madeleine to hear him say *that* than to listen to an undeserved reproach; but she led the way to her boudoir without replying, and for the next hour Maurice sat beside her, and they conversed without any jarring note breaking the harmony of their communion.

CHAPTER XLV.

REPARATION.

MAURICE, with as much *nonchalance* as he could assume, informed his grandmother that he had engaged a *garde malade* to assist in the care of his father. When good Mrs. Lawkins made her appearance the next morning, looking as plump, rosy and " comfortable " as English nurses (and house-keepers) arc wont to look, the countess merely bestowed upon her a passing glance and then took no further notice of her presence. It never occurred to Madame de Gramont to inquire into the fitness of this person for her position and duties. Besides, the countess seldom addressed a " hireling," except to utter a command or a rebuke. Maurice was greatly relieved when he perceived his grandmother's perfect indifference to the individual whom he had selected. Mrs. Lawkins had been thrown " into a flutter " by Madeleine's cautions and the prospect of being obliged to parry a series of cross-questions; but the reception she received quickly restored her equanimity. Count Tristan was sitting near his mother; the worthy house-keeper made her obeisance to both in silence, then turned to Maurice for directions.

" You have brought your trunk with you ? " inquired the latter.

" I left it in the entry, sir."

The count looked up at the sound of that voice. Immediately recognizing one whose association in his mind with Madeleine struck the chord which vibrated most readily, he exclaimed, in a piteous tone, " Madeleine ! Madeleine ! Why don't she come ? Wont Madeleine come soon ? "

Maurice, Bertha, and Mrs. Lawkins were filled with consternation at these words, which they imagined must arouse the suspicions of the countess; but she had not condescended to waste sufficient attention upon the domestic her son had hired to perceive that Count Tristan's ejaculations had any connection with her presence. The disdainful lady's eyes sparkled with anger at the unexpected mention of one whose name she desired never more to hear. She drew her chair close to Count Tristan's and said in harsh accents, —

" I trust, my son, that you have no wish ungratified ? When your *mother* is by your side, *whom* else *can* you desire ? "

Count Tristan was too easily cowed by her manner to venture a reply, even if his disordered intellect could have suggested any appropriate answer.

"I rejoice at your restoration to me," continued his mother; "and the filial duty I have the right to expect prompts me to believe that you also rejoice at our reunion."

The invalid looked very far from rejoicing; but the countess solaced herself by interpreting his silence into an affirmative.

From that time he never breathed Madeleine's name in his mother's presence; but those who watched beside him, often heard it murmured when he slept, or just as he wakened, before full consciousness was restored.

From the day that he returned to the hotel, he sank into a state of deep dejection. He would sit or lie for hours with his eyes wide open, without apparently seeing or hearing what passed around him, while an expression of despair overshadowed his deeply furrowed countenance.

The manifest weakness of his brain was a severer trial to Madame de Gramont than his enfeebled bodily condition; but she dealt with it as with her other trials; she would not acknowledge to herself the existence of his mental malady; she refused to admit that he lacked power to reason, at the very moment when she was exerting the species of authority she would have employed to keep an unreasoning child in check. The idea that it would be well to divert his mind, and render the hours less tedious, never occurred to her, or, if it did, she was totally at a loss to suggest any means of pleasantly whiling away the time. Her own health had not wholly recovered from its recent shock; the slow fever still lingered in her veins, but the daily routine of her life was as unchanged as though her strength had been unimpaired.

Dr. Bayard had ordered his patient to drive out every day, and the countess considered it her duty to accompany him. The pillows which Mrs. Lawkins carefully placed for the support of the invalid were almost as much needed by his mother; but she sat erect, and drew herself away from them, as though the merest approach to a reclining posture would have been a lapse from dignity. The count no longer gazed out of the window with that calm look of enjoyment which Maurice and Madeleine had remarked; he usually closed his eyes, or fixed them on his son, sitting opposite, with a mournfully appealing look, which seemed to ask, —

"Can no help come to me? Will it *always* be thus?"

Week after week passed on. Maurice, in spite of his unremitting attention to his father, found time to pay daily visits to Madeleine.

She no longer made her appearance in the exhibition-rooms, or saw the ladies who came to her establishment, upon business; but when Count Tristan was removed she had no gracious plea for excusing herself to those who called as visitors. She received them with graceful ease and dignified composure. Not one of them had courage or inclination to make the faintest allusion to the past, or to their acquaintance with her as " Mademoiselle Melanie." It was Mademoiselle de Gramont in whose presence they sat. Even Madame de Fleury had too much perception to venture to ask her advice upon questions of the deepest interest, — namely, the most becoming shapes for new attire, the selection of colors, the choice of appropriate trimmings, or some equally important matter which engrossed that troubled lady's thoughts, and caused her many wakeful nights.

After Count Tristan and Maurice returned to the hotel, Bertha escaped from imprisonment. When she informed her aunt that she was suffering from want of fresh air, the countess requested her to accompany Count Tristan and herself upon their daily drive; but Bertha maintained that driving would do her no good ; she detested a close carriage ; she wanted more active exercise, — she would take a brisk walk with her maid. Madame de Gramont would assuredly have mounted guard over her niece in person, were it not that the fatigue experienced even after a couple of hours' driving, admonished her that she lacked the strength for pedestrianism. Bertha was allowed to go forth attended only by Adolphine. Her walk always lay in one direction, and that was toward the residence of Madeleine ; and, strange to say, she never failed to encounter M. de Bois, who was always going the same way ! These invigorating promenades had a marvellous effect in restoring Bertha's faded color and vanished spirits.; and in the small, sad circle of which the stern-visaged Countess de Gramont formed the centre, there was, at least, one radiant face.

About this time the quiet monotony of Maurice's life was broken by a letter from his partner, Mr. Lorrillard. This gentleman had only recently learned from Mr. Emerson the painful circumstances which had taken place in connection with the loan made to the Viscount de Gramont at Mr. Lorrillard's suggestion. Mr. Lorrillard prided himself upon being too good a judge of character and upon having studied that of Maurice too thoroughly, not to feel confident that some satisfactory explanation could be given to occurrences which wore a very dubious aspect. He wrote kindly, yet frankly, to Maurice, requesting to know whether the account of the transaction which he had received was thoroughly correct, and more than hinting his certainty that all the facts had not been brought to light. Maurice was sorely perplexed; but, in spite of his strong desire to shield his father, he finally decided that Mr. Lorrillard was entitled to a full explanation, and that his own position would never be endurable while a suspicion shadowed his name. He despatched Mr. Lorrillard the following letter.

" *My dear Sir :* —

" I cannot but be touched by the confidence you repose in me. I do not thank you less because you have done me the common justice which is due from one man to another. When I received the loan from Mr. Emerson, I as firmly believed that the security I gave him was unquestionable, as he did. I had been led to think that the power of attorney in my father's hands had not been used. I was mistaken. I pass over Mr. Emerson's proceedings, which, however severe, were authorized by the light in which he viewed my conduct. The ten thousand dollars he loaned me were, at once, repaid him by the generosity of one of my relatives, Mademoiselle Madeleine de Gramont, whose debtor I remain. My father's dangerous illness has detained me in Washington. The instant he is sufficiently convalescent I purpose returning to Charleston to resume my professional duties.

"I am, my dear sir,
"Yours, very truly,
"MAURICE DE GRAMONT."

Mr. Lorrillard was highly gratified by the simple, ingenuous, yet manly tone of this letter, and well pleased to find his impressions correct. He immediately despatched an epistle to Mr. Emerson which convinced the latter that he could only conciliate a valued friend by making every possible reparation.

A few days later Maurice was surprised by Mr. Emerson's card. He could not converse with him in the presence of Count Tristan and Madame de Gramont, and was obliged to receive him in the general drawing-room of the hotel.

When Maurice entered, Mr. Emerson extended his hand and said, with an air of frankness, —

" I am a just man, M. de Gramont, and I came to make you an apology. My friend, Mr. Lorrillard, has convinced me that I ought to have paused before I yielded to the conviction that one whom he esteemed so highly had wilfully taken advantage of my credulity. I am now convinced that you were not aware that your property was mortgaged, and I come to tell you so."

" You have again made me your debtor," replied Maurice, not a little gratified. " I give you my word, as a gentleman, that I had not the remotest suspicion the property in question was encumbered. I have no right to complain of the severity of your treatment; it was justifiable under the circumstances."

" Hardly," replied the other. " But I shall esteem it a privilege to make all the reparation in my power. Of course you are aware that the railroad mentioned passes through your property, and that the estate has already doubled its former value? I came here to say that I am ready not only to loan you the ten thousand dollars you originally requested me to advance, but a larger sum, if you so desire."

What a sensation of thankfulness and relief those words caused Maurice! He would not only be enabled to repay Madeleine the amount she had so generously loaned, but he would be in a situation to meet the heavy expenses which his father and grandmother were daily incurring! Count de Gramont had never given his son entire confidence, and the latter was not aware of the *exact* state of the count's affairs; but Maurice had too much cause to believe that they were in a ruinous condition. He had only recently become acquainted with the mortifying fact that, from the time his father left the Château de Gramont, Bertha had been the banker of the whole party.

" I will meet your offer as frankly as it is made," answered Maurice, after a moment's reflection. " If you feel justified in loaning me fifteen thousand dollars, instead of ten, upon the former security, I will esteem it a great favor."

" Willingly; come to my office to-day, at any hour you please, and we will settle the matter. Make haste, for I must write to Lorillard by this evening's mail, and I desire to inform him, in answer to his somewhat caustic letter, that I have made the *amende honorable.*"

CHAPTER XLVI.

A MISHAP.

MADELEINE was accustomed to see Maurice at a certain hour every day, and looked forward to that period with such joyous expectation that a sense of disquiet, amounting to positive pain, took possession of her mind when the time passed without his making his appearance. She could not help reflecting how sad and long the days would grow when she could no more listen for his welcome step, and feel her heart bounding at the sight of his handsome countenance ; and yet such days must come, and must be borne with the rest of life's burdens.

That was his ring at the bell, — those were his firm, rapid steps! His face glowed so brightly when he entered the little boudoir that Madeleine exclaimed, —

"Your father must be much better! You carry the news written in shining characters in your eyes."

Maurice related what had passed between himself and Mr. Emerson, to whom he had just paid the promised visit, and concluded by saying, —

"Now, dearest Madeleine, I am enabled to repay your most opportune loan, but not able to tell you from what misery and disgrace you saved me."

He laid a check upon the table as he spoke.

Madeleine was silent, and looked uncomfortable. Maurice went on, —

"You cannot *conceive* my happiness at being so unexpectedly able to pay this debt, though that of gratitude must ever remain uncancelled."

"At least, Maurice, I will not *deprive* you of the happiness, since it is one ; and perhaps you will be more pleased when you know that this money will enable me to make the last payment upon this house, which will now become wholly mine. It has grown more dear to me than I imagined it could ever become, — more dear through the guests whom it has sheltered, and the associations with which it is filled. I never thought of making it mine with so much joy."

"You will remain here then? You will continue your occupation?" asked Maurice.

"Yes, undoubtedly."

"But," persisted Maurice, "do you not look forward to a time when you will have another home?"

"I see no such time in the dim future," she returned. "Perhaps I may become so rich that the temptation to retire will be very great; but as I cannot live unemployed I shall first be obliged to discover some other, wider, and nobler sphere of usefulness."

"But the home I mean," continued Maurice, with an air of desperation, "is the home of another,—the home of one whom you love. Do you not look forward to dwelling in such a home?"

Madeleine's "No" was uttered in a low tone, but one of unmistakable sincerity.

"How can that be?" exclaimed Maurice, at once troubled and relieved.

"Do not try to read the riddle, Maurice. You will be happier in setting it aside as one of life's mysteries which will be revealed in the great day. Will you listen to a new song which I have been learning?"

"Will I listen? Will a hungry beggar gather the crumbs falling from a rich man's table?"

Madeleine laughed and seated herself at the piano.

The new song only made Maurice desire to hear some of the old ones, and then other new ones, and she sang on until an unexpected and startling interruption destroyed all the harmony of the hour. But that occurrence we will relate in due season. We must first return to the hotel which Maurice had left before his usual hour, that he might pay a visit to Mr. Emerson previous to calling upon Madeleine.

The palatable delicacies which Madeleine daily sent to the invalids always reached the hotel at an hour when Maurice had promised to be at home. Robert had strict orders to deliver the salver to one of the hotel servants, and never to appear before the countess. This morning, however, the arrival of a large number of travellers had occupied all the domestics; not a waiter was to be found. Robert was anxious to inquire about a silver milk-jug which had not been returned. He carried his salver to the door of Madame de Gramont's drawing-room, though without intending to enter. The door happened to be open; he could see that the room was only occupied by Count Tristan, who was asleep in his arm-chair, and Mrs. Lawkins. She was the person whom he wished to see. The temptation was too great to be resisted. He entered with soundless feet, and placed upon the table a salver bearing a bowl of beef tea, two glasses of calves'-feet jelly, a plate of those Normandy cakes which the countess had so much relished, and a dish of superb white and red raspberries.

Approaching his mouth to Mrs. Lawkins' ear, Robert said, in a whisper, —

" Mrs. Lawkins, I had to come in, for you were just the person I wanted to see. You never sent back the silver milk-pitcher."

" The milk-pitcher?" replied Mrs. Lawkins. " Bless my heart! You don't say so? It's not here! I hope it's not been stolen. It must have got mixed up with the hotel silver and gone downstairs."

" You'll be sure to hunt it up, Mrs. Lawkins. I have said nothing to Mademoiselle Melanie, — Mademoiselle Madeleine, I mean ; but I am responsible, as you know, for all her silver, and I can't have what I bring here mislaid; as you were here I thought it was quite safe. How is the poor gentleman?"

" Ah, not so well as he was under Mademoiselle Madeleine's care. I'll see after the silver jug, and keep a sharp look-out for the silver in future."

Robert and Mrs. Lawkins stood with their backs to the door of Madame de Gramont's apartment, which opened into the drawing-room. What was their consternation on finding the countess herself standing in the door-way! Her countenance was perfectly appalling in its white, distorted wrath. She strode toward the two abashed domestics, and cried out, in a voice which broke the count's slumbers, and caused him to sit up in his chair with terror-dilated eyes, —

" Woman! What is the meaning of this? Of whom are you talking? Whose silver is that?" (pointing savagely to the salver.) " And who are you?"

Mrs. Lawkins was dumb.

" Am I to be answered?" demanded the countess, imperiously. Then she turned to Robert. " Whose silver is that? Whose silver did you say was missing?"

" Mademoiselle de Gramont's," Robert faltered out.

" And Mademoiselle de Gramont has the unparalleled audacity to send her silver here for my use? Do you mean to tell me that this salver and what it contains are from her?"

Robert could not answer.

" Great heaven! that I should endure this! That Madeleine de Gramont should have the insolence to *force* her *bounty* by stealth upon me, and that I should not have suspected her at once! Remove that salver out of my sight, and if you ever dare " —

Mrs. Lawkins had now partially recovered her self-possession, and interrupted the countess politely but very firmly, —

" Madame, you will do M. de Gramont great injury. Do you not see that you are exciting him by this violence ? "

" *Who* are you that you dare dictate to me ? Leave this house instantly! Were you sent here by Mademoiselle de Gramont to institute an *espionage* over me and my family ? Go and tell your mistress that neither she nor anything that belongs to her shall ever again defile my dwelling! I shall watch better in future! I will not be snared by her low arts, her contemptible impostures ! "

Mrs. Lawkins, though she was a mild woman, loved Madeleine too well to hear her mentioned disrespectfully without being roused to indignation; affection for her mistress overcame her awe of the countess, and she replied with feeling, —

" She is the noblest lady that ever walked the earth to bless it ! and her only art is the practise of goodness! Those who are turning upon her and reviling her ought to be on their knees before her this blessed moment! Didn't she nurse that poor gentleman night and day, as though he had been her own father ? Did she not bear all the slights put upon her by those who are not half as good as she ? — yes, that are not worthy to wipe the dust from her holy feet, for all their pride ? Didn't it almost break her heart when they forced the poor sick gentleman out of her house, to cage him in this cold, dreary place, where his own mother takes about as much care and notice of him as though he were a *Hindoo* or a *Hottentot !* " (Mrs. Lawkins was not strong in comparisons.) " And don't he mourn the night through for Mademoiselle Madeleine, crying out for her to come to him, as, I warrant, he never did for his mother ? And isn't that mother murdering him at this very moment ? "

" Leave the house ! Leave the house ! " cried the countess, in a voice that had lost all its commanding dignity, through rage. Leave the house, I say ! Do you dare to stand in my presence after such insolence ? "

" Yes, madame I dare ! " replied Mrs. Lawkins, coolly. " I am not afraid of a marble figure, even though it has a tongue ; and there's not more soul in you than in a piece of marble ; there's nothing but stone where your heart should be ; but even stone will break with a hard enough blow, and perhaps you will

" Go ! I say, go !" vociferated the countess, pointing to the door. " Am I to be obeyed?"

" No, madame !" replied Mrs. Lawkins, undaunted. " Not until I receive the orders of M. Maurice de Gramont. He placed me here, and here I shall stay until I have his leave to resign my duties."

Count Tristan had caught his attendant's hand when he conceived the idea that she was to be sent away from him, and when she refused to leave him, he pressed it approvingly.

"I am mistress here !" said the countess, with something of her former grandeur of bearing. " M. Maurice de Gramont has no authority to engage or discharge domestics, or to give any orders that are not mine. I will have none of Mademoiselle de Gramont's spies placed about my person ! Go and tell her so, and say that after this last outrage, I will never see her face again. Would that I might never hear her name ! She has been my curse, — my misery ; she shall never cross my path more !"

The count rose up as if sudden strength were miraculously infused into his limbs ; he raised both his arms toward heaven, and wailed out, " O Lord God, bless her ! bless her ! Madeleine ! Good angel ! Madeleine !"

The next moment he fell forward senseless and rolled to the ground.

The countess was stupefied ; — she could not speak, or stoop, or stir.

The alarmed house-keeper knelt beside him. Robert hastily set down the salver and lent his assistance. They lifted the count and laid him upon the sofa. The instant Mrs. Lawkins saw his face, and the foam issuing from his lips, she exclaimed, —

" It is another fit ! It is his second stroke ! Lord have mercy upon him ! and upon *you*," she continued, turning to the countess, solemnly ; " for, if he dies, so sure as there is a heaven above us, you have killed your own son !"

The countess' look of horror softened the kindly house-keeper, in spite of her just wrath, and she added, " He may recover, — he has great strength. Robert, run quickly for Dr. Bayard."

Then she unfastened the patient's cravat and dashed cold water upon his head, and chafed his hands, while his mother, slowly awakening from her state of stupefaction, drew near, and bent over him. But not a finger did she raise to minister to him ; she would not have known what to do, so little were her hands accustomed to ministration, — so seldom had they been stretched out to perform the slightest service for any one, even her own son.

We left Madeleine chasing away all heaviness from the soul of Maurice by her sweet singing. She was still at the piano, and he still hanging over her, when Robert burst into the room. He was a man almost stolid in his quietude, and his hurried entrance, and agitated manner, were sufficient to terrify Maurice and Madeleine before he spoke.

" Mademoiselle, it was my fault! Oh, if I had been more careful to obey your orders it would never have happened! "

His contrition was so deep that he could not proceed.

" Has Madame de Gramont discovered who sent the salver?" asked Madeleine, with an air of vexation.

"That's not the worst, Mademoiselle. The countess has found out how Mrs. Lawkins came there. She overheard us talking about the milk-jug I missed. Madame de Gramont was very violent; she said such things of you, Mademoiselle, that Mrs. Lawkins, who loves you like her own, couldn't stand it, and gave her a bit of her mind, and M. de Gramont was roused up also; he wouldn't hear you spoken against; he took on so it caused him another attack; down he dropped like dead! "

" My father, — he has been seized again, and " — Maurice did not finish his sentence, but caught up his hat.

" I've been for the doctor, sir," said Robert; " he's there by this time."

Maurice was out of the room, and hurrying toward the street door; Madeleine sprang after him.

"Maurice! Maurice! Stay one moment! Oh, if I could be near your father, — if I could see him! My imprudence has been the cause of this last stroke; yet I feel that he would gladly have me near him."

" He would indeed, my best Madeleine; but, my grandmother, alas! I have no hope of moving her."

" If her son were dying," persisted Madeleine, " her heart might be softened. If he asked for me, she might let me come to him; it would soothe *him* perhaps, and how it would comfort *me!* I shall be at the hotel nearly as soon as you are. I will wait in my carriage until you come to me and tell me how he is. Perhaps I *may* be permitted to enter if he asks for me. Do not forget that I am there."

Did Maurice ever forget her, for a single moment?

As soon as Madeleine's carriage could be brought to the door she followed her cousin.

It was perhaps surprising that she was moved with so much sympathy for one whom she not only had good reason to dislike, but toward whom she had formerly experienced an unconquerable repugnance ; but, with spirits chastened and purified, as hers had been, a tenderness is always kindled toward those whom they are permitted to *serve.* The very office of ministration (the office of angels), softens the heart, and substitutes pity for loathing, the strong inclination to regenerate for the spirit of condemnation. While Madeleine was daily ministering to the count, she found herself becoming attached to him, and, with little effort of volition, she blotted the past from her own memory.

The action of Count Tristan's mind had been peculiar ; when the discovery of his dishonorable manœuvring caused him a shock which planted the first seeds of his present malady, — when he had fallen into the depths of despair, — it was Madeleine's hand that raised him up, that saved him from disgrace, and saved his son from being the innocent participator of that shame. For the first time in his life a strong sense of gratitude was awakened in his breast. Again, it was through Madeleine that the votes of so much importance to him, and which he had believed unattainable, were procured ; she stood before him for the second time in the light of a benefactress. He had been seized with apoplexy while conversing with her ; when reason was dimly restored, his mind went back to his last conscious thought, and *that* had been of her, — hence his immediate recognition of her alone. Her patient, gentle, tender care had impressed him with reverence ; he was magnetized by her sphere of unselfishness, forgiveness and goodness, and some of the hardnesses of his own nature were melted away.

Count Tristan had practised deception until he had nearly lost all belief in the truth and purity of others, — had apparently grown insensible to all holy influences. Yet the daily contemplation of a character which bore witness to the existence of the most heavenly attributes silently undermined his cold scepticism, and tacitly contradicted and disproved his creed that duplicity and selfishness were universal characteristics of mankind, — a creed usually adopted by him who sees his fellow-men in the mirror which reflects his own image. Madeleine had discovered some small, not yet tightly closed avenue to Count Tristan's soul. Her toiling, pardoning, helping, holy spirit had done more to lift him out of the bondage of his evil passions than could have been affected by any other human agency.

CHAPTER XLVII.

INFLEXIBILITY.

"OH, you have come at last!" exclaimed the countess, with acrimony, as Maurice opened the door of his father's chamber. Then, pointing to the count, who still lay in a state of unconsciousness, she added, "Do you see what calamities you leave me alone to bear? — you who are the only stay I have left?"

By the aid of Mrs. Lawkins and the servants of the hotel, the count had been removed to his room. When Maurice entered, Mrs. Lawkins was standing on one side of the bed, Dr. Bayard on the other. The countess was pacing up and down the small chamber like a caged lioness.

Her grandson did not reply to her taunt, but addressed the doctor in a tone too low for her to hear. His answer was a dubious movement of the head which augured ill.

Bertha, who chanced to be in her own chamber, writing to her dyspeptic uncle, had only that moment become aware of what had happened. She stole into the count's room, pale with terror, crept up to Maurice, and clung to his arm as she asked, in a frightened tone, —

"Will he die, Maurice? Is it as bad as that?"

"I cannot tell; I have great fears. But see, he is opening his eyes; he looks better."

The senses of the count were returning; the fit had been of brief duration, and hardly as violent as the one with which he had before been attacked. In a short time it was apparent that he was aware of what was passing around him.

Maurice whispered to Bertha: "Madeleine is in her carriage at the door; put on your bonnet and run down to her, — you will not be missed. Tell her that my father is reviving."

Bertha lost no time in obeying, and was soon sitting by Madeleine's side, receiving rather than giving comfort.

Dr. Bayard, whose visits were necessarily brief, was compelled to leave, but he did so with the assurance that he would return speedily.

Count Tristan's eyes wandered about as though in search of some one; they rested but for one instant upon his mother, Maurice, Mrs. Lawkins, and then glanced around him again with an anxious, yearning expression, and he moaned faintly.

Maurice bent over him. "My dear father, is there anything you desire?"

The count moaned again.

"Is there any one you wish to see?" asked Maurice, determined to take a bold stand.

"Mad — Mad — Madeleine!"

The feeble lips of the sufferer formed the word with difficulty, yet it was clearly spoken.

Maurice turned bravely to the countess. "You hear, my grandmother, that my father wishes to see Madeleine; it is not usual to refuse the requests of one in his perilous condition. With your permission I shall at once seek Madeleine and bring her to him."

"Have you taken leave of your senses?" she asked with tyrannous passion. "Or do you think that I have not borne insults enough, that you strive to invent new ones to heap upon me? How can you mention the name of that miserable girl in my hearing? Has she not occasioned me and all my family sufficient wretchedness? Are you mad enough to imagine that I will allow you to bring her here that she may triumph over me in the face of the whole world?"

"My father asks to see her," returned Maurice, adding, in a lower tone, "and he may be on his death-bed."

Madame de Gramont, losing all control over herself, replied savagely, "*If* he were stretched there a corpse before me, — *he, my only son*, the only child I ever bore, the pride of my life, — Madeleine de Gramont should not enter these doors to glory over me! I know her arts; I know the hold she has contrived to obtain over him while he was at her mercy. That is at an end! I have him here, and she shall never come near him more, — neither she nor her *accomplices!*" and she indicated Mrs. Lawkins by a disdainful motion of the hand, as though she feared her meaning might not be sufficiently clear.

Maurice could not yield without another effort; for he perceived, by his father's countenance, that he not only heard the contest, but appealed to him to grant his unspoken wish.

"This is cruel, my grandmother! It is inhuman! You have nothing to urge against Madeleine, who has too nobly proved her devotion to her family, and her respect for your feelings; but if you *had* real and just cause of complaint, it should be forgotten at this moment. If my father desires to see her, she should be permitted to come to him."

"Do you presume to dictate to me, Maurice de Gramont? Is

this one of the lessons you have learned from the *mantua-maker?*
Do you intend to teach me my duty to my own child? *I swear
to you* that Madeleine de Gramont shall *never* see my son again,
while I live! I, his mother, am by his side, — that is sufficient.
No one's presence can supersede that of a mother!"

Maurice saw that contention was fruitless; he sat down in
silence, but not without noticing the look of compassion which
Mrs. Lawkins bestowed upon him. The count had closed his
eyes again, but low groans, almost like stifled sobs, burst at intervals from his lips.

The countess essayed to unbend sufficiently to attempt the
task of soothing him.

"My son," she said, in the mildest tone she could command,
"do you not know that your mother is near you?"

Without unclosing his eyes, he answered, "Yes."

"And her presence under all circumstances," she continued,
"should leave nothing to desire. In spite of what Maurice with
so little respect and consideration has attempted to make me
believe, I know you too well not to be certain that he did you
injustice."

No answer; but the countess interpreted her son's silence into
acquiescence with her observation, and remarked to Maurice
with asperity, —

"I presume you perceive that your father is fully satisfied.
It does not interfere with his comfort that you have failed in
your attempt. I well know you were instigated by one who
hopes to make use of your father's indisposition as the stepping-
stone by which she can again mount into favor with her family,
and force them into public recognition of her. This is but one
of her many cunning stratagems; there are others of which we
will talk presently."

She glanced at Mrs. Lawkins, who was arranging the count's
pillows, and raising him into a more comfortable position.

Maurice bethought him that it was time to let Madeleine know
there was no hope of her obtaining admission to his father. As
he left the apartment, the countess followed him into the drawing-
room.

"I have something further to say to you, Maurice, and I
prefer to speak out of the hearing of that woman. Am I to understand that you were privy to her introduction into this house,
and that you were aware that she was a spy of Mademoiselle de
Gramont?"

"A spy, madame?"

33 *

"Yes, a spy! Why should Mademoiselle de Gramont wish to place her menials here except to institute *espionage* over my family ? "

" Mrs. Lawkins was sent here by Madeleine because she is an efficient nurse, — such a nurse as my father needs and as he could not readily obtain. *I* brought her here, and I did not do so without knowing her fitness for her office."

" Her chief fitness consists, it appears, in her having been in the employment of the mantua-maker. I have no more to say on this subject, except that the woman must quit the house this evening."

" That is out of the question ; she cannot leave until I have found some one to take her place."

" Do you mean to dispute my orders, Maurice de Gramont? I shall not entrust to you the task of dismissing her. I shall myself command her to leave, and that without delay."

" You will do as you please, madame ; but may I ask by whom you intend to replace her ? "

" Somebody will be found. I will give orders to have another nurse procured. In the mean time, Adolphine can make herself useful."

" Adolphine ! " replied Maurice, contemptuously. " A butterfly might turn a mill-wheel as efficiently as Adolphine could take charge of an invalid."

" Be the alternative what it may," replied the countess, peremptorily, " I am unalterable in my determination. That woman sent here by Madeleine de Gramont leaves the house to-day ! "

Just then her eye fell upon the salver which Robert had left upon the table when he ran for the doctor ; that sight added fresh fuel to her indignation.

" Have you also been aware that Mademoiselle de Gramont carried her audacity so far that she had even ventured secretly to send donations, in the shape of chocolate, beef-tea, cakes, jellies, and fruit, to her family ? "

" I am aware," replied Maurice, " that Madeleine's thoughtful kindness prompted her, during your indisposition as well as my father's, to prepare, with her own hands, delicacies which are not to be obtained in a hotel. I was aware that this was her return for the harsh and cruel treatment she had received at the hands of, — of some of her family."

" Mad boy ! You are leagued with her against me ! This is unendurable ! Oh, that I had never been lured to this abominable country ! Oh, that I had never known the shame of find-

ing my own grandson sunken so low! But I have borne the
very utmost that I can support! Now it shall end! I will
return with your father to our old home, that we may die there
in peace! If you are not lost to all sense of filial duty, you will
not forsake your father, but accompany him to Brittany; he
will henceforth need a son!"

Maurice avoided making a direct reply by saying, "Have
the goodness to excuse me, madame; I will return in a few
moments."

He descended the stair with slower steps than was his wont
when on his way to Madeleine. Bertha was still sitting in the
carriage beside her cousin. Maurice read anxious expectation,
mingled with some faint hope, in Madeleine's countenance. He
entered the carriage before he ventured to speak.

" Your father, Maurice? " she asked eagerly.

" I think he is better; the attack does not appear as severe
as the former one must have been."

" Did you speak to your grandmother of me? Did you plead
for me, and entreat that she would allow me to go to Count
Tristan? "

" She is not to be moved, Madeleine; she is implacable."

" But if your father should desire to see me? " persisted
Madeleine.

" He did desire, — he even asked for you, — but my grandmother was inflexible."

" Maurice, I must, — must go to him, if he wishes to see me.
I understand his wants so well, — I must, must go to him!
Madame de Gramont may treat me as she will; but if he wants
me, I must go to him! "

Madeleine was so carried away by her strong impulse to reach
one to whom she knew her presence was essential, that she was
less reasonable than usual, and it was with some difficulty that
Maurice pacified her. But to resign herself to the inevitable,
however hard, was one of the first duties of her life, and after
awhile her composure was partially restored, and, bidding Bertha
and Maurice adieu, she drove home.

CHAPTER XLVIII.

THE NEW ENGLAND NURSE.

MADELEINE, in spite of the positive denial she had received, experienced as strong a desire to be near her afflicted relative as though his yearning for her presence drew her to him by some species of powerful magnetism. The wildest plans careered through her brain. She thought of the days in Paris when she had so successfully assumed the garb of the *sœur de bon secours*, and kept nightly vigils beside the bed of Maurice. Was there no disguise under which she could make her way to the count? But the doubt that she could elude the countess's scrutinizing eyes, — the certainty of the violent scene which must ensue if Madame de Gramont discovered her, — made her reluctantly relinquish the attempt. Then she clung to the hope that her aunt would not, while Count Tristan lay in so perilous a condition, insist upon discharging Mrs. Lawkins. All uncertainty upon that head was quickly dispelled by the appearance of Mrs. Lawkins herself. The countess had peremptorily repeated her sentence of banishment, and refused to listen to her grandson's entreaties that she might be permitted to remain until a substitute could be procured. To search for that substitute was the sole work left for Madeleine's hands. She despatched the willing housekeeper to make inquiries among her acquaintances, and charged her to spare neither time nor expense. Few Europeans can imagine the difficulty of executing such a commission in America; but the Englishwoman had lived in Washington long enough to know that she had no light labor before her. She was too zealous, however, to return home until she had found a person who was fully qualified to fill her vacant post.

Maurice was sitting beside Madeleine when Mrs. Lawkins returned from her weary peregrinations and made known her success.

"I did not send for the nurse to come here," said Madeleine. "It seemed to me better for you, Maurice, to go and see her and engage her to enter upon her duties to-morrow morning. That will give you an opportunity this evening of preparing the countess for her reception."

Maurice acted upon Madeleine's suggestion, and, after a very brief conversation with Mrs. Gratacap, secured her services.

Mrs. Gratacap belonged to the " Eastern States," albeit the
very opposite of *oriental* in her appearance and characteristics.
She was a tall, angular, grave-visaged person, possessing such
decided, common-place good sense that she came under the head
of that feminine class which Dickens has taught the world to
designate as " strong-minded." There was no "stuff and nonsense " about her ; she had a due appreciation of her own estimable attributes, as well as a firm conviction of the equality of
all mankind, or, more especially, *womankind.* When she accepted a situation, it was in the conscientious belief that the
persons whom she undertook to serve were the indebted party ;
yet she was a faithful nurse and both understood and liked her
vocation. In spite of her masculine bearing toward the rest of
the world, she always treated her invalid charges with womanly
gentleness.

When Maurice informed his grandmother that he had obtained
a new *garde malade,* the countess at once asked, —

" Are you attempting to introduce another spy of Mademoiselle de Gramont into my dwelling?"

Maurice controlled his indignation and replied, " My cousin
Madeleine has never seen this person. I hope she will suit, as
I have engaged her for a month, that being the custom here ;
even if she does not meet *all* our requirements, we cannot discharge her until that period has elapsed."

" I shall not consent to any such stipulation," answered the
countess. " If she does not please me, I shall order her to leave
at once."

" The arrangement is already concluded," returned Maurice ;
" it is the only one I could make, and you cannot but see that it
is a matter of honor, as well as of necessity, to abide by the contract."

Maurice evinced tact in his choice of language. The imposing words " honor " and " contract " made an impression upon
the countess, and she said no more.

The next day, shortly after the morning meal, the sound of
sharp tones echoing through the entry, was followed by the
noisy opening of the countess' drawing-room door.

" This is the place, is it ? " cried a harsh voice. " I say, boy,
bring along that box and dump it down here."

Mrs. Gratacap entered with a bandbox in one hand, and in
the other a huge umbrella and huger bundle, while the box
(which was a compromise between a trunk and a packing-case)
was carried in without further ceremony. Mrs. Gratacap was

attired with an exemplary regard for *utility;* her garments were
too short to be soiled by contact with the mud, and disclosed
Amazonian feet encased in sturdy boots, to say nothing of respectable ankles protected by gray stockings. Her dress was
of a sombre hue and chargeable with no unnecessary amplitude ;
where it was pulled up at the sides a gray balmoral petticoat
was visible; crinoline had been scrupulously renounced (as it
should be in a sick-chamber) ; the coal-skuttle bonnet performed
its legitimate duty in shading her face as well as covering her
head.

The countess might well look up in stupefied amazement; for
she had never before been thrown into communication with
humanity so strikingly primitive, and so complacently self-confident.

"This is the nurse of whom I spoke," was Maurice's introduction.

Mrs. Gratacap who had been too busily engaged in looking
after her "properties" to perceive the viscount until he spoke,
now strode forward, extended her hand, and shook his with good-
humored familiarity.

"How d'ye do? How d'ye do, young man? Here I am,
you see, punctual to the moment. Told you you could depend
on me. Well, and where's the poor dear? And who's *this*, and
who's *that?* " looking first at the countess and then at Bertha.

Maurice was forced to answer, "That is Madame de Gramont,
my grandmother, and this is Mademoiselle de Merrivale, my
cousin."

"Ah, very good! How are you, ma'am? Glad to see you,
miss!" said Mrs. Gratacap, nodding first to one and then to the
other. "Guess we shall get along famously together."

Then, totally unawed by the countess' glacial manner, for
Mrs. Gratacap had never dreamed of being afraid of "mortal
man," to say nothing of "mortal woman," she disencumbered
herself of her bandbox, bundle, and umbrella, deliberately took
off the ample hat and tossed it upon the table, sending her shawl
to keep it company, walked up to Madame de Gramont, placed
a chair immediately in front of her, and sat down.

"Well, and how's the poor dear? It's a pretty bad case, I
hear. Never mind, — don't be down in the mouth. I've
brought folks through after the nails were ready to be driven
into their coffins. Nothing like keeping a stiff upper lip. Your
son, isn't he? Dare say he'll do well enough with a little
nursing. Let's know when he was taken, and how he's been

getting on, and what crinks and cranks he's got. Sick folks always have crumpled ways. Post me up a bit before I go in to him."

The countess's piercing black eyes were fixed upon the voluble nurse with a look of absolute horror, and she never moved her lips.

Maurice came to the rescue.

" My father has been ill nearly a month; he was attacked with apoplexy; he had a second stroke yesterday."

" You don't say so? That's bad! Two strokes, eh? We must look out and prevent a third; that's a dead go; but often it don't come for years. No need of borrowing trouble, — worse than borrowing money."

" Let me show you to my father's apartment," said Maurice, to relieve his grandmother.

" All right, — I'm ready! And then you'll let me see where I am to stow my duds; any corner will do, but I must have a cupboard of a place all to myself; it need only be big enough to swing a cat round in. It isn't much comfort I want, but a hole of my own I always bargain for. Aren't you coming along?" she said, looking back at the countess, who sat still.

Madame de Gramont did not betray that she even suspected these words were addressed to her, nor that she heard those which followed, though they were spoken in a stage-whisper which could hardly escape her ears.

" Is your granny always so glum? We must cheer her up a bit," was Mrs. Gratacap's encouraging comment.

The nurse's high-pitched voice was softened to a lower key when she entered the apartment where Count Tristan lay, and there were genuine compassion and motherly tenderness in her look as she regarded him. She continued to question Maurice until she had learned something of the patient's history, — not from sheer curiosity, but because she always took a deep interest in the invalids placed under her charge, and by becoming acquainted with their peculiarities she could better adapt herself to their necessities.

One word only can express the countess's sensations at the dropping of such a " monstrosity " into the midst of her family circle, — she was appalled! Never had any one ventured to address her with such freedom ; never before had she been treated by any one as though she were mere flesh and blood. She had not believed it possible that any one could have the temerity to regard her in the light of equality. One might almost

have imagined that the formidable New England nurse had inspired her with dread, for she could not rouse herself, could not
gain courage to face the intruder, and, during that day, never
once approached her son's chamber. But Mrs. Gratacap, in the
most unconscious manner, made repeated invasions into the drawing-room, and even extended her sallies to the countess's own
chamber, always upon some plausible pretext, — now to inquire
where she could find the sugar, or the spoons, now to beg for
a pair of scissors, or to ask where the vinegar-cruet was kept, or
to learn how the countess managed about heating bricks, or getting bottles of hot water to warm the patient's feet!

The countess, compelled by these intrusions to address the
enemy, and galled by the necessity, said sternly, " Go to the servants and get what is needful."

" Law sakes! You needn't take my head off! I haven't got
any other and can't spare it!" answered Mrs. Gratacap, not in
the least abashed. " I don't want to go bothering hotel help;
I always keep out of their way, for they have a holy horror of us
nurses, and the fuss most of us make; though I am not one of that
sort. I leave the help alone and help myself considerable; and
what I want I manage to get from the folks I live with. That's
my way, and I don't think it's a bad way. I've had it for thirty
odd years that I've been nursing; and I don't think I shall
change it in thirty more."

She flounced out of the room after this declaration, leaving the
countess in a state which Mrs. Gratacap herself would have described as " quite upset; " but the haughty lady had scarcely time
to recover her equanimity before the strong-minded nurse returned to the attack.

The countess had retreated to her own room; but Mrs. Gratacap broke in upon her, crying out, " I say, when will that young
man be back? He's gone off without telling me when he'd be
at his post again."

Madame de Gramont's usual refuge was in silence, ignoring
that she heard; but here it was not likely to avail, for she saw
that the unawed nurse would probably stand her ground, and repeat her question until she received an answer. The countess,
therefore, forced herself to inquire in a severe tone, —

" Whom do you mean?"

" Why, the young man, your grandson, to be sure! A very
spry young fellow. I like his looks mightily."

If Madame de Gramont had been an adept in reading countenances she would have read in the nurse's face, " I cannot say

as much for his grandmother's;" but the proud lady was not skilled in this humble art, and never even suspected that a person in Mrs. Gratacap's lowly station would dare to pass judgment upon one in her lofty position. She replied, with increased austerity, —

"I am not in the habit of hearing the Viscount de Gramont, my grandson, mentioned in this unceremonious manner; it may be the mode adopted in this uncivilized country, but it is offensive."

"Law sakes! You don't say so?" answered Mrs. Gratacap, as if the rebuke darted off from her without hitting. "I didn't suppose you'd go to fancy I was *snubbing* him because I called him a young man! What could he be better? He's not an old one, is he? But I know some folks have a partiality to being called by their names, and I have no objection in life to humoring them. Well, then, when will Mr. Gramont be back? I'd like to know!"

"M. de Gramont did not inform me when he would return;" was the freezing rejoinder.

"Now, that's a pity! I want somebody in there for a moment, for the poor dear's so heavy I can't turn him all alone. Aren't you strong enough to lend a hand? To be sure, at your time of life, one an't apt to be worth much in the arms. At all events, an't you coming in to see him? You're his own mother; and, I swan, you haven't been near him this blessed day."

"Woman!" cried the countess, lashed into fury. "How dare you address such language to me?"

"Law sakes!" exclaimed Mrs. Gratacap, lifting up her hands and eyes. "What *did* I say? You *are* his mother, an't you? There's no shame about it, I suppose. I hadn't a notion of putting you into a passion. I thought it mighty queer you didn't come in to see your own son when he's lying so low; and I said so, — that's all! But if you don't want to come, I don't want to force you. I can't put natural feelings in the hearts of people that haven't got them; it stands to reason I can't, and you needn't be flying out at me on that account."

Mrs. Gratacap, after delivering this admonitory sentiment, was returning to the patient when she encountered Bertha, and inquired, —

"Did Mr. Gramont say when he would come back?"

"He did not say; but I think he will be absent for a couple of hours," replied Bertha.

"Oh, if that's the case, I must get a helping hand somewhere.

"You're a young thing, and, I dare say, strong enough. Come along and help me move the poor dear."

"Willingly," replied Bertha, "if I am only able."

As they entered the count's chamber, Mrs. Gratacap again subdued her voice, and though her words and manner were always of the most positive kind, there was a sort of rude softness (if we may use the contradictory expression) in her mode of instructing Bertha in the service required.

When the count was comfortably placed, she sat down, and Bertha also took a seat.

"I say," commenced Mrs. Gratacap, in a half whisper, "that's the most of a tigress yonder I ever had the luck to come across. Why, she's got no more natural feeling than an oyster, — no more warm blood in her veins than a cauliflower. I wonder how such beings ever get created. Are there many of that sort in the parts you came from?"

"She is very proud," replied Bertha, "and I am afraid there is no lack of pride in France among the noble class to which she belongs."

"Pride! Why, I wonder what she's got to be proud of? She looks as though she couldn't do a thing in life that's worth doing? I like pride well enough! I'm awful proud myself when I've done anything remarkable. But I wonder what that rock yonder ever did in all her born days to be proud of?"

Bertha tried to explain by saying, "Her pride is of family descent."

"I suppose she don't trace back further than Adam, does she? And we all do about that," was the answer.

Here the conversation was interrupted. Bertha was summoned to receive visitors.

The instant Maurice returned his grandmother attacked him. "Maurice, that woman's presence here is insupportable; there is no use of argument on the subject; I have made up my mind, — go and dismiss her at once, and seek somebody else!"

May not Maurice be pardoned for losing his temper and answering with considerable irritation, — "Have I not clearly explained to you, madame, that I cannot do anything of the kind? I have engaged her for a month, and I cannot turn her away without a good reason; here she must remain until the time expires."

"Pay her double her wages, and let her go!" urged the countess.

" Then send her to me ! " answered the countess.

Maurice did not stir; she repeated, in a more commanding voice, " Send her to me, I say ! "

Maurice reluctantly went to his father's room and returned with Mrs. Gratacap. Before the countess could commence the formal address she had prepared, the good woman took a chair, and with complacent familiarity, sat down beside her, saying, " Well, and what is it? I hope you feel a little better. I'm afraid you've a deal of *bile ;* really, it ought to be looked after ; if you can just get rid of it you'll be a deal more comfortable."

" Woman " — began the countess.

Mrs. Gratacap interrupted her, but without the least show of ill-temper.

" Now I tell you, if it's all the same to you, I'd just as lief you'd call me by my name, and that's ' Gratacap '— ' Mrs. Gratacap !' Fair play's a jewel, you know, and you didn't like my calling your grandson a ' young man ' even, but politely begged that I'd term him ' Mr. Gramont ; ' so you just call me by my name, and I'll return the compliment."

" I choose to avoid the necessity of calling you anything," returned the countess, when Mrs. Gratacap allowed her to speak. " You are discharged ! I desire you to leave my house " (the countess always imagined herself in her château, or some mansion to which she had the entire claim), " leave my house within an hour."

" Hoighty-toighty ! here's a pretty kettle of fish ! But it's no use talking ; I'm settled for a month ! that's my engagement."

" I am aware of it ; you will receive double your month's wages and go ! "

" I'll receive nothing of the kind ! I don't take money I've not earned ; and I'll not go until the time's up ! That's a declaration of independence for you, which I suppose you're not accustomed to in the outlandish place you came from, where people haven't a notion how to treat those they can't do without. Do you suppose your paltry money would compensate me for the injury it would do my character, if it should be said I was engaged for a month, and before I had been in the situation a day, I had to pull up stakes and make tracks? No, — unless you can prove that I don't know my business, or don't do my duty, I've just as much right here, being engaged to take up my quarters here, as you have. Don't think I'm offended ; make yourself easy on that head. I've learnt how to deal with all sorts of folks. I saw at the first squint that you and I would have a rather rough time, and I made ready for it. If you've got nothing more to say, I'll go back to the poor dear, for he's broad awake and may be wanting something."

" And you dare to refuse to go when I dismiss you ? "

" *Dare?* Law sakes! there's no *dare* about it. *Who's to dare me?* or to frighten me either? You don't think you've come to a free country to find people afraid of their shadows, — do you ? I'm afraid of nothing but not doing my duty ; I always dare do that, to say nothing of asserting my own rights and privileges. So let's have no more nonsense, and I'll go about my business."

Mrs. Gratacap returned to her patient as undisturbed as though the countess had merely requested her presence as a matter of courtesy.

The torment Madame de Gramont was destined to endure from this straightforward, steady-of-purpose, unterrified New England woman, must exceed the comprehension of those who never felt within themselves the workings of an overbearing spirit. Mrs. Gratacap maintained her ground ; there was no displacing her ; and she had become thoroughly sovereign of the sick-room, as a good nurse ought to be. The only alternative for the countess was to avoid her ; but she was a pursuing phantom that met the proud lady at every turn, haunted her with untiring pertinacity. Madame de Gramont absented herself from her son's chamber, except when Mrs. Gratacap went to her meals ; but little was gained by that, for the nurse was always flitting in and out of the drawing-room, or dining-room, at unexpected moments, and only the turning of the key kept her out of the countess's own chamber.

The first time that Madame de Gramont bethought herself of visiting her son when the inevitable *garde malade* was absent, Mrs. Gratacap returned in one quarter the time which the countess imagined it would require to swallow the most hasty meal.

" Well, I *do* say, that's a sight for sore eyes!" exclaimed the nurse. "I am as pleased as punch to find you here; but I've been thinking that like as not, you're scared of sick folks; there's plenty of people that are ; but there's nothing to be skittish about; I think this poor dear will get all right again."

" Silence, woman ! " commanded the countess.

" Never you fear," replied Mrs. Gratacap, either misunderstanding her or pretending to do so. " I'm not talking loud enough for him to hear. I don't allow loud talking in a sick-room, nor much talking either, of any kind. If you'd stay here a little while every day, you'd get some ideas from my management."

The exasperated countess retreated from the apartment, falling back, for the first time, before an enemy.

As she made her exit Mrs. Gratacap said to Maurice, "It's a pity your grandmother is so cantankerous; but, I'm used to cranks and whims of all sorts of folks, and it's only for her own sake, that I wish she'd make herself more at home here. Who'd think she was the mother of that poor dear lying so low? and she never to have a word of comfort to throw at him. But people's ways an't alike, thank goodness! It may be the style over in your parts, but I'm thankful I was born this side of the great pond."

A fortnight passed on, and the count rallied again. The shadows which obscured his brain seemed in a measure to have passed away; but they were succeeded by a deep melancholy. No effort made by Maurice or Bertha (Madame de Gramont made none) could rouse him. His countenance wore an expression of utter despair. He never spoke except to reply to some question, and then as briefly as possible; but his answers were quite lucid. As far as mere *physique* was in question, he was convalescing favorably.

Maurice received another letter from his partner, urging him to return to Charleston as soon as possible, and giving him the information that there was a most advantageous opening in his profession. While the count remained in his present feeble state, Maurice could not leave him; besides the countess and Bertha required manly protection.

Bertha continued to resist all Gaston's entreaties to name the day for their union, always replying that the day depended upon Madeleine, and if the latter remained single, she would do the same.

Maurice decided that, as soon as his father had recovered sufficiently to travel, it would be advisable for the whole party to take up their abode in Charleston. Many and sharp were the pangs he suffered at the thought of leaving a city which Madeleine's presence rendered so dear; but he would be worthier of her esteem, and his own self-respect, if he resolutely and steadfastly pursued the course he had marked out for himself before she was restored to him. To prepare the mind of his grandmother, and to learn Bertha's opinion of the proposed change, were subjects of importance which demanded immediate attention. He spoke to his cousin first, seizing an opportunity when the countess chanced to be absent.

Bertha looked amazed, and asked, "How can you leave Madeleine?"

"When I think of it, I feel as though I could not; and yet I must. I cannot linger here in idleness. Madeleine herself would be the first one to bid me go."

"I dare say!" answered Bertha, pettishly.

"But you, Bertha," continued Maurice, "how will you leave one who has a dearer claim upon you, than I, alas! will ever have upon Madeleine? How will you be reconciled to part from M. de Bois?"

"I answer as you do, that I *must.*"

"But you, Bertha, have an alternative; Gaston, if he could induce you to remain, — induce you to give him a wife, — would be enraptured."

"I suppose so," returned Bertha, with charming demureness; "but that is out of the question. Wherever my aunt goes, I will go."

"But how long is this to last, Bertha?"

"Nobody knows, except Madeleine, perhaps. I shall not be married until she is."

That very suggestion sent such a shuddering thrill through the veins of Maurice, that he cried out, —

"Bertha! for the love of Heaven! never mention such a possibility again! When the time comes, if come it must, I trust I shall behave like a man, but I have not the courage now to contemplate a shock so terrible. The very suggestion distracts me. I shall never cease to love Madeleine, — never! Were she the wife of another man, I should be forced to fly from her forever, that I might not profane her purity by even a shadow of that love; yet I should love her all the same! My love is interwound with my whole being; the drawing of my breath, the flowing of my blood are not more absolute necessities of my existence; my love for Madeleine is life itself, and if she should give her hand, as she has given her heart, to another man, I, — it is a possibility too dreadful to contemplate, — it sets my brain on fire to think of it. Never, never, Bertha, never if you have any affection for me, speak of Madeleine as" —

He could not finish his sentence, and Bertha said, penitently, —

"I am so sorry, Maurice, I beg your pardon; and there's no likelihood at present; and so I have told M. de Bois, that he might reconcile himself and learn patience."

Madame de Gramont entered, and Maurice, endeavoring to conquer his recent agitation, said to her, —

" I have been talking with Bertha about our future plans. I purpose returning shortly to Charleston ; indeed, it is indispensable that I should do so. I trust you and my father and Bertha will be willing to accompany me as soon as he is able to bear the journey, — will you not ? "

" No," replied the countess, decidedly. " Why should I go to Charleston ? Why should I linger in this most barbarous, most detestable country, where I have suffered so much ? I have formed my own plans, and intend to carry them into immediate execution."

" May I beg you to let me know what they are ? "

" I purpose," said the countess, slowly, but with a decision by which she meant to impress Maurice with the certainty that there was no appeal ; " I purpose returning to Brittany, and there remaining for the rest of my days ! "

Bertha half leaped from her chair, her breath grew thick, and her heart must have beat painfully, for she pressed her hand upon her breast, as though to still the violent pulsations.

" To Brittany, my grandmother ? " said Maurice, in accents of consternation. " I trust not. In my father's state of health, I could not feel that I was doing my duty if I were separated from him, and my interests, my professional engagements, compel me to remain in this country."

" Your filial affection, Maurice de Gramont, must be remarkably strong, if you weigh it against your petty, selfish interests, — your professional engagements. But, do as you please, — I ask nothing, expect nothing from you, — not even the protection of your presence, though I have no longer a son who is able to offer me protection."

" But if you will allow me to explain, — if you will allow me to show you that my lot is cast in America, — that it would ruin all my future prospects to return to Europe ! My father's affairs are so much entangled that I must exert myself for his support and my own." (He might have said the support of his grandmother also, but was too delicate.) " There is no opening for me in France, no occupation that I am fitted at present to pursue."

" I do not undertake to comprehend what you mean by your *prospects* — your *engagements* — your *exerting* yourself — or any of the other low phrases that drop so readily from your tongue. These are not matters with which I can have any concern. I have nothing to do with your *prospects*, your *exertions*, your *engagements*, or your *intentions*. *My intentions* are plain and unalterable. As soon as the physician says my son is in a state to travel, I shall engage our passage upon the first steamer that starts for Havre, and turn my back upon this miserable land, to which you, Bertha, by your capricious folly, lured us. It does not matter who accompanies me, or who does not; my son and I will depart, — *that is settled.*"

Bertha and Maurice were silent through dismay. The countess finding that neither replied, said to her niece, —

"Upon what have you resolved, Bertha? Will you allow me to return alone? Do you intend to refuse to go with me, because my grandson has coldly disregarded all the ties of kindred and severed himself from his father and me?"

Bertha answered quickly, "I wish, oh! I wish you could be persuaded to remain here; but if not, — if you *will* go, — if you *must* go '— I will go with you."

It was long since the countess had looked so gratified, and she drew Bertha toward her and kissed her brow, exclaiming, —

"There is, at least, *one* of my own kindred left to me! Thank God!"

"Do not suppose," said Maurice, "if this voyage is inevitable, if you cannot be persuaded to think the step hazardous, that I shall allow you to take it without a proper escort. If you return to France, let the consequence be what it may, I will go with you. Circumstances render it impossible that I should take up my residence there, but I will make the voyage with you, — I will see you and my father in your own home, and then" —

The countess contemplated him approvingly. "That was spoken like yourself, Maurice! I have still a grandson upon whom I can lean. Now, let us hasten our departure; let us start the instant it is possible; we cannot set out too soon to please *me*."

The countess *never* thought of the *necessity, propriety,* or *charity,* of pleasing any one else. Could any one's pleasure be of importance weighed against hers?

CHAPTER XLIX.

RONALD.

Who cannot conceive the consternation of Gaston de Bois when he learned that Madame de Gramont had resolved to return to Brittany with her son, and that Bertha had promised to accompany them? The countess sat looking at him with a species of savage triumph; for since he had become Madeleine's champion, she had treated him with pointed coldness. Gentle and sympathetic as his affianced bride was in general, she seemed for once to be insensible to the wound she had inflicted, and gave no sign of wavering in her resolution.

The next morning she was on her way to Madeleine's, accompanied by her maid. M. de Bois joined them as soon as they were out of sight of the hotel. How suddenly Bertha's soft heart must have become fossilized! for, although his heavy eyes and disturbed mien bore witness to the sleepless night he had passed, she did not appear to notice any change in his appearance.

"Bertha," he said, reproachfully, "you cannot be so cruel, — so ungenerous! You will not leave me and return to Brittany with your aunt, instead of giving me the right to detain you!"

"It's very hard-hearted," replied Bertha, tantalizingly; "but I have promised my aunt to accompany her, and I cannot break my word."

"But your promise to me?"

"I hope to keep that, in good time, when the conditions are fulfilled."

"But you link that promise with conditions which may never be fulfilled, — never!"

"Then we must be happy as we are," said Bertha, naïvely.

Bertha's obstinacy was surprising in one of her malleable, easily influenced character; but it seemed prompted by an instinctive belief that Gaston would be forced to make some exertion, — take some steps (their nature Bertha did not define to herself) which would result in bringing about Madeleine's happiness, and in promoting her union with her unknown lover. This one idea had taken such full possession of Bertha's brain that it could not be dislodged, and all Gaston's fervent entreaties that she would not let his happiness depend upon such an unlikely contingency were fruitless.

"Then I have but one alternative," said Gaston, at last. "I will resign my secretaryship and accompany you to Brittany. You cannot imagine that I would let you go without me?"

Bertha did not say how much pleasure this suggestion gave her; but the glad radiance in her blue eyes told she had been unexpectedly spared one half the sacrifice which she had determined to make, if necessary.

When Madeleine learned from Gaston the proposed departure of the countess and her family, a death-like pallor suddenly overspread her countenance, and she gasped out faintly, "All, — all going?"

"Dear, dear Madeleine," cried Bertha, "do not look so; you frighten me. It's very sad to leave you in this strange land alone. It depends upon you to keep two of us near you, — I mean M. de Bois and myself."

Bertha's words imparted no consolation.

"If you would but unravel this mystery, Madeleine?" Bertha went on. "It depends upon you and you only, to bind me here. When you are ready to stand before the altar with the one you have so long loved, so shall I be! Yes, though it were to-morrow."

"Bertha," answered Madeleine with such sad solemnity that for the first time Bertha's hope that her ardent desire might be accomplished was chilled, "you do not know what an, — an almost impossibility you are asking. Believe me, when I tell you, in all seriousness, that I shall never stand before the altar as a bride. An insurmountable barrier forbids! I shall live on, — work on, alone, — finding consolation in the certainty that I am acting wisely, and bearing bravely what must be endured. Will not this declaration convince you that you have decided rashly, not to say *cruelly*, in making your wifehood dependent upon mine?"

Bertha shook her head pertinaciously: "No — no — no! If I were to yield I should have to relinquish my last hope of seeing you a bride. I do not mean to yield! You need not persuade me; nor you either, M. de Bois. I am as obstinate as the de Gramonts themselves; and yet, in this instance, I think I am more reasonable in my firmness."

Madeleine and Gaston did not forego entreaties in spite of this assertion; but they had no effect upon Bertha, though she was thankful to be relieved from their importunities by the entrance of Maurice. Neither Madeleine nor Gaston felt disposed, in his hearing, to run the risk of making Bertha repeat her desire that Madeleine should become a bride. Madeleine roused herself that Maurice might not perceive her sadness, and made an effort to speak of the proposed voyage as a settled plan. The gloom of Maurice was not diminished by her attempt. He would have been less chagrined if he had seen the emotion which her pallid cheeks betrayed when the intelligence of their approaching departure was communicated to her. Ungenerous manhood! he would have suffered less had he known that she whom he loved suffered also!

Later in the day, as he was slowly walking toward the hotel, plunged in one of those despondent moods to which he had been subject before his sojourn in America, he was roused by a clear, ringing voice, though so long unheard, still familiar, and ever pleasant to his ears.

" Maurice ! "

" Ronald! There is not a man in the world I would rather have seen ! "

" And you are the very man I was seeking. I came to Washington on purpose to see you," replied the young artist, who had exerted so strong an influence over the character of Maurice in other days, and who had done so much toward " shaping his destiny."

Ronald was somewhat changed ; the rich coloring of his handsome face had paled, or been bronzed over; a few lightly traced, but expressive lines were chronicles of mental struggles, and told that he had thought and suffered. There was more contemplation and less gayety in the brilliant brown eyes ; more reflective composure and less impulsive buoyancy in his demeanor. Heretofore his bearing, language, whole aspect had ever communicated the impressiom of possible power ; now it bespoke power confirmed and concentrated, and brought into living action.

The friendship of Maurice and Ronald had not grown cold during the years they had been separated. They had corresponded regularly ; their interest in each other, their affection for each other had deepened and strengthened with every year, as all emotions which have their root in the spirit must deepen and strengthen, — the elements of *progress* being inseparable from those affections which draw their existence from this life-source.

Maurice, during his sojourn in Charleston, had paid weekly visits to Ronald's parents, usually spending his Sundays beneath their hospitable roof; and this made the day a true Sabbath to him. During the two months he had passed in Washington, Maurice had only written brief letters to Mrs. Walton; for the rapid succession of exciting events had engrossed his time, though it could not make him forget one who was ever ready with her sympathy and counsel. Her replies also had been curtailed by the all-absorbing joy of welcoming her son after his long absence.

The young artist had now achieved an enviable reputation as a painter. His first works were characterized by a towering ambition in their conception, which his unpractised execution could not fitly illustrate; but they had disappointed no one so much as himself. ~ After many struggles against a sense of discouragement, inseparable from high aspirations, frustrated for the moment, he had broken out of his chrysalis state of imperfect action, and spread his wings in strong and serious earnest. His sensitive perception of the great and beautiful, allied to the creative power of genius soon blazoned his prodigal gifts to the world, and he had gloried in that sense of might which makes the true artist feel he has a giant's strength for good or evil.

" I have rejoiced over your new laurels ! " exclaimed Maurice, warmly; for he had learned Ronald's distinction through the journals of the day.

" They are so intangible," replied Ronald, smiling, " that I'm not quite sure of their existence. I did not tell you that my father and mother are here and most anxious to see you. When will you pay them a visit? Can you not come with me now ? "

Maurice gladly consented to accompany his friend.

" You are our chief attraction to Washington," continued Ronald. " My mother was the first to propose that we should seek you out. Your letters were so sad, and even confused, that she felt you needed her. I think she fancies she has two sons, Maurice."

" She is the only mother I have ever known," answered Maurice; " and life is incomplete when a mother's place is unfilled in the soul."

CHAPTER L.

A SECRET DIVINED.

"TAKE care! the 'Don' will be jealous!" exclaimed Mr. Walton, as he witnessed his wife's greeting of Maurice, — a greeting as tender as a true mother could have bestowed. "When Ronald was a boy he would rush about like one gone mad if his mother ever ventured to take another child upon her knee, — he would never have his throne usurped. Our 'Don' was always 'monarch of all he surveyed.'"

This jocular appellation of the 'Don,' Mr. Walton had bestowed upon his son on account of his early propensity to fight moral windmills, and the Quixotic zeal with which he espoused the cause of the weak and the fair. This knight-errant proclivity ripened from the Quixotism of boyhood into the chivalrous devotion which had manifested itself in his somewhat romantic friendship for Maurice, — a friendship productive of such happy results to the young viscount.

Ronald replied, "My affection has gained a victory over my jealousy, as Maurice discovered some years ago. I have just given him a new evidence of that fact by accompanying you and my mother to Washington in the hope of seeing him."

"Did you really come for my sake," asked Maurice, much moved.

Mrs. Walton answered, "How could we help being distressed about you? Your letters were so unsatisfactory. I shall know more of your true state in one tête-à-tête, — one good long heart-talk, — than I could learn by a thousand letters."

After this declaration, Ronald and his father jestingly pronounced themselves de trop and departed.

Maurice had long since given Mrs. Walton his full confidence, and now to sit and relate the events that had transpired during his stay in Washington was a heart-unburthening which lightened his oppressed spirit. It seemed to him as though some ray of hope must break through the clouds which enveloped him, if her clear, steady vision closely scanned their blackness; she might discover some gleam of light which he could not perceive.

When he finished the narrative she asked, —

" And have you no suspicion who this mysterious lover can be? No clue to his identity? "

" Not the faintest," answered Maurice.

" But since you have seen Madeleine at all hours of the day, since you have resided in her house, she could not have evinced a preference for any gentleman without your perceiving the distinction."

" She evinced no preferences; no gentleman was upon an intimate footing except M. de Bois, who is engaged to Bertha, much to Madeleine's delight."

" M. de Bois, you tell me," continued Mrs. Walton, " has been her devoted friend during all these years that she has been separated from you. Have you not been able to learn something from him? "

" I have too much respect for Madeleine to force from another a secret which she refuses to impart to me; but I am quite certain that if M. de Bois knows whom Madeleine has blessed with her love, Bertha is still in ignorance. Bertha would have told me at once."

Mrs. Walton mused awhile, then said, " I do not see any loose thread by which the mystery can be unravelled; but you will, of course, make me acquainted with your Madeleine? "

" *My* Madeleine," began Maurice, bitterly.

" I called her yours involuntarily, because your heart seems so wholly to claim her. She will receive me, — will she not? "

" Gladly, I am sure."

" Then we will go to-morrow."

There were too many chords of sympathy which vibrated responsively in the bosoms of Mrs. Walton and Madeleine, too many planes upon which they could meet, for them to remain merely formal acquaintances. It was Madeleine's nature to treat those with whom she was thrown in contact with a genial courtesy which rose to kindness, often to affection; but it was only to a few that she really threw wide the portals of her large heart. Mrs. Walton's devotion to Maurice was claim enough for her to be ranked among the small number whom Madeleine admitted to that inner sanctuary.

On the other hand, Mrs. Walton was by no means impulsive in forming friendships; her existence had been brightened by very few. She had much constitutional *reticence;* she enjoyed a secluded life; she was not dependent upon others for happiness. A rich, inexhaustible well-spring of joy, — the one joy of her days, — flowed in through her son, and that pure fount was all-sufficient to water the flowers that sprang in her path. Maurice had awakened her womanly compassion, first, because Ronald had found in him a brother; next, because he was motherless and almost heart-broken, and finally, because his noble attributes won her admiring affection. But, although Mrs. Walton had no facility in making friendships, when she did become attached, it was with a sympathetic and absolute devotion which extended itself involuntarily to the beings who were dear to those she loved; thus her attachment for Maurice awakened an affection for Madeleine before they met; and when she clasped Madeleine's hand, and looked into her fair face, the reserve she invariably experienced toward strangers at once melted away, and in their very first interview these two responsive spirits drew near to each other with a mutual sense that their intercourse must become closer and closer.

Madeleine had frequently seen Ronald when, habited as the *sœur de bon secours,* she kept nightly vigil by the bed of Maurice, and Ronald had marked the classic features of the "holy sister," and quickly recognized them again when he was presented to Mademoiselle de Gramont.

After Mrs. Walton had visited Madeleine, Ronald persuaded her to call with him on Mademoiselle de Merrivale. Bertha received her quondam partner of the dance with much warmth and vivacity; but the countess looked with freezing hauteur upon these American friends of her grandson. Though Mrs. Walton was naturally timid, she was unawed by the countess's assumption of superiority; her self-respect enabled her to remain perfectly composed and collected, and to appear unconscious of the disdain with which she was treated.

This initiative visit was quickly followed by others, and Mrs. Walton proved how little she dreaded the countess by inviting Bertha to dine with her.

"I shall be delighted to go," said Bertha, "that is, if my aunt does not object."

"Rather tardily remembered," answered the countess, with acerbity.

"Better late than never," retorted Bertha, gayly; "so, my dear aunt, you will not say ' No.' "

The countess would gladly have found some reason for refusing, but none presented itself, and Bertha was sufficiently self-willed to dispute her authority; it was therefore impolitic to make an open objection.

M. de Bois also received an invitation. Maurice and Made-

leine joined the little circle in the evening, — a delightful sur
prise to Bertha and Gaston. This was the first evening that
Madeleine had passed out of her own dwelling during her residence in America. She had necessarily renounced society when
she adopted a vocation incompatible with her legitimate social position ; but, on this occasion, she could not resist Mrs. Walton's
persuasions, and perhaps the promptings of her own inclination.

Once more Madeleine's vocal powers were called into requi-
sition. She was ever ready to contribute her *mite* (so she
termed it) toward the general entertainment, and she would
have despised the petty affectation of pretended reluctance to
draw forth entreaty, or give value to her performance. Her
voice had never sounded more touchingly, mournfully pathetic,
and her listeners hung entranced upon the sounds. Maurice
drank in every tone, and never moved his eyes from her face ;
but when the soft cadences sank in silence, what a look of anguish
passed over his manly features, and told that the sharp bayonet
of his life-sorrow pierced him anew. He turned involuntarily
toward Mrs. Walton, and met a look of sympathy not wholly
powerless to soothe.

Mr. Walton was loud in his praises of Madeleine's vocaliza-
tion ; he had a courtier's felicity in expressing admiration, never
more genuine than on the present occasion.

" We must not be so ungrateful as to forget to offer Mademoiselle de Gramont the only return in our power, however far it
may fall short of what she merits," said he ; " the ' Don ' here, does
not sing ; he is not a poet even, except in soul, and all his inspirations flow through his brush ; but he interprets poets with an
art which I think is hardly less valuable than the poet's own
divine afflatus."

Madeleine, delighted, seized upon the suggestion, and solicited
Ronald to favor the company. His mother placed in his hands
a volume of Mrs. Browning's poems, and he turned to that
surpassingly beautiful romance, " Lady Geraldine's Courtship."

Ronald was one of those rare readers gifted with the power
of filling, at pleasure, the poet's place, or of embodying the characters which he delineated. The young artist's rich, sonorous
voice ; obeyed his will, and was modulated to express every
variety of emotion, while his animated countenance glowed,
flushed, paled, grew radiant or clouded, with the scene he described. A master-spirit playing upon a thoroughly comprehended instrument manifested itself in his rendition of the author.

All eyes were riveted upon him as he read ; he possessed in

an eminent degree the faculty of magnetizing his hearers, taking them captive for the time being, and bearing them, as upon a rising or falling wave, whither he would. As the tale progressed, the silence grew deeper, and, save Ronald's voice, not a sound was to be heard, except, now and then, a quickened breath and Bertha's low sobbing; for she wept as though Bertram had been one whom she had known.

Mrs. Walton's eyes had been fixed upon her son, with an expression of ineffable soul-drawn delight; but, just before the poem drew to a close, they stole around the circle to note the effect produced by his masterly reading upon others. Every face mirrored such emotions as the poem might have awakened in minds capable of appreciating the noble and beautiful; but by Madeleine's countenance she was forcibly struck; a marble pallor overspread her visage, her eyes were strangely dilated and filled with moisture; if the lids for a moment had closed, the "silver tears" must have run down her cheeks as freely as ran Lady Geraldine's; but, when Ronald came to that passage where Lady Geraldine thrills Bertram with joy by the confession that it was him whom she loved, — though he had never divined that love, — him only! Madeleine's lips quivered, and, with a sudden impulse, which defied control, she covered her face with her hands as though she dreaded that her heart might be perused in her countenance. It was an involuntary action, repented of as soon as made, for she withdrew the hands immediately, but the spontaneous movement spoke volumes.

As Mrs. Walton watched her, a sudden flash of *clairvoyance* revealed a portion of the truth, and she ejaculated, mentally, —

"The man whom Madeleine loves is unaware of her love, as Bertram was of Lady Geraldine's."

This suggestion, born in the under-current of her thoughts, floated constantly to the surface awaiting confirmation. If her belief were well-grounded, one step was taken toward fathoming the secret which Madeleine had doubtless some motive for preserving, but which Mrs. Walton's sympathies with Maurice made her earnestly desire to bring to light. Madeleine might have conceived a passion for one whom she would never more meet, or for one who was unconscious of her preference, though that seemed hardly possible.

Under ordinary circumstances Mrs. Walton would have been one of the last persons to take an active part in searching out the hidden springs of any human actions; but she was so deeply interested, both in Maurice and Madeleine, that a strong desire to be of service to them made her break one of the rules of her life. A wise rule, perhaps, so far as it frees one from responsibility, yet a rule which generous and impulsive spirits will often disregard in the hope of wafting into a drooping sail some favorable breeze that will send the ship toward a wished-for port.

It chanced the very next day, when Mrs. Walton was visiting Madeleine, that the latter was summoned away, and as she left the room, she said, —

"I will not be long absent; here are books with which I hope you can amuse yourself."

They had been sitting in Madeleine's boudoir; Mrs. Walton's chair was close to Madeleine's desk; upon the desk lay several volumes, probably those which had been last in use. Mrs. Walton made a haphazard selection, and took up a little sketch-book. Her interest was quickly awakened when she found that it contained sketches which were doubtless Madeleine's own. There was the château of Count Tristan de Gramont at Rennes, and the memorable little *châlet,* — the château of the Duke de Gramont, Madeleine's father, — the château of the Marquis de Merrivale, and sketches of other localities in her native land, of which she had thus preserved the memory. Then followed fancy groups, composed of various figures, apparently illustrative of scenes from books; but Mrs. Walton could not be certain of the unexplained subjects.

One familiar face struck her, — a most perfect likeness of Maurice, — it was unmistakable. Prominent in every group, though in different attitudes and costumes, was that one figure. Maurice, — still Maurice, throughout the book. Mrs. Walton was pondering upon this singular discovery when Madeleine entered.

She flushed crimson when she saw the volume her visitor was examining, and said, in a confused tone, taking the book from Mrs. Walton's hands, —

"I thought I had locked this book in my desk; how could I have left it about? It only contains old sketches of remembered places, and similar trifles, not worth your contemplation."

"I found them very beautiful," replied Mrs. Walton, "and the likenesses of Maurice are perfect."

"Of Maurice?" was all that Madeleine could say, her agitation increasing every moment.

"Yes, I could not understand the subjects, but his face and form are admirably depicted. You have a true talent for making portraits."

Madeleine could not answer, but as Mrs. Walton glanced at her conscious and troubled countenance, woman's instinct whispered, " It is Maurice whom she loves."

———+———

CHAPTER LI.

SEED SOWN.

ONCE more Count Tristan was convalescent. He could move his limbs with tolerable freedom, — could walk without support, though with slow, uncertain, uneven steps; his articulation was now hardly impaired, though he never spoke except in answer to questions, and then with evident unwillingness. He took little or no notice of what passed around him, but ever seemed brooding over his own misfortunes, — that is, if his mind retained any activity, of which it was not easy to judge.

In another week the month for which Mrs. Gratacap considered herself engaged would expire. That worthy, but voluble and independent person determined that she would not submit to the slight of having due notice of dismissal given her, and therefore herself gave warning that she purposed to take her departure. At the same time she said to Maurice, —

" I vow to goodness that grandmother of yours hasn't got the least idea of manners. I wonder if that's the style in her country? Why, we shouldn't call it common decency here! Law sakes! she's had a lesson or two from me, I think. Would you believe it, this very blessed morning she had no more civility than just to bid me leave the room as she wanted to speak to the doctor. I vow to goodness, I wouldn't have stirred a step if it hadn't been that I knew she didn't know any better, and I never force myself where I am not wanted; so I just took myself off."

" It was better to try and bear with my grandmother," answered Maurice, soothingly.

" And it's bearing with a bear to do it! " responded Mrs. Gratacap. " I don't mind it on my own account, — I am accustomed to all sorts of queer folks, but I suspected the old lady was up to something that would worry the poor dear, and, to be sure, I was right."

" What do you mean? " inquired Maurice, anxiously.

" Why, I couldn't help catching a word or two of what the doctor said when he went out ; I just heard him say that the patient *could* make the voyage if it were necessary, though it would be better to keep him quiet. Mark my words, she wants to pack off, bag and baggage, at short notice, — and *she'll do it !* Never trust my judgment if she don't."

Mrs. Gratacap was right ; one hour later, the countess, with a look which reminded Maurice of the days when she swayed unopposed, informed him that Count Tristan had been pronounced by his physician sufficiently convalescent to bear a' sea-voyage, and that she intended to leave Washington that day week, for New York, and take the first steamer that sails for Havre.

Maurice could only stammer out, " So suddenly ? "

" Suddenly ? " echoed the imperious lady ; " it is a century to me ! a century of torture ! And you call it *suddenly ? Nothing* will prevent my leaving this city in a week, and this detestable country as soon after as possible. Do you understand me ? "

" I do."

" Then I depend upon you to make all the needful preparations. There will be no change in my plans ; the matter is settled and requires no further discussion."

Maurice knew too well that there was but one course left, and that was submission to her despotic will. He at once apprised Gaston of the determination of the countess. M. de Bois was more grieved for his friend than for himself, and said he could be ready to accompany the party in twenty-four hours.

After this, Maurice took his way to the Waltons. He could not yet summon resolution to go to Madeleine.

We have already said that Mrs. Walton, through her woman's instincts, thought she had discovered Madeleine's secret, and every day some trivial circumstance confirmed her in her belief. But her shrinking nature made it difficult for her ever to take the initiative, or to attempt to change the current of events by any strong act of her own. There was no absence of *power* in her composition, but a distrust of her own powers which produced the same effect. Hers was a *passive* and not *suggestive* nature ; if the first step in some desirable path were taken by another she would follow, and labor heart and hand, and by her judgment and zeal accomplish what that other only projected ; but she had a horror of taking the responsibility, of " meddling with other people's affairs," even in the hope of bringing about some happy issue.

Ronald's impulses were precisely opposite to his mother's. He had an internal delight in swaying, in influencing, in bending circumstances to his will, in making all the crooked paths straight and righting all the wrongs of mankind. He was always ready to form projects (his father would say in a Quixotic style) and carry them into execution, to benefit his friends. He was deterred by no constitutional timidity, and the rash impulsiveness of youth looks only to happy results, and is seldom curbed by the reflection of possible evil. Ronald would have served Maurice at all hazards, and by all means in his power, or *out of his power.* He was expressing to his mother the chagrin he felt at the sad position of his friend, and his fear that it would throw a blight over his energies, when the latter remarked, —

"I think I have made a discovery which concerns Maurice, though I do not see how it can benefit him. Yet I am sure I know a secret which he would give almost his existence to learn."

"Indeed !" exclaimed Ronald. "Tell him then at once !"

"I cannot make up my mind that it would tend to any good result. It would be better, I think, not to touch upon the subject at all ; let events take their natural course."

"We should build no houses, we should write no books, and paint no pictures, if we adopted that doctrine," answered Ronald. "At least, tell me what you have learned."

"I think I know," replied Mrs. Walton, "whom Madeleine loves."

"Is it possible ? "

"And that is Maurice himself ! "

Mrs. Walton went through the whole train of reasoning by which she had arrived at her conclusion ; and Ronald was only too well pleased to be convinced.

"But, my dear, impetuous boy," said she, as she looked upon his glowing face, "what good to Maurice can grow out of this ? "

"Let us plant the seed and give it some good chance to grow," returned Ronald, eagerly. "Here is Maurice himself. The first step is to tell him " —

Maurice entered in time to hear the last words, and took them up.

"You can hardly tell him anything sadder than he comes to tell you. In a week we must bid each other adieu ; my grandmother has resolved to return to Brittany without further delay."

"I should be more deeply moved by that news," replied Ronald, "did I not think that I had some intelligence to communicate in exchange which is very far from sad. Maurice, are you prepared to hear anything I may have to say?"

"When did your words fail to do me good?" asked Maurice. "Do you think I have forgotten our long arguments in Paris, when I was in a state of such deep dejection, and you roused me and spurred me on to action by your buoyant, active, hopeful spirit? But go on."

"I want to speak of your cousin, Mademoiselle de Gramont."

Maurice expressed by his looks how welcome that theme ever was.

"You ardently desire," continued Ronald, "for so my mother has told me, to know who Mademoiselle Madeleine loves."

"Yes, I desire it more than words can utter."

"I think I can tell you," returned Ronald.

"You? You are not in earnest?" cried Maurice, in amazement. "For the love of Heaven, Ronald, do not sport with such a subject!"

"I do *not* jest, Maurice. I only tell you what you ought yourself to have discovered long ago."

"How could I? There is no possible clew. Madeleine sees no one, writes to no one, whom I could conceive to be the man whom she prefers."

"Easily explained," continued Ronald. "That man does not know he is beloved by her."

"Incredible!" replied Maurice.

"Very credible, my dear Maurice, as you are bound to admit; for that man stands before me."

"Ronald, for pity's sake — this — this is inhuman!"

"Do not wrong me so much, Maurice, as to think me capable of speaking lightly upon such a subject. My mother's perception of character is really wonderful; and her instincts, I think, never fail her; she is convinced that it is *you*, and you only, whom Madeleine loves. Reflect how many proofs of love she has given you! Has she not, throug h M. de Bois, kept trace of all your movements during the years that you were separated? Did she not run great risk to watch beside your sick-bed in Paris? Did you not tell me that it was her prompt and generous interference which prevented your losing your credit with Mr. Emerson? Does not her every action prove that you are ever in her thoughts? And, Maurice, I tell you, it is *you* whom she loves."

Maurice listened as though some holy voice from supernal regions chanted heavenly music in his ears. But he roused himself from the delicious dream, for he did not dare to yield to its spell, and said, —

" Did she not herself tell me that she loved another ? "

" May you not have mistaken her exact words ? " asked Ronald. " It was necessary to renounce you, to take all hope away from you, and place in your path the only barrier which you could not hope to overleap. And may she not have given you the impression that she loved, that her affections were engaged, while you drew the inference from her rejecting your hand that her heart was given to some other ? "

The countenance of Maurice grew effulgent with the flood of hope poured upon it.

"Oh, if it were so !" he exclaimed, in rapture. " Ronald, my best friend, what do I not owe you? Mrs. Walton, why, why are you silent? Speak to me! Tell me that you really believe Madeleine loves me ! "

Mrs. Walton, alarmed by the violence of his emotion, began to turn over in her mind the unfortunate results which might ensue if she had made an error. Maurice still implored her to speak, and she said, at last, with some hesitation, —

" If Madeleine does not love you, and you only, I have no skill in interpreting ' the weather signs of love.' I ought not to be too confident of my own judgment ; and yet I cannot force myself to doubt that, in this instance, it is correct."

" Say that again and again. I cannot hear it too often. *You cannot force yourself to doubt,* — you are quite convinced then, quite sure that Madeleine, my own Madeleine, loves me ? "

" I am indeed," responded Mrs. Walton, tenderly.

Maurice folded his arms about her, bowed his head on her shoulder, and his great joy found a vent which it had never known before ; for never before had tears of ecstasy poured from his eyes. That Mrs. Walton should weep too was but natural. She was a woman, and tears are the privilege of her sex. Ronald had evidently some fears that their emotion would prove contagious ; for he walked up and down the room with remarkable rapidity, and then threw open the window and looked out, cleared his throat several times, and finally said, in tolerably firm accents, —

"But, Maurice, what are we to do if the countess is determined to return to Brittany at once?"

"If Madeleine loves me, I can endure anything! I can leave her, I can go with my father, or perform any other hard duty. The sweet certainty of her love will brighten and lighten my trial. Oh, if I could only be sure!"

"Make yourself sure as soon as possible," suggested Ronald, to whom promptitude was a second nature.

"I will go to her; I will tell her what I believe; I will implore her to grant me the happiness of knowing that her heart is mine. But O Ronald, if I have been deluded, — if you have given me false hopes" —

"You will fight me," answered Ronald, laughing. "Of course that's all a friend gets for trying to be of service."

"Go, Maurice," said Mrs. Walton, "and bring us the happy news that Ronald and his mother have not caused you fresh suffering."

"You said you had not a *doubt*," cried Maurice, trembling at the bare suggestion.

"And I have not. Go!"

CHAPTER LII.

A LOVER'S SNARE.

MAURICE was on his way to Madeleine's. Not for years, not since the day when he breathed his love in the old Château de Gramont, had his heart throbbed with such rapturous pulsations as now; not since that hour had the world looked so paradisiacal, —life so full of enchantment to his eyes. As he reached her door and ascended the steps, his emotions were overpowering. A few moments more, and the heavenly dream would become a glorious, life-brightening reality, or would melt away, a delusive mirage in the desert of his existence, leaving his pathway a blanker wilderness than ever.

He was too much at home to require the ceremony of announcement, and sought Madeleine in her boudoir. She was not there. She was receiving visitors in the drawing-room. Maurice sat down to await her coming; but his impatience made him too restless for inaction, and he entered the *salon*.

Madeleine's guests were Madame de Fleury and Mrs. Gilmer, — an accidental and not very welcome encounter of the fashionable belligerents; though since Mrs. Gilmer had received the much-desired invitation to Madame de Fleury's ball, she had affected to lay down her arms, and Madame de Fleury pretended to do the same.

Madeleine was listening with patient courtesy to the meaningless nothings of the one lady, and the stereotyped insipidity of the other. Madame de Fleury was tortured by a desire to consult her hostess concerning a fancy ball-dress which at that moment filled her thoughts; but Madeleine's manner was so thoroughly that of an equal who entertained no doubts of her own position, — the vocation of "Mademoiselle Melanie" was so completely laid aside, — that Madame de Fleury, with all her tact and world-knowledge, could not plan any mode of introducing the fascinating subject of "*chiffons.*"

The marchioness greeted Maurice with enthusiastic cordiality. It struck her, on seeing him, that she might broach the desired topic through his aid; and she said, with the most charmingly innocent air, as though the thought had just occurred to her, —

"Shall I see you, M. de Gramont, at the grand fancy ball which Madame Orlowski gives next week? I hear it will be the *fête* of the season."

"I have not the honor of Madame Orlowski's acquaintance," replied Maurice.

"What a pity! But I can easily procure you an invitation, and you will have time enough to arrange about a costume. I have not determined upon mine yet. I want something very original. I am quite puzzled what to decide upon. I am perfectly haunted with visions of dresses that float through my brain. I have imagined myself attired as nymphs, and heathen deities, and ladies of ancient courts, and heroines of books; but I cannot make a choice."

Madame de Fleury did not venture to look toward Madeleine, and the latter made no observation. Maurice rejoined, —

"My father's state of health forbids my availing myself of your amiable offer."

Madame de Fleury was slightly discomfited. It was difficult to keep up the subject which seemed to have dropped naturally; but for the sake of reviving it, and trying to draw some suggestion from the Queen of Taste, she even condescended to address her foe; and, turning to Mrs. Gilmer with a false smile, asked, —

" *You* are going, of course? Have you determined upon the character you mean to assume ? "

Mrs. Gilmer was flattered by finding her attire a matter of acknowledged importance to her rival, and replied, with a simper, —

" Not altogether, — my costume is under discussion, — I shall decide *presently*."

A significant glance intimated that she meant shortly to proceed upstairs, to the exhibition-rooms of " Mademoiselle Melanie."

Madame de Fleury grew desperate, and was resolved not to be baffled in her attempt; she now launched into a dissertation upon different styles of fancy dresses. Madeleine turned to Maurice to make inquiries about his father. Poor Maurice! as he noted the unruffled composure of her bearing, the quietude of her tone, the frank ease with which she addressed him, his hopes began to die away, and tormenting spirits whispered that Ronald's mother had certainly come to an erroneous conclusion.

Madame de Fleury, finding that her little artifices were thrown away upon Madeleine, took her leave ; Mrs. Gilmer lingered for a few moments, then also made her exit, closely copying the graceful courtesy and floating, sweeping step of her rival.

" Thank Heaven ! they are gone !" exclaimed Maurice. " I have so much to say to you, Madeleine, every moment they staid appeared to me an hour."

He could proceed no further, for the door opened, and Ruth Thornton entered with sketches of costumes in her hand, and said, hesitatingly, —

" I am sure you will pardon me, Mademoiselle Madeleine; Madame de Fleury insisted ; she fairly, or rather *unfairly* forced me to seek you with these sketches ; she seems resolved to secure your advice about her costume."

Madeleine knew how to rebuke impertinence in spite of her natural gentleness, and the very mildness of her manner made the reproof more severe. She had thoroughly comprehended Madame de Fleury's tactics, and had determined to make her understand that when she visited Mademoiselle de Gramont, the visit was paid to an equal, not to the mantua-maker upon whose time the public had a claim.

" Say to Madame de Fleury that I leave all affairs of this nature in your hands, and that I have perfect reliance on your good taste."

Ruth withdrew.

" Let us go to your boudoir, Madeleine," said Maurice.

Madeleine, as she complied, remarked, —

" You are troubled to-day, Maurice; two bright spots are burning upon your cheeks; you look excited; what has happened ? "

" Much or little, as it may prove," replied Maurice, taking a seat beside her. " In the first place, my grandmother has concluded to leave Washington in a week, and, after she reaches New York, take the first steamer to Havre."

Maurice had given this intelligence so suddenly that Madeleine was off her guard, and the rapid varying of her color, the heaving breast, the look of anguish, the broken voice in which she exclaimed, " So soon? so very soon ? " rekindled his expiring hopes.

" This has been but a brief meeting, Madeleine, after the separation of those long, sorrowful years. The future is all uncertain, I cannot fix a time, after I have said adieu, when I may clasp this dear hand again."

" But," faltered Madeleine, " your profession, — you will not abandon that? You will return to Charleston ? "

" It is my earnest desire to do so."

" Then you *will* return ! You will return soon ? "

Maurice must have been the dullest of lovers if he could not distinguish the intonation of joy in Madeleine's voice.

" If my own advancement is the only incentive to my return, circumstances may interfere ; my father's health, for instance, the necessity of attending to his affairs, or other considerations."

Madeleine did not reply.

"Madeleine, I shall offend you, perhaps, for I am about to transgress. At all hazards, I must touch upon a subject which you have banished from our conversation."

For a moment Madeleine looked disturbed, but this warning enabled her to collect herself; she soon said, with composure, —

" Even if you do not spare *me*, Maurice, do not touch on any theme which must give pain to yourself."

" I have not yet quite decided," returned he, " how much pain it may cost me. I will only ask you to answer me a few questions. As I am a lawyer, cross-examination, you know, is my vocation, and you must indulge me. Nearly five years ago you declared that you had bestowed your heart irrevocably. You were very young then, — you had had few opportunities of seeing gentlemen; yet you have remained constant to this mysterious lover? You have never repented that you loved him?"

"Never!" answered Madeleine, with fervor.

"And you believe that he loves you?"

Madeleine bowed her head.

"And you have loved him long? Perhaps you loved him early in your girlhood; perhaps you loved him from the time you first met?"

Madeleine bowed her head again.

"Even as *he did you?*"

"I do not know," she answered, in a low voice.

"That is strange; men are apt to boast of the length as well as of the strength of their passion," remarked Maurice. "Your lover must be an exception. But perhaps he is unaware that he is blest by your love?"

Without suspicion Madeleine fell into that snare, well-laid by the young lawyer, for she answered, thinking that it would calm the jealous pangs to which Maurice might be subjected, —

"You are right; he is *not* aware that I love him."

Had her eyes not been downcast, had she looked up for an instant into the face of Maurice, she would have known by its look of radiant ecstasy that she had betrayed herself.

In a tone which emotion rendered unsteady, he went on, —

"You would cast your lot with his, Madeleine? If he were poor, you would share his poverty? You would even abandon your dream of earning a fortune for yourself, — and I know how dear that dream is to your heart, — for his sake? You would do this were there no barrier to the avowal of your love, — no barrier to your union with him?"

"I would."

"And that barrier is the opposition of his proud relatives?" asserted Maurice.

Madeleine started, looked in his face in alarm; for the first time, the suspicion that he had divined her secret, flashed upon her.

But Maurice went on unpityingly, —

"You refused him your hand because you thought it base ingratitude to those relatives who had sheltered you in your orphan and unprotected condition, and who had other, as they supposed, *higher* views for him. You feared by letting him know that you loved him to injure his future prospects, and you nearly blighted that future by the despair you caused him when he lost you. And since you have been restored, at least to his sight, you have

with a martyr's heroism adhered to your plan of self-sacrifice
because you thought that to relinquish it would draw down upon
him and yourself the wrath of his haughty grandmother, — I
will not say of his father; because, too, you believed that you
would be accused of ingratitude. And you have allowed him to
suffer unimaginable torture rather than acknowledge that the
lover to whom you have been so true, — the lover for whom you
have sacrificed yourself, — the lover most unworthy of you
(save through that love which renders the humblest worthy), —
is the man you rejected in the Château de Gramont at the risk
of breaking his heart."

Madeleine dropped her face upon her hands with a low sob,
but Maurice drew the hands away, and folding his arms about
her said, fervently, —

"Madeleine, my own, my best beloved, it is too late for concealment now! I know whom you love, — it is too late for
denial. Look at me and tell me once, — tell me only *once* that
it is true you do love me; tell me this, and it will repay me
for all I have suffered."

But Madeleine did not yield to his prayer; she tried to extricate herself from his arms, but they clasped her too tightly;
and when she could speak she said, through her tears, —

"You ensnared me, — you entrapped me to this! I should
never have told you! And what does it avail, — I can never
be your wife."

"It avails beyond all calculation to know that you love me,
even if, as you say, you cannot be my wife. Madeleine, to know
that you love no other, — that you love *me*, — that I have a
claim upon you which I may not be able to urge until we meet
in heaven, — is heaven on earth!"

What could Madeleine reply?

"But why, Madeleine, can you not become mine? My father
would no longer object. Are you not sure of that? Do you
not see how he clings to you? And my grandmother" —

"It would kill her," broke in Madeleine, "to see you the husband of one whom she detests and looks down upon as a degraded outcast. The Duke de Gramont's daughter only feels
her pride in this, that she could never enter a family to which
she was not welcome."

"Then her pride is stronger than her love! No, Madeleine,
though your firmness has been tested and I dread it, I will
not believe that you will continue so cruel as to refuse me your
hand."

" Did you not say that it was happiness enough to know that, — that," —

Madeleine had stumbled upon a sentence which it was not particularly easy to finish.

" To know that you love me! that you love me! Let me repeat the words over and over again, until my unaccustomed ears believe the sound ; for they are yet incredulous! But, Madeleine, you who are truth itself, how could you have said that you loved another, even from the best of motives?"

" I did not. I said that my affections were already engaged: yet I meant you to believe, as you did, that I loved another ; and the thought of the deception, for it *was deception*, has caused me ceaseless contrition. *I do not reconcile it to my conscience ;* I spoke the words *impulsively* as the only means of forcing you to give up all claim to my hand ; *but I do not defend those words.*"

" And I do not forgive them! You can only win my pardon by promising me that you will openly contradict them, and atone for your error by becoming my wife."

Madeleine's agitated features composed themselves to a look of determination which made Maurice tremble with apprehension ; and he had cause, for she said, —

" I cannot, Maurice, — I cannot, — must not, — will not be your wife without the consent of your father and your grandmother! "

" But if it be impossible to obtain my grandmother's ? "

" Then you must prove to me that you spoke truth by being content with that knowledge which you declared *would* satisfy you."

Maurice remonstrated, argued, prayed, but he did not shake Madeleine's resolve. Believing she was right, she was as inflexible as the Countess de Gramont herself.

CHAPTER LIII.

RESISTANCE.

MAURICE could not tear himself away ; he was still lingering by Madeleine's side when Bertha and Gaston entered to pay their daily visit. The perfect joy that rendered luminous the countenance of Maurice, and the happy confusion depicted upon

Madeleine's face, demanded but few words of explanation. Bertha caught Madeleine in her arms, laughing and crying, kissing her and reproaching her, over and over again. Then she turned to Maurice, as if impelled to greet him hardly less lovingly ; but Gaston, jealous of his own particular rights, interposed. She darted away from his restraining arms and danced about the room, shouting like a gleeful child ; then she kissed Madeleine again ; then, suddenly calming down, said to Gaston, reproachfully, —

" And you, — *you* knew this all the time, and did not tell me ? What penalty can I make you pay that will be severe enough ? I will plot mischief with Madeleine. If we can punish you in no other manner, we will postpone to a tantalizing distance the day you wish near at hand. Confess that I was wise to wait ! I knew Madeleine's lover would claim her in good season, but I never suspected he was my own dear cousin Maurice, whom she so resolutely rejected."

" Nor did I ! " cried Maurice, joyously; " and if *I* can forgive Gaston, you must."

" All in good time; after he is fitly punished, not before ! What do you say, Madeleine ? Shall we promise these two hapless swains their brides a couple of years hence ? "

" Bertha, Bertha ! you have not understood," answered Madeleine, gravely, yet with a happy smile on her sweet lips. " Maurice has no promise of a bride ; he looks forward to no bride, though I trust, you will, before very long, give one to M. de Bois."

" Dear me ! " exclaimed Bertha, completely sobered by this unexpected announcement. " I thought you had confessed to Maurice that *he* was the mysterious but fortunate individual whom you loved, and whom I have been puzzling my brains to discover."

Madeleine did not choose to respond to the statement made with such straightforward ingenuousness by Bertha, and only replied, —

" Madame de Gramont would never give her consent to the marriage of Maurice with the humble mantua-maker. I have too much of the de Gramont pride, or too much pride of my own, or too much of some stronger feeling which I can only translate into a sense of right and fitness, to become the wife of Maurice in the face of such opposition."

Bertha looked sorely disappointed and vexed, but vented her spleen upon the one whom she loved best, according to the invariable practice of women. She said to Gaston, —

"There! you are no better off than you were before! That's just what you deserve for keeping this secret from me!"

"But, Bertha, you will not be so unreasonable," urged Madeleine.

"Why not, when you set me the example? Why should I not be unreasonable and obstinate when you teach me how to be so? You know, Madeleine, you have been my model all my life long, and it is too late to choose another."

Madeleine was silenced, but Bertha ran on petulantly, this time turning to Maurice.

"How *can* you look so happy when Madeleine says she does not mean to marry you? I never saw anything like you men! One would think you had no feeling."

Maurice replied: "It is so much happiness to know who possesses Madeleine's heart, that even if she remain unshaken in her resolution, I could not be miserable."

"And you will not mind leaving her and going to Brittany? Your plans are not to be altered?"

"Not unless she will alter them by consenting to accompany me. You know that my grandmother insists upon returning, and she is inexorable when she has once made up her mind."

"Like somebody else!" said Bertha, who was decidedly irritated.

Maurice resumed: "And it is my duty not only to protect her, but to watch over my poor father."

"And you will really, *really* go?" questioned Bertha, doubtingly.

"I have no alternative."

"Then L am more thankful than ever," she replied, tartly, "that when my aunt wished to make a match between us, I never thought of accepting you! I never could have endured such a patient, contented, stoical suitor, who would be perfectly happy in spite of his separation from me."

Maurice laughed at this sally, but Gaston remarked, seriously, —

"Yet you demand great sacrifices from one who is not as patient and well-disciplined. You make your wedding-day dependent upon Mademoiselle Madeleine's, when Mademoiselle Madeleine declares that she does not intend to name one."

"We are an obstinate family, you see!" retorted Bertha, her good-humor returning.

"Will not your father miss you?" suggested the ever thoughtful Madeleine to Maurice. "You have been absent very long;

that talkative nurse may not be able to restrain herself, and your presence may be needful to preserve harmony."

Maurice admitted that he ought to return; but, after bidding Madeleine adieu, he could not persuade himself to go back to the hotel until he had seen those to whom he owed his present happiness.

"Ronald!" he exclaimed, as he entered Mrs. Walton's drawing-room; "long ago I became largely your debtor, but now you have placed me under an obligation which cannot be estimated. Oh, if I only had your energy and promptitude of action, I might some day " —

Ronald interrupted him: "Then my mother was right, and I did not give you bad advice in spite of my Quixotism?"

Maurice related what had happened to sympathetic listeners.

Evening was approaching; his absence from his father had been far more protracted than usual, and before he had said half that he desired to say, or listened to half that he wished to hear, he was compelled to leave.

When the hand of Maurice was on the door of his grandmother's *salon*, he could distinguish the sound of angry voices within, — his grandmother's sonorous tones and the sharper voice of Mrs. Gratacap. As he entered, the latter was saying, —

"It's a sin and a shame, I tell you! And I'll not have the poor dear made miserable in that way, while he is under my charge. I'm not going to submit to it; and you know you can't frighten me with all your high ways."

Mrs. Gratacap was standing beside the count, as though to protect him; Madame de Gramont was seated directly before him, and looking highly incensed. Count Tristan himself appeared to be in great tribulation, and grasped the hand of his nurse with a dependent air. As soon as he caught sight of Maurice, he cried out, —

"I'm not going! I'm not going, I say! Maurice, come, come and tell her!"

"What has happened?" inquired Maurice, with deep concern.

The countess attempted to speak, but Mrs. Gratacap was too quick for her.

"Here's the madame has been talking to the poor dear until she has driven him half wild. I never saw anything like it in my born days; she wont give him one moment's peace! He was doing well enough until she began *jawing* him."

It is to be hoped that the countess did not understand the meaning of this last, not very classical expression.

" Will you be silent, woman ? " said she, wrathfully.

Mrs. Gratacap was about to answer; but Maurice silenced her by a reproving look, and then asked again, —

" What has happened ? Why does my father seem so much distressed ? "

" I have been preparing his mind " — began the countess.

Mrs. Gratacap broke in, " Upsetting his mind, you mean."

Before Madame de Gramont could answer, Maurice said to the nurse, in a persuasive tone, " Pray leave us, for a little while, Mrs. Gratacap."

" I wouldn't contrary you for the world ! " returned the nurse. " Only when *she's* done, just you come to *me* and I'll give you the rights of the case."

Mrs. Gratacap departed, and the countess continued, —

" I have been explaining to your father that we are shortly to leave this execrable country and return to Brittany, and that he has great cause for congratulation ; but he did not seem to comprehend me clearly, and that woman, who is always intruding her opinions, chose to imagine that he was groaning and crying out on account of what I said. The liberties she takes become more intolerable every day ; she is enough to drive your father distracted."

" What does she mean ? " asked Count Tristan, piteously. " Where do they want to take me ? I'm not going."

" My son," replied the countess, " I have informed you ; but that insolent woman prevented your understanding ; we are to return very soon to Brittany, to the Château de Gramont ; I expect you to rejoice at this pleasing intelligence."

" No — no, I cannot go ! I cannot leave " —

He stopped as though his mother's flashing eyes checked the words ready to burst from his lips.

" You will not have to leave *Maurice,*" she said, coldly ; " he is to accompany us."

" But Madeleine ! Madeleine ! " he sobbed forth as if unable to restrain himself.

The countess was on the point of replying angrily, when Maurice interposed.

" I beg you, madame, not to excite my father by further discussion. Come, my dear father, you are tired; it is getting late ; I know it will do you good to lie down."

And he conducted the unresisting invalid to his own chamber, leaving the countess swelling with rage, yet glorying in the certainty that she would carry out her plans, in spite of every op-

CHAPTER LIV.

AN UNEXPECTED VISIT.

Another week passed on. The day preceding that on which the countess and her party were to set out on their journey had arrived. All the necessary preparations were progressing duly.

Maurice, from the hour that he had learned Madeleine's secret, had lived in such a dream of absolute happiness that he felt as though he could ask for nothing more, — as though the cup presented to his lips was too full of joy for the one, ungrateful drop of an unfulfilled desire to find room. He comprehended Madeleine's character too thoroughly, — respected all her instincts and principles of action too entirely, again to urge his suit, or seek to obtain her promise that she would one day be his; she *was his* in spirit, — he could openly recognize her as his, — that sufficed! and he believed it would still suffice (if her sense of duty remained unaltered) through his whole earthly existence; for all his days would be brightened by her love, and the privilege of loving her.

Bertha, after her first, petulant outbreak, had also ceased to press Madeleine on the subject of her possible marriage, and with meek demureness reconciled herself to the uncertainty of the future, and the certainty of tormenting her lover in the present.

M. de Bois's devotion to Madeleine sealed his lips. Madeleine had formed a resolution which she declared unalterable. Bertha had announced a determination dependent upon Madeleine's, and the suitors of the two cousins had only to submit and hope.

The labor of packing Madame de Gramont's wardrobe, as well as that of Bertha, devolved upon Adolphine; she had not quite filled the trunks of her young mistress when she was summoned by the countess. This was on the morning of the day preceding the one appointed for their departure. Adolphine was heedless and forgetful to a tantalizing degree. The countess deemed herself compelled to superintend her movements; that is to sit in an arm-chair and look on; the lofty lady would not have deigned to assist by touching an article, though she now and then issued an order or indulged in a rebuke, and by her presence greatly retarded Adolphine's operations.

Count Tristan had driven out every day. His mother and

Maurice always accompanied him. This morning, when Maurice went to announce to his grandmother that the carriage was at the door, he found her watching Adolphine, who was on her knees before an open trunk.

"It will be impossible for me to accompany you to-day," said the countess. "I will speak to your father; it will be his last drive, and he must excuse me."

She rose and passed into the drawing-room where Count Tristan was waiting.

"My son," said his mother, raising her voice as she now always did when she spoke to him, seeming to imagine that by this means she could make him comprehend better. He was not, however, in the least afflicted with deafness, and the loud tone was more likely to startle him than to calm the perturbation which was usually apparent when she addressed him. "My son, you are to take your airing this morning without me. You understand that this will be your *last* drive in this detestable city. You perfectly comprehend, I hope, that you leave here to-morrow; and before long we shall be safely within the time-honored walls of the old château which we ought never to have left."

The proposed change had been so constantly impressed upon the count's mind by his mother that he seemed, at times, to be thoroughly aware of it; yet at others the recollection faded from his memory. At first, when the voyage was mentioned, he would remonstrate in a piteous, feeble, fretful way, declaring that he would not go; but of late he had appeared to yield to the potency of Madame de Gramont's will.

Maurice offered his arm to the count and they left the room. As the door closed after them, Count Tristan turned, as though to assure himself that it was shut, then looked at Maurice significantly and nodded his head, while a smile brightened his countenance. It was so long since Maurice had seen him smile that even that strange, half-wild, inexplicable kindling up of the wan face was pleasant to behold. As they descended the stair, the count looked back several times, and gave furtive glances around him, smiling more and more; then he rubbed his hands and chuckled as though at some idea which he could not yet communicate. At the carriage-door he paused again, and again looked all around, continuing to rub his hands, then fairly laughed out. Maurice began to be alarmed at this unaccountable mirth. They entered the carriage and the coachman drove in the usual direction; but the count exclaimed impatiently, —

"No, no — that's not the way! stop him! stop him!"

Maurice, at a loss to comprehend his father's wishes, did not immediately comply with his request, and the count, with unusual energy, himself caught at the check-cord and pulled it vehemently.

"This is not the way,—not the way to *Madeleine's!*"

Then Maurice comprehended his father's exultation; he had conceived the project of visiting Madeleine! But what was to be done? The countess would be enraged if she discovered Count Tristan had seen Madeleine; and the agitation caused by the interview might prove harmful to him. Yet would it not do him more injury to thwart his wishes? And would it not be depriving Madeleine of an inestimable joy?

The count grew impatient; he shouted out, in a clearer tone than he had been able to use since his first seizure, "To Madeleine's! To Madeleine's, I say! I *will* see Madeleine!"

Maurice hesitated no longer and gave the order. His father's agitation was, every moment, on the increase, though it was now of the most pleasurable nature; he gave vent to little bursts of triumphant laughter, muttering to himself, "I shall see her! I knew I should see her again!"

"My dear father, you will endeavor to be calm,—will you not? I am fearful this excitement will injure you, and my grandmother will never forgive me if you become worse through my imprudence. She must not know that we have been to Madeleine's. It would render her uselessly indignant; but Madeleine will be so overjoyed to see you once more that I could not refuse to comply with your wishes."

The count murmured to himself, rather than replied to his son,—

"Good angel! My good angel! We are going to her! We are very near—there! that's the house yonder. I'd know it among a thousand! Maurice, I'm well! I'm strong! I want nothing now but to see Madeleine! It's all right—is it not? She settled about that mortgage—she obtained us those votes—there's no more trouble! Nobody knows what a scoundrel I have been! I remember all clearly. I am very joyful; I must tell Madeleine; I must say to her that she—she—she brought something of heaven down to me; there must *be* a heaven, for where else could Madeleine belong?"

Maurice had not heard his father speak as much or as connectedly for a month. His face was pleasantly animated, in spite of its unnatural expression, and he moved his arms about

37

so freely it was evident the weight which had pressed with paralyzing force upon them was removed.

The carriage stopped. Maurice could scarcely prevent his father from springing out before him and without assistance.

The silent Robert looked his surprise and gratification as he opened the street door. While Maurice was inquiring where his mistress would be found, Count Tristan pressed on alone, walking with a firm, rapid step. He entered the first room. It was Madeleine's bedchamber; the one he himself had occupied during his illness. It was vacant. He passed on, crying out, —

"Madeleine! Madeleine!" He looked into the drawing-room, then into the dining-room, still calling, "Madeleine! Madeleine!"

He hurried on toward the well-remembered little boudoir. There Madeleine was sitting at her desk, quietly sketching. When, to her amazement, she heard the count's voice, she thought it was fancy; but the sound was repeated again and again. Those were surely his tones! She started up and opened the door. Count Tristan was standing only a few paces from it, — Maurice behind him.

"Madeleine! Madeleine! I see you. I am happy. I can die now."

As these words burst from his lips, the count staggered forward and sank on Madeleine's shoulder; for she had involuntarily stretched out her arms toward him. The next instant he slipped through them and dropped heavily upon the floor. One glance at his distorted face, and at the foam issuing from his lips, one sound of that stertorous breathing was enough. Maurice and Madeleine knew that he had been struck with apoplexy for the third time!

Maurice and Robert carried him to the bed he had before occupied; and Madeleine sent for Dr. Bayard in all haste.

The count lay quite still, save for that heavy breathing and the convulsive motion of his features. Madeleine and Maurice stood beside him in silence, with hands interlocked.

Dr. Bayard arrived, looked at the patient, shook his head, and, turning to Maurice, said, in a low tone, —

"There is nothing to be done."

"But see," answered Maurice, clinging to a faint hope, "he is getting over it, — he seems better."

"It is the third stroke," replied the doctor, significantly, as he was leaving the room.

Madeleine heard these words, though they were spoken in an

undertone, and she followed Maurice and the physician from the apartment.

"Do you mean," she inquired of the physician, in accents of deep sorrow, "it is *impossible* for Count Tristan to recover from this shock?"

"My dear young lady, I am unwilling to say that anything is *impossible.* The longer a physician practises, the more he realizes that we cannot judge of *possibilities;* but, in my experience, I have never known a case of apoplexy that survived the third stroke."

"He will die, then? Oh, will he die?"

"His life, for the last two months, has been a living death," replied the physician, kindly. "Could you wish to prolong such an existence?"

The doctor took his leave, promising to return, but frankly avowing that his presence was needless. As soon as he had gone, Madeleine said to Maurice, who appeared to be so much stunned by this new blow that he was incapable of reflection, —

"Your poor grandmother, — O Maurice, what a terrible task lies before you! You will have to break this news to her. She must want to see him once more, and he may not linger long. You have not a moment to lose."

"I feel as though I could not go to her," answered Maurice. "What good can she do here? She will only insult you again; and, if my father should revive, her words may render his last moments wretched. Let him die in peace."

Madeleine replied, —

"She may be softened by the presence of the angel of death. She may long to hear one parting word of tenderness from his lips, and utter one in return. Go, I beseech you! Go and bring her!"

And Maurice went.

CHAPTER LV.

AMEN.

MAURICE, when he opened the door of his grandmother's drawing-room, found the apartment vacant. The countess was still in her own chamber issuing orders to the bewildered Adolphine, whose packing process advanced but indifferently. Bertha had retired to her room. Maurice passed into his father's apartment, where Mrs. Gratacap sat knitting, and, in a few words, told her what had occurred.

" Poor dear ! " cried the compassionate nurse. " I feared it would be so. I saw it coming this last week ; and a third stroke is a death-knell — that's certain ! But it will be a blessed escape for the poor dear ; so don't take on, Mr. Morris " (this was her nearest approach to saying "*Maurice* "). " You'll need all your spirit to get along with the old lady ; though, if she were the north pole itself, I should think this blow would break up her ice."

" Will you have the goodness to desire my cousin to come here ? I had better tell her first," said Maurice.

" Mrs. Gratacap withdrew and quickly returned accompanied by Bertha who was trembling with alarm ; for the messenger had lost no time in making the sad communication.

" I cannot tell my grandmother, Bertha, in the presence of Adolphine. Will you not beg your aunt to come to me in the drawing-room ? " said Maurice.

Bertha had scarcely courage to obey, she had such a dread of witnessing the countess's agitation ; for she felt certain it would take the form of anger against Madeleine and Maurice. With hesitating steps the young girl entered the apartment where the countess sat. She had been much irritated by Adolphine's stupidity, and cried out, —

" Positively, Bertha, this maid of yours has been totally spoiled by her residence in this barbarous country. She is worth nothing ; she has no head ; and she even presumes to offer her advice and suggest what would be the best mode of packing this or that ! It is fortunate for us that this is our last day in this odious city, and that we shall soon be on our way back to Brittany. But Adolphine is completely ruined ; there is no tolerating her."

" I am very sorry," said Bertha, putting her handkerchief to her eyes.

" You need not cry about it," retorted the countess, angrily. " How often have I tried to impress upon you that this habit of evincing emotion is, in the highest degree, plebeian ! Tears are very well for a milk-maid, but exceedingly unbecoming a lady. They are an unmistakable sign of vulgar breeding. I cannot endure to see a niece of mine with so little self-control."

Bertha removed her handkerchief and tried to force back her tears, as she said, —

"Maurice begs to speak to you for a moment."

"Very good. Can he not come to me?"

"He entreats that you will go into the drawing-room."

"Do you mean to intimate," asked the countess, sternly, "that my grandson ventures to *summon me to his presence*, instead of coming to mine? What indignity am I to expect next? Since he has forgotten his duty and the deference due to me, go and remind him."

"He has something very serious to tell you," faltered Bertha; "he wants you to hear it there,—it is so sad."

Bertha, in spite of her aunt's contemptuous glances, could not help burying her face in her handkerchief again.

"What absurdity!" sneered the countess; but she began to experience a vague sensation of uneasiness.

"Come! come! do come!" pleaded Bertha.

"Since it seems the only way to put an end to this hysterical exhibition of yours, Bertha, I will go and reprove Maurice for his lack of respect."

But the countess did not literally carry her threat into execution; for, noticing the absence of Count Tristan, she said hurriedly,—

"Where is your father?"

"Pray sit down one moment, my dear grandmother"—

She interrupted him by asking again, more anxiously,—

"Where is your father?"

"I will explain, but"—

"Why do you not answer my question?" she cried with increased violence. "Where is your father?"

Could Maurice answer "At Madeleine's?" He still hesitated, and the countess, with more rapid steps than she was wont to use, hastened to Count Tristan's bedroom.

Mrs. Gratacap greeted her with "Oh, poor dear, don't take on about it! We couldn't but expect that it would come soon, and"—

The countess did not wait to hear the close of her sentence, but with a cold horror creeping through her veins, hurried back to Maurice, and once more asked, imperiously,—

"Maurice, where is your father? I command you to answer at once! I will hear nothing but the answer to that question."

Driven to extremity, Maurice replied, "My father is at Madeleine's!"

"Miserable boy! How did you dare to set my wishes at

defiance? You shall repent this, — be sure you shall! How had you the audacity to fly in the face of my command?"

"I heard no commands on the subject," returned Maurice; "and if I had done so, my father's wishes would still have held the first place. As soon as we left the house he insisted upon going to Madeleine's; he would take no refusal; his affection for her is so strong that" —

"How dare you talk to me of his affection for that artful, designing girl, who is a disgrace to us all, — whose low machinations have placed her beneath my contempt? Henceforth, thank Heaven! we shall be out of the reach of her vile manœuvres."

This was beyond endurance. Maurice forgot everything but the insulting epithets applied to Madeleine, and said, with a dignity as imposing as Madame de Gramont's own had ever been, —

"My grandmother, never shall such language be applied to Madeleine again in my presence, by you or any one! Madeleine is not merely my cousin, she is the woman I love best and honor most in the world; — the woman who, if I ever marry, will become my wife."

"Never! never!" cried the countess, fiercely. "That shall never be, come what may!"

Maurice, recovering himself somewhat, went on, —

"It is upon a far sadder subject that I wish to speak to you, — I meant to break the news gently, — I hoped to spare you a severe shock, but you force me to come to the point at once. My dear father has had another seizure of the same nature as the two former.

"Parricide!" shrieked the countess, "you have done this! You have killed your father! The agitation occasioned by your taking him to that house and letting him see that unhappy girl has caused this attack; if he should die you will be his murderer!"

What reply could Maurice make which would not enrage her more? The countess went on, furiously, —

"Go, — bring him back to me quickly! He shall not remain there! By all that is holy, he shall not."

"I come to ask you to go to him since he cannot come to you," said Maurice, with as much mildness as he could throw into his tone.

"Yes, I will go, I will go!" replied his grandmother. "I cannot trust you; I will go myself, and see him brought here."

She retired to her own chamber to make ready, and Bertha quickly followed her example.

Meantime Madeleine with Mrs. Lawkins, watched beside the count. His attack was briefer than the former ones. When it was over, he fell into a deep and placid slumber. During that sleep his face changed! Those who have watched the dying and recognized the indescribable expression which marks the countenance when it is "death-struck" will understand what alteration is meant. He waked slowly and gently,—first stirring his hands as though clutching at something impalpable, then gradually opening his eyes. They looked large and glassy, but as they fixed themselves upon Madeleine's face, bespoke full consciousness.

"Madeleine!" he murmured feebly; but his voice was distinct, and pathetically tender. "I am with you again, Madeleine,—that is great happiness,—great comfort. I am going soon, Madeleine;—do you not know it?"

"Oh! I fear so!" answered Madeleine, weeping; "but you do not suffer? You are calm?"

"Very calm,—very happy with my good angel near me. Madeleine, you have much to pardon; but you will pardon,—all,—all!

"I do, I do. If there be anything to pardon, I do, from my soul, a thousand times over."

"You have made me believe in God and his saints, Madeleine, and I bless you."

Madeleine was holding both of his cold hands in hers, and had bowed her head, that his icy lips might touch her forehead; but she rose up suddenly, for she heard the wheels of a carriage stop, and the street door open; she deemed it well to prepare the count.

"I think your mother and Maurice have arrived."

A cloud passed over the face of the dying man, but did not rest there. He was beyond fear! His haughty mother could no longer inspire awe!

A moment after, Maurice opened the door and the countess entered the room. Approaching the bed, as though unconscious of Madeleine's presence, she exclaimed,—

"My son, my son, what brought you here? How could you have paid so little respect to my wishes? I will not reproach you" (this was much for her to say), "only make the effort to let yourself be removed at once."

"I am going fast enough, mother; I am dying!"

" No, — no!" cried the countess, vehemently. "You could not die *here!* You are not dying! You cannot, *shall not die!*"

She spoke as though she believed that her potent volition could frighten away the death-angels hovering near, and prolong his life.

Madeleine had attempted to withdraw her hand from his, for his mother had seized the other clay-cold hand ; but he said, with a faint smile, "Don't go, Madeleine ; do not leave me until I cannot see you and feel you more." Then making a great effort to rally his expiring energies, he continued, "Mother, love Madeleine ! We need angels about us to lift us up when we fall. Keep her near you if you would be comforted when the hour that has come to me comes to you !"

The countess did not reply, but the hand she held had grown so clammy, she could no longer refuse to believe that her son might be dying. Still she was not softened ; she could not turn to Madeleine and embrace her, as the dying man so obviously desired.

"Maurice," said his father.

Maurice approached, and the countess instinctively drew a step back, to give him room. She had dropped the marble hand, and Maurice took it in his.

"Maurice, you, too, have much to pardon. Madeleine has forgiven, — will not you?"

"Oh, my father, do not speak of that! All is well between us ; but, if we must indeed lose you, — tell me, — tell Madeleine that you give her to me. She loves me, she has never loved any other ; and I never *have* loved, — never *can* love any woman but her. Bid her be my wife, for she has refused to let me claim her without your consent and my grandmother's."

Count Tristan tried to speak, but the words died upon the lips that essayed to form themselves into a smile of assent. He lifted Madeleine's hand and placed it in that of Maurice.

A convulsed groan, or sob, broke from the countess, but it was unheard by her son ; his spirit had taken its flight.

It had gone, stained with many evil passions, — perhaps crimes, — but what its sentence was before the High Tribunal, who shall dare to say ? That erring spirit had recognized good, and therefore could not be wholly unsanctified by good ; it had repented, and therefore sin was no longer loved ; all the rest was dark ; but He who, speaking in metaphors, forbade the " bruised reed " to be broken, or "smoking flax" to be quenched, might have seen light, invisible to mortal eyes, even about a soul as shadowed as that of Count Tristan de Gramont.

The countess had been the only one who doubted that he would die, yet she was the first to perceive that he was gone. She uttered a piercing, discordant cry, and with her arms frantically extended, flung herself upon the corpse. Her long self-restraint, her curbing back of emotion, made the sudden shock more terrible; she fell into violent convulsions.

Maurice bore her into the adjoining apartment, followed by Madeleine, Bertha, and Mrs. Lawkins. When the convulsions ceased she was delirious with fever.

Madeleine ordered the room Maurice had occupied to be speedily prepared for her reception. Her delirium lasted for many days. Had she recovered her senses, she would assuredly have commanded that the corpse of her son should be removed to the hotel, that his funeral might take place from thence; but Maurice thought it no humiliation that the funeral of the proud Count Tristan de Gramont should move from the doors of that mantua-maker niece who had saved his name from dishonor by the products of her labor.

Count Tristan had few friends, or even acquaintances in Washington. Maurice and Gaston were chief mourners. The Marquis de Fleury and his suite, Mr. Hilson, Mr. Meredith, Mr. Walton, and Ronald, accompanied the corpse to its last resting-place.

Bertha had taken up her residence at Madeleine's. Maurice remained at the hotel, — that is, he slept there, but the larger portion of his hours was passed beneath Madeleine's roof.

That Madeleine was his betrothed was tacitly understood, though no word had been spoken on the subject, and her manner toward him was little changed. She loved him with all the intensity and strength of her large nature, but her love could not, like Bertha's, find expression in words, in loving looks, and caressing ways. Maurice was content, even though he could never know how inexpressibly dear he was to her. His was one of those generous natures which experience more delight in *loving* than in *being loved*. He never believed that Madeleine's love *could* equal his, and he argued that it *could not because* there was so much more to love *in her* than there was *in him*, and a true, pure, holy love, loves the attributes that are lovable rather than the mere person to whom they appertain. Maurice asked but little! A gentle pressure of the hand, — a soft smile, — a passing look of tenderness, though it was certain to be

quickly veiled by the dropped lids, — a casual word of endearment timidly, reluctantly spoken, or, oftener, spoken unpre-
meditatedly and followed by a blush ; these were food sufficient
for his great passion, — the one passion of his life, to exist upon.
Indeed we are inclined to think that with men of his temperament love is kept in a more vigorous, more actively healthy state
by its (apparently) receiving only measured response. A woman who is gifted with the power of throwing her soul into looks,
and language and loving ways, runs the risk of producing upon
certain men an effect approaching satiety. The woman who has
instinctive wisdom will never dash herself against this rock ; yet
few women are *wise;* fewer give *too little* of their rich, heart-
treasures than *too much.*

CHAPTER LVI.

THE HAND OF GOD.

WHEN the fever gradually abated, and consciousness returned
to the countess, she lay in a state of half-dreamy exhaustion
which precluded the power of thought or the stir of her high
passions. It was manifest that she recognized those who moved
about her bed, for she now and then addressed Bertha, Maurice,
and even Madeleine by name. Madeleine's heart throbbed with
joy when she dared to believe that there was no unkindness in
Madame de Gramont's tone. Maurice and Bertha had made
the same observation and augured future harmony and happiness
from the unanticipated change. But their delusion was quickly
dispelled, for it soon became apparent that the countess believed
herself to be in the Château de Gramont, and that her mind had
gone back to a period previous to the one when Madeleine had
awakened her displeasure. Either the objects by which she
was surrounded had grown familiar to her eyes, or as she beheld
them indistinctly in the dim light, imagination lent them olden
shapes, for she assuredly fancied herself in her own chamber, in
that venerable chateau to which she had so earnestly longed to
return. It was somewhat remarkable that she never mentioned
Count Tristan, though she several times spoke of her antiquated
femme de chambre, Bettina, and of Baptiste, and desired Made-

leine to give them certain orders, just as she would have done in by-gone days.

It was not deemed prudent to make any attempt to banish the hallucination under which she was laboring, and which unavoidable circumstances must gradually disperse.

Maurice received a second letter from Mr. Lorrillard, again urging him to return to Charleston, and apprising him that his services would be particularly valuable at that moment, as he (Mr. Lorrillard) was occupied in preparing to conduct a case of much importance, which needed great care in collecting authorities, and these researches it was the province of Maurice to make.

Maurice placed the letter in Madeleine's hands, less because he needed her counsel than because it was so delightful to feel that he had the right to consult her.

" What do you advise, Madeleine ? " he asked, after she had perused it.

" I would have you send the answer you have already concluded to send."

" How do you know that answer ? "

" I have read more difficult books than your face, Maurice ; besides, there seems to me only one answer which would be advisable. Your grandmother is safe under Bertha's care and mine ; she does not absolutely need your presence."

" And nobody else needs it, I am to infer ? " retorted Maurice, a little ungenerously.

He deserved that Madeleine should give him no answer, or, at least, one that implied a rebuke ; but such women are usually tardy in giving men their ill deserts, and she answered softly, " It will be less hard to part than it has been."

" You have uttered my very thought," returned Maurice. " It is less hard to part now that we know how closely we are linked, —now that separation cannot any longer disunite, and love's assurance has taken the place of doubt and anguish. Were we *less* to each other in spirit, we should feel the material space that can divide us *more*, — is it not so ? "

If Maurice expected any answer, he was forced to be contented with the one which, according to the proverb, gives consent through silence.

It was needful to prepare the countess for his departure. Maurice went to her chamber, and, after a few inquiries concerning her health, to which she hardly replied, said, —

" I am truly grieved that I am forced to leave you, my dear grandmother. I am summoned away by urgent business."

At that last word her brows were slightly knitted, and she murmured contemptuously, " *Business,*" as though the expression awakened some old train of painful recollection.

" If it were not needful for me to go," continued Maurice, " I would not leave you ; but you have the tender and skilful care of Madeleine and Bertha, and I shall be able to return to you at any moment that you may require me."

" Where are you going ? " asked the countess, but hardly in a tone of interest."

" To Charleston."

" Charleston ! " she repeated with a startled, troubled look, " Paris, — you mean Paris ? "

" No, — not so far as Paris, — you remember the journey is but short between Washington and Charleston."

Maurice had not deliberately intended to force upon the countess the consciousness of her present position ; but it was too late to retract.

She raised herself in the bed, leaning with difficulty upon her wasted arm, and asked, in a frightened tone, —

" Where, — where am I then ? "

" In Washington, my dear grandmother. Have you forgotten how my poor father was " —

" Hush ! hush ! " she gasped out, " I cannot endure it. Let me think ! let me think ! "

She sank back upon the pillow with closed eyes, and the workings of her features testified that recollection was dawning upon her.

After a time she cried out, — for it was a veritable cry, — " And *this house,* — *this bed* where I am lying, — O God ! it is too much ! "

Maurice was at a loss to know what to do. He waited to see if she would not question him, would not speak again ; but, as she lay silent and motionless, he retired and sought his cousins.

" Do not be so much distressed," prayed Madeleine, when she heard what he had to relate. " This was unavoidable, — your grandmother's intellect was not disturbed, — her memory only seemed quiescent ; the most casual circumstance might, at any moment, have awakened her recollection of the past ; it is as well that it should be recalled to-day as to-morrow. Come, Bertha, we will go to her."

Madeleine and Bertha entered the room together, but the ever cowardly Bertha drew back, and Madeleine approached the bed alone. The countess opened her eyes, looked at her a moment, as though to be quite certain of her identity, then turned her face to the pillow and murmured, " Where is Bertha ? "

" Bertha is here," said Madeleine, motioning Bertha to take her place, as she drew back.

Madeleine felt that the countess had turned from her because her presence was painful; with a light step, but a heart once more grown heavy, she withdrew.

Bertha stood by her aunt's side without daring to disturb her by a word. After a time the countess unclosed her eyes again and looked around the room; then, gazing at Bertha, said slowly, —

" It all comes back, — it was like a frightful dream at first, — but the reality is more terrible! Bertha, — Bertha, — I have so little left! *You* love me? *You* will not forsake me?"

Bertha had never before heard her imperious aunt make an appeal to any human being; what wonder that she was melted?

The countess resumed, with increasing agitation, " You were to have gone back with me to Brittany, — you, and Maurice, and his " —

There came a break, — she could not name her dead son. Death to her was the harsh blow dealt by a merciless hand, snatching its victim away in retributive wrath, — not the wise and mild summons that bids suffering mortality exchange a circumscribed, lower life for a larger, higher, happier existence.

It was some time before Madame de Gramont could continue; then she said, " I must go back, Bertha! I cannot die out of those old walls! It was you, you who lured me from them. We will return to them. You will go with us, Bertha?"

" I will," replied Bertha, though her heart sank as she uttered the words. She had thought that the project of returning to France was wholly abandoned.

" And we will go soon, — as soon as I am able to travel, that time will come quickly. I am growing stronger every minute. Let me depart speedily; it is all I can look forward to that can sustain me, that can lift me up after the abasement to which I have been subjected."

Though they conversed no more, Bertha did not leave her aunt until she had seen her sink to repose.

When Bertha repeated to Maurice, Madeleine, and Gaston the conversation which had just taken place, a heavy gloom fell

38

upon all. Maurice's return to Brittany, at this crisis, would be a great disadvantage to him, and when the countess was removed to a distance from Madeleine, it was more unlikely than ever that she would yield consent to Madeleine's union with Maurice ; the chances were that she would not allow Madeleine's name to be uttered in her presence.

Gaston had given up all idea of altering Bertha's repeatedly expressed determination to be married upon the same day as her cousin, and not to marry at all if that day never came ; but since Count Tristan had joined the hands of Maurice and Madeleine, he cherished the hope that the countess would no longer refuse to sanction their union, and that this voyage to France would be wholly relinquished.

Maurice listened to Bertha in silence, but that night his step could be heard pacing up and down his chamber through the still hours, and he scarcely attempted to rest. During this period of painful reflection, he formed a resolution which he proposed to carry into execution as soon as his grandmother was ready to receive him.

As he took a seat by her side he motioned Mrs. Lawkins to leave them together.

" Are you well enough to listen to me, my dear grandmother? I must speak to you on a subject of great importance to me ; I ought to add, of some importance to yourself."

The countess signified that she listened by a slight affirmative movement of the head.

" Bertha has told me that you still desire to return to Brittany. Though at this moment my accompanying you will force me to make some heavy sacrifices, still, there is one condition, — *and only one*," — Maurice emphasized these last words, — " upon which I can consent."

The countess made no observation. He was forced to proceed, —

" You were present when my dying father placed Madeleine's hand in mine, — do not interrupt me, I entreat ! Madeleine and I have loved each other from our infancy ; she has rejected me solely that she might not cause grief to you and my father; he has given her to me, — he bade you love her; will *you* not give her to me also ? "

" Never ! " answered the countess ; and though the tone was low it was steady and resolute.

Maurice went on, disregarding her reply. " I will return with you to Brittany on the condition that she accompanies us, as my affianced bride, or as my wife. You have lived beneath Madeleine's roof; my father died there; gratitude, if nothing else, should bind us to her. Can you urge any reasonable objection to her going with us to Brittany, and as my wife ?"

The countess was roused. "Would you have me show my runaway niece to the world? Would you have me publicly patronize, associate with, caress the *mantua-maker*, in my own land, before my own kin? Never!"

"Then," returned Maurice, resolutely, "I do not return with you to Brittany. Bertha may do so, and you will, doubtless, have the escort of M. de Bois; but if you renounce Madeleine, you renounce me! Madeleine will not become my wife without your consent, — I do not conceal *that* from you; but I remain in this land, where she will continue to dwell. If *you* so wholly disregard my father's last wishes, you cannot hope that *I* can forget them, or that I can feel as bound to you as though they had been respected. If your decision is final, I will not urge you further."

"It is final!" was the laconic answer.

"And so is mine!" replied Maurice, rising. Without longer parley he left the room.

At this crisis, the conduct of M. de Bois threatened to give a new turn to events. We have had abundant proof of his gratitude and unwavering devotion to Madeleine. His aversion to the countess had increased with her persecution of her defenceless niece, and when the inexorable lady remained unmoved by the dying prayer of her son, and refused to sanction Madeleine's union with Maurice, M. de Bois's detestation culminated. He was inspired with an earnest desire to stretch out his arm to shield and aid Madeleine, and humble her oppressor; but an effectual method of accomplishing this act of justice did not present itself to him until Maurice communicated the result of his last interview; then Gaston conceived the project of following up that masterly move with another which would give it force. If he could only have counted upon Bertha as an ally he would have been confident of the success of his plan; but he knew that Bertha's timidity — say, rather, her *cowardice* — was insuperable, and she held her aunt in too much awe to dare to take any decided stand. M. de Bois called all his energies into play to influence the weak medium he was compelled to employ.

Madeleine was occupied in a different part of the house when Maurice, finding Gaston and Bertha in the boudoir, told them the result of his interview with Madame de Gramont. By and by Gaston lured Bertha into the garden. They made one or two turns in silence; Bertha looked up wistfully into her lover's face, and said, in a tone of reproach, —

" How silent you seem to-day ! "

" Yes, I feel grave, — I have something to accomplish, and I greatly need, but fear to claim, your aid."

" Mine ? What lion is there in a net that needs such a poor, wee mouse as I to gnaw the meshes ? "

" No lion already in the snare, but a lioness to be lured into our net. Bertha, do you truly love Mademoiselle Madeleine ? "

" What a question ! "

" Do you love her so well that your love for her could surmount your dread of your aunt ? "

" Yes, that is, I think it could. What would you have me do ? "

" Follow the noble example of Maurice ; tell Madame de Gramont that you will not return to Brittany with her unless Maurice and Mademoiselle Madeleine return also. She detests this country, and the fear of being compelled to remain here will conquer her."

" But how could I do this ? " questioned Bertha, feeling that she had not firmness for the task. " I have promised to go with her. What excuse could I offer ? "

" The excuse," answered her lover, " that you could not travel with her alone."

" Alone ? "

" Yes, for I do not count the light-headed Adolphine any one."

" But you, — you are going with us ? "

" I shall not go unless Maurice and Mademoiselle Madeleine go," replied M. de Bois.

" And you can let me go without you ? You can let me take such a journey with my aunt in her broken state of health ? "

" I will not let you go at all if I can prevent your going."

Not a few persuasions were needed before M. de Bois could obtain Bertha's promise to inform her aunt that she could not accompany her except upon the conditions Maurice had made. Bertha looked like a culprit awaiting sentence, rather than a person who came to dictate, when she entered Madame de Gramont's apartment. The countess had been highly incensed by her conversation with Maurice, and was wrought up to such a pitch that she seemed to have gained sudden strength, and almost to be restored to health. Bertha stole to her side, but the young girl's good intentions were oozing away every moment. The probability is that that she would not have had the courage to introduce the subject at all had not the countess asked, —

"Have you heard of the unnatural conduct of Maurice? Do you know that my own grandson abandons me?"

"I have heard," replied Bertha, hesitatingly. "Oh! what are we to do? How could you ever travel to Brittany alone?"

"Alone?" cried the countess, catching hold of the blue silk curtains that draped her bed, and raising herself by clinging to them. "Alone? Do *you*, too, forsake me? But what else could I expect when my grandson, my only child left, has abandoned me?"

Bertha's determination was put to flight by her aunt's woful look as she spoke these words with despairing fierceness, while she grasped the curtains more tightly and bore heavily upon them for support.

These draperies were suspended over the centre of the bed from a massive gilded ornament, shaped to represent a huge arrow, and the countess in her agitation gathered the folds around her, and hung upon them in her efforts to sit up.

"Oh, no, aunt, I have not forsaken you," returned Bertha. "I will go with you; but what shall we do alone? M. de Bois refuses to go unless Maurice and Madeleine go."

"Does M. de Bois expect to dictate to *me*?" demanded Madame de Gramont, haughtily. "Let him remain; you will go with me, Bertha, and I shall hire a courier."

"I am afraid we will not be able to find a courier in America," Bertha ventured to suggest.

"Then we will go without one! We will go the instant I am able; and I feel so much stronger at this moment that I could start at once. It is settled that we go, and I defy Maurice or any one else to keep me."

Madeleine had been visiting the working-room, and, without being aware of what had just taken place, she now entered her aunt's chamber. Madame de Gramont's convulsed features, and her singular attitude as she sat up in the centre of the bed, tightly grasping the curtains, which had been drawn from their usual position, impressed Madeleine so painfully, that she was running toward her; when the countess, raising herself up, with sudden strength, exclaimed, — "Madeleine de Gramont, keep from me! — do not come near me! All my sorrow has come through you! — Go! go!"

She gave such a violent strain upon the curtains, as she

38 *

passionately uttered these words, that Madeleine's quick ears caught a sound as of some fastening giving way. With a cry of horror, she sprang to the bed, flung her arms around the countess, and dragged her from it just as the heavy ornament fell!

Madeleine's piercing cry, and Bertha's shriek summoned not only Mrs. Lawkins, who was sitting in the adjoining chamber, but Maurice and Gaston. The curtains partially concealed the bed and the two who lay prostrate beside it ; the white, haggard, terrified countenance of Madame de Gramont was alone visible. As Mrs. Lawkins endeavored to extricate her from the folds of the curtain, Maurice and Gaston removed the fallen arrow to which the drapery was still attached. Afterwards Gaston, who was nearest to Mrs. Lawkins, assisted her in raising the helpless countess and placing her upon the bed. Then the form of Madeleine became visible. She was stretched upon the ground motionless and senseless ; her beautiful hair, loosened by her fall, enveloped her like a veil, and wholly concealed her face. What a groan of agony burst from Maurice as he knelt beside her and swept away the shrouding tresses! They were wet, and the hands that touched them became scarlet. The outermost edge of the arrow had struck Madeleine's head, inflicting a deep gash, and, as it fell, tore her dress the whole length of her left shoulder and arm, making another wound which bled profusely.

Maurice was so completely stupefied with horror that he had scarcely power to lift her light form.

" Here! here! place her here!" cried Mrs. Lawkins; "don't stir her any more than possible."

Maurice mechanically obeyed and laid Madeleine upon the same bed which bore the countess.

The nurse was the only one whose presence of mind had not completely departed, and she hurried from the room to send for medical assistance.

Maurice, as he clasped Madeleine in his arms, groaned out, " She is killed! she is dead! Oh, my Madeleine, my Madeleine! are you gone? Madeleine! Madeleine!"

Madeleine gave no sign of life, though the blood still flowed.

Mrs. Lawkins, who had returned, tried to force him away — entreated him to let her approach Madeleine, that she might bind up her head and stanch the blood; but he did not hear, or heed, — he was lost in grief. M. de Bois also appealed to him, but in vain; then Gaston attempted to use force to recall him to reason, and, seizing both of Maurice's arms, essayed to unclasp them from their hold of the inanimate form, saying as he did so:

"For the love of Heaven, Maurice, collect yourself; she may bleed to death if you prevent Mrs. Lawkins from doing what is needful to stop the blood."

Maurice struggled with him, as he exclaimed, hopelessly, "She is dead! she is dead!"

"She is *not* dead, but you may kill her if you refuse to let Mrs. Lawkins bind up her wounds."

Maurice no longer resisted, and Mrs. Lawkins wiped away the blood, and commenced bandaging the fair, wounded head. The pale features had been stained with the crimson flood, and, as Mrs. Lawkins bathed them, their marble whiteness and stillness were appalling.

Bertha had not ceased to sob, though Gaston, the instant he could safely relinquish his hold of Maurice, essayed by every means in his power to soothe her.

The countess was gazing upon Madeleine with an air of stupefied grief. Bertha, who had no control over her passionate sorrow, as her eyes fell upon Madame de Gramont, cried out, reproachfully, —

"Aunt, but for her, you would have been killed! You who never loved her! She has lost her life in trying to save yours!"

The countess did not appear to heed the cruel words, though they were the echo of her own thoughts.

Mrs. Lawkin's skilful ministry had stanched the blood and Madeleine's head and arm were bound up; but still she lay like some lovely statue, her lips apart and hueless, — her eyes closed, and the dark lashes sweeping her alabaster cheeks; while her long hair, still dripping with its crimson moisture, was lifted over the pillow. As Mrs. Lawkins, having accomplished her sad task, drew back, Maurice pressed into her place, and Bertha crowded in beside him, loading the senseless Madeleine with caresses and tender epithets; then, as she turned to her aunt, who had raised herself on her elbow, and was also bending over the lifeless figure, exclaimed impetuously, —

"Oh! how could you help loving her? We all loved her so much! Cousin Tristan said she was his good angel, and she has been the good angel of all our family; but our good angel is gone! We have lost her through you!"

Bertha's overwhelming sorrow had swept away all her former dread of her aunt, whom her reproaches deeply stung. They were the first Madame de Gramont had ever heard from those timid lips. At that moment the conscience-stricken woman would have made any sacrifice, even of her pride, to have seen Madeleine restored to life. While contemplating that angelic face, now so still and white, torturing fiends recalled all the harsh words she had used to pain this defenceless being, — all the cruel wrong she had done her, — all the misery she had caused her; and now she inwardly prayed that Madeleine might live; but with that prayer arose the thought that the supplication of such a one as she would remain unheard in heaven.

Mrs. Lawkins, aided by Maurice, was applying restoratives. With his arm beneath Madeleine's head, he was holding a spoon to her lips, and, with gentle force, pouring its contents into her mouth, watching her with the most thrilling anxiety. He thought a slight movement of the lips was perceptible; then they quivered more certainly, and she made an effort to swallow.

The countess was the first one that spoke : " She is not dead! I am spared that ! "

She sank back upon her pillow and wept.

No one present had ever seen her weep; but now she did not try to hide her tears ; they gushed forth in fierce torrents, like a stream that breaks forth through severed icebergs; for in her soul the ice that had gathered to mountain heights was melting at last.

Maurice had echoed the words, " She is not dead," pressing his own burning lips upon those pale, feebly-stirring, cold ones, and catching the first returning breath that Madeleine drew. At that long, fervent kiss her eyes unclosed ; they saw his face and nothing beside.

" Madeleine, my beloved, you are spared to me! My life returns now that you are given back."

Madeleine faintly murmured " Maurice," and then her eyes wandered from his face to those around her, and she added, " What is it ? "

Bertha's transition from grief to joy was so clamorous that no one could answer. If Gaston had not restrained her, Madeleine's bandage would have been endangered by the young girl's vehement embraces, which were mingled with incoherent exclamations of rapture.

" What is it ? " again questioned Madeleine ; but, as she spoke her eye caught sight of the fallen curtain, thrown in a heap, and remembering the recent danger, she turned quickly to the countess, and said, feebly, —

" You are not hurt, aunt, — madame ? The shaft did not strike you, — did it ? "

The countess felt that a shaft had fallen and struck her, indeed, but not the one Madeleine meant. She stretched out her hand and clasped that of her niece as she said, —

" I am uninjured, Madeleine ; it is you who received the blow. God grant that this may be the last that will fall upon you through me ! It is in vain to struggle against His will. It was His hand, — I feel it ! I resist no longer ! "

She looked toward Maurice, who exclaimed joyfully, " My dear, dear grandmother, have I regained Madeleine doubly to-day ? Do you mean " —

The countess finished his sentence solemnly, " That it shall be as my son said."

Madeleine, overcome with joy and gratitude, tried to raise herself up that she might reach the countess, but sank back powerless, and the effort again started the crimson current which trickled through the bandage and ran down her face.

" Don't move ! " cried Mrs. Lawkins. " See, see, what you have done by agitating her. Go, all of you, away. Mr. Maurice, go, or you will do her more mischief. Take him away, M. de Bois."

Maurice was so much alarmed at the sight of the blood that he could not, at first, listen to these expostulations ; but Mrs. Lawkins continued to threaten him with such evil results if he did not obey, and to urge M. de Bois so strenuously to compel him, that Gaston succeeded in leading him away ; Mrs. Lawkins bade Bertha follow them, and then locked the door.

As she prepared a fresh bandage she said apologetically, " I was obliged to send them away, Mademoiselle Madeleine ; you must be quiet and not speak a word until the doctor comes ; it is very, very important."

And Madeleine did lie still in a trance of pure delight, and the countess lay beside her almost as motionless.

CHAPTER LVII.

CONCLUSION.

THE wound in Madeleine's head was dangerously near her temple. Her long swoon had been caused by the severity of the blow, and she was completely exhausted by her great loss of blood. When Dr. Bayard had examined her injuries and read-justed the bandage, Maurice bore her gently to her own chamber, clasping her closely in his arms as he went, and breathing over her words of tenderest endearment. He left her in Mrs. Lawkins' charge to be undressed and laid in bed, but even during that brief process, knocked several times at the door to urge the good house-keeper to make haste and admit him.

For nearly two months Maurice had been chained to the bedside of his suffering father, or his grandmother; he had been fully initiated into the duties of ministration, and upon the strength of his experience he claimed the entire care of the new invalid. What a luxury to him it was to watch over his beloved Madeleine! It seemed ungrateful of her to deprive him of the happiness by getting well too rapidly. As Ruth Thornton occupied the same room, Madeleine needed no watcher at night; but Maurice scarcely left her during the day. Her light food, her cooling drinks and calming potions, she received from his hands alone. Hour after hour, he sat and read to her, — sat and talked to her, — sat and looked at her, — and never was weary, — never was so superlatively happy in his life! He was jealous of any one who attempted to share his vigils; when Mrs. Lawkins approached, he playfully reminded her that they had agreed upon a division of labor, and Madame de Gramont was her patient; when Ruth and Bertha tried to press upon him their services, he had always some plea to peremptorily dismiss them both. Mrs. Walton was the only one in whose favor he relented a little. He allowed her to sit beside his charge for a couple of hours every day. How could he refuse when the presence of this invaluable friend gave Madeleine such true pleasure, and when Mrs. Walton was filled with such evident delight in watching the intercourse of these two kindred spirits, who to her eyes seemed created for partnership?

Madame de Gramont had daily, with a sort of ceremonious affection, inquired after Madeleine's health. Madeleine's first visit, when she was able to rise, was to her aunt; but Maurice would not allow his patient to attempt to walk without his supporting arm about her waist. We will not say that Madame de Gramont greeted Madeleine *cordially;* but she received her with marked consideration, and expressed satisfaction at beholding her able to move; this was the sole allusion she made to the accident. Maurice, who had grown thoroughly tyrannical, would only permit Madeleine to remain a few moments with his grandmother, and brought the interview to a sudden close.

Now that Madeleine was convalescent, she found great enjoyment in long, pleasant drives with Bertha, Maurice and Gaston. On bright days they left the carriage, and wandered into the woods to gather wild flowers, and rest beneath the trees. On one of these occasions, Madeleine was sitting upon a fallen tree, her lap filled with the flowers she had culled, and which she was weaving into a wreath. Bertha aided her work by selecting and handing the requisite flowers. Maurice was supplying her with luxuriant moss which she mingled among the bright blossoms. Gaston, lying at Bertha's feet, contemplated the lovely picture before him. The wreath was finished, and Madeleine wound it about Bertha's picturesque little hat, — not one of those unmeaning abominations which neither cover the head, nor shade the face, but a round straw hat, slightly turned up at the sides, and ornamented only by a single, black plume.

" Look, M. de Bois," said Madeleine, " is not my chaplet successful? Could anything be more becoming to Bertha?"

" Yes," answered Gaston, "there is one chaplet in which she would look still lovelier, — a wreath of orange-blossoms. Come, Bertha, are you not ready to reward my patience and forbearance? Will you not let me remember this day as one of our brightest, by telling me when you will wear that orange-blossom wreath?"

Bertha laid her head upon Madeleine's shoulder at the risk of crushing some of the wild flowers, and answered, " That depends upon Madeleine. I told you long ago that Madeleine should name the day."

" Come then, Mademoiselle Madeleine," Gaston pleaded ; " do you speak!"

Maurice's eyes fervently seconded the adjuration.

Madeleine answered, with the perverseness of her sex, " You ought to return to Charleston, Maurice."

" I know I *ought;* but do not imagine I mean to do what I ought to do, until you have done what you ought to do as an example ; if you do *that,* you will tell me when I may return to claim my bride."

" You shall know to-morrow," said Madeleine, " but only on condition that neither of you gentlemen mention the subject again to-day."

Both lovers promised ; but, simply because a condition had been made, they every moment experienced the strongest temptation to disregard the stipulation.

That night Madeleine and Bertha had a long conversation, —

" a woman's talk," such as maidens, and matrons too, delight in, all the world over. They decided that Maurice must leave at once for Charleston, and remain three months, only returning the day before the one appointed for his nuptials. The double wedding was to take place in church ; the bridal party to return to Madeleine's and, after a collation, leave for Philadelphia, and the day following for New York. The countess, accompanied by Gaston and Bertha, would sail at once for Havre, and Maurice and Madeleine take up their abode in Charleston. Bertha's plans, after she reached France, were left to be determined by circumstances.

Madame de Gramont was the first one apprised of this arrangement, and it met with her full approval. She rejoiced at the certainty of seeing her beloved château again ; and, though she spoke not one word to that effect, experienced great relief at being spared the necessity of appearing in Brittany with Madeleine, whose presence must necessarily cause abundant gossip.

Maurice and Gaston were warned that the penalty of a single remonstrance against these plans would be a month added to their period of probation. Maurice compromised by pleading that instead of leaving Washington at once, he might be permitted to remain until the close of the week.

The French ambassador had been much chagrined at the prospect of parting with Gaston. It was tolerably difficult to find a person who was not always seeking his own interests, or meddling in diplomatic affairs, to supply M. de Bois's place. When M. de Fleury was informed that the period for Gaston's departure was settled, he urged him to promise to return within six months, saying that he would only engage a secretary *pro tem.* in the hope of M. de Bois occupying his former position.

As the young French maidens were orphans, and of high family, M. de Fleury offered to assume the office of father in giving them away, and the flattering proposition was particularly acceptable to the countess.

Ronald Walton was to be the groomsman of Maurice, and Madeleine made her humble friend Ruth, the happiest of maidens, by inviting her to officiate as bridesmaid. Bertha needed a bridesmaid and groomsman, since her cousin would be thus attended, and she chose Lady Augusta Linden and her *fiancé.* Mr. Rutledge, through whose influence Madeleine had obtained a vote of so much importance to Maurice.

These nuptial arrangements seemed to give general satisfac-

tion, with one exception ;. Mr. Walton declared that he was unfairly treated; that he meant to be assigned some office ; and as
his son was Madeleine's groomsman, and as he was not himself
qualified to be Bertha's, he must be allowed to act as the father
of the latter. M. de Fleury, he said, ought to be contented
with the *rôle* of father to one of the brides. Bertha, who had
been charmed by the courtly manners and delightful conversation of this agreeable gentleman, cordially consented.

Once more Madeleine and Maurice were to be parted; and
even this brief separation tested their fortitude. The Waltons
accompanied Maurice, and were to return with him to Washington.

On his arrival in Charleston, he had cause to be flattered by
the hearty greeting of his partner. Maurice plunged at once
into professional duties ; but another employment helped to
speed the time, — a truly charming occupation, — the preparation
of a home for his bride.

Mrs. Walton assisted the young lawyer in the agreeable task
of selecting furniture, and making those arrangements which
demanded a woman's hand.

A never-failing happiness flowed to Maurice from the exchange of letters with Madeleine. Each day commenced with
the sending, and closed with the receiving, of one of these precious paper messengers. But Madeleine's letters, by no means,
came under the head of "love letters." She could not have
poured out upon paper, any more than she could have spoken,
the fulness and depth of her affection ; but Maurice found inexhaustible delight in what she wrote, which was always suggestive of so much left unsaid.

Madeleine rented her house to Ruth, who now became the
head of the establishment which "Mademoiselle Melanie" had
rendered so popular. At Madeleine's suggestion, Ruth had
written to her widowed mother and young sister and requested
them to make their future home with her. That letter was
read by streaming eyes, and its contents filled to overflowing
two joyful hearts.

Mrs. Lawkins was to accompany Madeleine to Charleston and
take charge of her household there.

Madeleine proposed closing her establishment on the day of
her wedding ; for she well knew that her *employées* would desire
to witness the ceremony. And she further evinced her thoughtfulness by ordering a bountiful collation to be spread in the
apartments usually devoted to business, at the same time that

the table was prepared for her own bridal party in the apartments beneath.

Madeleine and Bertha had both apprised their bridegrooms elect that they preferred to forego the French custom of receiving the usual *corbeille*, containing laces, India shawls, jewelry, etc., etc., adding that some simple bridal token would be more acceptable.

The day before the wedding arrived, and with it Maurice and the Waltons.

We will not attempt to paint the meeting between Maurice and Madeleine, — it was too full of joy for language, too sacred for description, — but pass on to the events of the evening when the exchange of bridal gifts was made.

Maurice fastened about Madeleine's white throat a small chain of Venetian gold, to which was suspended a cross of rare pearls; and on the back of the cross were inscribed these words of the prophet, —

"Labor is worship."

M. de Bois, knowing that Bertha was only too well supplied with gems, had experienced great difficulty in selecting a bridal gift. But, after many consultations with Madeleine, he chose a set of cameos cut in stone. The necklace and bracelets were composed of angel heads; but his own likeness was cut upon the brooch, and that of Madeleine on the medallion that formed the centre of the bracelet. Who can doubt that Bertha was enchanted with her gift?

Madame de Gramont presented each of her nieces with a handkerchief of rich old lace, very rare and no longer purchasable.

Madeleine placed in Bertha's hands a magnificently bound volume; it contained Mrs. Browning's poems illustrated, in water colors, by Madeleine herself. Many of the paintings were exquisite, but those which represented "Lady Geraldine's Courtship," far surpassed all the others.

And now came the great surprise of the evening, — the disclosure of a secret which Gaston and Bertha had carefully guarded. Bertha, in her clingingly affectionate way, knelt down beside Madeleine, and laid in her lap two ancient-looking jewel-cases, her bridal gift to Madeleine. How Madeleine started and trembled at the sight! Well she knew those caskets, but her shaking hands could not press the springs by which they were secured. Bertha lifted their lids and disclosed the diamonds and emeralds which had been the bridal jewels of Lady Katrine Nugent, Madeleine's great-great-grandmother; the jewels which Madeleine had been forced to part with to obtain herself subsistence; the jewels whose design she had imitated on the dress which first made her "fairy fingers" known to Vignon; the jewels Bertha had recognized when they were worn by Madame de Fleury; the jewels which in attempting to trace to their owner, Maurice had suffered so terribly. These memorable jewels were restored through Gaston's agency. He had related to M. de Fleury their history, and Mademoiselle de Merrivale's desire to repurchase them. The marquis had promised acquiescence in the young lady's wishes if Madame de Fleury's consent could be obtained. Gaston and Bertha paid the ambassador's wife a visit of persuasion. Gaston was an especial favorite, and Madame de Fleury loved Madeleine as well as it was possible for her to love any one. Her yielding up these jewels was a high proof of the noble *conturière's* power over her frivolous heart.

What bride does not smile when she sees the sun shine into her chamber on the nuptial morning? The sun shone gloriously on the bridal day of Madeleine and Bertha. The ceremony was to take place at any early hour, — no invitations were issued, — the bridal party was to meet at Madeleine's to go to church.

Madeleine and Bertha were attired precisely alike, and with severe simplicity; they both wore dresses of white silk, made close to the throat. (A *décolté* attire would not be tolerated at a Parisian bridal.) Their veils were circular and of point lace; their chaplets of natural orange blossoms woven by Madeleine herself. Madeleine had not intended to wear any ornament, save the cross Maurice had presented her, but Bertha insisted on clasping Lady Katrine Nugent's bridal bracelet on her cousin's arm, and fastening her tiny lace collar with the lily and shamrock brooch. Bertha, herself, wore Gaston's cameos, and could scarcely restrain her joyful tears when she fastened on her fair bosom the brooch which represented her lover's countenance, and the bracelet that bore her beloved Madeleine's. She was adorned with the images of the two most dear on earth.

Need we say that both brides were supremely lovely? Gazing at Bertha's sweet, unclouded face, that looked out from among the wealth of golden ringlets, and noting the soft light in her blue eyes, the delicate rose-flush that came and went on her cheeks, one might well declare that nothing more beautiful could be found, until the gazer turned to Madeleine. Her face was colorless with emotion, yet its paleness only rendered the sculpturesque beauty of her features more striking; her eyes were downcast, and thus one missed their clear lustre and holy expression; yet the long lashes were some compensation, and her look was so spiritual, so saint-like in its beauty, that nothing mortal could have been lovelier.

For one moment only were Maurice and Gaston permitted to greet their brides, and then they were hurried into the carriages which awaited them.

Though no invitations had been given, the church was densely crowded. When the nuptial procession entered, the suppressed murmur of many voices sounded like the rushing of distant waves. First came Madame de Gramont, leaning on the arm of Maurice; they were followed by Ronald and Ruth Thornton; Madeleine, led by the Marquis de Fleury, followed. Then came the second party, Gaston with Mrs. Walton on his arm; Lady Augusta and Mr. Rutledge; Bertha, led by Mr. Walton, not the least proud and happy man of that large assembly.

At times, during the ceremony, low sobs were audible; they came from Madeleine's *employées*, who could not wholly control their grief, as the certainty of losing their gentle mistress forced itself upon them.

The newly made wives passed out of the church conducted by their husbands and returned to Madeleine's residence.

During the collation the brides stood together at the head of the table. The French ambassador and Mr. Walton were the life of the festive board, and infused an element of gayety which the small assemblage would have lacked without their aid, for a happy silence had fallen upon the nuptial party. Besides these gentlemen, Mr. Meredith and Mr. Hilson were the only strangers present.

The brides left the company to assume their travelling attire; but Madeleine, before she made this change, stole to the apartment where her needle-women were at table, with Victorine at the head, and spoke a word of kindly farewell to each, in turn. There were no dry eyes in that room.

Maurice was more than satisfied with Madeleine's approval of the pleasant abode he had chosen. Many and joyous were the years he and his beloved companion passed under that roof. One year after their marriage it also sheltered for a time Gaston and Bertha. Madame de Gramont died soon after her return to Brittany.

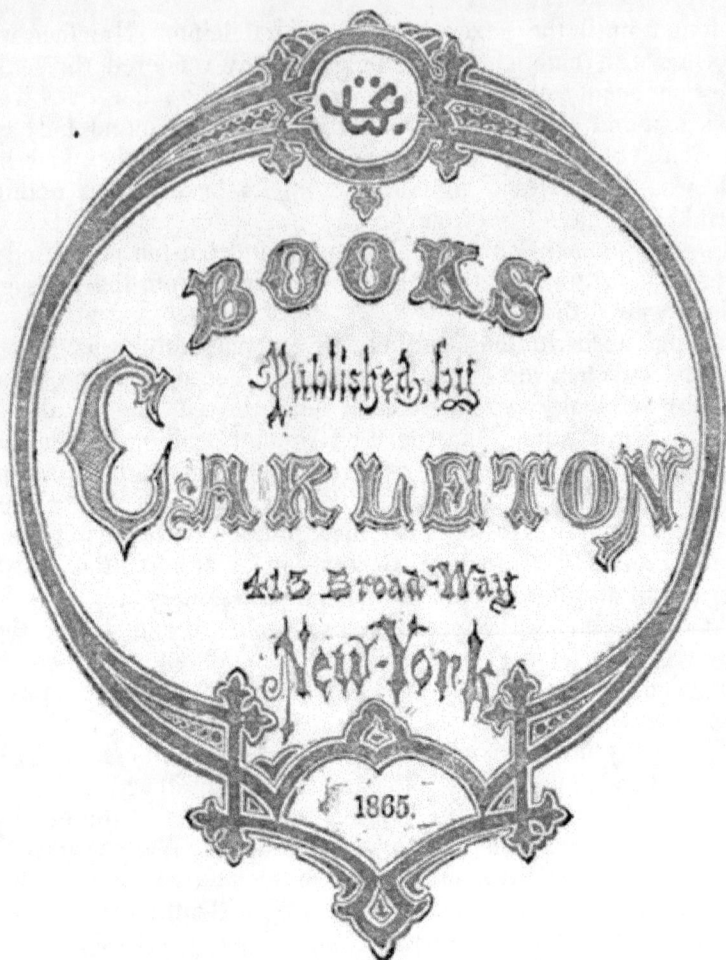

BOOKS

Published by

CARLETON

413 Broad-Way

New-York

1865.

" There is a kind of physiognomy in the titles
of books no less than in the faces of
men, by which a skilful observer
will know as well what to expect from the one as the
other."—BUTLER.

NEW BOOKS

And New Editions Recently Issued by
CARLETON, PUBLISHER,
NEW YORK.
413 *BROADWAY, CORNER OF LISPENARD STREET.*

N.B.—THE PUBLISHER, upon receipt of the price in advance, will send any of the following Books, by mail, POSTAGE FREE, to any part of the United States. This convenient and very safe mode may be adopted when the neighboring Booksellers are not supplied with the desired work. State name and address in full.

Victor Hugo.

LES MISERABLES.—*The best edition,* two elegant 8vo. vols., beautifully bound in cloth, $5.50; half calf, . . $10.00

LES MISERABLES.—*The popular edition,* one large octavo volume, paper covers, $2.00; cloth bound, . . $2.50

LES MISERABLES.—Original edition in five vols.—Fantine—Cosette—Marius—Denis—Valjean. 8vo. cloth, . $1.25

LES MISERABLES—In the Spanish language. Fine 8vo. edition, two vols., paper covers, $4.00; or cloth, bound, . $5.00

THE LIFE OF VICTOR HUGO.—By himself. 8vo. cloth, $1.75

By the Author of "Rutledge."

RUTLEDGE.—A deeply interesting novel.   12mo. cloth, $1.75
THE SUTHERLANDS.—   do.   .   .   do. $1.75
FRANK WARRINGTON.—   do.   .   .   do. $1.75
LOUIE'S LAST TERM AT ST. MARY'S.— .   .   do. $1.75
ST. PHILIP'S.— *Just published.*   .   .   do. $1.75

Hand-Books of Good Society.

THE HABITS OF GOOD SOCIETY; with Thoughts, Hints, and Anecdotes, concerning nice points of taste, good manners and the art of making oneself agreeable. Reprinted from the London Edition. The best and most entertaining wor ' of the kind ever published. .   .   12mo. cloth, $1.75

THE ART OF CONVERSATION.—With directions for self-culture A sensible and instructive work, that ought to be in th hands of every one who wishes to be either an agreeable talker or listener. .   .   .   12mo. cloth, $1.50

Miss Augusta J. Evans.

BEULAH.—A novel of great power. .   12mo. cloth, $1.75

4 LIST OF BOOKS PUBLISHED

Mrs. Mary J. Holmes' Works.

DARKNESS AND DAYLIGHT.—*Just published.* 12mo. cl. $1.50
'LENA RIVERS.— . . A Novel. do. $1.50
TEMPEST AND SUNSHINE.— . do. do. $1.50
MARIAN GREY.— . do. do. $1.50
MEADOW BROOK.— . . . do. do. $1.50
ENGLISH ORPHANS.— . . do. do. $1.50
DORA DEANE.— . . . do. do. $1.50
COUSIN MAUDE.— . . . do. do. $1.50
HOMESTEAD ON THE HILLSIDE.— do. do. $1.50
HUGH WORTHINGTON.— *Just published.* do. $1.50

Artemus Ward.

HIS BOOK.—An irresistibly funny volume of writings by the immortal American humorist. . . 12mo. cloth, $1.50
A NEW BOOK.—*In press.* . . . do. $1.50

Miss Muloch.

JOHN HALIFAX.—A novel. With illust. 12mo., cloth, $1.75
A LIFE FOR A LIFE.— . do. . do. $1.75

Charlotte Bronte (Currer Bell).

JANE EYRE.—A novel. With illustration. 12mo. cloth, $1.75
THE PROFESSOR.—do. . do. . do. $1.75
SHIRLEY.— . do. . do. . do. $1.75
VILLETTE.— . do. . do. . do. $1.75

Edmund Kirke.

AMONG THE PINES.—A Southern sketch. 12mo. cloth, $1.50
MY SOUTHERN FRIENDS.— do. do. . $1.50
DOWN IN TENNESSEE.—Just published. . do. $1.50

Cuthbert Bede.

VERDANT GREEN.—A rollicking, humorous novel of English student life; with 200 comic illustrations. 12mo. cloth, $1.50
NEARER AND DEARER.—A novel, illustrated. 12mo. clo. $1.50

Richard B. Kimball.

WAS HE SUCCESSFUL?— A novel. 12mo. cloth, $1.75
UNDERCURRENTS.— do. do. $1.75
SAINT LEGER.— do. do. $1.75
ROMANCE OF STUDENT LIFE.— do. do. $1.75
IN THE TROPICS.—Edited by R. B. Kimball. do. $1.75

Epes Sargent.

PECULIAR.—One of the most remarkable and successful novels published in this country. . . 12mo. cloth, $1.75

A. S. Roe's Works.

A LONG LOOK AHEAD.—	A novel.	12mo. cloth,	$1.50
TO LOVE AND TO BE LOVED.—	do. . .	do.	$1.50
TIME AND TIDE.—	do. . ;	do.	$1.50
I'VE BEEN THINKING.—	do. . .	do.	$1.50
THE STAR AND THE CLOUD.—	do. . .	do.	$1.5C
TRUE TO THE LAST.—	do. . .	do.	$1.50
HOW COULD HE HELP IT.—	do. . .	do.	$1.50
LIKE AND UNLIKE.—	do. . .	do.	$1.50
LOOKING AROUND.— *Just published.*		do.	$1.50

Walter Barrett, Clerk.

OLD MERCHANTS OF NEW YORK.—Being personal incidents, interesting sketches, bits of biography, and gossipy events in the life of nearly every leading merchant in New York City. Three series. . . 12mo. cloth, each, $1.75

T. S. Arthur's New Works.

LIGHT ON SHADOWED PATHS.—A novel.		12mo. cloth,	$1.50
OUT IN THE WORLD.—	do. .	do.	$1.50
NOTHING BUT MONEY.—	do. .	do.	$1.50
WHAT CAME AFTERWARDS.—*In press.* .		do.	$1.50

Orpheus C. Kerr.

ORPHEUS C. KERR PAPERS.—Three series. 12mo. cloth, $1.50
THE PALACE BEAUTIFUL.—And other poems. do. $1.5C

M. Michelet's Works.

LOVE (L'AMOUR).—From the French. 12mo. cloth, $1.50
WOMAN (LA FEMME.)— do. . . do. $1.50

Novels by Ruffini.

DR. ANTONIO.—A love story of Italy.	12mo. cloth,	$1.75
LAVINIA; OR, THE ITALIAN ARTIST.—	do.	$1.75
VINCENZO; OR, SUNKEN ROCKS.—	8vo. cloth,	$1.75

Rev John Cumming, D.D., of London.

THE GREAT TRIBULATION.—Two series. 12mo. cloth, $1.50
THE GREAT PREPARATION.— do. . do. $1.50
THE GREAT CONSUMMATION.— do. . do. $1.50

Ernest Renan.

THE LIFE OF JESUS.—Translated by C. E. Wilbour from the celebrated French work. . . 12mo. cloth, $1.75
RELIGIOUS HISTORY AND CRITICISM.— 8vo. cloth, $2.50

Cuyler Pine.

MARY BRANDEGEE.—An American novel. . • $1.75
A NEW NOVEL.—*In press.* $1.75

Charles Reade.

THE CLOISTER AND THE HEARTH.—A magnificent new novel, by the author of " Hard Cash," etc.   8vo. cloth, $2.00

The Opera.

TALES FROM THE OPERAS.—A collection of clever stories, based upon the plots of all the famous operas.   12mo. cl., $1.50

J. C. Jeaffreson.

A BOOK ABOUT DOCTORS.—An exceedingly humorous and entertaining volume of sketches, stories, and facts, about famous physicians and surgeons.   12mo. cloth, $1.75

Fred. S. Cozzens.

THE SPARROWGRASS PAPERS—A capital humorous work, with illustrations by Darley.   .   .   12mo. cloth, $1.50

F. D. Guerrazzi.

BEATRICE CENCI.—A great historical novel. Translated from the Italian ; with a portrait of the Cenci, from Guido's famous picture in Rome.   .   .   12mo. cloth, $1.75

Private Miles O'Reilly.

HIS BOOK.—Comic songs, speeches, &c.   12mo. cloth, $1.50
A NEW NOVEL.—*In press.*   .   .   .   do. $1.50

The New York Central Park.

A SUPERB GIFT BOOK.—The Central Park pleasantly described, and magnificently embellished with more than 50 exquisite photographs of the principal views and objects of interest. A large quarto volume, sumptuously bound in Turkey morocco, ... $30.00

Joseph Rodman Drake.

THE CULPRIT FAY.—The most charming faery poem in the English language. Beautifully printed. 12mo. cloth, 75 cts.

Mother Goose for Grown Folks.

HUMOROUS RHYMES for grown people ; based upon the famous " Mother Goose Melodies."   .   .   12mo. cloth, $1.00

Mrs. ——

FAIRY FINGERS.—A new novel.   .   12mo. cloth, $1.75
THE MUTE SINGER.—   do.   *In press.*   do. $1.75

Robert B. Roosevelt.

THE GAME FISH OF THE NORTH.—Illustrated. 12mo. cl. $2.00
SUPERIOR FISHING.—*Just published.* do.   do. $2.00
THE GAME BIRDS OF THE NORTH.—*In press.*   . $2.00

John Phoenix.

THE SQUIBOB PAPERS.—With comic illustr. 12mo. cl., $1.50